New York Glory

New York Glory

Religions in the City

EDITED BY

Tony Carnes and Anna Karpathakis

New York University Press

NEW YORK AND LONDON

NEW YORK UNIVERSITY PRESS
New York and London

Library of Congress Cataloging-in-Publication Data
New York glory : religions in the city / edited by Tony Carnes and
Anna Karpathakis.
p.   cm. — (Religion, race, and ethnicity)
Includes bibliographical references and index.
ISBN 0-8147-1600-8 (hardcover : alk. paper) —
ISBN 0-8147-1601-6 (pbk. : alk. paper)
1. New York (N.Y.)—Religion—20th century.   I. Carnes, Tony.
II. Karpathakis, Anna. III. Series.
BL2527.N7 N49 2000
200'.9747'1—dc21   00-011334

New York University Press books are printed on acid-free paper,
and their binding materials are chosen for strength and durability.

Manufactured in the United States of America
10 9 8 7 6 5 4 3 2 1

Contents

Acknowledgments

The editors gratefully acknowledge the following people for their kind assistance with this book: Anatoliy Khotsyn, Arthur Vidich, Darilyn, David Harris, David Singer, Debbie Harkins, Dmitriy Nikolayev, Ezra Williams, Friedhelm Radandt, Glen Kleinknecht, Guenther Roth, H. Dean Trulear, Harvey Conn, Helen, Henry Woo, Ifhan Bagby, John Kennedy, Jose Casanova, Joseph Maier, Marie Salerno, Masha Chlenova, Members of the Columbia University Seminar on Contents and Methods in the Social Sciences, Michael Faulkner, Morgen Kleinknecht, Paul Shapiro, Peter Benda, R. Stephen Warner, Richard and Joan Ostling, Richard Kaufmann, Robert Orsi, Roderick Caesar Jr., Ruth, Samuel Heilman, Samuel Kliger, Stanford M. Lyman, Susan Farrell, Susan Lachman, Tal Brooke, Tatiana Svoyskaya, Tim Keller, Timothy Morgan, Hubert, Jennifer Hammer, Despina Papazoglou Gimbel, David Roozen, and Rena Yufufova.

Preface

New York Glory

Richard John Neuhaus

When you're tired of London, the great Dr. Johnson observed, you're tired of life. The same might be said of New York City. In fact, in various ways, people have been saying essentially that about New York for more than two hundred years. In his fine overview in the next chapter, Tony Carnes touches on the ways that visitors to New York from Europe and elsewhere have sensed, to either their satisfaction or alarm, that the city betokens the future of the modern (postmodern?) world.

When lecturing in England on the religious and cultural situation in the United States, I was impressed by an Oxford don who politely dissented from something I had said but then quickly added, "From my years there, I concluded that America is so vast and so various that almost any generalization made about it is amply supported by the evidence." And that, too, may be said of New York.

Shortly after being appointed archbishop of New York in 1984, John Cardinal O'Connor visited Pope John Paul II. The pope greeted him with outspread arms and declared, "Welcome to the archbishop of the capital of the world!"

But New Yorkers are regularly reminded, and not always in the kindest tones, that New York is not America. They just as regularly, and happily, agree. One way in which New York is presumed not to be like the rest of America is that the rest of America is very religious, whereas New York is determinedly secular. It is one of the great merits of this book that it challenges, sharply and convincingly, that assumption.

I have encountered sociologists who, with respect to America's religiosity and New York's secularity, speak of "New York exceptionalism." My own experience of living here for more than thirty years, which is reinforced by the stories and data in these pages, suggests that we should view such a notion with great skepticism. In general, secularization theorists have made something of a turnaround in recent years. In the more militantly secular versions of the eighteenth-century Enlightenment and up through recent times, it was thought that secularization was something of an unstoppable juggernaut. As the world became more modern (that is, enlightened), religion would either wither away or be hermetically sealed off from public life as a private eccentricity. Secularization theorists tended to be European and agreed with Max Weber that there appeared to be an unbreakable link between modernization and the "disenchantment" of the world. All is rationalized, specialized, bureaucratized, functionalized. In short, all is secularized.

Those subscribing to this general theory are often puzzled as to why religion, in maddeningly diverse ways, is so vibrantly alive in America, even though America is a modern—perhaps the most modern—society. The agreed-upon answer to this puzzlement was expressed in the notion of "American exceptionalism." Today there is a growing consensus that it may be more accurate to speak of European exceptionalism, or at least of western European exceptionalism. While Germany, France, and the Netherlands, among others, seem to be in thrall to a numbing secularization, around the world—in Africa, Asia, Latin America, and elsewhere—there is a resurgence of religion, with all the attendant cultural and political consequences. This is the reality examined by Harvard's Samuel Huntington in his much controverted, but I think essentially accurate, "clash of civilizations" thesis. I am inclined to risk going a step further and say that if the proverbial man or woman from Mars asked about the most important single thing happening on planet Earth at the beginning of the twenty-first century, a very good answer might be the *de*secularization of world history. This is not, according to the textbooks still used from grade school through graduate school, how history was supposed to turn out.

This book suggests that the myth of New York exceptionalism is as dubious as the myth of American exceptionalism. With respect to religion, because America is more like than unlike the rest of the world, so New York is more like than unlike America. But of course, New York is also different. The difference, however, may be quite the opposite of what is usually supposed. The conventional wisdom for a long time was that the city is the preeminently modern expression of Weber's rationalized "disenchantment." It seems to me more likely, however, that the raucously variegated disjunctions of everyday life in New York open up spaces of enchantment—both wondrous and bizarre—unknown in more domesticated forms of human society. The city is a city of many cities, a world of many worlds.

My first parish assignment was to a medium-size town of fifteen thousand people in far upstate New York. The life of that town was tight as a drum, predictable, rational, and, in all its dimensions, run by the rules of a family, a business, and an Episcopal church that had dominated it for generations. I and the small flock I shepherded were most decidedly outsiders. Then, still in my mid-twenties, I came to Brooklyn, New York, and plunged into the community activism that in those days went with being the pastor of a poor black parish. Within months, I was leading demonstrations, testifying before the city council, meeting with the mayor, and generally playing the part of a public person of importance in a way that would have been impossible in the upstate town of my first parish. A person of importance? It was partly true and partly a delusion, and the truth and the delusion were hard to separate. That is what is meant by saying that New York is a world of many worlds.

Everybody with a taste for it and a modicum of talent gets a chance to be important in New York. There are so many worlds in which to be important, or at least to feel important. It is the city of finance and business, of fashion and theater, of publishing and the arts, of hustling and fervent piety. This book is mainly about the last dimension of life in New York. Former Mayor Edward Koch frequently said that religion, and the Catholic Church in particular, is the glue that holds the city together. I don't know if that is the most apt image, but for many New Yorkers, religion defines a place to be, a piece of the whole from which it is possible to view the whole through the eyes of enchantment. As the late Christopher Lasch wrote of the family as a refuge in a heartless world, so too it is possible to view the religious communities described in these pages as such refuges. For many members of these communities, they may be that. Yet it is the case, I expect, that for many others, religion provides the story line by which to make sense of, and to make livable, the whole.

I have sometimes suggested that over the heavenly gates will be a sign: "From the Wonderful People Who Brought You New York City, the New Jerusalem!" I add that those who in this life did not like New York City will have another place to go. I say that less than half-jokingly, but not very much less.

Carnes notes, correctly, that Roman Catholicism in New York is very much slighted in the accounts provided here. I share his puzzlement as to why that should be. After all, somewhere around 42 percent of all the people in New York claim to be Catholic, and it is a Catholicism of stunning variety. I am told that in New York the Mass is said every week in thirty-two different languages. (Some say it is thirty-nine different languages, but I think they are counting somewhat similar Chinese dialects.) So the dearth of research on Catholicism is hardly due to lack of "color" or variety. And in many ways the presence of Catholicism in the city is religiously overwhelming. As comedian Lenny Bruce said back in the 1950s, "The Catholic Church is the church you mean when you say 'the Church.'" In terms of public presence, no religious figure is in the same league as the cardinal archbishop. When gay activists decide to protest what they view as religion's oppressive ways, the demonstration is, of course, at St. Patrick's.

It is not as though the media, theater, and entertainment worlds based in New York ignore Catholicism. On the contrary, at any given time, half a dozen or more plays are deploring or deriding (and usually both) the allegedly terrible things done to pupils by Sister Immaculata in parochial school, and sitcom and talk show jibes about Catholic guilt (usually sexual) are a staple. Yet academics in the social sciences seem to be paying little attention to the reality of Catholicism in New York. Perhaps it is like the elephant in the living room. Everybody knows it is there and has rather definite views about it, but there seems to be little to be done about it except to ignore it in the hope that it will go away.

Perhaps one reason for neglect is the academic vogue for minorities, preferably minorities of color. Catholicism is still viewed by many as huge and monolithic. Some even think of it as a pillar of the establishment in New York. At the same time, there is a vestigial suspicion of Catholicism as an alien immigrant force. In 1984, when John O'Connor first came to New York, the institute of which I am president held a number of dinners to introduce him to various leadership sectors of the city. One such dinner was with the movers and shakers in the media. This came in the aftermath of public controversy over the new archbishop's having challenged the public claim by vice-presidential candidate Geraldine Ferraro that Catholic teaching permitted support for the abortion license decreed by the Supreme Court in 1973. At the dinner, the then executive editor of the *New York Times* opined that when John F. Kennedy ran for president, "the question of whether you Catholics belong here, whether you understand how we do things here, had been settled once and for all." "But I have to tell you, Archbishop," he said to O'Connor (who was not yet a cardinal), "in the few short months you have been here, some of us are asking those questions again." This to the religious leader of almost half of the population of the city.

I do not have a satisfying answer to Tony Carnes's puzzlement about the lack of academic interest in Catholicism in New York. I do know that G. K. Chesterton was right when he said that Catholicism is ever so much larger from the inside than from the outside. There are such rich lodes to mine in research and writing. Based on my own experience in the archdiocese and the Brooklyn diocese, I would love to see, to cite but one instance, a thorough examination of the Filipinos in New York. In the past half-century, in parish after parish, the Filipinos have been a catalyst of change in charismatic renewal, catechesis, and the revival of popular eucharistic and other devotions. Then there are the many determinedly disciplined "renewal movements"—from Opus Dei and Focolare to the Neocatechumenal Way and the Legionaries of Christ. Who are all these people, mainly young people, who are bent on evangelizing the capital of the world and thus—or so they believe—changing the world?

Suffice it to say that *New York Glory* should be viewed as a beginning. Religion in New York City is a subject as inexhaustible as the human story itself. And were a definitive account ever to be written, it would immediately need to be rewritten. When I came here as a young man, I was showing around a friend from out of town. Pointing to all the construction sites where buildings were being torn down and others erected or rehabilitated, I said in my innocence, "This is really going to be a beautiful city when they get it finished." But of course, the finishing of New York City is an eschatological concept. Meanwhile, *New York Glory* provides overviews, assessments, and snapshots of a city on its way to the New Jerusalem.

Part I

Overview

Chapter 1

Religions in the City
An Overview

Tony Carnes

The three big headlines about the new New York are that the economy is booming, crime is way down, and the soul is back. The numbers of churches, synagogues, temples, and other religious institutions are growing at a record pace. Does anybody still really think that New York is just hard streets with no soul? Name a religion, look around, and you'll find its believers in this city, sometimes a lot of them. Who would have ever thought that the late-twentieth-century migrations into New York would turn out to be pilgrimages of the soul? New York also is attracting one of the most diverse concentrations of religions that the world has ever seen. As Catholic writer G. K. Chesterton once observed, the masses in New York are bringing "rooted truths" with them. If not quite Mecca, Jerusalem, or Vatican City, New York is increasingly being transformed into a city of faiths. Consider the following statistics:

- New York City has more Roman Catholics, Muslims (Fareed 1992), Hindus, Rastafarians, Jehovah's Witnesses, Greek Orthodox, Russian Orthodox, and religious Jews than any other city in the United States.
- More than one-half of Asian immigrants are churchgoers; 70 percent of all immigrants to New York are Christians (ICMEC 1999); and the fastest-growing institution in Hispanic neighborhoods is the church.
- About one out of five schoolchildren is in a religious school (Ravitch et al. 2000).
- In the last ten years, Korean churches alone have founded more than a dozen local colleges and seminaries. The number of Seventh-Day

Adventists has grown 900 percent, mostly since the 1980s; and the number of Mormons, 300 percent in the 1990s.

- Eighty-two percent of New Yorkers say that religion is very or fairly important to their lives; 90 percent identify with a religious group and believe in God; and 46 percent attend religious services once per month or more (December 1991 Gallup poll for *New York Newsday*; *New York Times*/CBS Survey, May 10–14, 1994).

The goal of this book is to gather original material from some of the most current social research on religions in New York City. It draws on all the major research groups on city religion, including the City University of New York's (CUNY) Program for the Analysis of Religion among Latinos (PARAL) (Stevens-Arroyo 1995; Stevens-Arroyo and Díaz-Stevens 1994; Stevens-Arroyo and Pantoja 1995; Stevens-Arroyo and Perez y Mena 1995), the American Jewish Committee's survey research of American and new Russian immigrant Jews (AJC 1997, 1998, 1999), Queen's College Asian religion studies, the Project on the Religion and Incorporation in New York at The New University, and the New Ethnic and Immigrant Congregations Project.

No volume can cover everything, and we have left much for future researchers to explore, such as the social impact and humanitarian practices of religion, various ethnic beliefs, religions' use of space, economics, and second-generation religionists.

We looked at religion in the city through a wide-angle lens, searching for trends rather than using the congregational approach championed by sociologists such as R. Stephen Warner (Warner 1993, 1994, 1999a and b). Certainly Warner is right that "congregationalism" is an American pattern adopted by most immigrant religions. The congregations become "worlds unto themselves . . . where new relations among the members of the community . . . are forged" (Warner and Wittner 1998, 3). Accordingly, this book includes several rich examples of congregational studies. However, we believe that the congregational approach needs to be situated within the larger context of world, nation, city, sociocultural process, and inter- and intradenominational relations. Indeed, sometimes scholars come to see congregations as "worlds unto themselves" a little too much.

As Max Weber reminded us, all minds, hearts, and social action live under authorities, fundamentally religious, but also political and social, in order to reject the chaos and meaninglessness of the world (Weber

1973). Authority is someone or something that has the right (or takes the right) to govern or control our lives. The sociologically most significant authorities claim that they are the ultimate and final arbiters of what is right or wrong, what is real and unreal, and what is meaningful and un-meaningful. So, successful authorities are able to claim legitimacy, that is, that they have a right to rule. Consequently, authorities engaged in legiti-mation battles try to pin the label of "illegitimate" on one another. Reli-gious and secular apologetics, then, are strategies of legitimation and delegitimation. Gods are proclaimed glorious, and their faults are hidden behind a normative system of signs (see Sennett 1980, chap. 6). Today, it appears that religions are again growing strong enough to push for a new balance of power among the fundamental authorities that govern the lives of New Yorkers.

Religion, ethno-racial identity, political parties, and political/social movements "are . . . in competition . . . and [derive] from the same exis-tential need for affiliation. . . . If people have accepted one such identity-conferring vision, they cannot give equal billing to another, so the various alternative visions are to some extent in competition" (Light and Lee 1997, 29). In New York City, power, fame, money, and sex are, in this sense, also time-tested popular religions.

In *New York Glory*, we consider religions as those organizations or movements that self-consciously identify themselves as religions. In other words, although we are reporting on what is commonly called *institution-alized religion*, it is not possible to ignore entirely a broader sense of reli-gion. Furthermore, we cannot cover all institutionalized religions or every important facet of the ones that we do cover.

As religions ascend, their adherents may demand a reworking of the boundaries of city social life. Warner notes that in the United States, reli-gion establishes difference as well as, sometimes, the basis of inclusion.

> The prototypical religious form in the United States is not the (inclusive, geographically delimited) "parish" but the (exclusive, culturally distinct) "congregation" . . . congregations provide cultural space for immigrants and other cultural minorities, . . . a home away from home, a place where the language of the home country and its codes of honor enjoy a privilege they do not enjoy in most of the host society. As I like to put it, they are re-membrances of Zion in the midst of Babylon. (Warner 1994, 220, 222)

Religions organized through parishes morally charge their neighbor-hood boundaries so that resistance to outsiders may be more fierce, and movement to outside the city may be slower (Gamm 1999). In contrast, people in congregational religions can sell their buildings and move pretty quickly, although they may recycle their sacred spaces to another religious group (Warner 1999a).

Until the riots of the 1960s, scholars commonly thought that religion was one of the most important organizing features of New York City. In *Beyond the Melting Pot* (1963), Glazer and Moynihan claimed that the two most important causes of social and political relations in the city were religion and race (also see Herberg 1955). But after the riots, Glazer concluded that race had overwhelmed the importance of religion in New York City (Glazer 1969).

Most of New York's social scientists, however, had already left religion behind with the great classical sociologists like Max Weber and Emile Durkheim and their functionalist successors like Talcott Parsons. The sociology of religion lost prestige to such fields as the study of class, race, and politics. The turn away from religion by the city's social scientists was not unprecedented among city intellectuals, who for much of the city's history had fled to New York to escape Middle American provincialism and morality. Indeed, New York's social analysts, in their haven from the heartland, were prepared to turn a blind eye to religion. Jewish intellectuals of east European origin also were eager to shed their religious background (Howe 1976). As John Miller of the Center for Religion and Civic Culture in Los Angeles put it, "The marginalization of religion in sociology caused a blindness to a major dimension of the new city" (Miller 1999; see Kivisto 1993).

Consequently, the scholarly coverage of religion in New York City has been very spotty, amounting to historical studies of specific groups, plus a few specialized surveys and ethnographies. Recently, Anthony Arroyo-Stevens led a group examining Latino religion in the city, and Jewish organizations have funded a number of studies worrying about Jewish continuity and decline. Yet one is most struck by the meagerness of such scholarly coverage. For example, until recently, there were very few works on new immigrant religions in New York or elsewhere. Stephen Warner, a leading sociologist of religion, lamented in 1998, "These 'new' ethnic and immigrant peoples share . . . a nearly complete neglect of their burgeoning religious institutions by researchers and the public" (Warner and Wittner 1998, 6). There are surprisingly few contemporary studies of the city's Roman Catholics except for some recent work on Hispanic religion. Some scholars, like David Yoo, feel that they have encountered an anti-religious bias in social science that casts religion "as an opiate of the masses and as ephemeral in nature" (Yoo 1996, xv). Yoo may have forgotten that his fellow Asian American scholars are also trying to shed their immigrant parents' "parochialisms" and are embarrassed in front of their secular academic peers.

It Was Not Always That Way

The great German sociologist Max Weber arrived in New York City early one September morning in 1904 eager to see the economic results of American Protestantism. Beholding the blaze of lights "like a burning city," his close friend and theologian Ernst Troeltsch wrote his wife that New York was like a sacred city of "fire worshipers" (Rollman 1993, 366).

Weber saw New York as a peculiar combination of materialism and idealism that restlessly combined with and contradicted each other in individual hearts and cultural panoplies. Troeltsch observed, too, that the "life and bustle" went with "a people of working brains" (Rollman 1993, 383). For Weber and Troeltsch, New York was "The City," the manifestation of the highest "capitalist spirit" in the world. But even Weber was not oblivious to the tragedy of the Christian inspiration of capitalism—what his friend Georg Simmel called the tragedy of culture—as it dissipated while impelling and justifying the creation of unprecedented rationalizations of life. On these shores, Weber observed, many people had struggled and died to establish their faith, and now many were struggling and dying under the dominance of its bureaucratic capitalist aftermath. Troeltsch also saw that "the churches are numerous, but small, and disappear almost among the towering buildings. It is the picture of a city not characterized by church steeples" (Rollman 1993, 368). As he rode past the huge Brooklyn cemetery, Weber was moved by the spiritual hopes and struggles of New Yorkers living in the overwhelming and deadening structures of capitalism without a saving, freeing spirit.

Intellectuals' concern about religion in New York City likewise declined, matching the general social secularization. The city's Protestant establishment was becoming disestablished. The great African American migration to the north was also a migration out of the churches. Many Jews were anxious to leave the unmodern tyrannies of the rabbis. Many Italian immigrants felt unwelcome in Irish Catholic churches or were anticlerical.

The history of religion in New York City has always been framed by a higher degree of tolerance, secularization of public institutions, and pluralism than usually found elsewhere in the United States. Still, the city has also been the site of a fair number of religious wars and moral conflicts, such as the Dutch Reformed oppression of other religions in New York's founding period, the Great School Wars between Protestant and Catholics in the nineteenth century, and the Protestant-Catholic political-moral wars culminating in Manhattan's Calvary Baptist Pastor John Roach Stratton castigating "Rum, Romanism, and Rebellion" in the 1920s. Today, Jews, Protestants, and Catholics continue to fight over institutional control, prejudice, and discrimination. Roman Catholic and Jewish ethnics have also fought to overcome the invidious effects of the Protestant establishment.

Since the 1920s, the Protestant establishment has tried to institutionalize a liberal Protestant ethic in an internationalized, universalized, rationalized religion and image of the city—a sort of cartelization to promote harmony and modern rationality—through the New York City Council of Churches, Union Theological Seminary, Riverside Church, the Interfaith Center, and the UN chaplaincy. These efforts intensified the "modernist-fundamentalist" debates, which reached their peak intensity in Rev. Harry Emerson Fosdick's modernist jeremiad "Shall the Fundamentalists Win?" Since the 1950s, the fundamentalists have regrouped and started to rebuild their presence in New York, although this rebuilding did not achieve any significant success until the 1990s.

African American church leaders led the city's civil rights movement while the black Muslims aimed to put fear into the hearts of their enemies. Conservative ethnic religionists fought against secular liberals' bulldozing and busing their neighborhoods. And a new religious particularism arose in reaction to the intrusion of the secular elites' programs for social reform.

In 1957, evangelist Billy Graham warily approached New York for his first Madison Square Garden crusade. Protestant establishment intellectual leader Reinhold Niebuhr repeatedly attacked Graham and refused to meet with him; others were also skeptical. Graham admitted that he was "prepared to go to New York to be crucified by my critics" (Martin 1993, 225). Twenty-five years later, in 1991, another of Graham's crusades signaled a turning point in the visibility and role of religion in New York City. This time, Graham, with Roman Catholic support, held in Central Park the largest religious gathering in New York City history, according to the *Daily News*. This highly symbolic punctuation mark in New York City's religious history was soon followed by a highly successful papal visit and, in 1993, by the ousting of the New York City public school chancellor José Fernandez by a coalition of Catholics, Jews, and ethnic evangelicals.

Denominational Reorientations

In the absence of a state church system, all religions in the United States become denominations, varieties of organized religion competing in the spiritual marketplace. In this section, we look at two big New York City religions, Protestantism and Catholicism, and two relatively new imports.

Catholicism in New York has undergone three reorientations since its introduction to New York. Its vast Irish immigrant population gave New York Catholicism a pronounced Irish lilt that offended the Italians arriving in the late nineteenth and early twentieth centuries. Mary Brown shows how the church's adjustment to the Italians laid the foundation for today's Roman Catholic immigrants, now mostly from Spanish-speaking countries. The church's parish system, which is organized on the basis of geography, has been supplemented by parishes whose leaders conduct religious services in multiple languages, as well as some parishes' ethnic and linguistic specialization. Much of this specific ethnic and linguistic specialization, however, has been centralized in the diocese headquarters.

The Protestant establishment as exemplified by the Episcopal Church of the Vanderbilts and Morgans declined precipitously between 1950 and 1990. Robert Carle portrays three successful but diverse efforts at an Episcopal comeback: liberal, traditionalist, and evangelical. What all three have in common is a closer connection to the Episcopalian church's biblical roots and a deeper, more challenging religious life.

The African American Protestant churches have undergone generational, doctrinal, and educational sea changes. Wuthnow's observation (1988) that education has underlain denominational reorientation in the United States as a whole applies here. New York City African American church leaders are much better educated than those of previous generations and have assimilated the liberal-conservative fault lines of contemporary Protestantism. The post–Civil Rights generation is much more specific about their theological identities and views of the Bible while shifting somewhat to a more conservative political stance. The popularity of the charismatic/Pentecostal religion has made tremendous headway among New York City African American church leaders, though not with an increase in theological conservatism.

Conservative religions have found ways to thrive in New York. Lacking an accredited seminary for several decades, local evangelicals and charismatics/Pentecostals have erected a large number of Bible institutes and unaccredited seminaries to train their lay members and clergy. Korean ethnic institutes and seminaries sustain a Korean church denominational orientation that harks back to the more conservative theology of Korea. Consequently, many Korean churches are much more conservative than their American denominational partners. Hi-tech, hi-education Hindu immigrants swing not toward secularization and liberalism but toward Hindu fundamentalism and ethnic particularity. In India, the hi-techers were complaisantly religious, if not secular. But here in New York, they adopt religious-ethnic fundamentalism to sustain their ancestral identity and, particularly, that of their children. This ethnic-religious fundamentalism, which has displaced pan-Hinduism, is continuing its ascendancy as the new immigrant generation achieves economic and social success. This fundamentalism will undoubtedly lead to clashes with the larger society, and even more so with the Hindus' own children.

Some religions find their roots in New York. Santeria, a Cuban-style, Catholic-influenced religion, was adopted and reformed back to its African origins, becoming the "Yoruba religion" for former Protestant African American adherents. Could this form of Yoruba religion be its Protestant form, the Cuban Santeria its Catholic form, and the African religion the original?

Conversions and Religious Switching

In New York, conversion and religious switching[1] almost always involve changes, revivals, or invocations of ethnic identities. According to Samuel Kliger, Jews from the former Soviet Union feel like "Russians" discovering a new or renewed Jewish identity that is often more ethnic than religious. Segundo Pantoja proposes that religious Latinos in New York can pass back and forth between Roman Catholic and evangelical churches because of their common underlying Latino religiosity. Eastern Orthodoxy is losing members as its ethnic congregants become assimilated as American suburbanites, according to Cimino, and are being replaced by converts who are drawn to the "otherness" of Orthodoxy and who often bring a different attitude toward their new religion. As Cimino and Karpathakis note, the converts are "modern Americans" who conflict with the established believers over culture and power. Likewise, new Russian Jewish immigrants often resent the expectations of American Jews and are quietly struggling for control over their ethnic-religious destiny.

Because of the overlap of deeply held ethnic identities and religious affiliation, New York has not always been a site of massive conversions and religious switching. Although Irish and Italian identification with Roman Catholicism remained fairly constant during much of the twentieth century, in times of great migration to the city, New York tends to become a very active switchboard for spiritual pilgrimages. In fact, many local religious leaders believe that interest in religion and openness to conversion or religious switching are highest during migrants' first two years in New York.

Many newcomers enter New York already predisposed to conversion and religious switching. The new Russian immigrants, Kliger notes, went through a period of widespread disillusionment with Communist ideology and a subsequent search for a new faith in the former Soviet Union starting around 1990 or 1991. Latinos come to New York from countries that already have a large number of converts to evangelicalism, so they arrive "preevangelized" or "prenetworked" to the numerous evangelical denominations here in the city. The Yuppies who were swept into the city by the financial services boom in the 1980s and 1990s often report being given the names of "hot churches or synagogues" like B'nai Jeshurun or Redeemer Presbyterian.

Quite a few of the conversions or religious switching reported in this book are to more demanding religious regimes like charismatic Catholicism, evangelical Protestantism, "hard-core" Eastern Orthodoxy, or Hindu fundamentalism. The flourishing of conservative religion in New York has accompanied massive migrations. New Russian Jewish immigrants are more likely to join Orthodox synagogues if they join any at all. The conversion process may be partly a function of tradition meeting modernity (see Ammerman 1987). Eastern Orthodox converts reject certain aspects of modernity. However, Russian and Latino converts seem to be responding to social and existential crises in their homeland and to the unsettling and liberating effects of migration. Indeed, many Russians speak of their conversions as entering "a normal modern life" ruled by socially ascendant transcendent ideas, absolute morality, law, and reason.

Even though conversion and religious switching may take place in

New York City, it is often with a cultural vocabulary from the home country. Pantoja's Latinos come with a pan-Latino understanding of religion that mandates a supernaturalistic, effervescent, personalized relationship with the divine and presupposes simultaneous religious identities, codes, and affiliations. Most of the new Russian immigrants define their Judaism in Russian Orthodox terms, seeing religion as something intensely personal and private, not communal. Public rituals, then, are not favored but when performed become simultaneously public moments and private inner pilgrimages.

New York is also a place where people can leave religion. Many Russian Jews come to New York expecting to leave ideological *diktat* for a freer humanism and are surprised by American Jews' religious expectations. Sometimes religion seems uncomfortably close to their memories of Soviet violations of conscience.

Many of the chapters in *New York Glory* consider strategies for winning converts, retaining more members, or bringing back the "fallen away." Pantoja wonders whether an ecumenical strategy of a pan-Latino religiosity might facilitate a return of "evangelicos" to his church. The conclusion to Kliger's chapter could have been a call for Russian-led synagogues and Jewish organizations with a Russian religious sensibility that contradicts the "Protestantism" of American Jews. Cimino highlights the strategic appeal of Eastern Orthodoxy's literature and tradition as an antidote to "shallow modernity." Lucas wonders what the Mormons can do to raise their retention rate, and Farrell and Perez-Gonzalez outline strategies that religious feminists have used.

No religion can attract converts or build a significant social movement without creating symbolic enemies to overcome. "Satan," a good example, is the culmination of many threats. The enemies come from within as inner temptations, contradiction, and emptiness (see Warner and Wittner 1998) as well as from without. Converts come to Eastern Orthodoxy decrying shallow evangelicalism and Roman Catholic hypocrisy. The new Russian immigrants have rather obvious bogeymen in the form of Soviet Communism and Russian social chaos. Now, however, they are beginning to resent the overcontrol and denigration by American Jews. African American church leaders inveigh against violence and drugs. Middle- and upper-class Episcopalians and Upper East Side evangelicals are likely to talk about stress. Most immigrants also speak of religion as a way of preventing the immoral American society from contaminating their children. Urban Muslims repeatedly castigate the easy sexuality of American culture. But the problem with the parents' symbolic strategy of rejecting American society is that as their children assimilate, they are likely also to reject their parents' religion.

Several religious groups consider immigrant New York a training ground for winning converts overseas. But they usually do not take into account that immigrants' backgrounds, identities, and life plans are very different from those of most of their compatriots. Orthodox Lubavitchers combed the former Soviet Union and found that the Jews remaining there are quite different from those who emigrate to Israel or the United States. Kliger reports that Jews in Russia are much more likely to be atheists than are new Russian Jewish immigrants in New York and Boston. Consequently, the opportunities to convert them would seem to be greater in immigrant entrepôts. Ebaugh believes that immigrants to the United States are creating transnational religions (Ebaugh 1999). But just as religions become transnational for some, other home-country religionists find immigrants' religions strange and even distasteful. In addition, U.S. immigrants face the dilemma of the second generation's leaving their religion through intermarriage or assimilation to American secular culture, particularly at elite universities.

Ethnic Diversification

The history of New York City's religions has been and continues to be intertwined with the history of immigration. Each wave of immigrants brings its own religions. Sometimes the immigrants come because of their religion, and in other cases, they come for other reasons but bring their religions along (see Barkan 1995). Finally, a number of New Yorkers come in order to flee organized religion.

First the Dutch came with their Dutch Reformed Protestantism. Then the English and German Protestants came, along with a few Jews. Starting in the nineteenth century, a large wave of Roman Catholic Germans, Irish, and Italians arrived, followed by another large wave of both Buddhist Chinese and Jews in the late nineteenth and early twentieth centuries. African American Protestants migrated to New York City in large numbers starting during World War I. Then "la migracion" of Puerto Ricans during and right after World War II brought Hispanic religions to New York City.

The Hart-Cellar Immigration Act of 1965 commenced the latest wave of religiously significant immigration, and now the population of New York City is more than one-third immigrant. Roger Sanjek says that the ethnic and immigrant diversity of Elmhurst-Corona, Queens, is the future of us all (Sanjek 1998). But Rose Coser Ebaugh, head of a study group on immigrant religion in Houston, Texas, wonders whether the impact on religion is different from that of the nineteenth century's wave of immigrants (Ebaugh 1999). Stephen Warner observes that like those of the nineteenth century, today's new immigrants are mostly Christians (Warner 1999a).

New York City is the most ethnically diverse place on the globe. My newsstand alone carries papers in fourteen languages, but this is small potatoes next to the 196 nationalities who have passed through the city schools. "More than 56% of the city's population are foreign born or the children of foreign born." In 2000, approximately 37.5% of the city's population was foreign born, a percentage that rivals the high point of immigration for New York City, when 40% of the city's population was foreign born. (Moss, Townsend, and Tobier 1997, 1; NYC Dept. of City Planning 1999; for the United States, see Hirschman, De Wind, and Kasinitz 1999; Portes and Rumbaut 1996; for diversification in Chicago, see Livezey 2000).

Until recently, Mormonism was a white religion, consigning all the other races to the lower regions of heaven (Ostling and Ostling 1999, chap. 6). Black Muslims were, well, black. Now, Mormonism in the city and elsewhere has grown tremendously among nonwhites, and the Black Muslims of Malcolm X's old Temple no. 7 have shed the "black" and acquired many colors. Likewise, Seventh-Day Adventism, a religion that got its start upstate as the Mormons did, as all-white, is now an overseas and immigrant religion. Something has happened.

Some religionists, like Malcolm X's Muslims, needed an ideological change to match their growing psychological openness to other diverse ethnicities before they could diversify their own religions. For Malcolm X, the ideological change came first from disillusionment with the leader of his religion and then an experience with and the acceptance of the dominant strand of Islam. Imam Pashah, the current leader of Malcolm X's old mosque, used to "hate white people" but now is proud of his congregation's diversity.

The Mormons' ethnic diversification also came after an ideological change in 1978 when church tradition was reinterpreted in a radically new way. But the Mormons' ethnic diversification seems more closely related to the church's determination to gain social acceptance as a variant of normal

Christianity. Mormons have thus adjusted to the American public philosophy of racial equality, hoping to leave behind such embarrassments as the protests over its visitors' center across from Lincoln Center.

The Mormons and Seventh-Day Adventists also illustrate that much of the city's ethnic diversification of religions started overseas that then came here. The Protestant missionary movement originated as perhaps the largest social movement in the nineteenth century and is still strong today. It went everywhere, and now much of the religion in the city is its echo (see Miller 1999). Korea, the Philippines, and other countries are even sending missionaries to New York. Recently, a Brazilian missionary came to assume the leadership of a multimillion-dollar urban church-planting center. Converts overseas naturally feel an affinity with the home country of their religion. The immigration of religionists is not simply the movement toward home base, however. Many religions have become transnational, and the movement from the home country to another resembles more the migration to a common meeting ground.

Since the mid-nineteenth century, Roman Catholicism has been the city's largest religious denomination. According to the 1990 National Survey of Religious Identification (Kosmin and Lachman 1993), 42 percent of New Yorkers identified themselves as Roman Catholics. Parochial schools educate more than 170,000 children in the city and adjoining counties of New York State (Kosmin and Lachman 1993). More than 70 percent of New Yorkers of Irish, Italian, and Polish backgrounds identified themselves as Catholic in the 1990 National Survey of Religious Identification. Historically, New Yorkers of German background have also been heavily Catholic. Although the Catholic Church seems to be identified mainly with New York Irish and Italians, the church's largest group is the Latin Americans in the New York Archdiocese, which covers Manhattan, Staten Island, and the Bronx. (The Diocese of Brooklyn includes Queens.) In addition, 7 percent of Catholics in New York State are black (Doyle and McDonald 1996).

Although Catholic white ethnics have been moving out of the city, causing the closing of many churches and schools, the vast immigration to New York has revitalized many congregations. Ruth Doyle, director of research for the Archdiocese of New York, says, "One of the great untold stories of the Catholic Church in New York City is the filling up of the parishes with new immigrant liveliness." Every week, mass is now celebrated in more than two dozen languages. Recently, new nationality parishes were opened for Arabs, Portuguese, Koreans, and Albanians, to name only a few of the newcomers.

Every Good Friday, the people of the Church of the Incarnation in Queens Village march around the neighborhood, their leaders proclaiming the Gospel in Spanish, English, and French. Once primarily an Irish parish, the diversity of people there have learned to live with one another. Parishioner Hermina Jaramilo observes that Catholic parish life has changed in both diversity and tolerance: "The faces and the language have changed, but not the Word."

By the 1940s, a number of African Americans in New York were converting to Roman Catholicism. Using a then-current baseball allusion, priests and nuns called their campaign to convert "working in the Negro League." Black New Yorkers have been most impressed with Catholic education. In Harlem, for example, 75 percent of the students in Catholic schools are black Protestants, and in Brooklyn and Queens, the number of Haitians and Trinidadians has significantly expanded the ranks of black Catholics.

In the United States—and these numbers are probably reflected in New York—66 percent of Hispanics are Catholics, although they increasingly prefer evangelical and Pentecostal/charismatic Protestantism (Deck 1994). In 1990, Puerto Rican and Latin American high school students had a significantly lower preference (52% to 54%) for Catholicism than their parents' generation and a proportionally greater preference for Protestantism (Kosmin and Lachman 1993, 138–139).

The defections from Catholicism begin with the low rate of religious practice among Hispanic Catholics (23% nationally) and a scarcity of Hispanic priests (4% nationally) (Gonzalez and LaVelle 1988).[2] Immigration also causes them to look for new attachments. In addition, the "explosion of Protestantism" in Latin America preevangelizes many Hispanics before they arrive in New York City; David Martin suggests that the evangelical stress on intimacy, the administration of their own churches, and a new work ethic appeal to upwardly mobile Hispanics (Martin 1990). One does not have to be in a Spanish-speaking evangelical church long before being asked by its leader to become involved in the church's spiritual life.

New York City Religion and the Psyche

Is religion an opiate, as Marx claimed, or is it a fuel that empowers, as an African American congregant asserts in Mary McRae's chapter 15? Karl

Marx is infamous for debunking religion as a narcotic that numbs the pain of poor people at the expense of blinding them to the source of their oppression, capitalism. Religion as therapeutic, then, is the lobotomy for the underclasses. Marx introduced New Yorkers to this view in the 1860s in his newspaper columns in the *New York Herald Tribune.*

From the evidence offered in the following chapters, New Yorkers of all classes and religious persuasions feel oppressed. While inmates at Sing Sing State Prison as described by Victoria Erickson and H. Dean Trulear quite naturally feel degraded, Upper East Side evangelicals (according to Hannibal Silver) also suffer real or imagined emotional trauma from being stereotyped as rigid, bullying, fatalistic, irrational bigots who are sexually frigid and use religion as a crutch. Leah Davidson's Zen Confucian Korean medical student, J, feels his world is collapsing, whereas McRae's black Protestants rest up after wrenching experiences with workaday racism.

Therapeutic programs help many people by giving them strength to reveal and sustain an alternative social identity, taking advantage of the city's allowance "for play with the possibilities of concealment and revelation" (Orsi 1999, 49). Because prison inmates and African Americans feel that their humanity is often hidden from view, seminary teachers and church leaders proclaim them as worthwhile and fully human. Upper East Side evangelicals believe that their religion's good qualities are hidden from view by stereotypes, and their counselors help persuade them to assume a new, more acceptable public identity. A Zen therapist tries to show his Korean American patient that his abusive father does not represent the real fatherhood of the Zen Confucian tradition.

The emotional tone of these religionists is set by family trauma. Most of the Upper East Side evangelicals are single without the nearby support of their families, who face the problems of modern dating and family formation. The Sing Sing inmates have hurt and silenced their families but through a religious program are learning how to be responsible family members again. J's relations with his parents and wife seems to be on the breaking point. Most of the African American congregants are women without men, although one church in Brooklyn has managed to attract more men through an aggressive male-centered program.

Therapists, religious leaders, and lay religionists provide familial warmth and acceptance (see Warner and Wittner 1998, 369–371). Bill Webber, the seminary leader at the Sing Sing prison program, acts as a father figure, and the seminary's graduates act as an extended family to the new students. One suspects that Redeemer's counseling center is a crisis center for many people without families in New York. J finds a home in the *zendo?* and perhaps a father figure in his Zen master. The African American congregants have made their churches function and feel like extended families. Although the chapters in this book do not explicitly say so, religions in New York create a feeling of being part of a family of coreligionists, a social circle of strangers (see Kadushin 1966) who nonetheless feel like kin when they see another studying the Bible on the subway, sporting a yarmulke, or discussing the latest qigong exercises.

Religions try to soothe emotional trauma by offering alternative authority for one's self-identity and social presence. But the new authority is not necessarily or purely as religious as these religions imagine it to be. God is sometimes redefined or joined by other gods, idols in the older sense.[3] The Christian teachers at Sing Sing offer God the Creator, but with a touch of self-creation thrown in. The African American churches offer Moses and Jesus as touchstones to human dignity. The result is the stand-on-my-dignity manner of African American church people, ranging from the dignified military-like Sunday marching of white-clothed and -gloved church ladies to the permanently insulted dignity of Rev. Al Sharpton. Sometimes it is hard to discern where the dignity of God ends and tradition and self-effrontery begins (Seltser 1995).

The Upper East Side evangelicals and the Korean Zen Confucian therapist of Flushing seem to be fellow travelers with today's therapeutic culture. In *Habits of the Heart*, Robert Bellah and his colleagues warn that religion loses its salt when it becomes psychological smelling salts. Although praising the warm caring of small groups in American churches, Robert Wuthnow cautions that the small groups do not seem to be leading to deeper theological understanding or a larger social identification.

Indeed, some religious and ethnic circles are wary of psychological therapies. Some evangelicals see them as secularizers and a displacement of pastors. New York University's Paul Vitz, a convert to Roman Catholicism from Psychological Religion (as he calls it), now proclaims from pulpits and lecterns around the city that "psychology as it is conventionally understood is atheism" (Vitz 1994, 1999). Nonetheless, among evangelicals and other religionists, the popularity of psychological counseling is growing quickly. According to Gary Collins, president of the American Association of Christian Counselors, "There's no more exciting time to be in this field." His organization's membership now tops 18,000 (Rabey 1996). Populizers such as evangelical child psychologist James Dobson, author Larry Crabb, and Orthodox Jewish psychologist Laura Schlesinger regularly reach tens of thousands in New York through their radio broadcasts.

Many Jewish New Yorkers see in psychoanalysis a liberation from rabbinical irrationality and Christian triumphalism. In New York, Freud was a prophet of liberation from religion and a Moses to the promised land of rational thought. But Freudianism was bivocal in its moral teachings. On the one hand, Freudian psychology could be used to undermine moral, particularly sexual, boundaries. Yet interpreted in a different way, psychotherapy demanded that one take responsibility for one's actions and develop a maturity defined by self-discipline. In fact, Freudian and other psychologies became veritable substitute religions. No place else in the world has as many psychological healers and devotees as does Manhattan. Forty-four percent of its inhabitants have consulted a psychological counselor (Penn and Schoen 1995). There are even quasi-religious psychotherapy communes, and many of the New Age religions contain psychological elements.

Therapy helps establish boundaries. The Presbyterian Church uses counseling to convince its adherents that New York City is not outside the boundaries of the Bible Belt. Indeed, the church wonders whether the hinterland can really be deeply Christian (see Zerubavel 1991, 6–9). As is typical of many Asian immigrants, J, a Zen Confucian patient, is concerned about the limits of parental authority. The prison inmates want to leave the confines of prison, both literally and psychologically, and once released, they also want people to place them in an acceptable social category (Zerubavel 1991, 12–13). African American congregants want simultaneously to bind themselves racially in the church while unbinding themselves racially in society.

These attempts to redraw the city's emotional boundaries are still experiments. The Upper East Side evangelicals are mainly young and single, a group that is quite optimistic about life in the city. But what happens when the Seinfelds get married and have children? Or are laid off from their Wall Street firm? How will the one-and-a-half- or second-generation Asians like J resolve their emotional ambivalence, even anger, toward parental authority? At present, the Asian Christian churches offer four main remedies. Some accept patriarchal authority while staying in the first generation's churches but try to soften it gradually. Others form English fellowships, usually after some conflict, and others go to non-Asian churches like Redeemer Presbyterian Church (which is more than one-third Asian). A few form purely second-generation churches, a phenomenon currently more common in California than in New York. Many Asians leave their parents' authority and religion behind. Karen Chai has written about this struggle in a Korean church in Boston (Chai 1998). But the booming Korean churches may be followed by a bust (see Mullins 1987). From whom or what will the second generation get its emotional cues and sustenance?

In New York, the aforementioned four remedies are clearly displayed in the members of the evangelical Protestant Overseas Chinese Mission (OCM), one of the largest local Chinese religious organizations in the United States. After some conflict, one-and-a-half- and second-generation members established an English congregation in the 1980s. Then as more second-generation Chinese Americans graduated from college, some started attending the predominantly white Redeemer Presbyterian Church on the Upper East Side while also going to the OCM. Despite some internal tension, the OCM's English congregation leaders responded by establishing in 1999 the Vision Church on the Upper West Side as an independent congregation modeled on Redeemer. The patriarchal authority structure at OCM has also caused some of its second-generation leaders and members to drift away, sometimes leaving the Christian religion entirely.

The outside world is not necessarily sympathetic to religious beliefs or memberships, causing believers to feel caught between religion and world. Robert Merton, a sociologist at Columbia University, portrayed this dilemma as a sociological ambiguity that produces emotional tension with various reactions. The individual or individuals may feel that their membership in a church, temple, *zendo?*, or mosque conflicts with their position in a school, business, friendship circle, or other religion. At that point, both the politics and therapy of religion may become intertwined.

The Social Basis of Feminist Religious Persuasions

Catholic feminist ethicists form a network of the intellectual-academic feminists who started modern feminism in New York. They march to battle in a cloud of papers, books, conferences, organizational acronyms, and foundation money. In sociologist Anthony Giddens's terms, these feminists are modernists of abstract reason and truth. Farrell ends on the note that these modernist feminists are withdrawing from their battles with the Catholic Church, leaving the lesbian and gay activists to renew the charge.

The lesbian and gay synagogue that Harris describes refers to feelings and community. This feminist (and obviously not just female) social formation is the feminism of late modernism, to use Giddens's terms (1990, 1991), which opposes feeling and community against the rationalism of high modernism.

The feminism of the Latinas and Rastafarians is an example of an immigrant gender development. However, the Latinas in ministry whom Perez y Gonzalez describes seem more old-fashioned than the female Rastafarians. The Latina feminists are isolated exemplars who have used traditional culture, experiences with poverty and migration, and their religious beliefs to secure a place for strong women leaders. The next stage of their development seems more likely to be the traditional city politics of demanding more attention and resources for the Latino community than a widespread feminist movement. The Rasta women seem much more hip and modern with their reggae music and poetry, much more part of a modern social movement adept at using symbols and organization.

The Latinas in ministry also remind us that many of the religious changes in New York started overseas. Perez y Gonzalez says that the Latinas' activism had its roots in Latina culture of catering to the needs of others. In addition, the Pentecostalism of Latina women is a backfire from its tremendous success in overseas Latino communities.

New York's religious feminists were among the founders of modern feminism and have dominated the headlines about church and gender. But gender conservatives have not been neglected. In this book, the chapters about Orthodox converts, African American church leaders, Manhattan evangelicals, Mormons, and others all portray religious communities with conservative gender perspectives that are wrestling with liberal feminism. In 1993, their coalition ran School Chancellor Fernandez out of town after he tried implementing a "2 Daddies, 2 Mommies" curriculum legitimizing gay and lesbian family styles.

Family and children also have moved to center stage. The Latinas in ministry have created an ensemble of social justice actions because of their traditional cultural concern for children and family. The Rastas have started to form congregations as an appropriate format for housing families and educating children (also see Hepner 1998b). These new family-oriented feminisms join a rising conservative profamily agenda. While Manhattan public policy advocates like the Manhattan Institute and the Institute for American Values offer a scholarly panache to profamily policies, in the trenches of the city's religions even feminism assumes a family style.

Consequently, the new religious attention is on the role of the father and church leader. In 1998, Promise Keepers, an evangelical ministry for male responsibility, held its inaugural city meeting in the Jets' stadium with forty thousand male church members in attendance. Several fast-growing African American churches like Johnny Youngblood's East New York Baptist Church and E. R. Bernard's Christian Life Centre have an aggressive male-centered approach. Korean men compensate psychologically for the downward social mobility that often accompanies their immigration to the United States by assuming leadership positions in church (Hurh and Kim 1990). Where these efforts will lead and how religious feminists will respond is uncertain. However, if we judge by the Latinas in ministry and Rastafarians, feminists' future success in having a grassroots impact among the religious may depend on how seriously they deal with family, fathers, and children. Indeed, a "family values" discourse flows through other new religions like those of the Hindus (Kurien 1998) and the Iranians (Feher 1998).

The prevalence of American egalitarianism is an influential force among New York religionists. As a result, traditional gender conceptions are frequently contested within religions, as we see in the Latina and Rasta examples. Other instances in the city are the exit of Muslim women from strong patriarchal mosques (see Abusharaf 1998) or in the numerous second-generation disputes over gender roles in immigrant congregations.

One growth area for old-style feminism may be among second-generation immigrants dissatisfied with the fierce patriarchies of their churches and families. In one of the most "staggering declines in church history, many Korean churches are changing from churches of family members to churches of parents" (Kim and Kim 1996, 14). Most of the Korean American second generation fall into two groups, which may be called Generation 2A and Generation 2B. Generation 2A wants its own English-speaking congregation and is comfortable with authoritarian structures. So far, the so-called second-generation churches in the city are really Generation 2A churches. Generation 2B wants a more Americanized style of spirituality and generally either drops out of church or goes to Anglo churches like Redeemer Presbyterian. Generation 2B is much more open to feminist perspectives.

Religion and Politics

For years, New York City's police commissioner went once a week to brief Cardinal John O'Connor on current police affairs affecting the Roman

Catholic Church. The meeting demonstrates how ethnicity/nationality (Irish), religion, and politics have intersected in New York. In 1949, Puerto Rico elected its first governor, Luis Muñoz Martin. At the same time, a militant independence movement also arose, which in 1950 attempted to assassinate President Harry Truman and in 1954 gunned down and wounded five members of the U.S. Congress. The independence fervor also affected New York City's Puerto Rican churches and Bible institutes. In 1957, a substantial part of the Assembly of God Puerto Rican churches declared their independence by taking with them the Hispanic mother church in New York City and its Bible institute to form a new denomination.

Karpathakis's chapter on Greek Orthodoxy illustrates how immigrant religions bring home-country politics into the city. Politics in the churches, mosques, and synagogues also has created internal conflicts regarding the proper role of religion. In the Greek Orthodox Church, the Americanizers want to leave Greek politics and ethnicity out of the church, a desire that angers other members of the Greek Orthodox Church. Most African American church leaders have either wanted to stay out of politics or have opted for a brokerage politics of bargaining for resources from the white establishment in exchange for votes. In U.S. politics, about 34 percent of Catholics identify themselves as conservatives, 34 percent as moderate, and 26 percent as liberal (*New York Times* poll, November 29–December 5, 1999). Politically, West Indian evangelicals are conservative on many issues, although they often vote for Democrats. Kliger indicates that fewer of the recent Russian immigrants are Republicans than the 1970s wave but still are more conservative and independent than other city Jews. The new Russians overwhelmingly approve of Mayor Rudy Giuliani. Ten to 20 percent of Dominican Christians vote for Republicans, and more than half of the Christian Colombians and Ecuadorians supported Republican mayoral candidate Giuliani (Hispanic Research Center 1995; also see Dao 1999).

According to chapters 24 and 25, members of the Greek Orthodox Church and African American church leaders usually favor the Democrats. However, Archibishop Iakovos and some new converts supported George Bush over the Democratic presidential candidate and former Massachusetts governor Michael Dukakis. As Carnes shows, New York City's African American church leaders are politically conservative on many issues and are less committed to the Democratic Party than they used to be. As Taylor makes clear, Brooklyn's African American church leaders have been liberal Republicans espousing New Deal policies.

As religion returns to the public square (Neuhaus 1984), it "simultaneously introduces . . . intersubjective norms into the private sphere (analogous to the feminist dictum 'the personal is political'), and morality into the public sphere of state and economy (the principle of the 'common good' as a normative criterion)" (Casanova 1994, 217). Issues like busing, racism, education, budget allocations, abortion, and sexual and gender issues have invoked religious and ethnic-religious activism as well as inner debates.

Religion often enters politics through events like wars. Citizenship for many Puerto Rican immigrants did not acquire a real meaning until World War II, in which many of them served with great valor. In fact, Hispanics earned more Congressional Medals of Honor per capita than any other group. So this generation thought they should be fully integrated into American society and fought for it through groups like ASPIRA and the American GI Forum.

The killing in 1999 of the African immigrant Amadou Diallo at first brought to the fore American and African immigrant Muslim leaders, who then lost the stage to Rev. Al Sharpton and his Baptist allies, and Diallo's memorial service was held at the Convent Avenue Baptist Church. The U.S./NATO-Yugoslavia conflict was another such event that aroused many new Russian immigrants, who felt pulled by their Russian, Jewish, and American identities.

In sum, the magnitude of religion's impact on New York City's social and cultural life has been underappreciated. *New York Glory* aims both to capture the richness of religious life in New York City and to provide a foundation for our understanding of the current and future shape of religion in urban America.

NOTES

1. Definitions of conversion vary widely among religions, peoples, and academic disciplines (see Malony and Southard 1992; Snow and Machalek 1984). Conversion may be defined as the transformation of one's system of authority and meaning. Religious switching emphasizes changing self-identities and organizational affiliations without necessarily transforming one's system of authority or meaning.

2. Protestant seminaries and schools of theology have three times the number of Hispanic students as do Catholic seminaries (Kosmin and Lachman 1993, 138). Bishop Edwin O'Brien of St. Joseph's Seminary in Yonkers says that only

about a dozen new priests are ordained each year for the whole archdiocese of New York.

3. This may not be so much a result of a cultural merging (Bastide 1960; Herskovits 1941) as a result of interaction with ideals of self and salvation.

Chapter 2

The Religious Demography of New York City

Vivian Z. Klaff

On a recent visit to New York City, I spent a few hours in a local library gathering a list of references concerning the historical development of the city and its specific religious groups. Most of the books about Catholics, Jews, various Protestant denominations, Eastern philosophies, and other religions are ethnographic case studies of a historical period, a specific neighborhood, or a unique institution or are stories about immigration and efforts at integration. I could not, however, find any book that systematically summarized the area's religious composition.

Public opinion surveys show that a high percentage of the American population believe in a supernatural entity, even though this belief is not necessarily reflected in practice (National Opinion Research Center 1996). In addition, religion is at the center of a number of controversial issues related to prayer in school, abortion, the fundamentalist movement, and the connection between belief in a particular religion and the legitimacy of prevailing laws. Although it is fairly easy to find information about most of a population's compositional variables at different levels of geography, identifying individuals by religion is more complicated. Difficult as it is to gauge the size of a population subgroup, it is even more difficult to determine the characteristics of a religious group and, more important, to compare the characteristics of different religious groups.

The history of New York City is also the history of diversity, and this book shows how this diversity is manifested in its religions. As Binder and Reimers observed in *All the Nations under Heaven* (1995), "At the outset of the American Revolution at least twenty-two houses of worship representing at least twelve denominations existed. When Major Samuel Shaw of

Boston visited the city in May 1776, he described its people as 'a motley collection of all the nations under heaven'" (Binder and Reimers 1995, 1).

In 1860, the U.S. census listed only white, black, and mulatto (three-eighths to five-eighths black) as population categories, but by 1990, the census offered a wide variety of racial and ethnic categories. Of the approximately 250 million persons counted in the 1990 census, 74 percent were classified as non-Hispanic white, 12 percent as African American, 10 percent as Hispanic, 3 percent as Asian, and just under 1 percent as Native American. Each of these groups was further divided according to ethnicity and country of origin. In 1990, about a quarter of the population was foreign born, and since then, the proportion of non-English-speaking immigrants has increased. At the end of the twentieth century, the population of the New York City metropolitan area, defined as the five boroughs, was estimated at about 9 million, compared with 7.3 million in 1990. However, almost no representative national demographic data were collected with reference to religion.

Collecting Data on Religion

Studying religious identification and the various data sources regarding religious affiliation presents a number of methodological problems. The first is the restrictions on asking people about their religious affiliation, and so no religious data are available from federal data collection systems. Our analysis of religion therefore relies on data from a wide variety of sources in which religious affiliation is usually collected as a "background" variable (see Christiano 1987).

Between 1850 and 1936, the U.S. government collected information on religious organizations and their members. This information has many methodological flaws, however, and according to Glock, "there simply are no reliable historical statistics on church membership and it is extremely doubtful that accurate statistics can be produced through manipulating the unreliable ones" (Glock 1959, 39). Nevertheless, historians and social scientists have used these data in a number of ways to document and analyze the changing cultural and religious diversity of the American population. But after the 1930s, even the flawed data available until then were eliminated when the entire federal government removed from the data collection system all questions about the religious identification of individuals or organizations.

The history of New York City is closely tied to the cultural and religious diversity of the American population. A large portion of the early settlers of "New Amsterdam" (New York City) were refugees seeking religious freedom and security. Even though many of them were not welcomed, eventually immigrants were permitted to retain (or establish) their religious convictions. Consequently, as the demographic profile of the American population has changed over the past few decades owing to the greater number of immigrants from a wide variety of cultures, the religious identification of the population has become much more diverse.

The second problem in quantifying New York City according to religious categories is defining a religion. Religion and ethnicity are usually voluntary expressions of identity, and people construct their identities and practices as they desire or require. Religious identification can be based on self-identity, membership in a religious institution, formal definitions proposed by different subgroups within the larger religious grouping, or other characteristics related to a particular group. There are no standardized definitions for collecting and analyzing data on religion, and definitions vary from one religion to another and even within a religion across time. For example, Catholics view church membership as deriving from traditional practices such as infant baptism, and not necessarily "registration." In contrast, most Protestant denominations rely more on the voluntary decision of adherents to state their religious conviction. Membership in religious bodies can therefore be based either on persons formally registered as members of an organization or on the church's recognition that a person has met certain requirements.

In many situations, data are obtained from membership records, interviews with "expert witnesses," or the impressions of a local religious leader who has estimated the size of a congregation. Information on "religious identification" and "religious preference" is also often obtained just by asking people, "What is your religion or your religious preference?" Although there a reasonable correlation between identification and preference, this correlation is weaker when analyzing membership. For example, the *National Survey of Religious Identification* (Kosmin and Lachman 1993) points out that many more Americans claim to identify with a number of the major Christian religious denominations than the membership figures of those groups bear out. Conversely, sometimes religious organizations inflate their membership numbers to demonstrate the success of their leadership.

The third problem is the consistency of religious identity. Through either conversion or the internal restructuring of subgroups within a larger religious group, the number of people identified with a particular group can and often does change over time. For some religious groups, joining or leaving is a simple matter of voicing a choice. Other groups have very rigid norms with which one must comply before one can join, and leaving the group often means breaking with one's family and community. For example, Orthodox Jews are discouraged from marrying outside their group, and conversion to Judaism is extremely difficult. Rates of entering and leaving vary and are very difficult to obtain.

The fourth problem is the changing pattern of immigration and the religious composition of new immigrants. When immigration patterns are highly differentiated, it is difficult to use data from previous years to represent current estimates. New research is required. In addition, the recent large number of immigrants from a wide range of societies has made New York City's religious environment extremely diverse, and thus the idea of a triple melting pot of Protestant, Catholic, Jew (Herberg 1955) has become a somewhat simplistic categorization. Furthermore, some of the chapters in this book demonstrate that the immigrant population has been instrumental in altering the size and character of religious groups. One example is Seventh-Day Adventism: "the face of Seventh-Day Adventism in metropolitan New York has changed dramatically over the past 30 years, as it has been transformed from a church of primarily Caucasians and Afro Americans . . . to a church that is now 90 percent immigrant" (Lawson 1998, 329).

The 1990 General Social Survey (GSS), a national random sample of U.S. adults, revealed that most of the respondents had some religious feeling and were willing to identify their religious affiliation. The GSS also revealed that about 90 percent of adult Americans believe in a supernatural being; about 75 percent pray every day; and 60 percent say religion is very important to them.

It appears, then, that Americans are aware of their religious spirituality even if they do not formally belong to a religious organization. According to GSS data, about six in ten Americans are formally linked to a religious congregation, but attendance at religious services has declined since the 1950s and was about 40 percent in the 1980s. This statistic means that we need to understand the limitations of using membership data to generalize about the characteristics of any religion. To use such data, we must prove that members of a religion are the same as those stating they are adherents of a particular religion but are not members of the religious institution. The evidence suggests that the mainstream "middle-of-the-road" Protestant denominations are losing members and that the more fundamentalist groups are gaining (Roof and McKinney 1987). In addition, the evidence shows that a larger share of the American adult population is not identifying with any religion.

New York City and the National Survey of Religious Identification

The 1990 National Survey of Religious Identification (NSRI) has helped determine the religious composition of the New York City metropolitan area. About 113,000 households were contacted, and information was obtained from respondents aged eighteen or older (a detailed description of the NSRI data set can be found in Kosmin and Lachman 1993).

The randomly selected sample represented about 175 million adults and used a weighting procedure. For this chapter, I selected those respondents living in the five boroughs and those living in New York State. Based on this selection, the NSRI sample represents about 5.7 million adults in the boroughs (NYC) and about 13.2 million adults in New York State (NYS).

Table 2.1 presents the adult religious composition of the United States, New York State, and New York City in 1990, based on data from the NSRI. Note that the NSRI's data do not include children under age eighteen. Although I have assumed that the adult population represents the distribution of the entire population, this is not necessarily accurate. Where fertility rates and/or migration rates differ among groups, the adult population may not be a correct representation of the children. Each of the denominations represented in the table contains at least 1 percent of the New York City NSRI sample except for the Mormons, who numbered less than 1 percent in New York City but more than 1 percent in the United States as a whole.

The largest group were the Catholics (42.4%), and the next two largest groups were the Baptists (10.8%) and the Jews (10.7%). A small group of respondents stated that they were Protestant (4.5%) and Christian (2.7%), and if we could have reinterviewed them, many would probably have been redistributed among the Protestant denominations. In addition, 7.5 percent of the respondents stated that they were agnostic or had no religion. Comparing the religious composition of New York City with

TABLE 2.1
Religious Identification, Persons Aged 18 and over for the United States,
New York State, and New York City

	U.S. Total (%)	New York State (%)	New York City (%)
Catholic	26.2	44.3	42.4
Protestant	9.8	6.9	4.5
Baptist	19.4	8.3	10.8
Christian	4.6	2.3	2.7
Episcopalian	1.7	2.0	1.6
Evangelical	0.3	0.3	0.4
Jehovah's Witness	0.8	1.0	1.1
Lutheran	5.2	2.7	1.2
Methodist	8.0	6.1	3.0
Mormon	1.4	0.2	0.2
Pentecostal	1.8	1.5	2.4
Presbyterian	2.8	2.4	1.3
Protestant Total	(55.8)	(33.7)	(29.2)
Christian Total	(82.0)	(78.0)	(71.6)
Jewish	1.8	6.9	10.7
Muslim	0.3	0.8	1.6
Hindu	0.1	0.6	1.0
Agnostic/None	8.2	7.0	7.5
Other, Refused	7.6	6.7	7.6
Total Percent	100.0	100.0	100.0
Number (1,000s)	175,441	13,227	5,666

SOURCE: National Survey of Religious Identification, 1990.

that of the United States, we see that New York City has a considerably higher proportion of Catholics (42.4% compared with 26.2%) and Jews (10.7% compared with 1.8%) than does the United States as a whole. Of the larger groups, those underrepresented in New York City are the Baptists (10.8% versus 19.4%), Lutherans (1.2% versus 5.2%), and Methodists (3.0% versus 8.0%).

In sum, 71.6 percent of the respondents in New York City were Christian, compared with 78 percent in New York State and 82 percent in the United States. A higher proportion of the three non-Christian groups lived in New York City than in either the state or the nation as a whole. Although the data for the other smaller religious groups are not reliable because of the small number, New York City appears to contain a considerably larger number of non-Christian and recent immigrant group religions than does the nation in general. The attraction of New York City to immigrants and the networking available to them suggests that the diversity of religious organizations has expanded in recent years. An analysis of the General Social Survey (GSS) data from 1972 through 1998 for the country as a whole verifies this assumption. The GSS data for three decades were combined, and of those respondents interviewed between 1972 and 1980, 1.34 percent identified themselves as other than Catholic, Protestant, Jewish, or none. Between 1981 and 1990, this percentage increased to 1.98, and between 1991 and 1998, it rose to 3.43. In general, we can conclude that the religious composition of New York City is less Christian than is that of the nation and is fairly heterogeneous in religion as well as race.

Religious Diversity by Race

The racial and ethnic diversity of New York City's five boroughs is well documented. The 1990 U.S. census reported that 52 percent of the population was white, 29 percent was black, and 7 percent was Asian. A fairly large group, 12 percent, listed another ethnic/racial origin. Based on a different enumeration, about 24 percent identified themselves as Hispanic in origin. Because "Hispanic" combined persons defining themselves as white, black, and other, the percentages do not sum to 100 percent. Table 2.2 shows the distribution of each of the religious groups by race and Hispanic ethnic identity, based on the NSRI data set, which used a somewhat different subjective definition of ethnicity. In the New York City area, just over half of the population is white (54%), about a third is black (37.5%), and the remainder would not or could not identify themselves by the black-white racial classification. Three groups (Catholic, Jewish, and Lutheran) are predominantly white, and ten groups are predominantly black. About two-thirds of the Hindus and one-third of the Muslims were not willing to define themselves according to the black-white racial classification. Interestingly, most of the Baptists (89.5%) and the Pentecostals (93.9%) are black.

A separate classification of the population by Hispanic ancestry reveals that about 15 percent in the New York City area consider themselves to be of Hispanic origin. Within the Hispanic population, only two groups contain a majority of whites, the Catholics and the Pentacostalists. All the other groups are predominantly Hispanic nonwhite. Although we cannot make assumptions from these data about the extent of racial or ethnic integration, they do show a fairly clear overall racial and ethnic differentiation for most of the clearly defined denominations.

TABLE 2.2
Racial-Ethnic Composition of New York City by Religious Identification (%)

	White	Black	Don't Know/ Refused	Total %	Hispanic White	Hispanic Nonwhite	Don't Know/ Refused	Total %
Catholic	75.6	19.3	5.1	100	24.9	74.5	0.6	100
Baptist	4.1	89.5	6.3	100	2.3	96.0	1.7	100
Jewish	95.5	3.2	1.3	100	1.7	97.5	0.8	100
None	50.9	35.4	13.7	100	13.4	84.8	1.8	100
Protestant	39.9	52.1	8.0	100	5.9	93.3	0.8	100
Methodist	12.0	83.3	4.7	100	4.1	95.2	0.7	100
Christian	37.5	48.7	13.9	100	14.8	85.2	0.0	100
Pentecostal	2.3	93.9	3.7	100	37.8	62.2	0.0	100
Episcopalian	39.1	53.1	7.8	100	0.0	100	0.0	100
Muslim	16.9	48.3	33.7	100	2.2	96.7	1.1	100
Presbyterian	44.4	48.7	7.0	100	7.5	83.9	8.6	100
Lutheran	71.9	21.1	7.1	100	3.9	91.5	4.6	100
Hindu	18.9	13.3	67.7	100	4.2	93.3	2.5	100
Seventh-Day Adventist	0.0	91.3	8.7	100	9.3	90.7	0.0	100
Mormon	11.1	88.9	0.0	100	9.1	81.8	0.0	100
Total	54.3	37.5	8.2	100	14.6	83.8	1.6	100

SOURCE: National Survey of Religious Identification (1990).

Religious Diversity within New York City

Table 2.3 contains data regarding the sixteen groups identified in table 2.1, disaggregated for the five boroughs. The groups again are divided into seven categories. As we noted earlier, the largest religious group in all the New York City boroughs in 1990 was the Catholics, which is a continuation of a trend dating back to the nineteenth century. According to data on church membership compiled by Christiano (1987, 174), about 68 percent of all New York City church membership in 1890 was Catholic, which increased to 77.9 percent in 1906.

The proportion of Catholics in each borough ranges from the low of 31.7 percent in Manhattan to a high of 67 percent in Staten Island. As one would expect, the Protestant population is the next largest group in all the boroughs, particularly the Bronx, where Baptists (15.3%) make up just under half of the Protestants. Baptists are also fairly strongly represented in Brooklyn and Manhattan. The third-largest group in all five boroughs is the Jewish population, with the greatest numbers living in Brooklyn and Manhattan.

TABLE 2.3
Religious Identification for New York City and the Five Boroughs, Adult Population Aged 18 and Over, Based on NSRI Study, 1990 (%)

	Manhattan	Brooklyn	Queens	Bronx	Staten Island	NYC Total	NYC Number
Catholic	31.7	40.0	50.3	41.0	67.0	42.4	2,402,000
Protestant	4.4	4.7	4.3	4.1	6.6	4.5	257,000
Baptist	11.6	13.0	6.7	15.3	1.8	10.8	613,000
Christian	1.8	3.5	3.0	1.7	2.1	2.7	150,000
Episcopalian	2.8	0.7	0.6	3.4	2.2	1.6	93,000
Jehovah's Witness	0.5	1.8	1.0	0.9	0.0	1.1	60,000
Lutheran	1.0	1.1	2.0	0.1	1.5	1.2	69,000
Methodist	5.0	1.9	2.4	3.7	1.1	3.0	167,000
Mormon	0.0	0.2	0.0	0.6	0.4	0.2	11,000
Pentecostal	3.3	1.8	1.2	3.8	2.7	2.4	133,000
Presbyterian	0.8	1.0	1.3	2.5	1.3	1.3	74,000
Total Protestant	(31.2)	(29.7)	(22.5)	(36.1)	(19.7)	(28.8)	1,627,000
Jewish	12.5	13.1	9.9	6.1	5.8	10.7	605,000
Hindu	1.4	1.6	1.6	1.8	1.5	1.6	91,000
Muslim	0.4	0.9	1.2	1.5	0.0	0.9	53,000
Agnostic/None	13.6	6.5	5.6	5.5	3.5	7.5	427,000
Other/Refused	9.2	8.1	8.9	8.0	5.6	8.1	461,000
Total %	100.0	100.0	100.0	100.0	100.0	100.0	
Total #	1,270,000	1,720,000	1,518,000	882,000	276,000		5,666,000

SOURCE: National Survey of Religious Identification (1990).

Ethnic Comparisons within Boroughs

New York City

The largest religious group in New York City is the Catholics (42%), followed by the Baptists (11%) and the Jews (11%). Seventy-three percent of Hispanics and 53 percent of whites are Catholic, with Jews accounting for the second-largest group of whites. Twenty-nine percent of blacks are Baptist, and 19 percent are Catholic. In all the boroughs, of the three ethnic groups, the black population is more widely dispersed among religious categories.

The Bronx

The Catholic population (41%) of the Bronx is the largest religious group, followed by the Baptists (15%) and the Jews (6%). Sixty-eight percent of Hispanics and 62 percent of whites are Catholic, and 22 percent of whites are Jewish. Thirty-three percent of blacks are Baptist, and 18 percent are Catholic.

Brooklyn

The Catholic population (40%) of Brooklyn is the largest religious group, followed by the Baptists (13%) and the Jews (13%). Seventy-nine percent of Hispanics and 48 percent of whites are Catholic, and 30 percent of whites are Jewish. Thirty-two percent of blacks are Baptist, and 22 percent are Catholic.

Manhattan

The Catholic population (32%) of Manhattan is the largest religious group, but it is proportionately lower than that of the other boroughs. Manhattan also differs from the other boroughs in that besides fairly large concentrations of Baptists (12%) and Jews (13%), it contains a large group of people stating that they have no religion (14%). Seventy-four percent of Hispanics and 31 percent of whites are Catholic, and 26 percent of whites are Jewish. Twenty-nine percent of blacks are Baptist; 15 percent are Catholic; 13 percent are Methodist; and 11 percent have no religion.

Queens

The Catholic population (50%) of Queens is the largest religious group, followed by Jews (10%) and Baptists (7%). Sixty-nine percent of Hispanics and 60 percent of whites are Catholic, and 15 percent of whites are Jewish. Twenty-five percent of blacks are Baptist, and 21 percent are Catholic. About 10 percent each of blacks in Queens define themselves as other Protestant or Methodist.

Staten Island

The Catholic population (50%) of Staten Island is the largest religious group, followed by Jews (10%), Baptists (7%), and those with no religion (7%). Sixty-nine percent of Hispanics and 60 percent of whites are Catholic, and 15 percent of whites are Jewish. Twenty-five percent of blacks are Baptist; 22 percent are Catholic; 8 percent have no religion; 9 percent are Methodist; and 12 percent are Protestants who have not specified their denomination.

Ethnic Comparisons among the Boroughs

Catholics

The Catholic population of New York City in 1990 was 42 percent. Of this, 67 percent lived in Staten Island; 50 percent in Queens; and about 33 percent each in the Bronx, Brooklyn, and Manhattan.

Whites made up more than half of New York City's Catholic population, more in Staten Island and the Bronx and considerably fewer in the other three boroughs. Blacks made up less than one-fifth of New York City's Catholic population, with about 66 percent in Queens; 50 percent in Brooklyn; many fewer in the Bronx, Brooklyn, and Manhattan; and only about 10 percent in Staten Island. Most of New York City's Hispanics were Catholic, in all the boroughs, where their percentage ranged from a high of about 80 percent in Brooklyn to a low of about 68 percent in the Bronx.

Baptists

The Baptist population of New York City was 11 percent, with slightly more in the Bronx, Manhattan, and Brooklyn; fewer in Queens; and very few in Staten Island. Fewer than 3 percent of whites were Baptist, in all the boroughs. Similarly, very few Hispanics in New York City identified themselves as Baptist. Baptists were the largest of the black religious groups in the city, representing about a third of the black population. In all the boroughs except Staten Island, slightly more than 30 percent of the Baptists were black. In Staten Island, about 14 percent of the Baptists were black.

Jews

The Jewish population of New York City was 11 percent, slightly more in Manhattan and Brooklyn, about the same percentage in Queens, and somewhat less in the Bronx and Staten Island. Twenty-two percent of New York City's white population was Jewish. Their proportion of the white population ranged from a high of 30 percent in Manhattan to 16 percent in Queens, with only 7 percent in Staten Island. New York City's Hispanic Jewish and black Jewish populations made up less than 2 percent of that of the entire New York City area.

No Religious Identification

About 8 percent of the New York City population stated that they had no religion, with the highest proportion (14%) in Manhattan. The highest percentage was whites, followed by blacks, and, last, Hispanics. The greatest numbers of whites and blacks with no religion were in Manhattan, and a fair number of blacks in Queens also reported having no religion.

Conclusion

The ability of researchers to describe the religious composition of an area such as New York City is limited by the lack of data. The NSRI data set used in this chapter was collected in 1990, and even though it is the largest and most recent national randomly collected sample on religion, the smaller the religious group was, the less likely there were to be a sufficient number of respondents for a meaningful count. Nevertheless, the NSRI does enable us to paint a broad picture of the distribution of religions in New York City.

New York City's Catholic population clearly is dominant, followed by the smaller but significant numbers of Jews and Baptists. Note, however, that a respondent labeled Catholic may manifest this identification in many ways, such as more liberal or traditional or evangelical. Similarly, the city's Jews may be either Orthodox or less traditional. Those groups not large enough to show up in the NSRI distribution, such as Rastafarian, Greek Orthodox, and Eastern Sacred Philosophy, also play important roles in the city's life and culture. Demographically, however, because these groups are small, they must be examined using a different methodology, such as ethnographic research or case study research, as is demonstrated in this book.

Part II

Denominational Reorientations

Chapter 3

Continuity and Change in Episcopal Congregations in New York City

Robert Carle

Despite sociologists' expectations of a decrease in the significance of religion and of its replacement by scientific education and thought in urban areas, cities like New York are anything but wastelands of the sacred.

In this chapter, I examine the recovery of the sacred among New York's artistic and professional elites using as case studies three thriving Manhattan Episcopal churches.

Episcopal New Yorkers: The Historical Context

Despite its status as a minority faith, the Anglican (named Episcopal after the American Revolution) Church throughout its history has maintained a powerful civic presence in New York. Indeed, Trinity Church (Anglican), Wall Street, chartered in 1697, was colonial New York's quasi-official church (Carle and DeCaro 1997, 11–12). After independence, the Episcopal Church was joined by a cluster of other Protestant denominations—Presbyterians, Methodists, Lutherans, Baptists, and Congregationalists—in functioning as New York City's unofficial religious and cultural establishment, the "mainline churches." Mainline Protestant theologians encouraged their denominations to assume responsibility for the world at large, and their social location assured them of the resources to do so (Carroll and Roof 1993). In the 1920s, only one out of seventy New Yorkers was Episcopalian. Although numerically weak, H. L. Mencken wrote that "the Episcopalians are the religious aristocrats. Just as the hoi polloi [common people] cannot hope to contend with the 400 in the Sunday supplements, so neither can the outcast religions cope with the Church of the Vanderbilts and the Morgans" (*American Mercury* 1926, 129).

Since the 1960s, many of these assumptions about Episcopalian New Yorkers have changed. Mainline denominations have suffered losses in membership in nearly every part of the country, and in New York the losses have been staggering. During the 1950s, parochial reports of the Episcopal Church of the Diocese of New York recorded more than ninety thousand communicants, but in the 1990s, parochial reports record fewer than fifty thousand. Because the diocese has maintained virtually the same number of churches throughout this period of decline, most churches in the diocese are, as one priest put it, "hanging on by their fingernails."

Today, mainstream Protestantism is dominated by what Nancy Ammerman calls Golden Rule Christianity. "What matters most in this view," she writes, "is how you live your life, how you treat others, whether you leave the world a better place" (Ammerman 1997a, 11). Such efforts usually consist of charitable donations and volunteer activities. The biggest challenge for Golden Rule Christians is constructing a prayer life and an explicit religious language, stories, and precepts. Without these, Golden Rule Christianity becomes little more than a self-righteous moral do-goodism that fails to sustain people in the crises of life. A strategic challenge for Protestant churches is thus to build up the moral, religious, and doctrinal capital that has historically empowered members to live good and caring lives.

Huston Smith, a former professor of philosophy at MIT, defined the central contemporary theological problem of the Protestant mainline as its failure to offer

> a clear alternative to the prevailing world-view of liberal, well-educated people who look to science to tell them what things are finally like. . . . If people do not hear from mainline churches the news of a world that is vastly more real than the one science reports and we normally experience, they will go where they do hear the news. (Smith 1996, 1)

And yet there remain in New York City thriving Episcopal churches that continue to reach the educated, professional classes of people who exercise a disproportionate influence on the city's social and cultural life. The three churches discussed in this chapter represent as wide a range of styles and theology and religious practice as one can find in the entire Episcopal denomination. All Angels' practices an evangelical-charismatic brand of Christianity. St. Bartholomew's seeks to draw New Yorkers by adapting its theology and liturgy to contemporary sensibilities. St. Thomas's maintains a staunchly Anglo-Catholic liturgical and musical tradition in the European cathedral tradition of the Middle Ages. All three have had strong rectors whose commitments have produced churches with colorful identities, and the distinctive characteristics of the three congregations seem to be key to their success. In sum, they all are controversial places that elicit strong feelings from people—feelings that range from enthusiastic support to deep apprehension.

Three Journeys

The following stories of three laypeople contain themes that I build on throughout the chapter.[1] The first person is Jane Garrison,[2] who attends All Angels' Church; the second is Sasha Von Scherler, who attends St. Bartholomew's Episcopal Church; and the third is Lee Whitley, who attends St. Thomas's. In significant ways, Jane, Sasha, and Lee are representative of the people in their parishes. All of them were drawn as adults to the Episcopal churches that they attend, but for different reasons. Jane found in All Angels' a Christian supernaturalism that met her need for emotional, physical, and spiritual healing. Sasha found in St. Bartholomew's a spirit of inclusion and a stance against injustice that contrasted with her earlier experiences with the church. Lee Whitley found in St. Thomas's an excellence in both music and architecture that satisfied his deep yearning to worship God using all his senses. The healing power of the Holy Spirit, the spirit of inclusion, and liturgical excellence came up again and again in interviews and surveys as qualities that drew people to All Angels', St. Bartholomew's, and St. Thomas's.

Jane Garrison

Jane Garrison holds a B.A. in art history from Yale University and an M.A. in art education from New York University. She lives on the Upper West Side of Manhattan and works as a freelance writer and illustrator. Jane's spiritual journey over the last decade has brought her into the spirit-filled and charismatic-renewal wing of the Episcopal Church. Today, her worldview combines the vivid supernaturalism of the New Testament with twentieth-century concepts from psychology, literature, and science. Jane's favorite Scripture story is Jesus' healing of the blind man in the Gospel of John. Like the blind man, Jane does not know why she has had to endure all the pain in her life, and also like the blind man, she has experienced healing in gradually coming to see who Christ is.

Jane grew up in a liberal Protestant church where she learned self-help principles that were little different from those found in secular society. "It didn't seem like the church would solve anything," she observed. A few years after Jane graduated from Yale, a series of financial, health, and family crises began to compel her to search for spiritual answers to her life. This marked the beginning of a "zigzag" spiritual quest that would, a decade later, bring her into the Christian fold. "In the 1980s when everyone was prospering, I was doing worse and worse. I was in New York struggling to be a writer and an artist, and my external world of security was being taken away. I needed desperately to have hope that my life would get better."

Jane tried New Age solutions and was for three years a devotee of Christian Science. During this time, Jane met a born-again Christian at an advertising agency who introduced her to a "thoughtful loving network of people" at a neighborhood "house church" affiliated with Grace Episcopal Church in the Village. "I was blown away," Jane said, "These people are smart and nice and they study the Bible every week. They prayed for each other and prayed for me. They were warm and welcoming and not fake."

Jane ended up attending All Angels' Church, which is located in her neighborhood. At a Francis McNutt conference attended by members of All Angels', Jane experienced the "baptism of the Holy Spirit, " a supernatural experience described in the New Testament book of Acts. This Pentecostal baptism produced an inner experience of peace and joy and was accompanied by special gifts of the spirit (charisms), including "the gift of tongues."

Especially important to Jane was an experience of deliverance from the spirits of fear and depression that were oppressing her. "Hooked into emotional wounds that needed to he healed over time," Jane pointed out, "were evil spirits that made my situation seem intractable and particularly painful, like there is no hope."

Although praying in tongues is not normative at All Angels', several other aspects of Jane's spiritual journey are. Eighty percent of the parishioners at All Angels' did not grow up Episcopal; 89 percent report that they know Jesus Christ as Lord and Savior, most reporting having entered into this relationship as adults; and "community of healing" is in the mission statement and comes up again and again in interviews as a metaphor to describe the parish.

Sasha von Scherler

Sasha von Scherler is an actor and a psychotherapist living in Manhattan whose ambivalence toward organized religion is rooted in events that predate her conscious memory. She was christened in a Lutheran Church in Nazi Germany. Her godfather was a member of Hitler's S.S., and her grandfather was a Nazi Party leader. In Nazi Germany, it was illegal to mention in church that Jesus Christ was a Jew.

During her christening ceremony, Sasha's father was in exile in Italy for tearing down a Nazi flag and mimicking Hitler on the radio. The contrast between Sasha's staid, conservative, religious grandparents and her activist, irreverent parents shaped her spiritual life in profound ways. "I was taught to be extremely irreverent," she says, "not to suffer hypocrisy gladly, to be suspicious of dogma. . . . You don't trust churches if your own good, sweet, dear, churchgoing grandfather can be capable of such evil."

Sasha's spiritual journey includes memories of Shinto shrines, Hindu swamis, and selections from the Bhagavad Gita and the Bible. "The evangelical thing is very hard for me," Sasha says, "How dare I tell anyone how to believe? The Gospel that holds me by the throat is what ye do to the least of my brethren, ye do unto me. The bottom line for me is love. What loves is good; what doesn't love is bad." Sasha's favorite Bible text is Jesus' cleansing the temple. "He is getting rid of something cruel and unjust, and he loses his temper a little."

Exclusion and alienation are themes in Sasha's experience of church, and *inclusive* is the adjective that Sasha uses to describe her standard for church. "I could never accept a Christianity that doesn't accept everyone." In 1958, Episcopal priests in New York City would not let her marry in their church because she had been divorced, but she finally found a United Church of Christ church in the Village that would perform the ceremony. It was not until her grandchildren were baptized at St. John the Divine (Episcopal) that Sasha decided to look for a parish. She went to St. Bartholomew's, which exhibited the "inclusiveness" that she so often missed in her other parishes. "I offered a little pledge and began attending."

Lee Whitley

Lee Whitley grew up Baptist in a small town in Georgia and has a B.A. and an M.A. in advertising from the University of Georgia in Athens. Lee now lives in midtown Manhattan and is a marketing consultant for classical concerts. He is a fan of opera, art museums, cutting-edge media, and the engaging conversations that New York City offers. "Many people are experts here," Lee observed, "They make intellectual demands of you."

In New York, the spectacular music program at St. Thomas's drew Lee into the Episcopal fold. St. Thomas's also has a residential boarding school that trains boys for its all-male choir. In the European cathedral tradition of the Middle Ages, the soprano parts are sung by young boys whose voices are still high.

St. Thomas's is also one of the few churches in America that still use the 1928 prayer book, which was superseded in most American Episcopal churches by the 1979 version. Whereas others might be confused by the older prayer book's archaic expressions, Lee finds that they aid him in his spiritual journey. "If you change the wording around, it introduces problems."

The excellence that Lee finds at St. Thomas's is reflected in the church's spectacular architecture and in the people who attend there. "There are strong personalities here who are into the arts and intellectually alive. These people are in control of their destinies and take initiative in life. There is very little hand-wringing here." Lee admits that "some might call St. Thomas's too stiff," but he was originally attracted to a church that lacks "effusiveness." At St. Thomas's you won't get the "forced friendliness, and probing personal questions" that you encounter in some Protestant settings.

Restoring the Faith: All Angels' Episcopal Church

Father Perini is from Australia and is serving for six months as an interim priest at All Angels'. His impressions of All Angels' were formed at a dinner that he attended at a parishioner's home in Greenwich Village.

> There was an economist, a dancer, a writer, two teachers, a Metro Transit worker, a historian, a singer, and two persons who had been homeless; white and black, outwardly successful and unsuccessful; it was a variation that reflected New York. Yet there was genuine respect; great laughter and

joy; a sense that we can all learn from one another; incredible equality. It was the richest evening I have spent in years. I feel greatly privileged to be part of a group like that.

All Angels' has built a parish that truly reflects the diversity of the neighborhood in which it is located. What holds people together is not identity along lines of class or race but a clear and intentional identity as an evangelical, Bible-centered, service-oriented Episcopal church. The current congregation was twenty years in the making and took some extraordinary risks along the way.

In 1979, a beleaguered group of parishioners de-consecrated their twelve-hundred-seat church facility, auctioned off its contents, sold the church property, and moved their church into the narrow, five-story parish house on West Eightieth Street between Broadway and West End Avenue (Carle and DeCaro 1997, 216–217). Twenty years later, All Angels' is a bustling Upper West Side congregation whose simple, oak-paneled chapel is packed with between one hundred and two hundred people for each of its three services.

After a service tailored to the needs of families, a service is held at 11:30 A.M. that is attended mainly by young, single professionals. "Worship is vibrant," church warden Bobby Gross writes, "with energetic singing accompanied by instrumentalists. The Episcopal liturgy is complemented by congregational prayer huddles, liturgical dance, and original drama sketches" (Carle and DeCaro 1997, 218). The music at the service is a stunning blend of traditional hymns, folk songs, jazz, calypso, and gospel.

The 5:00 P.M. service contrasts sharply from the morning services. Gross writes,

> Attendance ranges from between 150 and 200. [Approximately] 80 percent are African American and 20 percent white or other ethnicity (just the reverse of the racial mix in the morning). A large number of these parishioners are homeless, unemployed, or drug addicted. The worship form is still Episcopal liturgy, but the style is black, urban Gospel. The preaching tends toward the evangelistic, and the racially mixed All Angels' Gospel Singers are backed by piano, electric bass, and percussion. (Carle and DeCaro 1997, 218)

Many factors contributed to the transformation of All Angels' from a beleaguered parish on the margins of diocesan life to the vibrant institution that it is today, but perhaps the most important was the call of the

Reverend Carol Anderson as the congregation's rector. Parishioner Mary Johnson recalls Anderson's encouragement through evangelical preaching: "Every sermon that first year was on the same theme: Trust God," remembers Mary. "And in year two she preached 'Know Jesus' and then 'Go deeper' (in relationship with Christ)." Anderson taught people to pray aloud in their own words and introduced nontraditional music. She explored and developed a ministry of healing prayer. "She evangelized the church," says Paul Johnson, "and slowly we began to be a genuine spiritual community" (Carle and DeCaro 1997, 219).

When Carol Anderson left All Angels' in 1986, the church had a strong evangelical identity, a growing congregation, and a large Sunday afternoon feeding program. The Reverend Martyn Minns assumed leadership in 1988, and among the most dramatic achievements of his tenure was integrating into the Sunday evening worship the large crowd at the feeding program.

Both Minns and the music director Ron Melrose worked hard to shape the service to the needs of this new group of worshipers. Melrose formed the All Angels' Gospel Singers, a choir composed of both white and black, homeless people and professionals that now performs at both the morning and evening services as well as at various other venues in the city.

The Reverend Colin Goode assumed leadership of All Angels' in 1993, with a vision of training and empowering laity for leadership in keeping with Ephesians 4:11–13: "The gifts he gave were that some would be apostles, some prophets, some evangelists, some pastors and teachers, to equip the saints for the work of the ministry, for building up the body of Christ until all of us come to the . . . measure of the full stature of Christ."

A key component in this leadership development was a network of "house churches" in neighborhoods throughout Manhattan. In these small groups of ten to eighteen people, parishioners meet weekly in homes to share their joys and struggles, pray with one another, study the Bible, and grow together in faith. Because each group selects its own meeting time and place, "house churches" are adaptable to New Yorkers' busy lives. For many parishioners at All Angels', these home fellowships are central to their journeys of faith. Several respondents cited house church attendance as among the most significant spiritual practices that brought them closer to God. "It horrifies me to think of any Christian not attending a house church," Carry Barker says "The larger [church] experience is fun, but the house church is where I talk about my own journey, share in depth, and am made accountable."

All Angels' is a powerfully unified congregation in belief and practices, forming a distinctive moral community shaped by a clearly defined Christian identity and evangelical love. Although All Angels' is a diverse community ethnically, racially, economically and culturally, it is nonetheless a united community.

Adapting the Faith: St. Bartholomew's Episcopal Church

St. Bartholomew's is located in a stunning domed building on the corner of Park Avenue and Fifty-first Street in the middle of midtown Manhattan. It was described by its architect as "Romanesque of the Italian type." The church is built in the traditional crucifix pattern, facing east, and has a seating capacity of 1,250. The soft colors of the limestone and marble interior create an atmosphere that is warm, comforting, and womblike.

Inclusion is a word you hear a lot around St. Bartholomew's, and it refers to several initiatives taken by the Reverend Bill Tully during his tenure at the church. First, he created a church home for gays and lesbians. Second, he launched an aggressive campaign to reach religious seekers and people alienated from the church. Third, he began a music program that has attracted large numbers of ethnic minority youth to the church. Fourth, he has opened the communion table to all who come, regardless of belief or behavior. Father Tully's metaphor for the contemporary church is "house of return." "We have consciously created," Tully pointed out, "as wide a zone with as permeable borders as possible to make it easy for people to enter."

When Bill Tully came to St. Bartholomew's in 1994, he found a "vaguely homophobic atmosphere" that he has worked hard to change by supporting the formation of a gay and lesbian fellowship "that is openly announced and contributes to the life of the church." In April 1999, St. Bartholomew's hosted a conference entitled "Beyond Inclusion," a ministry out of Pasadena, California, whose mission is to "proclaim in the pulpit and shout in the streets—the central voice of Christianity, Jesus, does not denounce same-sex love!"

If Tully's activism on sexual issues places him in the liberal camp, his simultaneous commitment to Alpha, an evangelical and charismatic program to introduce seekers to Christianity, places him in the conservative camp. Under Tully's leadership, St. Bartholomew's hired the Reverend Nancy Hanna as senior associate minister for evangelism to make

Bartholomew's the "Alpha poster child in the diocese" (*Episcopal New Yorker* February/March 1999, 10). In the past three years, five hundred people have participated in St. Bartholomew's Alpha courses, and several hundred of them have begun attending the church. St. Bartholomew's received a grant from Trinity Church in Wall Street to introduce Alpha into parishes throughout the diocese.

The Alpha program is a practical introduction to the Christian faith, designed primarily for nonchurchgoers. The course consists of a series of weekly meetings in people's homes, each of which includes an informal meal, a talk, and small-group discussions. The meetings, fifteen talks about the basic principles of the Christian faith, are given over a ten-week period and conclude with a retreat weekend.

"Solid at the core, loose around the edges" are the words Bill Tully uses to describe his ecclesiology. This means that his aspiration is to be open to and accepting of persons wherever they are on their spiritual journeys. "Everyone has a place here, no matter what their lifestyles or their beliefs. We expect diversity."

St. Bartholomew's does not stress theological and moral coherence. "We are working on the heart," Father Tully explains, "We'll deal with the head later." The norms that he has introduced into the church are a welcoming inclusiveness for people, regardless of their background or achievements; a commitment to respect people's shared humanity; a respect for people's right to hold different views; and a Eucharist-centered worship style, expressed in a multitude of services in different forms.

The resulting diversity may, in the long run, make it difficult for St. Bartholomew's to settle on a common identity on which to build a strong church family. But at the moment, St. Bartholomew's is doing exceedingly well. Average attendance at the 11 A.M. Eucharist averages six hundred people, and since 1995, annual giving has grown from $400,000 to $1.5 million. People who had simply attended services are now attending church several times a week and assuming pastoral care responsibilities.

Keeping the Faith: St. Thomas's Episcopal Church

On the fifth floor of St. Thomas's exquisite parish hall, Father Harry Krauss delivers the final of his five Tuesday night lectures on vestments—the clothes that priests wear. Like witnesses monitoring the proceedings, dignified portraits of stern male clergy from previous rectorates adorn the walls above the lectern. Draped over dummies and resting on tables are woven and embroidered surplices, cassocks, gowns, capes, hoods, miters (bishop's headgear)—red and gold and purple and green. Father Krauss points to a huge scarlet piece of fruit embroidered on a gold background and quizzes the class about last week's lesson. "It's a pomegranate," one parishioner answers. "A symbol of fertility, and therefore of Mary," says another. Vestments are serious business for Father Krauss. "These vestments are fossilized costumes, Roman streetware from the time of our Lord," he says. "Vestments reveal to us faith in Jesus Christ. They say Jesus is our Lord and Savior; Jesus died for us; Jesus gives us new life."

Father Krauss describes himself as an "eighteenth-century high churchman." "We believe that traditional Catholic faith speaks to our own age and to all ages." One characteristic of the faith that St. Thomas's emphasizes is its sacramentalism. Sacramental traditions teach that God communicates with his people through the beauty and order of material things. Whereas many Protestants are suspicious that religious art figures might become "idols" that interfere with people's spiritual journeys, Anglicans and Catholics have historically claimed that art is a window onto the divine.

There are few places in the world where the love of art is more enthusiastically embraced than at St. Thomas's. The church was built entirely of stone, in exactly the way that the churches of the Middle Ages were built. The vault of the nave rises nearly 100 feet above the floor and is 215 feet long. The reredos, or altar screen, is the church's outstanding interior feature. Made of Duville stone, the reredos is 40 feet wide and 80 feet high with eighty figures depicted on it. St. Thomas's historian Harold Grove explains, "The high central figure is Christ in Glory, the Virgin Mary at [Christ's right], and St. John the beloved disciple at [Christ's left]."

When discussing their spiritual journeys, people at St. Thomas's are much more likely to describe the architecture of their church than are people at either St. Bartholomew's or All Angels'. "The beauty of St. Thomas's—the building itself, the music, the liturgy—reminds me of how much God is part of my life"; "What matters most to me in church is the glorious liturgy, the special sound of boy choristers, and the incredible architecture of St. Thomas's"; "I feel closest to God in St. Thomas's Church, just sitting and looking at the reredos."

"Making our liturgy live up to the architecture" is one way in which Father Andrew Mead describes his role at St. Thomas's. Although the liturgy is the same at St. Thomas's services, the masses are set to different composers. When you attend St. Thomas's, you receive an education in Stravinsky, Brahms, Byrd, Tallis, Allegri, and myriad other musical masters. In the European cathedral tradition of the Middle Ages, St. Thomas's has an all-male choir composed of men and boys, and it also has an all-male clergy.

Father Andrew Mead is one of seven of the 548 priests in the New York Diocese who still oppose the ordination of women. "I thought the search committee would rule me out because I am so conservative," he remarked. But his conservatism was part of the reason that St. Thomas's called Mead to be the rector. "They love their liturgy here and hold on to it tenaciously."

Joan Hoffman, St. Thomas's junior warden, remembers the search process.

> We surveyed the congregation when we were looking for a rector, and people wrote that they wanted the liturgy to stay the same; they wanted the music to stay the same; they wanted a high church conservative. Not one person wrote that we should have a woman or someone interested in hiring a woman priest.

Although many homosexual persons attend St. Thomas's, Father Mead is against the sort of redefinitions of sexuality that are taking place at St. Bartholomew's. "To be allergic to gay people is against the nature of Catholicism and of Christianity," he explained. But the church challenges people to "find their identities in Jesus Christ," not in their sexual orientations. Father Mead's prayer is that "no one will hear anything from me beneath New Testament standards of truth and mercy."

St. Thomas's has the only church-affiliated boarding choir school in the United States and one of the three remaining in the world. Founded in 1919, the choir school is a fully accredited academic institution with an outstanding academic program of English, mathematics, history, geography, science, Great Books, languages, theology, music theory, and instrumental study for grades 4 through 8. An enrollment of only forty-five boys ensures that each student receives individual attention from the school's ten full-time teachers and numerous part-time instructors. And a $20 million endowment ensures that each boy's education is heavily subsidized.

St. Thomas's is the largest—and the most liturgically conservative—church in the Diocese of New York, and it thrives precisely because it is conservative. Whereas All Angels' and St. Bartholomew's have expended impressive human and material resources in remaking themselves to fit the needs of a changing city, St. Thomas's success is a result of its tenacity in keeping things the way they are—or were. St. Thomas's offers people a religious experience that is rare in the modern world and is what keeps the church full.

Mainline Churches and the Spiritual Bazaar

A number of sociologists and theologians have shown that a new "search for spirituality" is now a major preoccupation of many Americans. Even the most secular adults have been swept up by the recent surge in American spirituality into what has become a religious bazaar.

This preoccupation poses both an opportunity and a challenge for mainline churches. On the one hand, people are more open to the idea of religious mystery than they have been in decades. But on the other hand, people no longer live in the types of spiritual enclaves in which mainline denominations have historically thrived. Whereas a limited cluster of mainline churches once wielded enormous cultural and social authority in the city, today churches are one stream alongside many others that are competing for the hearts and minds of New Yorkers.

The successes of the three parishes in this study suggest that there is no single strategy for rejuvenating the Protestant mainline in New York City's competitive marketplace. Although the three churches represent diverse styles and theologies in the Episcopal denomination, in their distinctive ways, all three also satisfy the postmodern yearning for religious mystery and experience. The three congregations celebrate the Eucharist several times a week, and a majority of respondents in the parishes identified Holy Communion as central to their spiritual growth. But in all three parishes, evangelistic and liturgical patterns of spirituality coexist fairly haphazardly. To varying degrees, the three parishes honor two classically Anglican forms of spirituality—one centering on the Bible, life-changing spiritual experiences, and small groups and the other centering on the prayer book, liturgy, and tradition. The unique blend of these spiritual practices empowers members to connect God's presence in prayer and sacrament with God's presence in church and the world.

All three congregations are arenas for conversation about spirituality and spaces in which the work of discerning God's will takes place. In a city where alienation is normative and the life of the spirit is elusive, these congregations are, for their members, places of belonging that are grounded in the transcendent realities that they celebrate (Ammerman 1996).

For the cosmopolitan persons described in this chapter, their churches nurture an "elective parochialism" (Warner 1988) rather than a sectarian withdrawal from society. Parishioners are attuned to the larger social world in which they live—they understand and respect the contributions of the marketplace and of psychology. In their congregations, cosmopolitans learn yet another language and way of life that they find both demanding and deeply satisfying. According to Ammerman,

> Congregations are thoroughly modern institutions. Yet they are communal gatherings . . . that afford their members an opportunity for connections with persons, groups , divine powers, and social structures beyond their individuality. They are affective, calling people beyond the calculating rationality of the state and market. They are diffuse, arenas where persons deal with each other in some measure of wholeness, not merely as role incumbents. And they are particularistic, highlighting the things that set them apart rather than looking for underlying universalisms. (Ammerman 1997a, 11)

Churches are spaces of sociability in a city where bureaucratic structures dominate public life. They are places where relationships of trust are formed and identity and a sense of belonging are nurtured. They are places that offer parishioners opportunities to be compassionate without being absorbed or depleted by the effort. Perhaps most important, congregations equip their members to make moral sense of the "the sordid surging realities of humanness," enriching a culture of utility and therapy with communitarian and biblical visions of our life together (Ammerman 1997a, 11).

NOTES

1. The information about these parishes was gathered from a variety of sources. I visited the churches on numerous occasions to attend services and to interview the priests on staff, church wardens, and dozens of lay parishioners. All three congregations provided me with newsletters, parish profiles, Sunday bulletins, program materials, and congregational surveys conducted over the last five years.

2. Her name was changed at her request.

Chapter 4

A Profile of New York City's African American Church Leaders

Tony Carnes

The late Benjamin Nelson, a sociologist at the New School University, once gave a remarkable presentation on the very simple question "Where do blacks get soul?" In the 1960s and 1970s, we had soul music, soul food, and declarations of possession of soul. Where did this large and central vocabulary come from?

In the New York African American community, soul is the idea or feeling that no matter who you are, you are special and going somewhere better. A person is still special even if oppressed. In the *Daily News*, columnist Stanley Crouch mused about New York African American soul:

> I recently found myself in the cancellation line, sitting on the Grim Reaper's lap [through a diabetes crisis]. . . . My response was that I didn't need to go [to the hospital]. But my wife is a Negro woman with the kind of Manhattan soul you can't get anywhere else in America. That soul—regardless of race—has special qualities. In terms of our town, it is urbane, sensitive and extremely stubborn, the latter quality being what allows our human essence to rise above all the limitations of this city's pressures and disappointments. When she puts her foot down, the building rocks to its foundation. (1997, 20)

Out of Harlem, Sylvia Brown markets Sylvia's Soul Food Spice. Hymns like "Swing Low, Sweet Chariot," "Amazing Grace," and "the Holy Ghost Vibe" by rapper Big Brother D continue the soulful tradition. The idea of soul is important to both the African American identity and the American identity. Every African American leader uses this vocabulary. Many of these leaders are pastors, and all come out of the African American churches.

Where did African Americans get soul? From the church. African Americans are a very religious group; 95 percent say that they are "religious" and that religion is very important to their lives; 78 percent belong and go to churches, and pastors are pivotal in the community (Emerging Trends 1987b; Roof and McKinney 1987, 91; *The Unchurched* 1989, 37). Sixty-nine percent of African Americans in the northeast United States say that "the Christian Church is a central part of the lives of most black people in America" (Barna 1999, 20). The community's key rhetoric comes out of the Bible, particularly from the Exodus story and the death and resurrection of Jesus.

In order to know the New York City African American community, we need to know and understand its longest-lasting and largest organization, the African American church. And in order to understand the African American church, we need to know and understand its leaders.

In New York City, the African American church is old and significant. The African American Zion Church, the second-oldest African American denomination, was founded in New York City in 1822. New York City includes some of the best-known African American churches in the United States. The Concord Baptist Church of Brooklyn, pastored by Rev. Gary Simpson, is one of the largest African American churches, with between twelve thousand and fifteen thousand members. The Abyssinian Baptist Church, pastored by Rev. Calvin O. Butts, and the Canaan Baptist Church, pastored by gospel and blues historian Wyatt T. Walker, epitomize the history of civil rights leadership in the city. A newer generation of influential pulpits are exemplified by Queens churches like the Allen AME Church, pastored by former congressman Rev. Floyd Flake; the Bethel Gospel Tabernacle, pastored by Bishop Roderick Caesar Jr.; and the Brooklyn churches like Rev. A. R. Bernard's Christian Life Centre and Rev. Johnny Youngblood's St. Paul's Community Baptist Church.

Since 1997, the International Research Institute on Values Changes has been interviewing hundreds of African American church leaders in New York City to construct its first in-depth group portrait. The following is part of the institute's story.[1]

Church

From Weakness to Pentecostal/Charismatic Revival?

Perhaps as a result of dissatisfaction with a merely social religion, New York City's African Americans seem to be shifting to Pentecostal/charis-

TABLE 4.1
Religious Profile of African Americans

Church Denomination	1997, NYC (%)[a]	1986, U.S. (%)[b]	1990, U.S. (%)[c]	1999, U.S. (%)[d]
Protestant	77	71	81.8	
Baptist	35	46.8	50.0	55
Methodist	4	18.2	9.1	12
Disciples of Christ	—	—	4.0	—
Pentecostal	17	16	4.0	—
Jehovah's Witness	0	—	2.1	—
Episcopalian	1	—	1.2	—
Presbyterian	6	—	0.8	—
Lutheran	1	—	0.7	—
Other Protestants	14	—	10.0	13
Catholic	<1	8.4	9.2	—
Muslim	0	—	0.9	—
Mormon	0	—	0.2	—
Smaller Black Communions	—	5.9	—	—
Largely White Protestant Groups	—	5.1	—	—
Refused	—	—	1.2	—
No Religion	—	—	5.9	—
Other Religions	1	—	0.8	6

[a] Church leaders. To code the self-identified theological identifications, we relied on the International Research Institute on Values Change (IRIVC)'s own coding list developed in surveys in New York and California, the Glenmary annual denominational books, and Mead and Hill's *Handbook of Denominations in the U.S.* We also tried to make sure that our code sheets included a thorough and accurate list of denominations with large numbers of African Americans.

[b] Church pastors. Lincoln and Mamiya 1990, 407.

[c] General population of African Americans. Kosmin and Lachman 1991, 131.

[d] General population of African Americans. Barna 1999, 26. "Other religions" includes Church of God in Christ, a Pentecostal denomination, Church of Christ, and nondenominational churches.

matic churches. Certainly, the proportion of young church leaders who are Pentecostal/charismatic has dramatically increased in the city. Forty-eight percent of those under age forty identify themselves as Pentecostal/charismatic, as opposed to just about 10 percent as evangelical/fundamentalist. Overall, church leaders prefer the label "Pentecostal/charismatic" (31%) to "evangelical/fundamentalist" (26%) (see table 4.1). Furthermore, although New York City's African American church leaders list more than forty-two different denominational affiliations, the affiliations are more often with Pentecostals/charismatic churches and less often with the Baptist church than is the case nationally.

The clear implication is that the charismatic churches have been much more successful in reaching younger generations of African Americans than their counterparts have been. However, despite the symbolic importance of the church, African Americans in northern central cities have had the lowest churched rate (28%) in the country (Nelsen 1988; Welch 1978), and northeast African Americans have the lowest rate of self-description as "religious" (50%, according to Barna 1999, 8). In contrast, nationally in 1987 an astounding 78 percent of the African American population were "churched," that is, claimed church membership and church attendance within the last six months (Emerging Trends 1987a, 5; Roof and McKinney 1987, 91; *The Unchurched* 1989, 37).

Many African American churches offer "a meaningless religiosity," claims William Turner, the director of Black Church Affairs at Duke University Divinity School (Tapia 1996). Once uprooted from a southern social setting where going to church was just the normal social thing to do, immigrants to northern cities like New York often did not have an ideological reason to reaffiliate with the church. Consequently, leaving the church was more a social act than an ideological one. For many African Americans, their childhood churches were more like neighborhoods or friendships that they loved but left behind when they moved away geographically, educationally, and socially. Journalist Beverly Hall Lawrence observed about her leaving the church, "It is not unlike what happens to some friendships that fade when one moves away" (Lawrence 1996, 6, 9). This drifting away from the church has consequently been countered by the movement of church leaders toward Pentecostal/charismatic churches that make high demands and foster a more intense spiritual life.

African American Church Leaders Are Theologically Divided

African American church leaders in New York City almost equally divided between conservative and liberal in their views of the Bible (see table 4.2), but you would not sense it by listening to their sermons, which often invoke the Bible. "You hear the Bible in their sermons," one prominent New York City African American pastor observed, "There is a thread of culture that keeps us together. So, unfortunately, people don't notice the theological change going on." In the northeast United States, 55 percent of African Americans say that they have read the Bible in the last week (Barna 1999, 30). Barna further suggested (66–68) that African American pastors may be blind to the shifting views of truth within their own congregations, with 90 percent of the pastors claiming that their congregants believe in absolute moral truth, while in fact only about one-third do. This theological bifurcation is found even among evangelical/fundamentalists and Pentecostal/charismatics. Nearly one-third of "evan-

TABLE 4.2
New York City African American Church Leaders' Views of the Bible, 1997

An ancient book of legends, history, and moral precepts	3%
A useful resource for teaching about the meaning of life and morality	10%
Authoritative in its teachings about the meaning of life and morality	26%
Without error in its teachings about the meaning of life and morality but makes some mistakes in its historical and scientific reporting	4%
Without error in its teaching about the meaning of life and morality but culturally accommodating in its historical and scientific reporting	2%
Without error in its teachings about the meaning of life and morality and in its historical and scientific reporting	47%

gelicals" (32%), "charismatics" (33%), "Pentecostals" (30%), and even "fundamentalists" (27%) break with the doctrine at the heart of the evangelical mode of faith, that is, the inerrancy of Scripture.

Indeed, conservative African American church leaders are reluctant to disturb the unity gained during oppression and civil rights struggles with a discussion of theological differences. As one prominent pastor explained, "If it was brought up, it would be a hostile intellectual debate. Besides, white people talk about it all the time, and it doesn't do any good. You know them by their fruits, not their doctrine." Still, the conservative views are much more in line with the beliefs of most (75%) African Americans, who maintain that "the Bible is totally accurate in all its teachings" (Barna 1999, 38).

Whose Word Do You Trust?

Many New York City African American pastors just laugh when they are asked whether they trust anyone. Michael Faulkner, a prominent African American pastor on the city's Police-Community Relations Task Force formed after the police abuse of Abner Louima, said, "Come on. You know why! Pastors don't trust anyone. As a pastor, you have had everyone lie to you!" (figure 4.1).

Trust has been a casualty of racial discriminations and prejudices. But without trust, a society cannot endure, and its culture cannot grow deep and rich. Fukuyama's *Trust* explored the theme that "a nation's well-being, as well as its ability to compete, is conditioned by a single, pervasive cultural characteristic: the level of trust inherent in the society" (1995, 7). Ernest Gellner (1994) identified webs of trust as the condition

Figure 4.1. Rev. Michael Faulkner, sometime Guiliani ally, Central Baptist Church, West Side of Manhattan. Courtesy of the collection of Tony Carnes.

of a liberal civil society. Whereas power or economics may bind a society together like wires twisted around staves, trust acts as an inner glue that gives a deep inner bonding that mere coercion or economic reward and punishment can seldom provide.

But if trust is the glue of society, then the African American church leadership is too loosely attached. New York City's African American pastors have very low levels of trust, and among them, about 10 to 15 percent are deeply alienated, almost phantomlike in their presence in the community. Francis Fukuyama suggests that this low-trust culture keeps African Americans socially fragmented and economically uncoordinated (1995). Consequently, a key question is how African American church leaders can rebuild trust.

Indeed, churches have a strong ideological commitment to speaking the truth and enforcing rules. Internally, they use social sanctions and discipline. Externally, churches fulminate, negotiate, and press their members into community action against deviants and free riders. As Fukuyama observes, "It is much harder to be a free rider when God (rather than, say, an accountant) is watching" (1995, 156).

New York City's African American pastors are most likely to highly trust their spouses (47%) and other pastors (67%). One out of every four highly trust their church members. But they do not trust many other people—not their neighbors, not their fellow ethnics, and hardly any representatives of the establishment. Rev. Floyd Flake of the Allen AME Church in Jamaica, Queens, says that one of his slogans is "Love your enemies and watch your back."

As church leaders, they expect to share the same values and struggles. Perhaps most important, African American pastors generally place great emphasis on "The Call," a special beckoning of God to the pastorate. The Call of God extends also to other believers, and church leaders do trust fellow church members, administrators, and classmates. However, African American church leaders are significantly more cautious about this wider circle of the church. For example, 37 percent say that they have only "some" trust of the word of "my church's members," although few would say that they have little or no trust. According to Barna (1999, 4), few African American pastors give any real authority to laypersons.

Church leaders place some trust in everyday acquaintances (around 50% with at least some trust) such as coworkers, neighbors, and local government workers like police and social workers. Perhaps this level of trust is about what is needed in the daily dance of life among strangers. In this regard, despite the bursts of antagonism toward the police from African Americans, it would seem that they accord the police a roughly ordinary amount of trust. A U.S. Department of Justice survey released in June 1999 found that about three-fourths of black New Yorkers were satisfied with the local police, and about one-fourth were dissatisfied.

The picture changes, however, when we notice that a relatively large number of church leaders highly distrust the police. Almost one-third have little or no trust in a policeman's word (or that of social workers). In sum, it seems that two-thirds of African American church leaders have an ordinary amount of trust in public law enforcers—with a wait-and-see attitude—but that one-third are highly distrustful and are probably much more ready to react angrily to police brutality in a city where nine out of ten black residents, according to a *New York Times* survey, say that the police often engage in brutality against blacks (Dan 1999).

This lack of trust might explain why an effective city leadership can mobilize African American church leaders' support for the police during times of social disorder. Conversely, ineffective or distrusted city leaders cannot easily rally the support for and trust in the police that already exists. In such cases, the one-third that is distrustful becomes an angry wave that brings the rest along with them. New York City Police Commissioner Howard Safir's frustration that critics only want to "smear the Police Department" defeats the opportunity to identify the likely avenues for building trust (Flynn 1999). That is, the real focus needs to be on building relations with the two-thirds already willing to trust (MacFarquhar 1999).

For African American church leaders, there is a group of "untrustworthies" who are mainly made up of the overclass and underclass, the establishment and the disestablishment. Very few African American church leaders in New York City trust the leaders of big institutions like government, business, and unions. Indeed, an African American church leader is more likely to highly trust a drug addict (2%) than an owner of a big corporation (1%), and he is only slightly more likely to highly trust a U.S. senator (3%).

Community and Politics

Compared with African American church leaders in the rest of the nation, those in New York City combine a relatively high political interest with a deteriorating community involvement (see table 4.3). The lower level of community involvement may reflect the fact that many African American pastors no longer live in the neighborhoods they pastor. Like the Eddie Murphys and Bill Cosbys of Englewood Cliffs, New Jersey, the pastors commute to their performance spaces. In fact, in contrast to their brothers across the nation (54%), New York City African American church leaders (46%) are not as likely to say that the church is their community.

The normal community life of most church leaders includes working with organizations that deal with many everyday concerns like business, professions, charity, and fellowship (Fischer 1982).[2] Bishop Roderick Caesar Jr. of the Bethel Gospel Tabernacle in Queens says he challenges his congregation and the forty other churches he oversees: "Does Heaven button up until 11 A.M.? Is that the only time the pipeline is open?" Yet, churches in New York City are less apt to encourage neighborhood involvement. Nationwide, almost three-fourths (74%) of the leaders' churches encourage their parishioners to become involved in their communities. In New York City, however, less than two-thirds (64%) of the churches do so, and twice as many churches are likely to discourage such involvement. Flake laments, "So many complain when their church is

TABLE 4.3
1997 New York City African American Church Leaders'
Involvement in Business or Civic Groups (%)

Charity groups	50
Support or fellowship groups	40
Business or civic groups	24
Professional associations	20
Neighborhood associations	19
Youth groups	16
School-related groups	13
Clubs	10
Sports teams	10
Ethnic organizations	10
Labor unions	9
Fraternal lodges	7
Cooperatives	7
Other	7
Political clubs	6
Issue groups	4

doing nothing, but they also complain when they feel their church is doing too much too fast."

Some church leaders are shocked into greater community awareness by a disaster like a murder or the sudden realization of a chronic dire situation. The Reverend Calvin Butts of the Abyssinian Baptist Church in Harlem crystallized his change of attitude toward community development in one electric sermon to his congregation in mid-1986. He recalls that one day he realized that Harlem had burned down around him, leaving empty shells of buildings facing the church as a rebuke. Out of that moment came the Abyssinian Development Corporation that has rebuilt hundreds of housing units and stores, in the process doing millions of dollars in business.

New York City African American Church Leaders Have a High Interest in Politics

New York City church leaders report that they vote significantly more often (64%) than do African Americans as a whole (between 40 and 50%). Sixteen percent of the leaders have attended a political rally. While these church leaders are not "militant," they are politically aware, reading the news and otherwise keeping involved.

Some social scientists have dismissed "black religiosity" as a drug that has kept African Americans from "political activism" and left-wing ideologies

(Lane 1959, chap. 16; Lipset et al. 1954; Marx 1969; Reed 1986; also see Marable 1983, 196).[3] Indeed, some church leaders see politics as a "worldly" activity or not very effective in the long run. They consequently steer their followers away from overly political churches to "more spiritual" ones. One prominent Harlem church leader went through a list of churches, noting about one, "Oh, at Abyssinian [Baptist Church] people do politics and religion" and suggested that another a church that was "very spiritual" might be "worth a visit."

A number of scholars have challenged the conclusion that African American religion and politics do not mix (Harris 1987, 29; Lincoln and Mamiya 1990, 213–214; Paris 1985; Ward et al. 1994). In 1976, U.S. Representative Andrew Young and Rev. Martin Luther King Sr. started Jimmy Carter on the road to victory in the 1976 presidential election with "the largest black vote in history," by bypassing the African American political establishment in favor of meetings like the Baptist Ministers Conference of Greater New York and Vicinity at the Convent Avenue Baptist Church (Vecsey 1976). In the 1989 New York City mayoral election that brought David Dinkins into office, African American voters were the most likely to report that "a religious leader had urged support for a candidate" (Arian 1991, 166).

Political Ideology Is Mostly Moderate, with Surprising Number of Conservatives

A plurality of African American church leaders say that they are politically moderate, with smaller numbers claiming to be conservative or liberal. It may seem surprising that almost one out of four African American church leaders in the city identifies himself as a "conservative" (see table 4.4).

A somewhat conservative trend can also be observed in African American church leaders' theory of poverty.[4]

Church leaders (2%) do not often give "discrimination" as a reason for poverty. Rather, their primary focus (47%) is limitations of family and educational background. Second in importance (12%) is that poor people have "sub-biblical" beliefs. In interviews, however, African American leaders are not likely to blame the victim (4%).

There is a growing emphasis on combining the Protestant work ethic with strengthening the family and using the church's socioeconomic resources as a way to solve poverty. For example, Floyd Flake preaches a

TABLE 4.4
1997 African American Church Leaders'
Political Ideology (%)

No answer	15
Most liberal	5
Very liberal	3
Liberal	15
Moderate	40
Conservative	12
Very conservative	6
Most conservative	4

"bootstrapper's ethic." Before becoming a pastor, Flake was in marketing at the Xerox Corporation, and now he encourages his flock in his "corporate way." In 1998

> while watching news about the stock market activity for the previous day, I wondered how many members of the congregation invested in stocks and bonds. Raising the question in a Men's Club meeting the following Monday night, I was shocked that out of over one hundred men, only five or six had an investment portfolio beyond insurance or a bank savings account. We took action by starting an investment club that was open to the entire church membership. Now, there are twelve investment clubs. (Flake and Williams 1999, 15–16)

Flake says his is a black Horatio Alger story, with the social and spiritual dimension that the black church experience adds. "You know the story. The quintessential rags-to-riches story" of our overcoming "all forms of adversity to rise to the top." But African American pastors are less likely to mention only self-help. As Flake noted, "There's no such thing as a self-made person. No one goes it alone" (Flake and Williams 1999, 15–16, 21, 43). Friends, family, church, government—all can and do help, and the most important is God.

In Brooklyn, another pastor has captured great attention for his version of the Protestant ethic. Like a boardroom prophet, a former Banker's Trust loan officer, A. R. Bernard of the Christian Life Centre, preaches godliness, capitalism, strong families, and self-discipline. Practicing what he preaches, he owns an accounting firm, a barbershop, and real estate. "Church is not a 'Sunday thing,'" he maintains. "It's a lifestyle. Unlike Marx, I think the church is a necessary institution."

Democratic Identification Is Relatively Low

African American church leaders are much less inclined to support the Democratic Party than African Americans are as a whole. In 1992, 82 percent of African Americans voted for the Democratic presidential candidate, but in 1997, only 57 percent of African American New York City church leaders identified with the Democratic Party (see table 4.5). Republican-leaning Michael Faulkner of the Central Baptist Church claims, "The Democratic Party uses the black church but doesn't leave $50 on the night table." Brooklyn pastor A. R. Bernard remembers how he felt himself treated "like an experiment" by liberals when they bused him as a fourth grader over to Queens. In fact, African American church leaders often do not feel akin to those Joe Klein calls the "Upper Left Side Liberals," that is, extremists from the Upper West Side and Greenwich Village.

But The Mayor Was Not Trusted

Although 20 percent of African Americans voted for mayoral candidate Rudolph Guiliani in 1993, only 5 percent of African American pastors in New York trusted his word. In fact, an astounding 56 percent claimed in 1997 to have almost no trust in the mayor's word. Faulkner, a sometime ally of the mayor, attributes the distrust to the nature of politics: "The mayor is going to lie; he is a politician." Calvin Butts, pastor of the Abyssinian Baptist Church, made news in 1998 by calling the mayor "a racist" and then embracing him in 1999. He explained that African Americans' relations with the mayor are governed strictly by politics, not trust. "There is a high distrust because of the way the mayor works. Dinkins had relations to the clergy, but the mayor is strictly a political animal."

So who trusts the mayor's word? The numbers are so small that our statistics yield only hints, not probabilities. Four characteristics of mayoral trusters do stand out, however. *All* the trusters are religious conservatives; two-thirds also trust the police; and two-thirds highly rate Christian involvement in abortion issues and tax reduction. Not surprisingly, most are Republican but not necessarily ideologically conservative. From these clues and the trusters' surprisingly high trust of unions, one could guess that the mayor is mainly supported by Republican evangelical or Pentecostal/charismatic cops turned church leaders.

TABLE 4.5
*1997 New York City African American Church
Leaders' Political Orientation (%)*

No answer	16
Republicans	13
Democrats	57
Other	14

TABLE 4.6
Ethnicity of New York City's Church Leaders (%)

No answer	41
Black	22
African American	18
Other	12
Hispanic/Latino	7

Race and Politics

In *The Closest of Strangers*, Jim Sleeper observes that African American New Yorkers favor candidates who promise to promote racial harmony, not division. Indeed, black racialist candidates often do not even win in black voting districts against white candidates. In the 1989 election for mayor, Sonny ("I hate all white people") Carson's involvement in the Dinkins campaign cost it votes in all groups, including African Americans (*New York Times*/CBS exit poll, 1989 mayoral election).

Increasingly, many people are resisting racial or ethnic labeling, a phenomenon that has led the U.S. Bureau of the Census to search for new strategies to uncover respondents' racial/ethnic heritages (see table 4.6). Forty-one percent of African American Church leaders in New York City refused to provide an ethnic identification, believing that ethnic or racial identity is about authority and affiliation (Light and Lee 1997, 29–30). Historically, ethnic identity was tied to divine origins. That is, a tribe or people would claim divine affiliation based on the fact that its ancestors sprang from the godhead or were specially selected for divine favor over against other tribes or peoples. Subsequently, religion and religious leaders have often played an important role in creating and perpetuating ethnic/racial identities and divisions that reinforce church solidarity. If religious leaders continue to refuse to reveal their racial identity, the impact over the long run may be significant.

Figure 4.2. Bishop Ezra Williams, Bethel Gospel Assembly, Harlem. Courtesy of the collection of Tony Carnes.

Many church leaders recall how they overcame their hatred of whites in favor of a universal human identity. Bishop Ezra Williams, one of the city's most respected Pentecostal leaders, remarked, "I used to think white people were the enemy. All I knew was Harlem. I thought I was Harlem born, Harlem bred, and when I die, I'll be Harlem dead." Then, interracial experiences in the army and attendance at a Bible study class in Harlem founded by a white woman started to change his thinking. "I started to realize that our society badly needs men and women who will exemplify the love of Christ. And he is color blind; we should be color blind" (figure 4.2).

The increasing number of people refusing to identify their ethnicity, the fragmentation of ethnic identities, and the rise of new hybrids like "multiracial" raise new policy issues for the church that have not been adequately addressed (see Kilker 1999). The old standard classifications mask a more complex diversity, more personally felt, though perhaps weaker in intensity, than they were before. This "intraethnic" diversity has long been a feature of New York City's neighborhoods, politics, and churches.

Because racial and ethnic categories overlap, we cannot be sure which category is more relevant to the respondent. Moreover, its relevance may change with the situation. For instance, West Indians see themselves as a group distinct from American blacks, but in politics they are more likely to list "black" as the relevant category.

For example, A. R. Bernard, pastor of the mostly "black" ten thousand-member Christian Life Centre, was born in Panama to a black mother and a white Spanish father. He therefore learned early the ambiguities of race. Rejected by her lover, his mother moved with her son to the Bedford-Stuyvesant section of Brooklyn. As a teenager, the young Bernard was attracted to the Nation of Islam, which "began to bring dignity to the black man." But he became tired of the hate-laden rhetoric. "Hatred has a self-consumptive destiny, once it consumes the enemy, it turns on itself." Bernard now preaches for the integrationist Promise Keepers' conferences that racial iniquity must be recognized and dealt with and then transcended. "There are two heritages to every man: that which is spiritual, and that which is natural. I found peace with my natural heritage by discovering my spiritual one."

The Future: The Post–Civil Rights Generation

Some analysts claim that the people born around 1960 or later are a post–Civil Rights generation (Smith 1996). They remember Martin Luther King Jr., Eldridge Cleaver, and Ralph Abernathy mostly as historical monuments, but Malcolm X seems more relevant to them because of his hard-edged style. Nearly all of the current leaders of the major civil rights organizations are a generation removed from the Civil Rights movement, and their newer vision has already guided their organizations into new strategies and styles (see table 4.7).

Some, like Rev. Calvin O. Butts of the Abyssinian Baptist Church, call this "the post-Dinkins era" because no younger African American church leader has yet emerged who could assume a leading public role like that of mayor. Indeed, African American church leaders are debating what kind of leader is needed for the twenty-first century. Eschewing charismatic civil rights confrontations, many like Butts and Floyd Flake of

TABLE 4.7
Habits of Civil Rights and Post–Civil Rights Generations (%)

	Civil Rights	Post–Civil Rights
Vote in most elections	71	56
Attended a political rally	21	11
Read a newspaper every day	30	19

Jamaica have opted for neighborhood-level victories like reclaiming blocks of housing, building schools, and opening stores.

In fact, the current church leaders in New York do differ from the older Civil Rights generation. They are better educated, as is the rising number of professional, middle-class parishioners. For example, many of the members of A. R. Bernard's Christian Life Centre are more likely to be carrying laptops and notepads than tambourines. By 1997, 43 percent of New York City's African American church leaders had completed at least college. They also are better educated as a whole than are the church leaders of other ethnic groups in the city.

Like those leaving the Baptist church of Martin Luther King (a drop of 20%), they are not as denomination minded as previous generations. One church leader asserted, "My focus is not on denomination. Church is just a way to get closer with the people that love God and each other." Moreover, they are wary of the old way of doing church business. When Rev. Henry Lyons, president of the National Baptist Convention, was indicted and later convicted for corruption (Gilbreath 1999), Abyssinian's Calvin Butts led an unsuccessful charge to censor him.

Baptist Michael Faulkner attributes the shift of leaders into Pentecostal/charismatic theologies from those of the evangelicals/fundamentalists as a result of the Baptist old guard. "In Baptist circles it is much harder to ascend to leadership for young people. So, they go to the Pentecostal churches where they can start tomorrow and instantly receive recognition. The Baptist hierarchy is much more tightly guarded."

The increased interest in high-emotion religion is not matched by a shift toward theological conservatism. These people's views of the Bible are split into 50 percent conservative and 50 percent liberal, just like those of previous generations. Emotional fervor does not seem to be producing a more biblically centered church. The shift to Pentecostal/charismatic theology also seems related to a national generational shift to focusing on oneself and feeling good. The current church leaders report much less involvement in groups outside Sunday church, except for sports and unions. They do not see themselves as victims suffering through life, but as spiritually empowered to transcend race and life's problems. Renita Weems of Vanderbilt University's Kelly Miller Smith Institute, who since 1992 has been studying what it means to be black and Christian, says that "the younger folk are seeking empowerment" to build positive relations and to cope with their careers. Indeed, Dallas pastor T. D. Jakes's psychospiritual texts are best-sellers in Christian bookstores here in New York City.

The younger generation is less interested in politics and social issues, and they are much less likely to vote or to engage in even minimal political activism. Not surprisingly, they are more likely not to identify with a particular political affiliation or ideology. A majority only occasionally pick up a newspaper to read about the world, national, or local events. They are even less concerned about Christian involvement in various political or social issues except for abortion and the environment.

To the extent that the post–Civil Rights generation is interested in politics, they are drifting toward Republicans with a more conservative ideology. Republican support among African American church leaders in New York City is strongest among thirty to thirty-nine year olds (19%). Consistent with the national trend, support for the Democratic Party is greatest among fifty to fifty-nine year olds (72%), the generation that came of age during the Civil Rights movement. It was the older members of this generation of African Americans that gave David Dinkins his highest vote in 1989 (Arian 1991).

The post–Civil Rights generation is much more supportive of Christian involvement in abortion issues and gives less priority to helping the poor or protecting minority rights. Indeed, they are less likely to blame the system for poverty and more likely to emphasize that the poor need to exercise self-control. Rev. Flake calls this "the way of the bootstrapper," which "is a mind-set that allows you to rise over and above the ordinary and become an extraordinary person by taking responsibility for your own thoughts, feelings, words, actions and life circumstances" (Flake and Williams 1999, 3). Many also strongly support Revs. Flake's and Wyatt T. Walker's attempt to establish charter schools.

Though still quite wary of Mayor Guiliani, the post–Civil Rights generation was twice as likely (7%) as the Civil Rights generation (3%) to trust his word. Revs. Floyd Flake, Arlee Griffin of Brooklyn's Berean Missionary Baptist Church, and Philius Nicolas, uncle of Abner Louima and pastor of the Croisade Evangelique Church, urged their parishioners to support Giuliani in the 1997 elections. The post–Civil Rights generation is better educated, better integrated into society, and more ready to lead.

Rev. Floyd Flake recalls his own remarkable path to Congress and the Allen AME Church in Jamaica, Queens:

> Born a slave, my grandfather became a sharecropper in New Ulm, Texas. But considering the advances that have been made by African Americans since the sixties in the social and political arenas, it is amazing how much we have regressed. Fortunately, we still have a legacy of values, work ethic and faith. We will change our future by the actions we take together. What will be our legacy? Will it be that we will hear the words of Scripture, "Well done, my good and faithful servant?"

NOTES

1. This study is based mainly on the New York City portion of a 1997 national survey of church leaders in theological certificate programs servicing African Americans, which itself was part of a larger study, "African American Theological Certificate Students and Social Services," funded by the Ford Foundation under the direction of H. Dean Trulear of the New York Theological Seminary (Carnes 1997). Most of these certificate candidates either are already pastors or lay leaders in New York City's African American churches or plan to be soon. We estimate that in the 1990s, almost one-half of African American pastors were trained in theological certificate programs at Bible institutes, seminaries, and denominational programs. As such, they constitute the largest schooled leadership group in the African American church. The other half of the pastors were most likely trained through apprenticeships.

This study is supplemented by surveys of New York City pastors conducted between 1993 and 1996, a 1995 survey of New York City evangelical church members, and a 1995/1996 survey of leaders and church leaders in New York City Bible institutes (including seven African American theological certificate programs).

Finally, refinements of interpretation of the statistical findings are based on forty-five qualitative interviews with New York City African American church leaders and some of their major interactional partners, like Mayor Rudolph Giuliani. My special thanks goes to the hundreds of New York City African American church leaders and members who listened, corrected, refuted, and expanded on my conclusions.

2. Most of these types of lists are modeled on the one in the 1983 General Social Survey ($S = 1599$), which asks what groups or organizations people belonged to (Davis 1983).

3. Some link religiosity, poverty, and political apathy (Linda Jones [pseudo-

nym], "I Don't Vote," *New York Times*, July 14, 1976, p. A-35). For alienation among the African American underclass, see Glasgow 1981; Wilson 1987.

4. Wells and Rice have a similar question concerning the origins of suffering. Because their focus is more theological, they use the language of theodicy ("suffering") in their question. Wells and Rice's approach in turn derives from Robert Wuthnow's research on the content of persons' meaning systems in California's Bay Area. My question is more narrowly and concretely focused on the causes of poverty. I am less likely to pick up any general theological tenet to which the students adhere, and I am much more likely to pick up their theology-in-practice or, at least, their theology-in-rhetoric about a real experienced evil (Wells 1993, 1994; Wuthnow 1976).

Chapter 5

The Yoruba Religion in
New York

Mary Cuthrell Curry

From Catholic Cuba came Santeria (also known as The Religion, Lukumi, Anago, Candomble, or Xango) to New York, where it became the Yoruba religion practiced by former Protestant African Americans.[1]

In this chapter, I summarize the transformation of the Yoruba religion in New York City, based on four years of field research among a group of African American adherents in Brooklyn, during which time I participated in the religious activities of the Yoruba and conducted intensive interviews with several dozen leaders and members.

The Yoruba religion is spreading in the United States as a result of recent Cuban immigration and efforts by some African Americans. It arrived in two stages: (1) through a huge influx of Yoruba slaves to Cuba (and Brazil) in the eighteenth and nineteenth centuries, and (2) through the subsequent Cuban diaspora caused by the 1960 Cuban revolution.

The Origins of the Religion in Yorubaland and Its Transformation during Slavery

The southwestern states in Africa that we now call Nigeria, Togo, and portions of the Republic of Benin (formerly known as Dahomey) and of Ghana constitute the ancestral home of the people now known as Yoruba. Yorubaland, as I call it, was composed of a number of city-states that were plunged into one hundred years of civil war until 1886 during which more than 1.2 million people were captured and brought as slaves to Cuba (Duany 1985, 106). Consequently, the Yoruba culture made a lasting impression on Cuba, where Lukumi, a variety of the Yoruba language, is still spoken. The roots of the Yoruba religion in the United States thus stem from the Cuban immigrants.

In Yorubaland, the religion was coterminous with the political empire and its culture. Each lineage had a specific orisha (or deity), and for the unity and well-being of the whole community, the Yoruba king ensured that all orisha were worshiped. Also, since some important people outside a given lineage might also worship another lineage's deity, orisha societies were established for all those who worshiped the same orisha, setting a precedent for the practice of worshiping multiple orishas.

The slaves' concern for the survival of the Yoruba religion produced both structural changes in their practice of the religion and a redefinition of community. Although the slaves lost their country and their lineages, they continued to practice their religion through symbolic ritual kinship. Furthermore, since there were too few members of any society in any one place, the priests of one society were initiated into the rituals of another orisha (Bastide 1971; Marks 1974; Weaver 1986). In this way, priests in the Western Hemisphere assumed the role of Yoruba kings in worshiping multiple orishas to ensure that all the divinities received their due and remained part of the religious tradition.

Cabildos de Nacion

During the period of slavery in Cuba, the Yoruba religion became the religion of an oppressed urban stratum, hiding its true nature behind the Spanish social institutions. Rather than being attached to the courts of kings and lineages, as it had been in Africa, the Yoruba religion went underground and fundamentally changed its structure in order to survive. Accordingly, under the guise of worshiping Catholic patron saints, the slaves worshiped the orishas (Cros Sandoval 1975; Sandoval 1994).

After being exiled from Africa, the Yoruba religion also acquired a new name, Santeria, from the word *santero*, which in Spanish originally meant a carver of images of saints. In Cuba, *santero* came to mean literally "a maker of saints" or "a creator of the path through which the deities could come to earth" and interact with human beings (James 1970, v).

Santeria Comes to the United States

The senior Yoruba priests I interviewed date from the 1940s the beginning of Cuban influence on the African American community. That influence was initially felt in the performing arts, for example, Afro-Cuban jazz and dance. The practice of Santeria, however, was kept very secret, and its most important rituals, such as initiations into the priesthood, continued to be performed in Cuba. In fact, the religion's main ceremonies were not practiced in the United States until the 1960s (Brandon 1983; Weaver 1986). According to a senior Yoruba priest,

> We didn't have that much on Santeria until the initiations in 1959 and 1960 and then the subsequent migrations here. Prior to that back in the 1950s, 1940s, etc., there were a lot of Afro-Cubans here, but they kept it in the closet. They would work, and then in the summertime, they would run down to Miami and take the ferry over to Havana and would work their initiations.

After the 1960 revolution, thousands of people left Cuba for the United States. Among them were initiated *santeras* and *santeros* (female and male priests of Santeria). In the United States, these Cuban priests discovered an interest in Santeria by African Americans and non-Cuban Latin Americans, as well as Jews and Italians. After the Cuban revolution, journeys to Cuba became difficult, and so Cubans began to perform initiations in the United States.

Even though the Yoruba religion also is practiced in Cuba, Brazil, Trinidad, and some parts of Haiti, all "houses" in the United States have Cuban roots, for two reasons, one structural and one historical. The structural reason is that as practiced outside Cuba, Yoruba was harder to transplant because it was practiced in temples with hierarchies of priests. But because the home of each Yoruba priest of Cuban origin was a shrine, transplanting the Cuban version of the religion required fewer people. The historical reason, of course, is the exodus of priests from Cuba during the Cuban revolution. Therefore, if we traced each line back far enough, we would eventually find just a few houses in Cuba, possibly even just one. Because most Cubans do not expect to return to their homeland, Santeria serves as a mark of Cuban social identity. In fact, the number of Cubans in the United States who practice the religion is even larger than that in Cuba (Brandon 1983; Cabrera 1970; Cros Sandoval 1975; Sandoval 1994).

The Yoruba Religion as an Expression of Africanness for Black Americans

While Cubanismo[2] is unlikely to appeal to other ethnic and racial groups, and the Spanish language and Cuban secretiveness are obstacles to many African Americans, black Americans nevertheless seek out the Yoruba religion to enhance their African identity.

A number of conflicts did develop between African American and Cuban practitioners of the religion. On the one hand, Catholicism, most of whose saints are white, undermines African Americans' use of the religion as a means of strengthening their African identity. On the other hand, Cubans interpret the black American desire to return to the religion's African roots as a denial of the Cuban role in transmitting it. Although some Cubans acknowledge the African origins of the Yoruba religion, others minimize it. Moreover, the original priests who established the religion in the United States were white Havaneros who downplayed its African roots. One New York City Cuban priest even claims that Santeria/Yoruba religion should be practiced only in the sacred language of Spanish. But the Afro-Cubans who center the religion in Matanzas, Cuba, usually emphasize its African origins (figure 5.1).

The great migration of blacks to northern cities in the United States earlier in the twentieth century was accompanied by the development of new religious movements outside the mainstream (Frazier 1974). These movements deviated from not only mainstream Christianity but also the Christianity of the black church. In Harlem, Marcus Garvey started a black nationalist movement that inspired many features of the Black Muslims and the formation of Rastafarianism in Jamaica. The Garvey movement redefined Christianity in blacker terms, and the groups that followed the Garvey movement were even more radical.

The common characteristic of all these groups was the redefinition of black identity outside the American mainstream definitions. For example, the black Jews of Harlem attempted to attain a sense of worth by portraying God, Jesus, and Jacob as black, and some Yoruba religionists came out of the Moorish Science Temple of Noble Ali Drew, which was the most nationalistic of the cults (Frazier 1974). These new religious groups viewed Africa as the home of a great culture and the sole origin of blacks. One of the most prominent of these new religious movements was the Yoruba religion. As a senior Yoruba religion priest declared,

It was like "Hey, what are you talking about? I'm black and I'm proud." Not only are we black and proud but we are religious and proud. It is a different frame of mind. We're more informed. We know more, we're learning more. We know about Africa. And for us, in this religion it's imperative that we know that. We're Americans in the sense that we are born and bred and we want all the goodies, just like everybody. But Sunday I step away from that bullshit. I don't have to go to church. No, no, I don't have to deal with that.

Figure 5.1. Store for Santeria and Yoruba religion devotees. Courtesy of the collection of Tony Carnes.

The First Afro-American Yoruba Priest

The first Afro-American Yoruba priest was Nana Oseijeman Adefunmi (born Walter Eugene King), who sought an African religious expression for black Americans. His search took him from Detroit, where he was born in 1928, to Cuba's Matanzas Province where on August 28, 1959, he was initiated as a priest of Obatala (the most senior deity in the Yoruba pantheon). Adefunmi was deeply influenced by the black nationalist tradition, as his father had been a Garveyite and was involved in the Moorish Science Temple of Noble Ali Drew (Hunt 1979).

Adefumni founded the Yoruba Temple, a well-known fixture of the Harlem scene from 1960 to 1970. Many members of the African American community first became aware of the Yoruba religion (which Adefunmi renamed Orisha-Voodun) through participation in the Harlem Yoruba Temple. Also under his influence, a number of African Americans took African names and began to wear African dress.

In 1970, Adefunmi left Harlem and established the village of Oyotunji (meaning "Oyo rises again") in Sheldon, South Carolina. Many of Adefunmi's former followers remained in New York, however, and some became members of Cuban or multiethnic Ocha houses. Mostly, the houses that Adefunmi and his followers built became African American houses, and because of their identification with Africa, the African American houses dropped the name Santeria and substituted the Yoruba religion (Brandon 1983; Clapp 1966). Many of the original followers of the Yoruba religion came from black nationalist backgrounds and were seeking a positive, public African identity. Consequently, they regarded the secret existence of orisha behind the guise of Catholic saints as a relic of slavery. Furthermore, since most African Americans were Protestant, Catholicism was also not a mark of their cultural identity as it was for the Cubans.

The Houses of Ocha in New York City

Today in New York City, the Yoruba religion is organized into structures of ritual kinship called Ocha houses or, simply, houses. The word *house* refers to a group of worshipers in a ritual kinship relationship and descended from orisha (deities).

An Ocha house is named for the priest who heads it, for example, Peter's house or Katherine's house. Members of the house are considered the godchildren of the priests in the house. Godchildren are godbrothers and godsisters to one another. Other terms modeled on kin relationships are grandparents in ocha, aunts and uncles in ocha, nieces and nephews in ocha, and the like. The key relationship is that between godparent and godchild (Gregory 1986, 67), and it is used as a master metaphor to describe the mutual links between parents and children, the living and their ancestors, and the orisha and humankind.

Godparents and godchildren have complementary responsibilities. The godparent is responsible for instructing the godchild in religious knowledge, ritual, and duties and oversees all necessary divinations, sacrifices, and initiations for the godchild. The godchild is expected to assist the godparent in rituals or do religiously related work in the godparent's home.

Most houses in New York City are structured around two major hierarchies: those called *alejo*, which have received the primary initiation of *ilekis*, and those initiated into the priesthood. *Ilekis* are bead necklaces strung according to the colors associated with each orisha. For example, Shango's colors are red and white, and Oshun's are orange and amber. Ilekis are said to extend the protection of the godparent's orisha to the initiated. Both the alejos and the priests are ranked according to seniority, that is, in the order of initiation. Moreover, all those who have been initiated into the priesthood outrank all those who have not.

The crucial stage of socialization into the Yoruba religion is initiation into the priesthood, which marks the highest membership category in a house. The initiate acquires an *ojubona* (a secondary godparent), who assumes the responsibilities of the godparent if the godparent dies or is incapacitated. Because the ojubona may come from another house, she may be the means of forming bonds between houses.

Very few practitioners of the religion become priests, because some view the role of godparent as onerous and unrewarding. Peter's house, for example, which had more than three hundred members in 1976,[3] had only sixteen initiations into the priesthood in the next twenty years. Katherine's house had many fewer members (approximately five in 1976), but by 1996, she had initiated eighteen priests. Of Peter's and Katherine's godchildren who are priests, only ten have initiated other priests.

Relationships among houses are formed through networks of kin or honorary kin. Subhouses of a line have built-in relationships. For example, houses whose heads are godsiblings interact closely, and marriages between priests of different houses also connect houses. Godparents usually serve as ojubona for a godchild's first priest initiated, and the ojubona of that godchild serves as the ojubona for the second priest.

Because growth comes from the priests' personal networks, an area as heterogeneous as New York produces ethnically diverse groupings. According to Gregory (1986) and Brandon (1983), houses of Ocha in New York City may be composed entirely of black Americans or Puerto Ricans, whereas others remain exclusively Cuban. Still others are multiethnic, although these houses tend to implode because of interethnic conflicts.

Yoruba Priests in New York City

A *babalawo* is a high priest who specializes in divination, and an *oriate* is an especially knowledgeable elder priest who ensures the correctness of rituals. The most noted of these ritual specialists was an Afro-Cuban babalawo named Pancho Mora, who was also known as If a Morote, who came to the United States in 1946 (Gonzalez-Whippler 1983). Until his death in 1987, Mora was the dean of babalawos in the United States. An oriate named Paolo, also known as Oosawede, was the first oriate to come to this country, and until his death, he was considered the ultimate teacher of priests of The Religion (Weaver 1986).

The primary role of a Yoruba priest is that of a mediator between human beings and the divine. A priest is also a counselor,[4] psychologist, father/mother confessor, and adviser on practical problems, all rolled into one. The priest, who is most often a woman, is the central figure in a hierarchical structure but is also subject to democratic controls and a familial ideology (see Deren 1953, 176). If a priest is thought to be disagreeable or lacking in knowledge or integrity, people will no longer consult her, although she will remain a priest.

In the United States, one of the priest's major functions is counseling people on "all the problems of life." In contrast to the Yoruba priests in Africa, U.S. priests define problems as problems of the self. For example, in West African religion, divination is like sociotherapy (Pelton 1980; Turner 1968, 1975a and b), whereas in the United States, priests describe it as psychotherapy. The focus of American priests is on the healthy functioning of the individual, which in turn helps the community function well. The shift in this country from the group-centered divination of Africa is probably a result of American individualism and also the fact that the religion serves a subgroup, not an entire society.

Priests may specialize. Some run kitchens during ceremonies; others become scholars of the religious tradition; and still others specialize in performing ritual ceremonies. Some priests make the religion a very small part of their lives, while others have an emotional attachment to the religion and make it the center of their lives. In New York City, some priests (the ritual experts known as the oriate and the babalawo) specialize in counseling priests. When someone presents to a priest a problem or requires a ceremony that is beyond her knowledge, she consults a ritual expert who functions as a consultant for a number of houses.

Beliefs and Rituals of the Yoruba Religion in New York City

The Yoruba religion as taught and practiced in New York City is difficult to summarize, as it is an interlocking system of beliefs and ritual practices. The Yoruba belief system includes both a cosmology and ideas of destiny and reincarnation. The ritual system consists of divination, sacrifice, and ceremonies.

Cosmology

A typical New York City adherent to the Yoruba religion believes that she stands at the intersection of a cosmos alive with the forces of God, the earth, the orisha (deities), and the ancestors. She visits a priest to ritually create pathways for her communication with the invisible divine.

Above all other deities, on another plane altogether, is God (called Olodumare or Olorun, the Owner of Heaven).[5] She/he is everything there is, the totality of all. God is supreme but receives no direct, organized worship and has no shrines. The Yoruba say, "Who would dare offer sacrifice to Olodumare?" since what would one have that Olodumare does not have or is not?

God is considered the creator of heaven and earth, omnipresent, omnipotent, and omniscient. She/he is the source of all destinies and the ultimate source of good and evil but is above human distinctions of good and evil. Rather, God is a combination of opposite polarities, the ultimate balance of all contradictions. Although God is not remote, the orisha (deities) are more approachable with requests for help and understanding of the cosmos.

Onile (the deity of the earth whose name means The-Owner-of-the-

Earth) sanctions the breaking of covenants and the shedding of blood. Unlike Olodumare, who is above gender, Onile is definitely female. She is the source of the necessities of life and the final resting place of the ancestors. Although sacrifices are not made to God, they are made to the earth (Onile).

Ancestors are the upholders of morality and are concerned with the behavior between kin and community members and with the good reputation of their descendants.

The divinities or orisha are complex multivalent beings. New York City Yoruba religionists consider the orisha to be aspects of God, forces of nature, or the universe viewed from different angles. According to John Mason and Gary Edwards, the orisha are specialized forms of the Supreme God, "a divine being who exists simultaneously on many levels. An orisha may be an historical figure, an ancestor, war leader, hunter or city founder, an animal, a tree or even a rock" (1985, 10). Orishas are analogous to the saints of the Catholic Church, since they are conceived to be intermediaries between human beings and God. The Yoruba, however, conceive of the relationship between humankind and the orisha as reciprocal, whereas the relationship between saints and human beings is supplicatory.

Orisha are also thought of as psychological forces in the human mind. The Yoruba believe that each person has an orisha assigned to her at birth and that this orisha and the person (called her child) share the same character. Yoruba religionists sometimes use a Haitian proverb to summarize this belief: "The character of the person is the character of the orisha."

Destiny and Reincarnation in New York City

New York Yoruba religionists say that their lives are governed by *ori*, the Yoruba word for "destiny." It means, simultaneously, a person's physical head, destiny, potentiality, the quality of a person's character, the ancestral guardian spirit, and a person's own deity, or orisha.

Divination and sacrifice are built around the concept of destiny. If the manifestation of a favorable destiny is the main concern of the practitioners in the Yoruba religion, then divination is the principal means of diagnosis, and sacrifice is the paramount means of setting things right.

Ori is the Yoruba word for "head" or "top." To Yoruba religionists, the physical head is sacred because it is the seat of divinity and the symbolic link between the divine and the human and between the ancestors and the living. The outer physical head is the manifestation of a person's inner head. *Ori* is also the word for "ancestral guardian spirit." The Yoruba believe that one component of the composite that creates a person is the soul of an ancestor, a guardian spirit that has chosen to come back to earth to protect that person. *Ori* is also the name given to one's personal orisha. No one can prevent what a person's ori ordains, and no other orisha can cause to happen what one's ori denies. Thus, for any person, the most powerful god is that person's own personal orisha.

Rituals of New York City's Yoruba Religion

Divination

Divination (the art or practice that seeks to foretell future events or discover hidden knowledge) must be performed to ascertain the pattern in Heaven, in order to remedy it through sacrifice or to ensure that those who work against it will not succeed. This potential destiny can be achieved only with struggle, the aid of supernatural forces, and the failure of those (human or otherwise) who would work to oppose its realization. Ori, then, is "choice/potentiality-to-be-realized-through struggle," a concept emphasizing a person's own self-creation.

Divination is also the communication between the human and the divine. Orunmila, the deity of divination, was present at each person's choice of destiny and therefore knows what is allotted to each. Consequently, if one needs such information, one goes to a priest to obtain it through divination. Three major forms of divination are commonly used by the New York City Yoruba: *if a, merindinlogun,* and *obi.* Each requires different degrees of initiation to practice.

Of the three, if a is the most prestigious. It is a kind of divination similar to geomancy, divination by figures or lines, usually drawn on the earth's surface. In the second form of divination, merindinlogun, the diviner uses sixteen cowry shells to generate the signs. The cowries are thrown onto a basket tray or a mat, and those that fall face up are counted, with a sign associated with each number. In New York City and elsewhere in the Western Hemisphere, a priest of either gender may use the merindinlogun. Consequently, this divination ritual is culturally more prominent here because there are many more women priests.

The third type of divination is obi. In Nigeria, obi is a kola nut that breaks into four lobes. Since kola nuts do not grow in either the United States or Cuba, coconuts are used. The diviner breaks a coconut and divides the meat into four pieces. The concave side of the coconut is white, and the convex is brown, which allows for a possibility of five (or $n + 1$) patterns when four pieces of coconut are thrown down simultaneously. Obi is capable of answering only yes/no questions.

Sacrifice

Sacrifice is the principal remedy recommended by divination. The basic pattern of most answers (*pataki*) is "So-and-so had such-and-such a problem and was told to perform such-and-such a sacrifice." From the priest's point of view, sacrifice has only one aim for sacrifice: to achieve or restore a state of balance between the individual and supernatural forces (Zuesse 1979, 218).

Ceremonies

The Yoruba religion in New York City holds four main types of ceremonies: life-passage ceremonies, priesthood-career ceremonies, cyclical ceremonies, and occasional ceremonies. Life-passage ceremonies are ceremonies held at transitional points in a person's life, such as birth, marriage, and death. Priesthood-career ceremonies are those receiving[6] ilekis, receiving warriors, and initiating people into the priesthood. Ilekis are bead necklaces made in color schemes appropriate to the various orishas and so vary from house to house. After people have received ilekis, it may be divined that they need to receive warriors. The orisha Elegba, Ogun, Osshosi, and Osun are collectively known as the warriors. Initiation into the priesthood is expensive in terms of time, money, and commitment. An initiation ceremony is a seven-day event, after which the priest becomes an *iyawo* (literally, "junior wife"), a year-long liminal state in which she or he is an initiate but not yet a priest.

CYCLICAL RELIGIOUS CEREMONIES

Every year, the New York City houses observe the same special days with ceremonies and the cessation of other activities. Each of the orisha has her own feast day or orisha day, usually associated with particular Catholic saint's day. On that day, priests of the orisha give their orisha her favorite sweets, appropriate fruit, a cloth in the appropriate color, and two candles. The orisha is seated on a mat, covered with cloth and surrounded with the fruit and sweets. People visit the priest of that particular orisha to pay homage, and while doing so, they can talk to the orisha, or the priest of the orisha may talk to the orisha for them.

On the anniversary of her initiation date, a priest celebrates her ocha birthday. It is a more important occasion than an orisha feast day, which it closely resembles, because on a birthday all the orisha and the priest must be given cloths, sweets, and fruits.

OCCASIONAL CEREMONIES: THE BEMBE

The Bembe is a possession dance whose purpose is calling the orisha to interact with the worshipers and give them advice. Bembes are performed when a particular orisha recommends one as a sacrifice and when someone is initiated into the priesthood, and on ocha birthdays. Bembes are elaborate ceremonies with hired professional drummers and singers.

During the Bembe, some priests are possessed. Then, when the possession is complete, the orisha who visits through the priest is led away and comes back dressed in her appropriate colors. The orisha may then give advice or answer questions. After a while, the orisha indicates that she wants to leave and is taken away. Shortly thereafter, the priest reappears in an unpossessed state. Meanwhile, the drummers play, and other priests may be possessed. This continues throughout the Bembe.

Conclusion: Yoruba Religion in Catholic and Protestant Cultures

The Yoruba religion is one example of the reproduction and transformation of a religious culture caused by a religion's moving from one culture to another. Its social structure was changed by its initial migration to Cuba and is currently being changed again in the United States. The social conditions of Cuban slavery and persecution produced a religious structure that proved the most transportable of all the Yoruba-derived religions in the Western Hemisphere.

The African American community in the United States, especially that in the urban North, was the first to embrace its African heritage. In the process, however, this embrace produced (and is still producing) other changes, for example, the de-syncretization or uncoupling of religious elements. In Cuba, the Yoruba religion encountered a largely Catholic milieu, whereas in the African American community, it entered a largely

Protestant environment. We could hypothesize that the Protestant setting greatly facilitated de-syncretization.

The Yoruba religion is finding some adherents in non-Cuban Latin communities and white ethnic communities. But because African Americans emphasize the African origins of the Yoruba community and Cubans emphasize its recent Cuban vintage, other communities probably will not find it as appealing. The ethnic communities that contain the largest numbers of whites are Italian and Jewish. We could thus hypothesize that Italian folk-Catholicism would be more amenable to syncretism and that the Jewish converts would be less attracted to a Yoruba-Catholic syncretism. We can expect, therefore, that the spread of the Yoruba religion into other sectors of American society will produce new patterns of reproduction and transformation.

NOTES

1. I wish to thank Helen Rose Ebaugh for her support, for reading multiple drafts of this paper, and for her insightful comments. I also wish to thank Janet Chafetz for her editorial comments.

2. The ideology of Cubanness.

3. All numbers are estimates, since there are no formal membership lists.

4. In Haiti, Brazil, and Cuba, one of the functions of a priest is that of herbalist and doctor. In the United States, this aspect of the priest's role has lost most of its prominence. Instead, if the diviner suspects medical problems, she advises the person to see a doctor.

5. Olodumare has no gender (or, rather, transcends sex and gender). She/he is spoken of as creator, but also some things are spoken of as being "in the womb of Olodumare."

6. In Yoruba parlance, to receive something means to acquire something and/or to undergo an initiation (not initiation into the priesthood, which is called "making ocha.")

Chapter 6

Hinduism in New York City

Ashakant Nimbark

Recent trends in information technology and cross-continental diffusion have created some curious contradictions among the approximately 200,000 NRIs (nonresident Indians), living and working in and around New York City.

This chapter is a part of an ongoing inquiry into what I call a trend toward *desecularization,* or a return to old-fashioned religiosity, this time with the help of postmodern computer technology.[1] I have incorporated into my work nearly one hundred semistructured interviews of recently immigrated computer scientists and technicians both in and around New York City.[2] They represent a highly urbanized, educated, and affluent community paradoxically coming from a supposedly traditional, relatively impoverished, and largely rural-agrarian multiethnic society of India, most of whose globally diffused religious groups are Hindu (more than 80%) but also include large numbers of Muslims, Christians, Sikhs, Parsis, Jains, and Jews. The New York–based Hindus encompass a wide variety of people, from the intellectually inclined followers of J. Krishnamurty and Rama Krishna Mission (who share many traits with the Unitarians) to the heavily ritualistic temple worshipers and youthful professionals who were agnostic or nonbelievers in India and were drawn to the Hindu temples only after arriving in America.

These professionals include many brown yuppies, who seem to be deeply involved in their traditional beliefs, even surpassing their elders and less affluent counterparts back home. They are quite comfortable dealing with horoscopes, palmistry, and religious rituals such as temple visits and recitation of prayers, all while continuing to pursue their high-tech, high-income, highly skilled careers and carrying out their professions in a postindustrial America.

A number of Hindu temples have been built in cities and suburbs from coast to coast. Several were constructed in Queens—including one in Flushing, which is modeled on the South Indian (high dome) temple—and are now full-fledged community centers (Sengupta 1999). In fact, more and more temple structures are being built with huge donations from their high-tech devotees, who explain,

> While we are busy with academic pursuits and career opportunities in America, we need to preserve our cultural roots, especially for the younger generations who would otherwise be vulnerable to the highly materialistic, promiscuous, and socially destructive behavior of this nonbelieving host society of America. To counter the local godlessness, we need to strengthen our faith in God and our ties with our traditional roots. (interview with a computer scientist in New York, June 1999)

These Hindu temples (community centers) conduct daily rituals and celebrations of important landmarks in the life cycles of their patrons—conception, birth, the naming of a child—in accordance with zodiac signs and horoscopes, the giving of holy thread (*upavita*), engagements, wedding showers, traditional weddings, huge feasts, celebrations of numerous holidays, prayers to bring health, well-being of the elderly, cremation, and postdeath ceremonies (figure 6.1).

The paradoxical trend, as illustrated by recent observations and interviews, is a process of desecularization, which may be creating the following "positive" rewards: (1) greater intergenerational communications and less "generation gap," (2) respect for the elderly and a lot of affection for the children, and (3) networking and mutual deference among devotees. On the other side of the coin are issues that these devotees will not even consider. Instead, they maintain (1) cultural isolation from other ethnic groups and have very little contact with other cultures; (2) a lack of individualistic, creative, and truly open communication across age and gender boundaries; (3) a retrogressive, ritualistic, and conformist behavior pattern which, ironically, causes its own contradictions.

How can we explain these contradictory patterns of spiritual serenity mixing with catchy commercialization and conspicuous consumption? First, let us briefly review the new, post-1965 immigration of technically skilled South Asians to the United States. The New York area has been the most favored place for these migrants, followed by California, with its high-tech Silicon Valley eager to absorb more and more information technologists from Asia, and its hot weather attracting enterprising Asian

Annual Support Form

THE HINDU TEMPLE SOCIETY OF NORTH AMERICA
(Sri Maha Vallabha Ganapati Devasthanam)
45-57 Bowne Street, Flushing, New York 11355
Phone: (718) 460-8484; Toll Free 1-800-99-HINDU
Fax: (718) 461-8055

Figure 6.1. City Hindu temples seek support to combat "local godlessnesss." Courtesy of the collection of Ashakant Nimbark.

investors and yuppies. Other popular host regions are Illinois, Michigan, Florida, and Washington, D.C.

Not too long ago, anthropologists and sociologists used to classify East Asian religions as more traditional, localized, and other-worldly than their West European counterparts, which were seen as rational, modern, global, and this-worldly. In the post–world war, postcolonial world, however, these classifications have become irrelevant (Hefner 1998).

The dichotomy between traditional religion and rational science, too, has been challenged, especially in the context of immigration. Many social scientists who assumed that modernization and scientific rationalism would make traditional religiosity obsolete, now increasingly acknowledge the coexistence of modernity and tradition (Berger 1967, 1999). Religious beliefs as well as practices have not only survived the worldwide growth of science and communication but also seem to have been revived and strengthened and have even used modern technology to popularize ancient traditions (Kurien 1999).

This paradoxical process of NRIs' maintaining (and even deepening) their traditional roots with the help of Hindu beliefs and rituals while assimilating (and even excelling) in America's professional-financial structure comes at the expense of unresolved issues leading to mental and physical stress, social-cultural tensions, and political-ideological inconsistencies. To examine this paradox, let us look closely at two different worship sites of Hinduism in and around New York. One is a large urban temple with an inclusive agenda; a multidenominational, multideity, multiregional, and multilinguistic structure; and a largely cosmopolitan membership. The other temple is relatively parochial, localized, and linguistically exclusive.

Following the classic work of A. R. Radcliffe Brown and Robert Redfield, anthropologists and sociologists distinguish localized "little traditions" from translocal "great traditions." The former are constructed around simple, preliterate, and rural or tribal rituals, and the latter take the form of more complex, classic, and universalistic worldviews. One might believe that this distinction also applies to the religious beliefs and practices of the Hindus being surveyed here and their relatives and families "back home." That is, the former may follow the great tradition, and the latter may be a part of the little tradition. The modernization of mass societies and the globalization of communication and commerce, however, do not allow us to validate such a dichotomy.

Whereas before 1965, when immigrants of South Asian background and predominantly Hindu affiliation were fewer and self-selected, the current South Asian immigrants are more heterogeneous. In addition, they often bring with them their less skilled and economically dependent parents and other relatives. Whereas the earlier immigrants developed inclusive, multilinguistic, and interregional associations, maintaining a unified pan-Indian "great tradition," the latter, ironically, tend to form more parochial and subcultural groups that can be termed "little

Figure 6.2. A "little tradition" priest in a temple in Corona, Queens.
Courtesy of the collection of Ashakant Nimbark.

traditions." And while the former paved the way for assimilation with
other Indians, Asians, and mainstream Americans, the latter tend to create what I call "cultural ghettos" (figure 6.2).

Earlier Indian immigrants celebrated cultural holidays and festivals
(mainly Deepavali, the festival of lights, and Holi, the festival of colors)

that were less sectarian and more secular. Later immigrants, however, have needed and demanded more regional and parochial associations in which persons from the same state, often the same province or even the same town, meet for much more exclusive gatherings. Their festivals and holidays, too, tend to be more subregional and narrowly based and frequently appear to be even more authentic and "pure" than the ones back home—that is, more "native" here than there! The religious rituals in such new/old settings claim to counter—but actually create and prolong—the patterns of ethnic segregation, self–isolation, nostalgia, and delayed assimilation.

Just as the megastores and large supermarkets like Wal-Mart often create a need for smaller and less impersonal 7-11–type convenience stores, the former "great tradition" Hindu temples and ecumenical ashramas, though still needed, are too intellectual, too colorless, or too impersonal for some homesick natives who are much more at home with their "little tradition" temples, with their personalized idioms, intragroup kinship, and familiar food. Their deities, too, are usually more colorful, locally dressed and capable of inspiring devotional chanting, dancing, and dietary feasts as well as fasts and personalized attention during devotees' times of trouble, joy, illness, accident, death, marriage, childbirth, new homes, and new jobs. In order to see how these two polar types of Hindu worship sites cater to the varying needs of their adherents, let us briefly review a typical day in each of these.

First, let us visit an "ecumenical" type of temple, variously known as Sanatan Dharma or Sarva Deva (inclusive religion/all-gods). Although many, if not most, temples have a main deity, the larger and more inclusive temples in and around New York City satisfy many types of Hindus by having niches for many more. The main deity usually is Vishnu or Shiva (the protector and the destroyer from the Hindu pantheon). Many posh temples follow the devotion of Ganesha (the elephant-headed deity, bringing good luck and a symbol of starting a new relationship, home, or business) or other deities. Even when a temple is dedicated to just one deity, it has sanctums for others. The deities are usually worshiped along with their consorts (Shiva with Parvati, Vishnu with Lakshmi, Rama with Sita, Krishna with Radha). These sanctums for the deities are situated around the perambulatory path of the devotees, enabling them to go from one to the next, worshiping and offering flowers and grains (and/or cash) to each.

A day at such an inclusive (all-deity) temple starts with Usha Pooja, or morning worship, at which the head priest makes an offering. The rest of the day consists of noon prayers, a noon food-offering followed by a luncheon, evening *aartis* (films) and music, and the final rite sending the gods (and their devotees) to sleep. Weekends have elaborate rituals and special feasts. Most of the temples observe all the Hindu festivals and also host innumerable regional and local festivals.

Devotees visiting a temple for worship are expected to make an offering in accordance with their ability and inclination. The offering can be anything from a simple *archana* (offering of flowers) to the sponsoring of all the *poojas* (rituals) in the temple from morning till night. Offerings like flowers, coconut, and *agarbattis* (incense sticks) are sold on the premises. Devotees can sponsor *langars* (free food for all) at many of the temples.

One thing that is quite noticeable about the temples in the United States is their ability and willingness to adapt. For example, in a temple I visited recently, the devotees were expected to sit down while the *aarti* was shown on closed-circuit TV, so that people could see it clearly instead of looking at the *poojari*'s backside. Most of the announcements were made over a microphone, and important rituals were videotaped. And the *yajna* (sacrificial fireplace) often has to be adjusted to meet local fire regulations, though not without the complaints from the priests as well as their congregations (*Newsday*, September 19, 1999).

These days, temples are becoming increasingly involved in issues of the temporal world. One factor that many temples are emphasizing is the need to cultivate religious awareness and faith in children as a panacea for social evils (figure 6.3). With this end in view, many temples conduct different levels of classes on Hinduism. In addition, many temples offer classes in languages such as Hindi and other regional languages. Temples also offer free medical checkups, provide relief in times of calamities, give out free food, and the like. All these services contribute to ethnic pride among Hindu American devotees, who are more supportive of the Hindutva movement (reglorification of Hinduism) in India led by the right-wing BJP Party than are Hindus in India (Kurien 1999, 654).

Asian Indians are united by one of the categories of the U.S. Bureau of Census but are increasingly divided by regional and subregional as well as religious and subreligious groupings (Warner 1993) that figure more prominently than, say, among the Chinese. In turn, these subgroups have been building more and more regionally based temples in and around New York City.

Figure 6.3. Mother "socializing" daughter in front of a goddess statue. Courtesy of the collection of Ashakant Nimbark.

Approximately 200,000 Indian Americans live in the Greater New York Metropolitan Area, and it is safe to assume that 80 percent of them are Hindus. Then there are the "hidden Hindus" from the Caribbean, who have been here for many generations. They now probably number more than 100,000 and, in many instances, are even more rigid regarding their beliefs and rituals than are Indians from the motherland (Melvani 1995). Our discussion thus centers on roughly 300,000 persons.

Compared with other smaller towns where ethnic groups have to function inclusively in their umbrella organizations (as the Indians did before 1965), the huge metropolitan New York environment sustains numerous subgroups divided along regional and linguistic lines. The Hindu community in New York would fit well into the characterization by Robert Bellah and colleagues of those who seek out like-minded others, with mutual narcissism (see 1985, 219–249). Thus the exclusive "little" Hindu communities draw more members now than their "great" counterparts do.

When we enter such a subregional temple in the New York area, its members speak the same language, have the same dietary preferences and taboos, and often find themselves in a more authentically parochial atmosphere than in large metropolitan areas like Delhi and Mumbai in India. Their holiday celebrations feature local songs, prayers, and dances. The food is more often prepared by the women devotees themselves and not catered, as in the inclusive temples. Elements of nostalgia, self-consciousness, and self-segregation are also more pronounced, as is the orthodoxy of rituals.

If the inclusive temple is identified by the traffic jams created by out-of town Mercedes and Volvos, the exclusive temple is usually near a subway stop, and those who come in their Nissans and Hondas use carpools, further facilitating their in-group interactions. The exclusive temple is almost a transplanted provincial Hindu island in the New York City ocean. All the devotees act like members of an extended family, a quasi commune, conversing on topics ranging from "What vegetable did you cook for lunch today?" to "When is the postdeath ceremonial feast for your late mother?" The imported, homegrown priests are supplemented by local retirees or moonlighting professionals. Temple priests take great pride in saying that rituals are carried out more authentically here than they are even in India. "Back home, you take everything for granted. Here, you have the hunger for it. When we are missing something, we want to be sure everything is getting done exactly the way it is to be done" (Sengupta 1999, 33).

A considerable portion of the Indians arriving in the United States these days are skilled workers for the computer industry. A survey of one hundred computer professionals revealed that they became more religious after moving to the United States. They go to the temple more often; they participate in religious functions, which they never did in India; and some have even given up eating meat and drinking alcohol after a few months in America because they believe that it is against their religion.

Most of the respondents were not strict followers when they were in India. For most of them, religious observation amounted to following and taking part in the family ceremonies, but they never initiated any religious functions on their own. They went to temple only on occasions like birthdays or festival days. And while they lived in India, only 24 percent of the respondents observed a day of the week as a vegetarian day, abstaining from all meat and fish. All the respondents recognized that they had changed after moving to America. While the pattern of religious ceremonies remained the same—that of following the family lead—they had become stricter in their observation of personal aspects of religion. In addition to the 24 percent who, while in India, had observed a day of abstaining from eating meat; 16 percent said that they had started such observance after coming to the United States.

Even the frequency of temple visits rose for all respondents, with one of the reasons being that the respondents enjoyed longer weekends in America. While in India, they did not own a car and had to depend on public transportation. Here it took just a few minutes to reach the nearest temple. Also, they felt that because their family was not around to guide them, it was incumbent upon them to take care of the religious aspects of their lives. Fifty-two percent of the respondents visited a temple at least once a week, and 28 percent visited a temple two to three times a month. Whereas 20 percent said that they did not visit a temple regularly, they did go at least once a month.

All the respondents were clear about wishing to visit a temple on special days like birthdays and festival days. Twenty-eight percent looked up the days for temple visiting on their own, and the rest got instructions from their family on which days to go to the temple. But more than half the respondents admitted that they did not do any *poojas* at home. The most common reason they gave was that their houses and apartments were not kept in a suitable condition to conduct the *pooja*, and they felt that a *pooja* conducted in an impure site might cause more harm than good. Some cited their ignorance of the procedure for not doing any *poojas* at home. All the respondents, however, had some object for worship in their homes. This was most often a picture of a deity, in some cases, an idol. And all of them were in the habit of folding their hands in front of it, either immediately after their bath or just before going to work. Forty-eight percent said that they also put a mark of worship like sandal paste or *vibhuti* on their forehead.

All the respondents stated that they made an offering to the temple when they were there, and they all appreciated and admired the temples' social activities.

Asked about the social contacts made at temple gatherings, the respondents were generally skeptical. Instead, they preferred to go to temples with their own groups of friends. And even when they talked to others at the temple, it was with people sharing the same values. Some sarcastic comments were made about ABCDs (American-Born Confused Desi, a term used to criticize a second-, or third-, generation Indian American) who do not want to participate in religious rituals.

Future plans for marriage, children, and retirement include religious customs. Almost all the respondents expected to marry Indians, often within the same caste, in a family-arranged marriage, representing a trend toward desecularization. By demonizing and selectively overprotesting the unstable marriages in America ("one out of two end up in divorce!") and glorifying the virtue of multigenerational extended families, they showed a clear preference for Indian (Hindu) values in their future families. Many believed that America was not the right place to bring up children and that they would return to India—at a later stage, of course, after profusely benefiting from their present technology-theology mix.

To compare these brown yuppies—the computer-skilled and horoscope-friendly new immigrants—I also interviewed fifty additional neo-Hindus, twenty-five from the longtime established elites and twenty-five proletariats (taxi drivers, 7-11 workers, and subway-newsstand workers) in the New York area. Those from the elites were generally concerned about their children's excessive assimilation into mainstream WASP America while also deploring their association with the nonwhite minorities and being ambivalent about other ethnic groups. Their desecularization, I noted, was in response to their overestimated uprootedness and overprojected fear of crime and drugs, disease, and family breakdown in America.

The proletariats more readily admitted their homesickness and nostalgia, which had sent them to temples with their families and relatives who shared their backgrounds. Unlike the elites who had lavish meditation lounges and elaborately decorated Hindu shrines, these families had simpler, smaller, and inexpensively imported ritual gadgets—small statues of local deities housed in wooden or brass cabinets comparable to (and usually next to) nineteen-inch TV sets. Their temple visits are more intensely devotional than public relation stunts.

The Asian-Indian media are heavily preoccupied with desecularized messages. About ten weekly newspapers are published in the New York area for this ethnic group. Half of them are in English, and the others are in local languages–Gujarati, Hindi, Punjabi, Bengali, Malayalam, and Teugu. More than one dozen radio programs and around twenty TV programs carry religious-devotional messages—news, advertisements, and "letters" from the readers, listeners, and viewers.

The NRI media scene in the New York area is filled with a mixture of worldly entertainment, intraworldly mobility and other-worldly worship. The coexistence of insurance agency ads, travel agency ads, and religious ceremony ads implies that the first ensures physical well-being, the second ensures constant touch with their roots, and the third should ensure well-being in the hereafter of these economically enterprising but socially marginalized NRIs. They spend millions of dollars inviting, sponsoring, and glamorizing religious discourses of jet-set orators such as Murari Babu, who offer elaborate Ramayana discourses laced with worldly wit, melodious music and how-to lessons. The basic premises of these popular neo-Hindu discourses seem to be that the Western world (especially America) is so secular, amoral, and crime ridden and the forces of globalization are so homogenizing that only their own religious tradition can offer them safety and identity.

Finally, the Hindu gods have arrived on the Internet. The Web offers to a large number of desecularized Hindus an opportunity to "surf and pray," shop and meditate. The Hindunet provides to its materialistically workaholic users calendars of holidays, lists of temples around the world, links to Hindu scriptures, and instruction on how to worship.

This paradoxical mixture of ancient faith and modern technology may still have another challenge. What about the next generation? The second-generation children of Hindu immigrants may still maintain familial ties that offer them the cozy comfort of extended households. The third and fourth generations, however, may find these contradictions too cumbersome to carry on (Mehta 1997). While their seniors are kept too busy in the temples to miss home, their women are still obedient, their kids are smart and well behaved, and others envy their community, the deceptively simplistic and narcissistically self-congratulatory way in which this topic has been discussed so far may soon backfire when their own resecularized youngsters start asking to drink the new wine of America.

NOTES

1. A draft form of this chapter was presented as "When Horoscopes and Computers Mix: Notes on the Hindus in New York" at the annual meeting of the Association for the Sociology of Religion, Chicago, August 1999.

2. I am grateful to Radhika Menen for conducting the interviews with the computer professionals and discussing the earlier phase of this study

Chapter 7

New York City
The Bible Institute Capital of the World?

Paul de Vries

Among New York City's least-known but most distinguishing character-istics is the fact that it has probably the largest concentration of Bible in-stitutes of any city in the United States, with more than seventy struc-tured programs of biblical inquiry and ministry training for people with a high school education.[1] Although most of these programs are not ac-credited, they participate in the usual higher-education traditions—stu-dents pay tuition, engage in serious study, write papers, prepare for tests, receive grades, and are honored at graduation, much as students in an ac-credited college program do.

In the nineteenth and early twentieth centuries, American churches trained most of their leaders through Bible institutes, Bible colleges, and similar programs. New immigrants, in particular, sought out Bible insti-tutes. Again today, in New York City there is a renewed demand for post–high school, entry-level training for ministries in the church. Al-most unnoticed, a number of new Bible institutes have been founded, particularly in the Hispanic and Asian churches. Indeed, about one-third of all churches in the New York City–New Jersey area are affiliated with a Bible institute.

Their students represent a significant leadership cohort in New York City. A New York City–New Jersey Pastors Survey found that 41 percent of all pastors had Bible institute training, with most then going on to col-lege (Carnes 1996b). For example, Rafael Reyes, director of education for the Eastern District Assembly of God, estimates that 80 percent of the New York City–area assembly pastorates contain Bible institute gradu-ates. The charismatic/Pentecostal churches are one of the fastest-growing organizations in New York City and are generally led by Bible institute graduates. City leader Rev. Ruben Diaz, who is also the president of the New York Hispanic Clergy Organization and pastor of the Christian Community Neighborhood Church in the South Bronx, graduated from Damascus Bible Institute before going to Lehman College. The fastest-growing African American church in New York City is probably the Pentecostal Church of God in Christ. Most of its pastorate comes from its mentoring relationships and two-year colleges, which are essentially Bible institutes.

Why are there so many Bible institutes in New York City? Three reasons stand out.

First, New York City is an education town, with more people enrolled in colleges and universities than in any other American city. Church people, too, want more substance than they can obtain from Sunday sermons or Sunday school lessons. The city also probably has more matriculated Bible institute students than other cities do.

Second, many of the evangelical churches in New York are especially popular among African Americans and Hispanics. Clearly, there are enough city residents for whom the Bible is, at least in theory, the final authority for faith and life and unquestionably worthy of concentrated study.

Third, Bible institutes in New York City are often vivid expressions of community and ethnic self-respect. While discrimination and misunderstanding remain common experiences in integrated colleges and universities, the Bible institute in one's own church—or in another church—can provide a safer haven for learning, growth, and affirmation.

Views of the Classroom

What is a class like in these institutes? The following glimpses highlight the cultural themes permeating Bible institutes as a whole.

Scene A: "Deeper Learning"

Seven African American men and women gather at a Bible institute for two hours every week for months to read and discuss the writings of Josephus, a prolific Jewish historian who lived shortly after the time of Jesus. In class discussions, they frequently refer to the Old and New Testaments.

This is the "research class" for the Bible Church of Christ Theological

Institute, in the Bronx. Together with their teacher, Minister Montrose Bushrod, these students examine passages from Josephus's *Jewish Antiquities* to better understand the events that occurred during the four hundred years between the times of the Old Testament and the birth of Jesus.

One evening the group discusses how a prophecy of Daniel hastened the breakup of the empire of a king from Greece. The next assignment was to read Josephus, book 14, chapters 10–15, "to learn about Julius Caesar, his dealings with the Herods, his death, Mark Anthony and his dealings with the Herods." That is a lot for students who have full-time secular jobs and heavy ministry responsibilities as well. Their teacher also assigned the study of six additional textbooks on the critical decades before Jesus. For example, a portion of Chicago preacher H. A. Ironside's book, *The 400 Silent Years*, is the assigned reading for tonight. The teacher explains that these years before the birth of Jesus defined the prevailing political power structure, including the Roman dominance of Israel and the strange role of the vicious but shrewd Herods. Based on their readings and research—as well as their personal spirituality and active ministry—these students often express thoughtful insights into the people to whom Jesus ministered, and they notice parallels with problems in their own churches.

Scene B: "Multicultural"

In one Bible institute in Brooklyn, the Vision Bible Institute at Bay Ridge Christian Center, the multicultural quality of New York City's evangelical church is evident (see Pier and DeCaro 1999, 126–141). Every class is offered at different times in both Spanish and English. In one class, the teacher is black, but all the students are Hispanic or white. In another class, the teacher is Jewish, but the class is entirely black. During a chapel service attended by all, about half the songs are in Spanish and half in English.

A global interest is evident as well. One instructor is teaching students how to read a map of Israel. The assistant dean, an Hispanic man, shows a short video of famine and persecution in Sudan. This institute also sponsors a ministry conference on the phenomenal growth of the evangelical church in South America and what lessons can be learned for similar growth in the United States.

Sometimes in multicultural settings, people are careful not to talk about disagreeable subjects, in a misguided effort to preserve the pluralist feeling. But all issues are discussed in these classes, surrounded by pictures and slogans of Jesus' baptism, Malcolm X, and Frederick Douglas.

Scene C: "Impact"

One of the oldest, the Manhattan Bible Institute, was founded in 1936 by Dr. Edward Howard Boyce, B.D., Th.D., and Ph.D., an alumnus of the Moody Bible Institute in Chicago and the Biblical Seminary and Columbia University in New York. Before he died after fifty-one years of leadership, Dr. Boyce appointed as his successor Dr. Richard Christie, his assistant for twenty-five years. Dr. Christie was an electrical engineer from Jamaica who had studied under Dr. Boyce at the Manhattan Bible Institute.

For many years, the Manhattan Bible Institute has trained thousands of leaders, primarily for the African American community. Among its most distinguished alumni are the famous late evangelist Tom Skinner and influential New York City bishops Ezra Williams of the Bethel Gospel Assembly in Harlem and Roderick Caesar Sr., the founder of more than twenty churches in the city and his native Trinidad (figure 7.1).

In fact, graduates of the Manhattan Bible Institute, located on 148th Street in Harlem, have gone on to establish ten Bible institutes. In turn, dozens of students from these second-generation institutes—including the Bible Church of Christ Theological Institute in the Bronx and the Bethel Bible Institute in Queens—have themselves established third and fourth generations of Bible institutes in the city and elsewhere, especially in the Caribbean. Thus at least seventy-five Bible institutes have been established through this one New York City institution. The mother and grandmother of these seventy-five programs are still going strong, with four hundred students representing twenty-three Christian denominations.

Scene D: "Changing Mission"

When describing New York City's Bible institutes, two words that repeatedly come to mind are *mission* and *vision*.

Consider this problem: a large, historic, African American church stands prominently in a South Bronx neighborhood. The senior pastor, Shellie Sampson Jr., D.Min., is a major leader among African American clergy, serving as the president of the influential Baptist Ministers' Conference of New York and Vicinity. He has been active in education, establishing an academy for children and a school of religion for adults and

Figure 7.1. Bishop Roderick Caesar Jr., Bethel Gospel Tabernacle, Jamaica, Queens. Courtesy of the collection of Tony Carnes.

helping establish an evangelical seminary for the city. This senior pastor himself is highly educated: he has a doctor of ministry degree from Drew University and is now working on his Ph.D. degree at Temple University. Training is so important to this church that seven years ago, it built adjacent to the church building a three-story cultural center for the schools.

The demography of the immediate Bronx neighborhood of this church, Thessalonia Baptist Church, has changed dramatically during the last five years. Now, in a neighborhood that very recently had been more than 95 percent African American, 75 percent of the church's neighbors are Hispanic Americans. In response, this Bible institute has introduced a course in conversational Spanish. In its first year, no fewer than twenty church leaders learned to speak some Spanish. Education, offered by the Bible institute, is a necessary prerequisite to crossing cultural boundaries.

Motivations

Theme A: "Deeper Learning"

What drives these students? What criteria do they use to decide where they will pursue their education? In general, their greatest concern is "doctrinal integrity." In a research project interviewing 856 Bible institute students, 72 percent indicated that doctrinal integrity was most important or very important for selecting a higher education program. Among the more than two hundred African Americans who were interviewed, 82 percent ranked doctrinal integrity even higher.

Some of the implications are obvious. Despite the considerable pressures of materialism and secularism in our society, substantial numbers in all races—but especially African Americans—regard religious integrity as paramount. Their devotion helps explain why many people study diligently, subject themselves to tests, and write papers for a course that may not even be accredited—because the perspective of the teacher and program has doctrinal integrity.

Of course, other factors matter as well. For the African American students, another important criterion was receiving a well-rounded education. In fact, African American students are more likely to have a college or graduate school education (24%) than any other ethnic group in the Bible institutes.

A high interest in a well-rounded education might indicate that Bible institute students are not strict seperationists from the world and its culture, knowledge, and affairs, and in fact, relatively few of their graduates hold to a strict "separationist" view. In a 1996 survey of New York City–New Jersey evangelical pastors' images of the world, less than 15 percent indicated that they believed that "worldly" knowledge or activities should be avoided, and 79 percent agreed that "the good person must be deeply involved in the problems and activities of the world (see Wells 1994, 233).

What do students want to study?

PRIORITY 1: "EVANGELISM"

One subject that has tremendous appeal to Bible institute students is *evangelism*, which they see as a way of sharing what has given meaning to their lives.

PRIORITY 2: "BIBLE AND MINISTRY SKILLS"

The New York School of the Bible (NYSB) at the historic Calvary Baptist Church is one of the better-known Bible schools, among a broad spectrum of ethnic groups. The NYSB offers three levels of certificates—preliminary, intermediate, and advanced—each covering areas of Bible knowledge and Christian ministry skills.

Several of the city's Bible institutes use materials produced by the Evangelical Training Association, based in Illinois. The general sequence of the institutes' four educational levels moves from (1) personal and spiritual preparation for ministry, to (2) Bible knowledge, to (3) theological awareness, and finally to (4) leadership skills.

PRIORITY 3: "SPECIAL TOPICS"

Christian higher education in New York City touches on a whole range of issues. Three options have recently attracted a lot of students. First, at least one Bible institute, the Bible Church of Christ Theological Institute, offers whole-day workshops on demonology, attended by hundreds of New Yorkers. Second, the New York School of the Bible is sponsoring a series of seminars on learning about institutional racism and working toward racial reconciliation. Indeed, teaching people about racial issues is a continuing priority of many Bible institutes. Finally, the program of one institute at the northern tip of Manhattan, Rocky Mount Bible Institute, exemplifies students' increased interest in eschatology. They want to know what the Bible says about the future—the future of life on earth as well as heaven and hell. What has sparked this interest? Perhaps it is general human curiosity, partly fed by the beginning of a new millennium.

PRIORITY 4: "NEED FOR CURRICULUM CHANGE"

Some of the Bible institutes, however, are using curricula that have not been reexamined for years, even though students often want to take courses in subjects like counseling that the institutes do not recognize or value. When the Assembly of God School of Ministry offered a one-day

TABLE 7.1

Ethnicities of Bible Institute Students in 1995 Compared with
General Population of New York City (%)

	Bible Institutes, 1995	Estimated 2000 U.S. Census
Hispanic	30	29
Black/African Americans	24	26
White	7	35
Asian	7	10
No Answer	32	—

SOURCE: *U.S. Bureau of the Census Report*, February1997.

seminar on counseling, it was surprised by the huge number of students who attended.

Theme B: "Multicultural"

In New York, the Bible institute phenomenon has a lot to do with ethnicity and race, but perhaps this should not be a surprise, since so much of life in the city is defined by these factors. Indeed, Bible institute students represent forty-six different ethnicities (see table 7.1). Most Bible institutes usually serve one ethnic group because they recruit from particular neighborhoodsand work through ethnic churches. Furthermore, much of the spiritual challenge that people face, individually and socially, is related to ethnicity. Lectures and discussions in the classes cover issues of discrimination, self-respect, justice, care, and the breakdown of barriers, concerns that are integral elements of the students' own and their parishioners' lives. "Is there a racial aspect to this problem?" a Bible institute student asked in one discussion. "Of course there is. There is a racial aspect to every problem," his teacher asserted. "This is just the way things are in this world."

Theme C: "Personal and Institutional Motivations"

Many students want to learn and study with people who have similar religious commitments and perspectives. Most churches do not have the same concentration of people (as a Bible institute does) who are serious about Bible study and spiritual growth, and most colleges lack a religious perspective.

Bible institute training is a requirement for some of New York City's offices of ministry, and so over the past two decades, more churches have revised their ministry education requirements for lay and ordained ministers. Some Bible institute students are likely to be interested in a B.Th. program, so accreditation and the transferability of credits are often important issues. Consequently, several institutes have special relationships with accredited colleges. Finally, each institute stays close to the active ministry of local churches. The director, the faculty, and the students all are engaged in many of the same local ministries, needs, problems, and opportunities.

Theme D: "Adaptation to a Changing City"

Since there are no endowments or established name recognition to sustain programs on their own, innovation is essential to the Bible institutes' mission and leadership. Consider two examples.

Andrew Chiu, Th.D., came from Hong Kong to establish the New York Theological Education Center in Queens. His potential students are spread out across the New York metropolitan area. Indeed, because more than 33 percent of Chinese Bible institute students were looking for correspondence courses, Chiu created correspondence courses. An added advantage of his particular program is that although the spoken languages of Mandarin and Cantonese are quite different, the written language is the same. Consequently, these correspondence courses now are also being used in Hong Kong and in the People's Republic of China.

Another innovator is Gershwin Grant, founder of the Global Bible Institute in the Bronx. He was puzzled by the fact that his students had a difficult time following the thinking processes and logic of St. Paul, such as in Paul's Letter to the Romans. Attributing the students' problem to the limitations of modern thought processes, Grant introduced a course in Plato and Aristotle to help them recognize and appreciate a broader range of logical and conceptual constructs. Consequently, students say that they have found more depth and comprehension in St. Paul's approach.

Theme E: "Founding Bible Institutes in Order to Have an Impact"

Bible institutes exist in part because they are founded and hosted by active churches. What motivates these churches? Frequently, it is the growth of interest in serious study of the Bible—a kind of sacred ladder up from adult Sunday school and seminars, to special Bible studies, to weekly classes with assignments, papers, and tests.

In other cases, Bible institutes spring fully grown from the sponsoring church. The direct benefits to the churches can be great. For example, the Antioch Baptist Church in Queens first opened its Bible institute in September 1996. During the academic year 1996/1997, it offered nine courses, including a survey of the Old Testament, African American church history, teaching techniques, spiritual maturity, English writing, and introduction to computers. All five of the students who took the teaching techniques course at Antioch Bible Institute are current Sunday school teachers at the host church, so they had ample opportunity to apply directly what they were learning. They immediately began experimenting with new teaching methods, which included role playing, discussion, student presentations, and group presentations. In a short time, Sunday school attendance more than tripled.

In this case, the ripple effect of the Bible institute went even further: at the host church two Bible study series unrelated to the institute swelled to four or five times the size they had been for years. The institute's director, Laura Sinclair, D.Min, attributes this change to the general growth of interest in the Bible stimulated by the institute's new teaching methods.

Trends

Bible institutes serve churches partly by raising the standard of accountability. When students know more about the Bible, their pastors know that their own sermons need to be based on the Bible and well prepared, since educated students are careful listeners, and particularly fine sermons become models. Bible institute education also seems to be feeding an increasing demand that ministry education be accredited.

Furthermore, while the students are studying the Bible in an institute, they regularly use the same material in sermons, radio talks, and Sunday school classes. The church thus benefits in both the short term (good lessons now) and the long term (well-trained leaders and examples for the future).

Because Bible institutes engage their students' spiritual interests, they educate hundreds of people who would not otherwise be in school. People who would never even apply to a college attend Bible institutes because of the training's religious purpose and the atmosphere of affirmation and encouragement that they find. Students often say that their Bible institutes are oases of empowerment and encouragement in the midst of the urban hostilities.

As a result, Bible institutes are often at the center of urban churches' ministry. Colleges, universities, and seminaries would do well to take notice and learn a few lessons from them. Much of the effective urban church leadership is being shaped by New York City's Bible institutes because they regularly teach and mentor people directly into the vital ministries of the church. Their practical and holistic perspective, in the context of the work of the ministry, nurtures and nourishes the Christian commitment, faith, and passion that people desire and that the urban church must possess for its difficult work.

NOTE

1. The statistics for this chapter are derived from Carnes 1996a, with the aid of Masha Chlenova, Dennis Day, Norma Fuentes, Gershwin Grant, Janel Hardaway, Mike Kitka, Priscilla Kwan, Esther Lee, Jin Fong Lowe, Carol Tom, Bella Tsai, and the Bible institute directors and educators and funds from the PEW Charitable Trust.

Chapter 8

Assimilation in New York City's Italian Parishes

Mary Elizabeth Brown

Parishes founded by Italians continue to exist in all five boroughs of New York City. Some, such as Saint Anthony on Sullivan Street, maintain an Italian identity through its feast day celebrations. In other cases, Italian American parishes have changed their identities over time; for instance, Holy Family, once an Italian parish in the East 40s, has become the parish of the United Nations (Andreassi 1999). Italian American Catholics' most lasting legacy, though, may be the precedents they set for the pastoral care of later Catholic migrants.

Presumptions of Geographic Stability and Uniformity of Authority in Roman Catholicism

The Roman Catholic Church is organized on the basis of geographical stability. The pope divides the world into dioceses, each named for the city where its head, or bishop, dwells. An archdiocese is the leading diocese in a province of several dioceses. The advantage of a geographical organization is that everyone's responsibilities are clear. One duty incumbent on the Catholic laity, that is, on Catholics who are not priests, is the support of their parish. Geographical boundaries tell the laity which parish to support and the pastor from which laity to expect support and requests for pastoral care.

One problem, however, is that geography does not mean homogeneity. If new groups of people with new needs move into the parish, the priests may not be prepared to care for them. This has been an important consideration in the United States, where high levels of migration have brought different Catholics into close proximity. During most of the nineteenth and twentieth centuries, U.S. Catholicism searched for a way to accommodate human mobility in a system that privileges stability.

On July 19, 1850, Pope Gregory XVI elevated New York to an archdiocese, and its boundaries have remained the same since. New York City is divided into two sees (the generic noun for dioceses and archdioceses). The Diocese of Brooklyn covers Brooklyn and Queens, and the Archdiocese of New York includes the counties of Bronx, New York (Manhattan), and Richmond (Staten Island) as well as the suburban counties of Westchester, Orange, Putnam, Rockford, Sullivan, Ulster, and Duchess.

It is the prelate's (the generic noun for bishops and archbishops) responsibility to divide the archdiocese and diocese into smaller units, called parishes, and to assign priests. Until 1908, the law of the Roman Catholic Church considered the United States a mission territory, which gave U.S. prelates greater power and flexibility to move priests around. Prelates had two sources of priests. Their first choice was diocesan, or secular, priests. Secular priests were usually trained at diocesan schools called seminaries and usually worked only within the see for which they were ordained. Prelates might also ask a religious order to staff a parish. A religious order is a group of persons who work together on their religious lives. One rule is that a parish be staffed by either diocesan clergy or a religious order, but usually not both.

Once appointed, pastors exercise great authority and responsibility. The Archdiocese of New York expects each parish to balance its own budget using income drawn from its own territory. The pastor works with assistants, parochial school–teaching sisters, and laity to raise funds, but it is the pastor who incurs episcopal wrath, perhaps even a transfer, if the parish falls into debt.

The Rise of Italian Parishes

Between the War of 1812 and the Civil War, the numerically superior Irish supplied to the New York Catholic Church the dominant culture and the majority of prelates, priests, women religious, brothers (men in religious orders who are not priests), and parishioners. But because Irish dominance interfered with the German minority's practice of its faith using its own language and devotional customs, the early-nineteenth-century New York

Catholics developed an informal system in which people crossed parish boundaries to attend their preferred parishes (Dolan 1975, 5).

The Archdiocese of New York experimented with ways to provide Italian pastoral care. The earliest records indicate that at first, Italians attended mass alongside coreligionists from other ethnic groups. But before long, the Italian immigrants instituted their own worship services. and scholars have suggested several reasons for this. After a brief period in which Italians intermingled with U.S. Catholics in established parishes, a system of "annex congregations" developed. This was an informal process in which individual pastors, realizing that they were acquiring increasing numbers of Italian parishioners but did not have the linguistic skills to care for them, set aside their basement chapels for the Italians' use and invited colleagues from religious orders to send Italian-speaking priests to staff these chapels (Lynch 1888; Smith 1905). The "annex congregation" stage lasted from the late 1870s until the 1910s. By the middle of the 1910s, it had given way to a third and final stage, that of the national parish (Colman 1953; Shipman 1916). Because of the great number of Italians, it is fair to say that in New York, national parishes had both linguistic and territorial borders, each parish caring for Italian-speaking Catholics within a particular area.

Some Italian communities skipped the annex phase and established their own parishes right away, usually in newly developed areas. The Italians came to these areas to construct housing, roads, or other urban infrastructures and then became the pioneer settlers in the new neighborhood. Examples include the Saint Philip Neri parish in the Bronx and many of the Long Island parishes (see, for example, Hanley 1988; La Gumina 1988). Once the general pattern of national parishes had been established, further changes in the institutional setting for assimilation were generational and took place largely within these national parishes.

Changes in Italian Parishes over Generations

The first important documented change in Italian national parishes took place among the clergy, some of whom were encouraged to preserve their language and particular ways of worship in the alien culture of the United States. One example is the Society of Saint Charles-Scalabrinians, named in part for its founder, Bishop Giovanni Battista Scalabrini. Concerned about emigration from his see, Scalabrini organized this community of priests and brothers to accompany the migrants on their journeys to their new homes and to provide comprehensive pastoral care. Afraid that the migrants might lose their faith in the new cultures they encountered in the Americas, Scalabrini advised his missionaries to maintain their own language and culture as safeguards to preserving their own faith.

Soon after they started working with Italian migrants in the United States, the Scalabrinian missionaries began to view assimilation differently. Then, during a visit in 1901, Scalabrini announced to his missionaries that he had chosen Boston as the site preserving the Italian language and culture, through an Italian-language parochial school. In a dramatic meeting, a local leader, Giacomo Gambera, argued to Scalabrini "that the proposed schools were excellent, but were neither needed nor possible at that time, for the reasons that the sisters did not know the language" (Gambera 1994, 131). Without realizing it, Gambera had committed himself to a new goal of helping Italians assimilate rather than preserve their language and culture.

Although the Scalabrinians and other Italian clergy had no established plan for assisting Italians in the adaptation process, their actions suggest some unarticulated strategies. Their first task was to make the parish an important institution to the Italian immigrants. A variety of concerns competed for the Italian immigrants' attention: their families, jobs, businesses, children's education, and so on. Italian pastors could thus attract them by pointing out that their parishes could help the immigrants achieve their goals.

The result was that first-generation Italian parishes appeared to be doing two things at once. While they did not preserve the Italian language, they did help the Italians conserve other aspects of their culture by providing space in which to practice some of their rituals. In Italy, whole communities might help celebrate the town patron saint's feast day. In the United States, the Italians lived among Catholics and non-Catholics who followed other customs, and so their parishes became centers for maintaining their particular rituals. Robert A. Orsi described how Our Lady of Mount Carmel in East Harlem became the site of the annual feast day celebration.

Italian parishes also provided material assistance for coping with day-to-day problems. An exemplary parish in this category was Our Lady of Pompei in Greenwich Village, whose pastor, Anthony Demo, became an amateur intake social worker (figure 8.1). Demo, who seems to have saved every piece of paper that ever crossed his desk, left thirty years' worth of communications about his parishioners' problems (Brown 1992a and b).

Figure 8.1. Father Antonio Demo of Our Lady of Pompei poses with a women's group from his congregation, ca. 1925. Courtesy of the Center for Migration Studies of New York.

Demo's help to the first generation fell into three categories. One group of supplicants knew exactly what they needed and also that Demo could provide it. Most of them requested prayers for help with a personal or family problem (Orsi 1996), and others needed baptismal or marriage certificates for the immigration authorities or in order to obtain work papers. A second category of people knew what they wanted and that Demo could not supply it but could help them get it. They wanted him to recommend them for jobs or their children for schools. In some cases, Demo heard about the request through a third party who gave him a character reference or confirmed an address. The third category were not ready to declare their problems to be beyond earthly help but were unsure of what else to do, and so they contacted Demo. Usually Demo referred them to an appropriate institution, such as unwed mothers to the foundling asylum, children to the orphanage, youngsters to schools or institutions for troubled youth, sick people to hospitals, and poor people to helping agencies (figure 8.2).

As the first generation died out and the second generation came of age, the Italian parishes began to perform another function, helping families raise their offspring. Such assistance served a dual purpose. It continued the strategy of attracting Italians to parishes by supplying services that met some other need. The assistance was also in the parishes' long-term interest. When American-born or -raised Italian youngsters grew up, they rejected many aspects of their parents' culture as too Italian and thus unsuitable for Americans like themselves (Child 1943; Ware 1994). The parishes, therefore, presented themselves as American institutions serving the young.

Traditionally, U.S. Catholic parishes have provided an important service for their youth, namely, education in parochial schools. But that education was so expensive that it was not accessible to every child in the Italian community, particularly because many Italian parents took their children out of school early. Thus, Italian Catholic parishes began by providing youth-oriented services but not parochial schools. Again, Our Lady of Pompei in Greenwich Village can serve as an example. Beginning in the 1890s, Pompei held catechism classes for children who did not attend parochial school, and in 1911, it opened a day-care center for the preschool children of working mothers. It also ran a drama program in

Figure 8.2. Interior of Our Lady of Pompei, 208 Bleecker Street, New York City, 1909. Courtesy of the Center for Migration Studies of New York.

Figure 8.3. Procession in honor of Maria SS delle Grazia, Our Lady of Grace, Mulberry Street, New York City, 1973. Courtesy of the Center for Migration Studies of New York.

which adolescents and young adults staged plays. Then, in 1930, Pompei finally had the space, money, and stability to open a parochial school. (Ironically, its teaching sisters were drawn from the same community that Scalabrini had intended to use for his Italian-language parochial schools a generation earlier, but at Pompei the sisters taught in English.)

We can date the rise of a new generation of Italian Americans and of new challenges for Italian parishes to about the time that World War II ended, in 1945. By that point, wartime and postwar prosperity had spread to almost all social classes via the 1944 GI bill, making it easier for Italians to leave the cities for the suburbs. Prosperity also made it easier for them to buy automobiles and to return to the home country to visit friends and relatives.

Italian parishes then found three new functions. First was the care of the elderly Italians who remained in the neighborhood (Candeloro 1994; Gillette and Kraut 1986; Weiler 1992). Our Lady of Pompei in Greenwich Village, for example, organized several programs for senior citizens, like day-long outings to religious sites and tourist attractions and a lunch program. Second, formerly all-Italian parishes began to care for the parishioners of other ethnic groups. A century ago, the Irish had moved out of their old neighborhoods, leaving their apartments and churches behind for the Italians. The remaining pastors and parishioners, however, did not welcome the newcomers. Only after the Irish population had dwindled to almost nothing did traditionally Irish parishes become known as Italian churches, though still with some continuing conflict. For example, Holy Rosary was founded on East 119th Street in 1884 to serve the Irish in East Harlem. Although in the 1910s, the archdiocese also set up a separate Italian rectory at Holy Rosary reflecting the growing presence of the Italians, not until 1925 did it appoint an Italian pastor, Gaetano Arcese, who was protested even then by the remaining non-Italian parishioners (Brown 1995) (figure 8.3).

What happened when it was the Italians who were the dwindling population facing newcomers in their churches? Sometimes history repeated itself. For example, the Irish at Transfiguration on Mott Street were so upset when their church was given over to the Italians that they attempted to take the parish name with them. (They failed, but it is worth noting that Transfiguration's ex-pastor gave his new parish in the West 40s of Manhattan a decidedly Irish name, Saint Malachy's, which has since become "the actor's chapel.") Not surprisingly, then, in 1950, when Transfiguration was assigned new priests to minister to the growing Chinese population, the Italian parishioners feared that their parish would become completely Chinese (Transfiguration Church 1977).

Other Italian parishes welcomed non-Italians. The Filipinos actually lived elsewhere but commuted to welcoming Pompei for mass, devotions, and programs. In the 1980s, the Italian Scalabrinians at Pompei took a Filipino secular priest into their rectory and started a new kind of ministry for Filipinos. In the 1970s, the Scalabrinians at Saint Joseph's on

Figure 8.4. Men carrying the *gigli*, a symbol of Saint Paulinus of Nola, Brooklyn, New York, 1975. Courtesy of the Center for Migration Studies of New York.

Catherine Street began making arrangements to care for the Chinese who were replacing the Italians in the neighborhood east of Chatham Square on the Lower East Side. The parish history as written in its yearbook was quite explicit as to why: "so that these Catholics will have the opportunity that was so often denied to early Italians to celebrate their faith within their local community" (Saint Joseph Church 1977) (figure 8.4).

Third, beginning with the first generation during World War I, Italian parishes became the public face of the Italian community. The war led the federal government to expect a great deal more of its citizens: all men had to register for the armed forces and some had to serve, and all people were expected to conserve food, buy war bonds, and report suspected espionage and sabotage. But the government wondered how to tell the people about these new demands. There was no television or radio, and the posting of public notices meant nothing to the people who did not read English or read at all. So the government asked the clergy to do their communications work.

Today, the commuting Italians need their churches to remind the city and their old neighborhoods about *their* presence and identity, so annual feasts have become historical notices of the Italians' presence. The annual feast of Saint Anthony, sponsored by the church of the same name on Sullivan Street, is a reminder of the Italian presence in SoHo, as are similar feasts in East Harlem and Brooklyn (Pope 1990; Posen, Sciorra, and Cooper 1983; Primeggia and Varacalli 1996; St. Anthony of Padua Church 1967). (Some readers might wish to add the Feast of San Gennaro in Little Italy to this list of feasts that preserve the Italian presence, but it is not sponsored by any of the parishes in the neighborhood.) Of course, being the public face of the community poses the special challenge of emphasizing spiritual devotion while making money from the tourists.

Assimilation above the Parish Level

While assimilation mostly took place at the parish level, in New York City, the diocesan, national, and international levels all have influenced the Italians' assimilation and were in turn influenced by them.

At the diocesan level, the presence of the Italians led New York's prelates to make changes in the archdiocesan bureaucracy, to assimilate, as it were, to the twentieth century. New York's nineteenth-century prelates, priests, and Irish majority shared more than Catholicism; they shared assumptions about that Catholicism. Because of these common values, the Archdiocese of New York functioned with little supervision. Each pastor knew the standards and communicated them to the laity. The advent of the Italians and other groups of Catholics, however, brought fears that these Catholics did not share the same values and that they would have to be more carefully supervised.

Archbishop Michael Augustine Corrigan solved this problem by recruiting an "Italian secretary," Father Gherardo Ferrante, for the archdiocesan bureaucracy. Some of Ferrante's duties were linguistic. Although Corrigan spoke Italian, translating was time-consuming for him, so Ferrante took up that task. Ferrante also served as a liaison between the chancery and Italian personnel in the archdiocese, particularly on marriage and annulment issues. During World War I, he transmitted information from the federal government, and he also took care of the finances of the Italian sisters' orders (La Guida del Clero Italiano di New York 1915). Corrigan died in 1902 and was succeeded by John Murphy Farley, better known as John Cardinal Farley after the Vatican appointed him a cardinal in 1911. (Traditionally, those people thus honored have substituted "cardinal" for their middle names.) Farley retained Ferrante but also began creating a series of "bureaus" to coordinate work among the most numerous ethnic groups: Italians, Slavs, Ruthenians, and Oriental Catholics (Eastern Europeans whose rituals were different from the mainstream Latin rite).

The Italian Bureau started work early in 1913. Its supervisor was Michael Joseph Lavelle, who was not Italian but a native New Yorker of Irish extraction. Ferrante served as his secretary. The other five members of the bureau were priests involved in caring for the Italians. Four were Italian, and the other was Daniel Burke, an Irish American active in Italian American pastoral care in the Bronx. After he died, Burke was succeeded by an Italian American priest, Gaetano Arcese, the first Italian American pastor of Holy Rosary in East Harlem.

The Italian Bureau and the other ethnic bureaus set a precedent for later action. The assimilation of the various ethnic groups was the first task that the Archdiocese of New York was unwilling to leave completely to the parishes, but it was not the last. Contemporary sees have many more offices to coordinate parishes on issues ranging from the assimilation of new immigrants to preparation for marriage, all previously taken care of at the parish level.

At the national level, authority was similarly concentrated. When the mass migration of Italians began, the Italians migrated on their own, relying on their wit and families, friends, and *padrone* to help them find work and avoid scams. One of Bishop Scalabrini's accomplishments was to publicize the unequal struggle between the individual immigrants and the forces of exploitation arrayed against them.

With a generation of experience behind them, the German Catholics had already found a solution to this problem. A Bavarian merchant and Catholic philanthropist, Peter Paul Cahensly, established the Saint Raphael Society for the Protection of German Catholic Immigrants, which provided chaplains to tend to immigrants traveling in steerage. A chaplain went among Germans arriving on ships to maneuver them past thieves and sellers of fake railroad tickets to a church hospice with good meals and beds at a reasonable price. There, the chaplains helped them contact relatives, employers, and rental agents. Following their example, Scalabrini and a layman organized a similar Saint Raphael Society for the Protection of Italian Immigrants with a chaplain and hospice at New York Harbor.

A number of forces led to a partial change in this system in the early 1920s. First, the chaplain of the Saint Raphael Society was replaced and the Society of Saint Charles-Scalabrinians was reorganized, which created an opening for others to enter the field of dockside immigrant care. Second, during World War I, U.S. prelates had organized the National Catholic War Council, and they wished to expand its work into issues that crossed diocesan borders. Immigration was one of these issues, and so the newly organized National Catholic Welfare Conference included a Bureau of Immigration with a New York office and a director.

Third, Mussolini came to power in Italy riding a wave of resurgent Italian nationalism, expressed in part as a desire to care for Italians abroad, so he funded a chaplain and Italica Gens to tend to Italians in New York Harbor and a hospice. Fourth, after Cardinal Farley died in 1918, his successor, Patrick Joseph Hayes, was interested in coordinating charity at the archdiocesan level and created Catholic Charities of the Archdiocese of New York. All this led to competition to care for the Italians passing through New York Harbor in the 1920s and 1930s. At first, Cardinal Hayes allied himself with Italica Gens by making their chaplain and hospice an auxiliary of his Catholic Charities. But after that chaplain died in 1934, the National Catholic Welfare Conference's Bureau of Immigration took over. Thus a new model for immigrant care emerged. Instead of immigrants caring for other immigrants, U.S. Catholics cared for the new immigrants. Perhaps substituting care by conationalists with care by U.S. Catholics hastened the process toward assimilation (Brown 1997).

Italian American migration also stimulated the organization of the pastoral care of Catholic migrants at the global level. On December 10, 1888, Pope Leo XIII (pope from 1878 to 1903) issued the first modern papal encyclical, or papal letter, concerning the issue of migration. Known by its first words in Latin, *Quam aerumnosa* or "With what bitterness" (the idea was that migrants left their homes reluctantly and bitterly), the encyclical claimed that the pope was naturally interested in "men sprung from the same soil as ourselves" (Leo was Italian born) and introduced Scalabrini's missionaries to U.S. Catholicism. Leo's words, however, must be balanced by his inaction in other cases (see Ellis 1956).

Leo's successor, Pius X (1903–1914) concentrated on issues concerning Italian migration, especially that of finding and training clergy to accompany the migrants (Swanstrom 1962). World War I and then the rise of Communism in the Soviet Union led the next two popes, Benedict XV (1914–1922) and Pius XI (1922–1939), to broaden their interest in migrants to include refugees from the war. Pius XII (1939–1958) issued norms and standards for providing pastoral care for migrant Catholics, especially those from one ritual who resettled in a place where another ritual dominated. One result was the creation of the Office of Delegate for Migration Affairs, which has grown into the Pontifical Commission for the Pastoral Care of Migrants and Itinerant Peoples. Through this office, the Catholic Church admitted that its established system was predicated on geographic stability and compensated by assigning to a specific institution the responsibility for people in constant movement: migrants, refugees, Bedouins, Roma (Gypsies), airline employees, and circus performers, among others.

Contemporary Experience

The pattern of immigration in the 1980s and 1990s resembles that between 1880 and 1920. Then, the Italians were the single largest Catholic group to enter the archdiocese, but they enjoyed a plurality, not an absolute majority. Other Catholic immigrants came, too. Similarly, in the late 1980s and early 1990s, migrants from the Dominican Republic were the largest single group to enter the archdiocese, but they were part of a diverse immigration (New York City Dept. of Planning 1996.) Also, while the Italians were baptized as Catholic, their conception of their faith was not the same as that of the Catholics already in New York, and the same is true for many contemporary Catholic migrants.

Migrants of the 1990s encountered a Catholic Church at a different historical stage. From 1840 to 1918, Catholicism in the Archdiocese of New York grew at the rate of one parish a year. Now, however, even though the influx of immigrants may increase the number of Catholics, it is unlikely to increase the total number of parishes or clergy. Land values and building costs in the areas where the migrants settle are too high to consider building new national parishes for new linguistic minorities.

So far, instead of an evolution from attending mass with other Catholics to annex congregations and then to national parishes, new immigrants have received care from established parishes. In some cases, the reason is that the archbishop has planned it that way. Díaz-Stephens (1993) described how when Puerto Ricans moved into the archdiocese, Francis Cardinal Spellman thought of variations of the national parish (he turned over to the Puerto Ricans Saint Benedict the Moor, erected for an African American congregation in Greenwich Village in 1883 and moved to West Fifty-third Street in 1898) and of variations of Cardinal Farley's ethnic bureaus (see also Coll 1989).

Sometimes, though, parish priests realized that a proper welcome could turn new migrants into new parishioners. At Our Lady of Good Counsel in Tompkinsville on Staten Island, the Augustinian priests on staff welcomed the Spanish community to what had been a largely Irish parish, with the result that the parish continues to grow in size, with many young families and a diverse spiritual life. It offers Spanish-language masses and celebrates the customs of Spanish-speaking countries in its parochial school (Rev. Francis J. Doyle, O.S.A., to Mary Elizabeth Brown, Washington, DC, February 28, 1998).

First-generation migrant Catholics continue to need special spiritual attention like access to clergy who speak their language. Although they still need the kind of material care that priests such as Antonio Demo extended to first-generation Italians, today governments and private agencies offer many more services through public relations campaigns on television, radio, and subway and bus posters.

Any agency must be able to predict what new needs will arise, and Father Demo's correspondence reveals how unpredictable immigrants' needs can be. Perhaps, it is here that intelligent, flexible priests with easy access to the first generation of an immigrant group can help guide resources to needs. Research is already under way comparing the children of post-1965 Hispanic and Asian immigrants with the children of previous generations (Portes 1994). It is likely that differences in the religious experiences of the school-age immigrants of the 1990s and of the second generation of Italian migrants lay in the different education of the two groups. As Miriam Cohen explained, Italian parents had every incentive to remove their children, especially their daughters, from school as soon as possible. The laws made it possible, and the combination of low family income and the availability of low-skilled jobs made it attractive. The situation changed only when truancy and child-labor laws were strengthened, when the supply of jobs for young unskilled workers dried up (this was between the end of the manufacturing era and the rise of McDonald's), and when it became obvious to parents that education, even for girls, had material benefits. Now, the second generation of post-1965 immigrants in New York have more educational opportunities, but it is not clear what effect that immigration will have on adolescents regarding religion.

Catholic parishes are already facing some third-generation challenges that Italian parishes did not have. This first mass migration consisted overwhelmingly of people of working age, and it was not until they grew old that the Italian parishes had to deal with senior citizens. But the post-1965 migration also includes a higher proportion of senior citizens, since new legislation gives high priority to the parents of migrants who became U.S. citizens. In some cases, such as the migration of Vietnamese refugees, whole families, including the elderly, migrated together. Thus, parishes starting care for new immigrants must also start care for elderly immigrants. Furthermore, because of high building costs, new immigrant groups must stay together at the same facility, immediately undergoing a multiethnic experience that it took some Italian parishes years to achieve.

One final issue of contemporary importance is the degree to which the presence of the immigrants will change U.S. Catholicism. In 1961, sociologist Francis Xavier Femminella proposed that the Italian emphasis on lay church responsibility contributed to a U.S. Catholicism ready for the lay-oriented teaching of Vatican II. Sociologist Andrew M. Greeley responded (1961) that the Italians had nothing to do with the United States' readiness for Vatican II; that what had happened was that Irish and German immigrants had entered the middle class and sent their youngsters to college, where they learned about liturgical reform and social justice. Information about these immigrants' specific contributions is sparse. Although there has been some research on the celebrations of the feast days of hometown patron saints, there has been little on the rituals that may have entered the U.S. mainstream.[1]

Still, even if nothing of Italian Catholicism enriched U.S. Catholicism, the presence of the Italians did matter. The hierarchy of the Archdiocese of New York could no longer assume a consensus among Catholics and had to implement bureaucratic means to ensure their unity. In contrast, the migrants of the 1990s have not inspired new archdiocesan bureaucratic models. A new office for Hispanic ministry simply followed precedents established by Cardinal Farley's ethnic bureaus. The new immigrants have, however, inspired experiments by the religious orders. For example, the

Scalabrinians have encouraged older Scalabrinians of Italian background and ministry to recruit young men from other countries to become priests and to accompany their people on their migration journeys.

NOTE

1. One example is the use of crèches or manger scenes, the little model stables with small statues of Joseph, Mary, the infant Jesus, angels, shepherds, the Three Wise Men, and the animals present at the first Christmas. Tradition credits Saint Francis of Assisi with building the first one, and one eighteenth-century Neapolitan manger scene is used for the Metropolitan Museum of Art for its holiday decorations. However, if this devotion was a part of U.S. Catholicism before the Italian migration, there is neither written evidence nor many antique manger scenes. On the other hand, visitors to Italian immigrant parishes comment on the displays (see Ware 1994, 313).

Part III

Conversions and Religious Switching

Chapter 9

Orthodox Converts in New York City

Richard P. Cimino

In East Greenwich Village as Father Christopher Cälin preached, an observer might have felt transported back to a Russian village, even though there were few elderly "babushkas" worshiping that evening. Instead, gathered around Cälin in the candle-lit sanctuary were about twenty-five young adults, who frequently crossed and prostrated themselves before icons during the long service. Through the darkness, one could see that the young, casually dressed women wore veils on their heads.

"Saint Herman brought hard-core Christianity to America. It wasn't watered-down. . . . It wasn't suburbanized, pick-and-choose Orthodoxy," preached Father Christopher Cälin during a Friday night service commemorating Saint Herman of Alaska at the Cathedral of the Holy Virgin Protection.

Eastern Orthodox churches throughout America are receiving a wave of converts, and many of these newcomers, at least in the cities of the Northeast, have been drawn to the old parishes whose sanctuaries were left empty after their ethnic members moved to the suburbs.

But the priest had something else in mind. The suburbanization and the resulting assimilation of ethnic members have tended to water down the intense mysticism and spiritual disciplines—such as fasting and even the wearing of veils—that have marked Eastern Orthodoxy. And it is these traditional components of the faith that are increasingly drawing converts to Orthodoxy.

On first impression, Eastern Orthodoxy does not appear to be a religion that would attract many Americans. The churches take pride in maintaining millennium-old traditions and teachings from foreign cultures, whereas Americans like to change and reformulate beliefs and theology from one decade to the next. Orthodox churches are communal in nature, emphasizing confession and spiritual oversight by a priest and requiring rigorous disciplines such as fasting. The tradition also has a vibrant mystical component. A typical Orthodox service, with its rich liturgical traditions of chanting and prayers and adoration of icons, can last for more than two hours. Conversely, American religious instincts are usually strongly individualistic and pragmatic, often adapting institutions to meeting individual needs.

While many Orthodox churches maintain connections to their "mother" countries such as Russia and Greece, their members have become increasingly assimilated into American society. And in many cases, the assimilation of Orthodox Americans has meant that they have left their Orthodoxy behind. The Orthodox Church in America (with an official membership of 1 million) is about half as large as it was thirty years ago, due to dropouts (Hopko 1986). Kosmin and Lachman estimated, however, that the actual Orthodox population is closer to 0.5 million adults, suggesting that many of the baptized members counted by officials no longer identify with the tradition. The newer figure may show that this "ethnic, ceremonial-focused religion is losing touch with the younger generations of North Americans" (1993, 290).

The wild card that may change this portrait of Eastern Orthodox assimilation and decline is the steady stream of converts who have been making their way into Orthodoxy in the past fifteen to twenty years. The converts come from a wide variety of backgrounds and perspectives, including former evangelical Protestants, high church Episcopalians, Lutherans, Roman Catholics, other mainline Protestants, followers of New Age spirituality, and those with no previous faith. The reasons given for such conversions are as numerous as the different kinds of people attracted to the faith. Ex-evangelicals say they find an ancient source of spirituality and a sense of tradition; former Anglicans (who have converted in the greatest numbers) and other mainline Protestants find a firmer base of doctrinal and ecclesiastical authority; and former Catholics value Orthodoxy's decentralized leadership structure and its preservation of spiritual disciplines no longer in place in many parishes since the modernizing influence of Vatican II.

The influence of converts is evident throughout Orthodoxy. The majority of the twelve bishops of the Orthodox Church in America (OCA) are converts from non-Orthodox backgrounds. For the past several years, about 40 percent of the seminarians at the OCA's St. Vladimir's Seminary in suburban Crestwood, New York, have been converts. The most dramatic example of conversion to Orthodoxy took place in 1987, when 2,400 Christians from the evangelical Campus Crusade for Christ joined en masse the Antiochian Orthodox Archdiocese. More recently, baby boomers and younger believers appear to comprise the "lion's share" of conversions to Orthodoxy, according to Father Peter Gillquist, director of evangelism and missions in the Antiochian Orthodox Archdiocese (telephone interview, December 13, 1995).

New York City has not been excluded from the convert phenomenon. The English-language parishes of the traditionalist Russian Orthodox Church Outside Russia (ROCOR) (which follows the old church calendar and has little to do with other Orthodox bodies) have also reported converts. Other, more ethnic churches have converts through intermarriages, particularly in the Greek Orthodox Church.

What draws converts to Orthodoxy, and how has this adopted faith affected the lives of these New Yorkers? Understanding these conversions may illuminate how believers maintain a tradition-based faith while living in a pluralistic and consumer society that tends to challenge and destabilize such loyalties. Between 1994 and 1998, seventeen New York converts to Eastern Orthodoxy were interviewed about their conversions and how their experiences affected their lifestyles (Cimino 1997, 64–101). Those interviewed were members from parishes of the Orthodox Church in America and the Russian Orthodox Church Outside Russia. Almost all the converts came to Orthodoxy on their own rather than through intermarriage.[1]

Seeking and Finding Orthodoxy

Many of the converts arrived at their destination after an exploration of today's religious marketplace. "You'll find that many of the converts have read their way into the faith," one member of the Cathedral of the Holy Virgin Protection told me when I first inquired about interviewing converts. Indeed, the bookshelves and tables of the converts' homes and churches are often filled with pamphlets and books explaining the faith in clear, straightforward terms.

Simeon Baumann, an intense-looking, twenty-seven-year-old teacher with a long beard, lives in a Lower Manhattan apartment filled with scholarly books. Bauman was raised in a devout Roman Catholic home, and while he was in college, he was particularly drawn to the Jesuits for their tradition of disciplined prayer and intellectual acumen. But when he actually began associating with a group of Jesuits, he found their concerns more worldly than spiritual. After deciding not to pursue a religious vocation, Baumann went to study at a divinity school. While taking courses on liturgy, he started reading such Eastern Orthodox theologians as John Meyendorff and Alexander Schmemann. "I wanted to learn how to pray, and these books were helpful. But I also thought that there was Orthodox rhetoric and then there would be the Orthodox reality, like with the Jesuits. After I attended my first Orthodox liturgy, I was pleasantly surprised, even enthusiastic. . . . It was the feeling that I found something that should have existed." Baumann was received into the faith a year ago. "It saved my life. I felt very much at home and welcomed," he said. He added that if the "Western [Roman Catholic] church had kept its liturgical integrity more faithfully, I would have stayed. Becoming Orthodox was not a matter of forsaking the papacy or anything like that."

Robin Genovese, a twenty-eight-year-old graduate student, discovered Orthodoxy through books and a personal search for the right church. She was raised in a "typical secular humanist New York family" with a Jewish mother and an unchurched Italian American father. She never went to church or synagogue and celebrated both Passover and Christmas. When she was young, she read the Bible as literature and found it fascinating. Then, when she entered college, she found herself "wishing to believe" in Christianity and started attending different churches while continuing to read about different faiths, including Eastern Orthodoxy. In looking for a church, she said her

> biggest anxiety was having my individuality absorbed into a religious community. With the Orthodox Church, the only reason to be there was worship. I didn't have my individuality threatened by social standards. . . . In attending all of the other churches, I never felt I was able to breathe. In Orthodoxy, I was able to breathe.

Orthodox spirituality and liturgy sharply contrast with other Christian and religious groups and practices. Thomas Day, a forty-seven-year-old social worker, was active in the Episcopal Church before adopting Eastern Orthodoxy. But he gradually began to feel that the Episcopal Church was losing its identity, that "they were diluting what they had to be in the mainstream." He was distressed with the divisions between the Protestant and Anglo-Catholic wings of the church and the fact that two different Episcopal parishes could seem to be "part of two separate denominations." He came to value Orthodoxy because it was "so esoteric, it's not mainstream and not watered down."

Wendy Kent, a twenty-six-year-old graduate student and former Episcopalian, was drawn to Orthodoxy when she was a junior in college, because its liturgy brought together the physical and the spiritual. "Your whole body is involved. It's not like your mind is away somewhere. In the liturgy you're always bowing, prostrating yourself, crossing yourself, kissing icons. It's holistic."

Of course, not all the converts were necessarily of a mystical and liturgical bent when they encountered Orthodoxy. Timothy Ness came to Orthodoxy in a way that one might expect from a lawyer. The twenty-seven-year-old Ness was brought up in Indiana as a Methodist and remained a devout Protestant until he came to New York City to attend law school. When his roommate converted to Orthodoxy, he was intrigued and began investigating the history of the different churches:

> There's overwhelming evidence that the early church looked like a continuation of the Jewish service. There's also evidence [for Orthodoxy] in the structure, method of making decisions and procedures for interpreting Scriptures that marked the early church. My thought process is logical. For others, it's experiential—the music, the incense, the feelings. For me, it was an intellectual exercise. Once you see how close the Orthodox Church [is to] the original church, it's not matter of debate.

Forming a Spiritual Community

"Chanting Praises to the Lord in the Spirit of Traditional Orthodoxy" reads the sign announcing the Orthodox Cathedral of the Holy Virgin Protection on East Second Street. The sign's reference to the popular practice of chanting refers to the fact that the cathedral speaks the language of spiritual seekers even while offering them an ancient and traditional faith. A steady wave of converts has brought life to an old cathedral that was ready to close down in the mid-1980s. Established in 1894, the cathedral was the mother church of the OCA, housing many of the denomination's fraternal organizations. The many Byelorussians and Eastern Ukrainians in the surrounding neighborhood comprised the parish membership.

The situation changed in the 1950s and 1960s as many of the ethnic members left the neighborhood for the suburbs. A new priest was called to the cathedral in 1985, and with the help of seminarians from St. Vladimir's Seminary, including Cälin, new life was injected into the parish. By the time Cälin became pastor in 1994, close to half of the membership was composed of converts.

Today the cathedral is a multiethnic mosaic of converts and ethnic members. With a membership of about 100, the parish draws about 150 people a week to the liturgy. Cälin said he takes a special interest in reaching out to the "disenfranchised, the Sufis and seekers, those who've tried everything." The youth-oriented and experimental atmosphere of the East Village provides a steady pool of prospective converts. Cälin tries to create as many access points as possible between the cathedral and the neighborhood, offering conferences, discussion groups, a bookstore, and special liturgies during the weekdays, some of which are held outdoors.

Under Cälin's direction, the more recent converts (those usually in their twenties and thirties) have been taking up increasingly traditional forms of Orthodoxy. Women are encouraged to wear head coverings during worship (a practice that has been discarded in many Orthodox parishes). Monasticism, with strict fasting and prayer rules, is regarded as the model of the Orthodox lifestyle. "[These converts] don't want compromised, easy-listening stuff. That's why we're succeeding. We don't water it down. We throw everything on the table and they eat as much as they can," Cälin explained. Some of these converts come to the cathedral from the suburbs, complaining that the parishes closer to their homes have no spiritual or liturgical life (interview with Father Christopher Cälin, January 1998).

Most of the converts selected parishes that were open to them and their concerns and questions and had a strong sense of spirituality and tradition. Simeon Baumann said that before he moved to Orthodoxy, he felt that "all the energy I had invested in the church was not of service to anyone." When he came to the Orthodox Church, he had the sense that "here was a place where I could invest my energy and it wouldn't be wasted." He sees the liturgy as "organically linking private prayer with public prayer." The required Orthodox disciplines of regular fasting, formal prayers, and confession provide the sense that "you're not doing it alone. The people from my own community are doing it, and that [sense of communal devotion] becomes a part of me."

Similar views of the communal nature of such spiritual disciplines as fasting, formal prayers, and spiritual readings were expressed by Jill Cook, a twenty-nine-year-old graduate student in theology. Cook converted to Christianity through the Episcopal Church, but she found the Episcopalians polarized between liberal parishes focusing mainly on social action and "Anglo-Catholics with English accents who opposed women priests—things that weren't part of my agenda." She attended an Eastern Orthodox church mainly out of curiosity. "I immediately felt at home. . . . There was the internal sense that prayer was going on here." As an Orthodox Christian, she values the rule of morning and evening prayers as well as fasting, "because it's part of the church discipline. Before [as an Episcopalian], I felt like this lone spiritual athlete. It was voluntary and I had all these standards I set for myself. Now there's just this ordinariness about being Orthodox; I'm just part of the community."

The guidance of "spiritual fathers" or confessors is an important spiritual discipline for the converts. This one-on-one mentoring relationship is often combined with confession, a practice that most of the subjects valued for providing a support system and initiation process into their new faith. Jill Cook pointed out that this relationship with her priest has been "very important. Not being a person who really had a father's guidance growing up, spiritual fatherhood has been very important to me, very healing of my relationship with men, as well as women."

Phillip Hays, a thirty-two-year-old writer and student, switched from a small OCA parish without a regular priest to a monastery connected with the traditionalist Russian Orthodox Church Outside Russia (ROCOR) because he wanted a spiritual father. "You need guidance in living a spiritual life. It's like in Eastern religions with a guru. You have to have obedience and be humble." Not having such guidance, "is like going to a physics class and not having a teacher there."

Conflict in the Church

As might be expected, the recent converts were the most religiously active and the least critical of Orthodoxy and their parishes. Those involved in the church longer, however, reported more struggles with the institutional and everyday realities of Orthodoxy. In the Manhattan office where she works as a political consultant, thirty-two-year-old Susan Miller keeps an icon of Jesus over a desk cluttered with pages of polling data. She admitted that there is an "unresolved" relationship between her faith and a career in which she consults for groups, as well as the issues with which she has had disagreements, such as the tobacco industry. "My beliefs as a

Christian should make me more considerate about how I use my talents in the workplace." But the church has not always helped her meet the challenges of the modern world. "There's a tendency of some Orthodox people to wish they were in another time and place. They might say, 'If only this was nineteenth-century Russia,' or 'If only we were all Orthodox.' It's very explicitly a rejection of the modern world . . . a kind of ghettoization of the faith."

Genovese remarked that in her eight years in Orthodoxy, she has spent months away from her parish and is always questioning her "faith, myself, and God." Her struggle often extends to her life in the church. After college, she became a regular member of an Orthodox Church in America parish in New York. She gradually became part of the church community, but such a sense of belonging has had its drawbacks. "The church is a lot like being in a giant family. You get a lot of support and you get a lot of blame; there's gossip and bickering like everywhere else. It's this thing of my being an individualist and rubbing up against the institution. . . . There's pressure to conform to certain standards." The conflict was brought home to Genovese in her plans for her upcoming marriage to a non-Orthodox man who has not been baptized (although he is a Christian), thus not allowing her to have an Orthodox wedding. "I know I'm doing the right thing. But there is the anxiety of not meeting up to the canon [church law]."

Many converts also saw the ethnic element in Orthodoxy as a point of conflict. Susan Miller said that although she has been a convert to Orthodoxy from Anglicanism for more than half her life, she is still seen as a convert "because I'm not Russian or Greek." Robin Genovese observed that the stress put on ethnicity in some Orthodox churches can be "very annoying. I'm Jewish and Italian and I feel a strong attachment to my own background, so I sometimes feel left out." Linda Burnham added that she was troubled by the nationalistic views of some traditionalist Russian Orthodox members. "It's a major conflict. I can't understand how they can be so holy to attain the rank of clergy and then be so unenlightened as to say that the church is not for all people."

Balancing Tolerance and Certainty

Even while practicing a comprehensive faith in a strong community, the converts showed a widespread acceptance of pluralism in their relations outside the church. Most of the subjects said that they had more non-Orthodox than Orthodox friends. Susan Miller said that the friends she has from the church exist in one orbit while her friends from college days or work exist in another, "like two hermetically sealed worlds." She added that she spends "a lot more time in church just because it's an easy habit," rather than forming new social ties. However, Simeon Baumann maintains that his involvement in the church is helping him form more solid friendships with non-Orthodox friends. He said he is more capable of friendship since becoming Orthodox and now holds friends to a higher standard.

While Robin Genovese was concerned about her conflict with the church about marrying a non-Orthodox man, she herself did not see such an action as wrong or sinful. Even now, Genovese said she does not pray that "God will make" her fiancé Orthodox. "I pray that we will love each other and be committed to each other." In her nine years of being in the Orthodox Church, Genovese said that she had never dated Orthodox men. After her marriage, she plans to bring any children she has to church (although they will not be baptized).

While several of the people interviewed said they had spoken to their friends about Orthodoxy, it was usually after someone had first expressed interest in the topic, and not always strictly for evangelistic reasons. In fact, the converts often frowned on active evangelism, even those who had actively "witnessed" for their faith in their former Christian churches. Genovese explained, "No one ever gets argued into the faith. I'll speak about my faith more because I want people to accept me and what I believe." Mariame Javic said she makes no attempt to evangelize friends, believing that "God will lead them" to the faith if he chooses.

Several of the converts said that since becoming Orthodox, they have felt more in common with traditional believers from other religions, such as Orthodox Jews and Muslims. Linda Burnham remarked that she views the Dalai Lama and Orthodox Jewish rabbis as the "next holiest" people after Orthodox priests and monks. All the converts felt that they could not say that other people would not find salvation in practicing their own faiths.

Intermingled with statements of religious tolerance, however, were the subjects' frequent affirmations of the truth of Orthodoxy over that of other Christian denominations and the importance of adhering to a comprehensive tradition rather than to selective parts of the faith. Mariame Javic maintained that "if you belong to a religion, you should believe all of it; you should take it seriously and try to understand it." She agreed with church teachings that Orthodoxy was the true church founded by Christ.

The converts were actually more uneasy about their relations with other Christians than with non-Christians. The traditional Orthodox prohibition of praying with "heretics," as well as different doctrinal understandings between Eastern and Western Christians, raised new problems for the converts in their everyday relations. Most believed that Western Christian churches had been secularized and diluted of spiritual truth—churches that as former members they were very familiar with—and for this reason, they were generally wary about plans for greater Christian unity in the future.

Joan Taylor, a thirty-two-year-old secretary, served as a missionary in an evangelical organization before becoming Orthodox. Since then, she has separated herself from much of her former life and finds that she has little in common with her old friends. Taylor no longer listens to much of the contemporary evangelical Christian music she had collected; instead she listens to Orthodox church music and more secular music. Her involvement in Orthodoxy has created a religious barrier between her and her parents, who also are missionaries. "We used to get together as a family and pray. It's not the same any more." Yet Taylor said she is more tolerant than she was as an evangelical, no longer believing that those in non-Christian religions are necessarily condemned if they do not believe in Christ.

Between Two Worlds

The move to Eastern Orthodoxy did not always cause drastic changes in the converts' lifestyles. For example, several of the converts' sexual attitudes and practices only gradually changed after they moved to the Orthodox Church. Several of them had had premarital sex before they adopted the faith and had difficulty in adhering to church teachings prohibiting such relations.

Genovese explained, "I was very different in my starting point than other people in relation to celibacy. I was sexually active early in life and was not raised valuing chastity." After her conversion, she continued to have sexual relations, although they were rarely casual. "On one hand, I felt what I was doing was right, but I also agreed with the church's teachings, so there was this tension." More recently, Genovese has "felt uncomfortable" with the level of sexual involvement she had with her fiancé and the tensions this has caused her in relation to the church, and so she has tried to live more within church guidelines. Susan Miller, who also had sexual relationships while a member of the church, said that some people's relatively lax approach to sexuality is in keeping with the "tendency of Orthodoxy to be flexible, to set up the ideal and then to recognize that you can't always live up to it."

Orthodoxy and the Culture Wars

The converts found a greater tension between traditional and modern views of gender roles and feminism. After she converted to Orthodoxy as a teenager, Miller said she went through an "antifeminist" period but added that "a few years in the working world cured me of that." She opposes radical feminist ideas that see men as the oppressors of women because "they tend to dehumanize people as some kind of artificial entities." Robin Genovese admitted that she is "unabashedly for women's rights" and believes that

> women could do almost anything as well as or better than men. But I also definitely believe in gender roles. I love the idea of being a wife. I have no problem with the husband being the head of the family. Saint Paul taught that husbands are the head of a wife. But I wouldn't put up with a husband who would not see me as an equal.

While she supports the church's rule of ordaining only men as priests, Genovese added, "I don't know why there are no women in the diaconate or tonsured to be [Scripture] readers." Joan Taylor said that in her transition from evangelical Protestantism to Orthodoxy, she has learned to balance the idea of submission to one's husband and "being one's own person." Mariame Javic observed that feminism had "damaged women a lot, although it also did some good. It made women more confident." She is particularly troubled by the view in some feminist circles that women are powerless and that there are few differences between the sexes. She remarked that

> women have power as much as men, but its a different kind of power. . . . Part of a woman's nature is different than the nature of men. Women can accept humility, while men have a lot more pride to overcome to be spiritual. . . . I don't think the church is biased against women. We have the Theotokos [Mary] and so many strong women as examples.

In general, the converts supported many of the advances of feminism, such as equal access to employment, while holding to the importance of differences between men and women. The female converts would, in varying degrees, be sympathetic to what Christina Hoff Sommers termed "equity feminism," which calls for fairness for women in society while arguing that such equality does not preclude differences between the sexes (such as in the male priesthood and a greater nurturing role for mothers in raising families) (Sommers 1994). The male converts exhibited a similar conflict regarding gender roles and feminism. Simeon Baumann said that while women in general should take a greater role in child rearing than men do, he could see many exceptions to this rule. "Each couple is unique. There will be more aggressive women who take more of a leadership role in the marriage. I have no problems with that."

Most of the converts agreed that since becoming Orthodox, they had been less active on political issues than before converting. The changing political involvement of converts is illustrated by Cynthia Hayes, a thirty-one-year-old black woman who works as a medical secretary. She grew up in a Methodist family that went to church only on holidays. While she was in college, she started dating a white man who was in the process of converting to Orthodoxy. Cynthia, an unwed mother, had her daughters baptized in the church, and it was during the baptism ceremony that she was struck by the power of Orthodoxy. "It didn't feel like the churches I grew up with. There was this other-worldly feeling. It seemed like everything was directed toward God, [including] the priest and people." She converted to Orthodoxy soon after and then married Phillip.

While she was in college, Cynthia was involved in registering voters for Jesse Jackson during his candidacy for the presidential nomination. "I was very militant in civil rights [and] trying to galvanize political power to overcome racial prejudice." But when she converted to Orthodoxy and then married a white man, that was too much for many of her friends. "They said I was selling out." Civil rights issues and racial prejudice in general gradually have had "less impact on me now. It's not blackness but God that saves. I still see prejudice, but it's not as important to me now."

A focus on the personal rather than the political dimensions of life was common among the converts. Mariame Javic is "trying to change things in my little part of the world. Politics is a corrupt and dirty game." Robin Genovese said that since becoming Orthodox, she is "much more cynical about the good we can do politically. We're better off acting on an individual level or on a subversive level, which would challenge certain structures and policies. I think political groups have a dangerous tendency to think things are perfectible." Jill Cook was involved in the peace movement before becoming Orthodox, but today she tends to "live on a more local, personal level. I'm not as likely to go out and protest for peace as I did in the past; now I'd treat people nicer on the cafeteria line."

Many of the converts even more strongly opposed the church's involvement in political issues. Simeon Baumann maintained that such opposition stemmed from Orthodox teachings. "The primary service of the church to the world is its liturgical life. Most of the other things the church does, such as its social services, can be done better by the world." They often dismissed the idea of greater Orthodox influence in society through political means as unrealistic or even utopian. Javic viewed the religious warfare in the former Yugoslavia with scorn. "I don't like it when people use Orthodoxy for politics. [Orthodoxy] is only a spiritual life." The intensity of the subjects' disdain for Orthodox political involvement was expressed in some of their views on abortion. Although not as involved politically in prolife issues as the Roman Catholics and evangelicals are, a growing segment of Orthodox believers have become involved in antiabortion activism. Javic said that when a bishop started speaking on prolife issues during one service, she and some of her friends walked out of the church in protest. "There we were all spiritual and boom—abortion! The church is no place to teach politics. The church shouldn't worry about being contemporary. It's timeless."

Even though she thinks her church, the Russian Orthodox Church Abroad (ROCOR), should maintain its prolife stance, Diane Greene was more prochoice than most of the other converts. "We are so corrupted as a society, you have to have ugly solutions for ugly problems. If you outlaw abortions, there will be more of them." On the other end of the spectrum was Timothy Ness's wife, Emily. She was active in prolife activities as a Catholic convert and after moving to Orthodoxy, she remained active. But while most were personally against abortion and distanced themselves from the prochoice movement, many of the converts were not convinced that political means would solve the problem.

The converts' rejection of political activism did not necessarily mean that they were not concerned with social and political issues. For instance, several of them worked with the poor and strongly supported environmental concerns, even to the extent of calling for the church to support them.

A Monastery Full of Converts

On a street on the far edge of the East Village known more for drug deals and poverty than incense and chanting is a monastery called Mercy House. The monastery was started in 1994 by the traditionalist Russian Orthodox Church Outside of Russia. Housed in the dignified-looking brownstone are two monks and several homeless people. Although some of the homeless have converted to Orthodoxy, it was more unexpected when Orthodox believers from throughout the city started flocking to the liturgy at Mercy House. "Our original purpose was doing acts of mercy, but we also found that there are a lot of the spiritually poor here," said Father Joachim Parr, a tall monk with a long beard covering much of his face.

Mercy House attracts about forty to sixty people each week for its liturgy, and the majority are converts to the faith. After a two-hour liturgy filled with incense, bowing, and chanting, most of the congregation heads down to the basement for brunch. A tangible sense of community pervades these gatherings, with the worshipers greeting one another with three kisses (to symbolize the Trinity) and spending much of their day at the monastery. Parr, himself a convert, said that it was not unusual for someone to convert to Orthodoxy in one of the more modern groups, such as the Orthodox Church in America, and then to make the transition to a more traditional body such as the ROCOR. "They come to the synod [ROCOR] because they want to have a more traditional faith. They ask themselves, what is the point of becoming Orthodox if they don't follow all the traditions of the church?" Many of the converts are attracted to the ROCOR's strongly preserved ascetic monastic traditions (interview with Rev. Joachim Parr, January 1998).

To one degree or another, the Orthodox mysticism and asceticism that reach their zenith at a place like Mercy House have shaped most of the converts' lifestyles and attitudes. One hears in their accounts a turning inward toward spiritual matters and a shift away from broader, "impersonal" concerns. The theological nature of Eastern Orthodoxy helps explain such attitudes, and the liturgy and the church itself are viewed as the manifestation of the kingdom of God on earth.

Several of the converts showed signs of at least a semimonastic lifestyle. Many of them use their chrismated names to emphasize their Orthodox identity, just as a monk assumes a new name upon joining a monastery. It is no coincidence that the converts most involved in such ascetic-based spiritual disciplines were also the least politically active and concerned. They often regarded their spiritual life as conflicting with political and worldly concerns, whether in the wider society or the church.

A Flexible Faith and Unique Community

All the converts emphasized the importance of spiritual disciplines and embracing Orthodoxy completely. But a certain degree of pluralism and even consumerism were evident in how they shopped around for a parish that met their spiritual needs, as well as how they applied church teachings to their lives. The converts valued Orthodoxy because it was flexible in its demands while also upholding high standards.

One reason for the greater degree of pluralism in the converts' social outlook and lifestyles can be found in the Eastern Orthodox tradition itself. As Susan Miller said in discussing sexuality, there is the "tendency of Orthodoxy to be flexible, to set up the ideal and then to recognize that you can't always live up to it." Eastern Orthodoxy is also highly decentralized and does not have an authoritative magisterium that might encourage more uniformity of views and interpretations of the faith.

The Orthodox liturgy, the central and sometimes only function of many parishes, also illustrates and may even help explain the flexible nature of the faith. Parishioners come late and leave early, with many not staying for the entire service. The sense of individual freedom allowed in the liturgy appears to have been carried over by the subjects into other parts of their lives. Robin Genovese exhibited this kind of individualism in her account of discovering Orthodoxy when she said she felt that her "individuality [was not] threatened by social standards," as it might have been in other congregations.

While the sense of community in Orthodox churches is often palpable, it is a unique community based on common rituals that provide members with an ideal vision of spiritual truth (through the liturgy and church traditions and teachings) and with the tools (through the spiritual disciplines) by which they can find such a reality in their own lives. All the converts had close connections with their parishes, and they all said they had benefited from the guidance they found in their relationship with priests and spiritual confessors. It is these central spiritual components of the faith rather than the common social values and views that provide the bond among these believers.

Some researchers found a unique sense of community among the

Orthodox. The researchers interviewed twenty-five Orthodox converts in Boston, who were mostly young adults, and found that they were

> not simply robotic followers of a rigid faith. Rather, they bounce their individual, implicit feelings off the traditions of the Orthodox faith. It is not that they abandon individual feelings but that what are still their individual understandings or private belief systems find communal support, despite differential interpretations, in the collective life that gives validation to their own social construction of reality. (Chalfont and Calvicanti 1994, 9)

The interviewees' accounts point to a central concern with the primacy of the spiritual and the personal dimensions of life over politics and ideology. Many of the issues that have been politicized by protagonists on both sides of the "culture wars," such as feminism and abortion, could not be fit neatly into either conservative or liberal categories. In contrast to Western thought, in which all truth is viewed as an "either-or" matter, some researchers maintain that in Eastern thought, "one can believe on different levels and that beliefs held on one level need not be consistent with those on another." Thus, conflicts between science and faith—or between modern gender relations and the teachings of the church fathers— can be "avoided simply because when one thinks theologically it is on one level; scientific thought is on another level" (Chalfont and Calvicanti 1994, 450–451).

Of course, the views of Orthodox converts, particularly the clergy and other leaders, can be very conservative. In reading the literature published by converts, one can find vigorous condemnations of feminism, theological liberalism, individualism, ecumenism, and many other modern ideas. In particular, the converts to Orthodoxy from evangelical Protestantism have created a more dogmatic and polemical strain in the American church—a fact that concerns some Orthodox leaders and intellectuals while comforting others who fear a loss of doctrinal substance in Orthodoxy (Guroian 1995; Rossi 1996). But the mystical and decentralized nature of Orthodoxy also leads to a more adaptive and flexible posture in relation to modernity. The Orthodox solution to the culture wars, and modernity in general, is not so much to form exclusive Christian communities with uniform worldviews but, rather, to cultivate a spirituality that challenges such modern dilemmas as materialism, secularism, and politicization. The converts regarded the discipline of fasting as a way of limiting materialism, while the liturgy itself offered them a zone of timelessness and sanctity in what they saw as a mundane world.

Many of the converts interviewed can be considered what Max Weber termed *religious virtuosos*. Eastern Orthodox parishes function as well-preserved enclaves of religious virtuosity. But it remains to be seen whether the reassertion of mysticism and ascetic disciplines that has drawn converts to the faith will be enough to protect Eastern Orthodoxy from the encroaching forces of assimilation and secularization.

NOTE

1. The converts' names were changed to protect their anonymity. This study is based on seventeen interviews with Orthodox converts in New York from 1994 to 1998. An account of these cases studies can be found in Cimino 1997, 64–101.

Chapter 10

The Religion of New York Jews from the Former Soviet Union

Samuel Kliger

"I will consider myself a Jew until I am dead!" declared Svetlana, a recent immigrant from Kharkov, Ukraine. But Svetlana, sixty-three, also says that her identity does not include following Jewish customs or religious traditions. Rather, her identity is etched by others' hostility into a defensive pride of being part of the Jewish nation. For her, then, being a Jew is "to support Israel in important aspects, but not in its ordinary life."

Former Muscovite Yuri, forty-six, agrees that being a Jew means "feeling compassion for the problems of Israel," but having become an American citizen in 1992, he cautioned that one "should not be unconcerned with what is going on in this country." Henrietta, seventy-two, invokes the cosmopolitanism of her native St. Petersburg, remarking that any national identity makes her uneasy. "Jews have to be internationalists; Israel is becoming a nationalist country."

Others are like Ida, in her seventies, who recently came from Kiev and admits, "It is difficult to answer what it means to be a Jew." At the extreme is Bela, thirty-nine, who is sure that he did not come from Tashkent, Uzbekistan, to join a religion: "It is humbug!"

So, Who Are the Jews from the Former Soviet Union?

Immigrants from the former Soviet Union (FSU) are often called Russian immigrants, Russian Jews, or just Russians. They comprise (or may soon comprise) up to 25 percent of New York City's entire Jewish community, yet we know little about their identity struggle, religious views, beliefs, and attitudes as newcomers in America.[1]

The Russians Are Coming: The New Wave

Since 1994, the largest group of immigrants to New York City has been from the FSU (NYC Dept. of City Planning 1999). The first wave of Russian Jews were part of the historic nineteenth- and early-twentieth-century immigration to the United States. A second wave came after World War II, and a third wave started with the change in the immigration law in the early 1970s. In 1989, the U.S. Congress designated Soviet Jews, along with evangelical Christians, Ukrainian Catholics, and Orthodox, as a category eligible for admission to the United States as refugees if they could prove they had a credible fear of persecution if they remained in the Soviet Union. This resulted in a "fourth wave" of Russian immigrants, who began arriving to the United States in the late 1980s.

More than 200,000 Russian Jewish immigrants have arrived in New York City as refugees since the early 1970s (Galperin 1996, 229). If we also add those who came on other types of visas (for example, relatives of American citizens, asylum seekers, employment-based visa holders, and green card lottery winners), the number of Russian (both Jewish and non-Jewish) immigrants to the New York metropolitan area has probably reached 400,000. In fact, new Russian immigrants now comprise almost a quarter of New York City's entire Jewish community (Onion 1996, 31).

In several ways, these immigrants are different from those who arrived in the 1970s.

First, although all Russian Jewish immigrants were persecuted, Russian anti-Semitism has changed over the past three decades. In the 1970 and 1980s, the state officially sponsored anti-Semitism in the guise of anti-Zionism. Now, on the surface, the state oppression has disappeared, and the state claims official neutrality in matters of ethnicity. But since 1989, Jews in Russia have still experienced hostility from the state in the form of anti-Judaism, in addition to the still popular anti-Semitism.

The notion that Judaism is a cruel and dangerous religion is widespread in Russia. Alexander Bovin, a Russian liberal intellectual and former ambassador to Israel, remarked in an interview with *Alef* magazine: "I am not quite sure that aspiration for higher justice is typical for Jews. . . . There is no religious tolerance in the Torah. . . . There are so many curses and punishments listed that how can this apotheosis of cruelty match the aspiration for high justice?" (Bovin 1996, 13).

In 1991, more than half of 4,200 Soviets questioned in a public opinion poll wanted all Jews to leave the country (*New York Post*, September 26, 1991, 9). Even in post-Communist Russia, attitudes toward Jews remain quite negative (Brym 1994; Gibson 1994; Gibson and Duch 1992). Gudkov and Levinson (1994) found widespread assertions that Jews avoid physical labor and place money and profit above human relations. Carnes concluded that in Russia, "more than any other xenophobia, anti-Semitism is a powerful activator and intensifier of negative stereotypes toward other people in general" (1995, 25).

In a study sponsored by the American Jewish Committee (1999), the Research Institute for New Americans found that 58 percent of new Russian immigrants strongly believe that anti-Semitism is a serious problem in the former Soviet Union. A second difference between the most recent immigrants and those of the 1970s is that the earlier immigrants were oppressed by a Soviet system that seemed to offer no friendly future for Jews, whereas the fourth wave is leaving Russia because they are afraid that the Russian government will not last into the future. Furthermore, the earlier immigrants saw their future blocked because of their Jewishness, whereas the new wave sees some advancements for Jews in Russia but do not believe the country is stable.

So, those who now come to the United States are not coming so much for Jewish reasons but for fear of a Russian collapse. Consequently, the new wave is not as eager to discover its Jewish identity in the United States, although the constant undercurrent of Russian anti-Semitism has kept the Jewish identity alive.

The fourth wave recognizes that Jews in Russia have achieved much more influence in the country's political life and economy than ever before in Russian history. Those Jews who now live in Moscow (including "half-Jews," "some-Jews," and those members of Jewish families placed in the "Jewish orbit") comprise a significant part of the new Russian elite. A well-known Russian journalist, Leonid Radzikhovsky, observed that even after twenty years of emigration, Jews in Russia are stronger than they were twenty years before; furthermore, despite feeling less comfortable in Russia than do Jews in other developed Christian countries, their weight in Russian politics and business is much more significant than in any other Christian country (Radzikhovsky 1996, 6; Shanks 1996; Stanley 1997).

Third, the fourth wave of Russian immigrants contain proportionally fewer Jews than did the earlier waves. Zhanna Zaionchkovskaya, chief of the migration laboratory of the Russian Academy of Sciences, stated that of the nonrefugee immigrants during the last two years of the early 1990s, twice as many ethnic Russians emigrated to America as Jews (Dubrovskaya 1995). Also, many members of refugee families are not Jewish but are related to Jews, mainly by marriage. For many of them, the traditional definition of who is a Jew is not so important to their self-identity (Blumenthal 1998).

As many as 29 percent of recent immigrants to Israel from the former Soviet Union could not prove their Jewish identity (Tabory 1995, 188). Based on this fact and some observations at the New York Association for New Americans, we can estimate that the proportion of non-Jews among the refugees is somewhere between 30 and 40 percent.[2] In a 1998/1999 study by the Research Institute for New Americans, 60 to 70 percent of the new Russian immigrants identified themselves as Jewish (AJC 1999).

Fourth, the latest wave of Jewish immigrants had an alternative that the previous waves did not. After the collapse of the Soviet Union, Jewish life in the republics of the former Soviet Union has flourished. This means that the fourth-wave Jews were not compelled to leave Russia for religious reasons but for some other reason like security, familial reunion, or economic opportunity. Various studies show that any Jewish activity, particularly religious, is at the periphery of the new Russian immigrants' interests and value systems. A recent poll by the Analytic Center of the Russian Academy of Sciences found that 53 percent of Jews (but only 21 percent of ethnic Russians) could not identify their religion; 23 percent of Jews (but only 7 percent of Russians) considered themselves atheists; and only 8 percent of Jews identified themselves as practicing Judaism (Chertok 1995; Kliger and Carnes 1994).

Although 95 percent of Jews in Moscow, Kiev, and Minsk wanted a "Jewish cultural revival" and 78 percent wanted a "Jewish religious development," only 17 percent (but 26 percent of American Jews) celebrated the Jewish New Year; 10 percent observed the Jewish Sabbath; and 5 percent (but 37 percent of American Jews) claimed to be members of Jewish organizations (Brym 1994, 25). According to Shapiro and Chervyakov's study of Jewish activists, 36 percent said they were believers or "rather believers than not"; only 3.5 percent wanted to learn more about Judaism; and 7 percent regularly recited Jewish prayers at home (1992, 10, 12). The recent wave of immigrants and the American Jewish community both wonder what their common fate will be in this country in the new millennium.

Russian Jews and the American Jewish Community: Mutually Broken Expectations

The American Jewish community expected that the new Russian Jewish immigrants, being cut off from Jewish life in the Soviet Union, would want to participate actively in Jewish religious and communal life in America. The newcomers were expected to bring "new blood" to the established American Jewish communities. But from the point of view of the organized American Jewish community, this is not happening yet. As they are seen by mainstream American Judaism, Russian Jews in America continue to be as indifferent to Jewish heritage and Jewish communal life as they were while they were living in the Soviet Union.

Moreover, while crediting the American Jewish community for helping them come to this country, Russian Jews nonetheless expect more practical assistance now that they have arrived. Dependent on the government in the former Soviet Union, they now need a patron in America. Emotionally, they expect love and friendliness, but instead they feel that American Jews are trying to impose on them an ideology (including "boring" religious practice), rather than helping them in their practical needs or expressing their "love" to them.

Although Russian Jews are acculturating more as Russians than as Jews, American Jews have tried to reach Russian Jews as Jews while derogating or failing to understand their distinctive Russian identity. The American Jewish community has thus been asking itself whether the Russian Jews really want to become a part of their community, to discover their Jewish heritage, or prefer to stay away from Judaism. Is it worthwhile to try to bring them closer to Judaism and the Jewish community?

Russians, in turn, ask different questions. Do American Jews really and sincerely want us, as Russian Jews, to join the American Jewish community, or do they intend to keep us as a "second-class" Jews? Should we participate in their odd and bureaucratic organizations, or do they merely want us Russian Jews to be a source of new revenues for their bureaucracies?

These questions arise from the cultural and historical divergences between the organized American Jewish community and the still disorganized Russian Jews. Furthermore, the organized American Jewish community has developed under the influence of the United States' prevailing Protestant culture, with its emphasis on communal religious practice, individual responsibility, charity, and communal life rather than ideology and theology (Shapiro 1996). From the beginning period (1895–1948), the Jewish Federation's main goal was assimilation into the mainstream (Protestant) culture, "helping Jews integrate into the United States, learning its language, its culture and its values, . . . to eliminate barriers to the Jewish understanding of America and to full Jewish participation in the American dream" (Feldstein 1995/1996, 5).

Since the 1990s, however, the emphasis has changed to ensuring the future of Judaism and fulfilling the increasing need for Jewish education and Jewish continuity (Feldstein 1995/1996, 9). Meanwhile, Jewish family values have been replaced by American cultural values. As Anita Friedman explained: "Many of us may pine for the idealized good old days. But after so many years in America, American Jewish behavior has become much like American dominant culture behavior, with few exceptions and with most of the same problems" (1995, 298).

Soviet Jews have formed their lifestyle, values, and mentality under two dominions: a Russian culture rooted in Russian Orthodoxy and the Communist totalitarian regime with its emphasis on ideology and the state. The idea of a Jewish religion and communal life is unfamiliar to them. At most, they know that the synagogue is a place for Jews to gather for service and prayer. But they do not understand why they should have to pay dues to belong to the synagogue. To Russian Jews, faith is very private and intimate and has to do with personal feelings and thoughts rather than action. Any explicit religious practice or communal identification (like wearing a yarmulka) and a separate Jewish communal life are not only unfamiliar but even seem shameful.

This experience is reflected in the language: Russian Jews prefer to use the word *vera* (Russian for faith) rather than *religia* (religion). To Russians, *religia* has the connotation of boring and tiresome rituals and observances, whereas *vera* popularly refers to an individual contemplating his own fate.

The Jewishness of most Russian Jews is a given fact. According to Markowitz,

> Soviet Jews regard their Jewishness as an intrinsic component of who they are. Jews are born Jews, and no one in the USSR challenges or questions their . . . Jewishness. As immigrants explain it, being a Jew is an immutable biological and social fact, ascribed at birth like sex and eye color. (1993, 139)

In answer to the question "In your view, what does it mean to be a Jew?" 41.4 percent of the respondents in a 1993 survey of Jews in Moscow and St. Petersburg said that it simply meant "to feel oneself a part of the Jewish people"; about 25 percent said, "to be a son/daughter of Jewish parents"; and for 12.1 percent, it meant "to be proud of the Jewish nation." Amazingly, only 1 percent connected their Jewish identity with "professing Judaism," and only 4 percent said that to be a Jew meant "to observe Jewish traditions and customs" (Shapiro and Chervyakov 1993, 3). The same was reported for those Russian Jews who immigrated to Israel (Tabory 1992, 273). A similar trend was also found in a 1998/1999 survey of Russian Jewish immigrants in New York. For less than 7 percent, being Jew meant "to observe Jewish custom and traditions," and for only 3.4 percent, it meant "professing Judaism" (AJC 1999).

In its core rabbinical tradition, Judaism is a practical religion or a lifestyle, requiring everyday practical action in fulfilling God's commandments. But for Russian Jews, their Jewish identity does not mean religious practice. That is, "Jew" means "to belong," "to know," "to have," "to be proud of," "to feel," "to think," "to be," even "to believe," but not "to do." Russian Jews explain their religious views in expressions like "I think there is someone above; it may be God," "I was born a Jew," "My grandfather was a rabbi," "I want more Jewish culture," "I speak Yiddish/Hebrew," "I believe Jews are a chosen people," "I feel more Jewish and/or religious in America than I did in Russia." In other words, they explain their identity and religion in a way that does not require or imply major changes in behavior, lifestyle, or religious practice.

When asked why they do not attend synagogue, Russian Jews reply, "I do not understand what is going on there," "this is all for business," "there is nothing attractive there," "God can hear me without synagogue," "I have many problems to solve first," "God doesn't need my prayer" (whereas an American Jew would say, "I need to pray because I believe it helps," or "my community needs my prayer").

Russian Jews expect the American Jewish community to provide the same kind of services that the community provided fifty to one hundred years ago: assimilation into American culture and economy in order to achieve the "American dream." American Jews, in turn, expect from Russians at least an openness to a Jewish lifestyle that Russians lost seventy years ago. The fact that both American Jews and Russian Jews still are Jews is much less significant than the fact that American Jews are Americans and Russian Jews are Russians. Traditional Judaism is no longer a uniting factor for parts of the tribe.

Jews and Russians

Jewish immigrants in New York City who are from the former Soviet Union are commonly called Russians, regardless of their origins from quite different parts of the country. Indeed, most of those from the European part of the former Soviet Union consider themselves "Russians." This is not the case, however, for the so-called Bukharian Jews from Central Asia, especially those from the towns of Bukhara and Samarkand in Uzbekistan. In the 1990s, about thirty thousand Bukharian Jews arrived in Forest Hills, Queens. Although they had adopted the secular culture of their Uzbek and Tadjik neighbors, growing xenophobia and Islamic fundamentalism drove them to America and a distinct Bukharian Jewish identity (Bialor 1994).

Jews from all over the former Soviet Union are very similar to Russians in their religious attitudes, cultural norms, moral values, and identities. In a 1993 poll, almost half the Jews from Moscow and St. Petersburg said the Russians in their city were closer to them culturally and spiritually than Ukrainian or Byelorussian Jews, and only 17.2 percent felt Ukrainian and Byelorussian Jews were closer to them than the Russians in their city (Shapiro and Chervyakov 1993, 3, 13).

Ethnic Russians and Russian Jews also have similar religious attitudes (Hill 1989, 337). Forty-four percent of the Jews consider themselves believers or rather believers than not, and only 3 percent attend synagogue at least once a month (Shapiro and Chervyakov 1993, 9,11). Likewise, 45 percent of all Russians consider themselves believers, while only 10 percent of Russian Orthodox attend church at least once a month. Experts say the church's appeal has more to do with culture and ethnicity than spirituality (Glastris 1996; *Izvestiya* June 4, 1993, 3). Thus, both ethnic Russians and Jews see Russian Orthodoxy and Judaism, respectively, as merely cultural and symbolic forms of their shared national identity.

In fact, if they convert, Russian Jews in New York are more likely to become Russian Orthodox than another Christian denomination.[3] When asked, "Which of the religious doctrines is the most attractive for you?" 14 percent of Jews from Moscow and St. Petersburg stated Christianity (Shapiro and Chervyakov 1993, 11), by which they mean, in most cases, Russian Orthodoxy (see table 10.1).

In New York, the number of Russian Jews converted to "Jews for Jesus" may be much smaller than that for converted American Jews. The number

TABLE 10.1
Which Religion Is Most Attractive to You?

	Jews in Moscow and St. Petersburg, 1993 (%)	Russian Jews in New York, 1999 (%)
Judaism	34	49
Neither	33	24
Christianity	14	8

of American Jews joining messianic groups is growing every year, with more than 300,000 Jews joining messianic Jewish groups, whereas fewer than 1,000 Russians have accepted Yeshua as the Messiah (Onion 1996, 31).

In many cases, conversion to Russian Orthodoxy takes place as a result of intermarriage. According to 1988 marriage registration statistics, 63 percent of mixed marriages in Russia involved at least one Jewish spouse, 45 percent in the Ukraine, and 40 percent in Belarus (Tolts 1992). Most of the children in such families are completely assimilated into the Russian culture. Because the Russian culture is dominant, the Jews in mixed marriages are more likely to convert to Russian Orthodoxy than vice versa. This is especially true for non-Jewish men whose conversion includes being circumcised. If they are pressured by the American tradition of belonging to a religious group, such couples usually find the Russian Orthodox church the easiest entrance to a religious community (Brym 1994, 20).

Immigrants and Religious Practices

Judaic life revolves around a set of practices that makes its participants holy. As given by the Torah and the Talmud, these practices create the boundaries between their participants and the rest of society and symbolizes Jewish identity in relation to God. Boundaries, as Douglas showed, symbolize the beginnings of identity and society. "The objective of these [boundary-symbolizing] rituals is not negative withdrawal from reality.... The rituals enact the form of social relationships and ... enable people to know their own society" (Douglas 1966, 153).

Practices of the Body: Circumcision

Although Jewish religious law requires all male Jews to be circumcised (the Hebrew *bris* for "covenant"), the vast majority of young Russian Jews are not circumcised. As Shanks noted, "Now, five years after the Soviet Union disintegrated and Jews have been free to practice their religion and observe their customs, almost no Jewish boys are being circumcised" (1996, 46).

Since Orthodox tradition requires unconditional circumcision, a debate has arisen. Some Jewish leaders do not consider circumcision a first priority for new immigrants, and so many remain uncircumcised. For example, Belkin, twenty-seven, a Russian Jewish immigrant who does not want to be circumcised, said: "It's not the pain. It is just that for immigrants there are too many problems to solve. I did not have a chance to become religious." Rabbi Elijahu Shain, a circumciser famed for having performed eight thousand operations, admits that even among those who have decided they want a bris, cancellations are in a rate of one in five (*New York Times*, March 15, 1995, 21,23).

Practices of Time: Sabbath and Holidays

Religious Jews often claim that their concept of Sabbath is the most powerful ritual for Jewish identity and community. Noted Judaic scholar Rabbi Kaplan put it this way:

> It is not exaggeration to say that the Jew has survived . . . largely because he had the Sabbath. . . . It has been said that as much as the Jew has kept Sabbath, so has Sabbath kept the Jew. As long as Judaism exists as a vibrant, vital force, the Sabbath is its most outstanding ritual practice. (1984, 5)

However, Russian Jews do not place much importance on keeping the Sabbath. According to a 1993 poll by the Jewish Research Center, 79 percent of those questioned in Moscow and St. Petersburg said that their parental families observed no Sabbath duties; only 2 percent regularly did so (Shapiro and Chervyakov 1993, 6, 8).

Russian Jews observe Passover more than any other Jewish religious holiday. In 1993, about a third of the respondents in Moscow and St. Petersburg said that they observed Passover regularly. But Russian Jews commonly interpret "observance" to mean "remembrance," without any ritual or moral actions. For example, when asked, "Did you take part in Passover Seder this year?" less than 20 percent said yes (Shapiro and Chervyakov 1993, 10–11).

Two nationwide studies of Soviet Jews in the United States revealed a controversial set of data about Jewish immigrants' religious behavior (see

Kosmin 1990a; Simon, Simon, and Schwartz 1982). According to Simon and colleagues (1982), 50 percent of Soviet Jews fast on Yom Kippur, but according to Kosmin (1990a), 84 percent fast on Yom Kippur and 67 percent attend a Passover seder. Steven Gold (1994, 5), who did the most comprehensive overview of studies of Soviet Jews in the United States, explained why the findings of some studies are controversial:

> Studies of this sort . . . are less likely to capture the rich, complex, and often contradictory nature of the Soviet Jews' experience. [They] . . . tend to suffer from small sample sizes and from the fact that those willing to cooperate with a researcher may not be representative of the entire community. Finally, there is a good reason to question the validity of former Soviets' responses to telephone surveys, since they are noted for their distrust and manipulation of bureaucrats.

Still, other studies also show that a high rate of Russian immigrant Jews observe rituals and holidays. New York Federation (1984) data suggest that 78 percent of Russian Jews fast on Yom Kippur and 75 percent attend a Passover seder. The data from the 1991 New York Jewish Population Study—the most recent and most comprehensive survey of a sample of Jews from the former Soviet Union—obtained even higher figures: 78 percent fast on Yom Kippur, and 90 percent attend a Passover seder.

Practices of Nature: Dietary Laws

The laws of kosher food, found in Leviticus 11 and Deuteronomy 14:4–21, identify what foods Jews are permitted to eat and how they must be prepared. But Russian Jews know and observe very little about this. Only 1.2 percent of Jews in St. Petersburg said they kept kosher regularly (Shapiro and Chervyakov 1993, 8). But the 1991 New York Jewish Population Study found that 70 percent of Soviet Jews in New York City kept two sets of dishes (Gold 1994, 55), although surveys in Russian show that most Russian Jews did not follow Jewish religious prescriptions, even after living for several years in United States.

A Four-Level Religious Attitude

Russian Jews' religious views may be described as having four levels of attitude (Kliger 1999).

In God We Trust

Generally, Russian Jews see religion as a cultural, traditional, or philosophical concept. For them, the meaning of a belief in God is quite ambiguous. Although almost 40 percent of Jews in Moscow and St. Petersburg in 1993 were "sure that God exists," only about 20 percent definitely considered themselves believers (see table 10.1). Thus, many Russian Jews combine belief in God with low religious identification.

Moreover, the number of atheists among Jews in Russia is significantly higher than it is for American Jews or ethnic Russians. This does not necessarily mean that Jews are less religious than the Russians, since ethnic Russians reject atheism as one of the features of Communist propaganda (Dunstan 1993). But for Jews in Russia, atheism was and still is a way of assimilation. For a Jew to be accepted in a dominant Russian culture, it is still easier to be an atheist than either to be a religious Jew or to convert to Russian Orthodoxy. By and large, a nonreligious, atheistic, secular Jew is considered in the Russian consciousness to be "less Jewish" than a religious Jew.

In our 1996 in-house survey we found that more Russian Jewish immigrants (42%) believe that God exists, which is slightly higher than the percentages for both the general population in Moscow (Kliger and Carnes 1994) and for Jews in Moscow and St. Petersburg (Brym 1994), though significantly less than that for American Jews (AJC 1997).

In a 1990 survey, 22 percent of the Moscow respondents were sure that God exists, and 17 percent were sure that such a being does not exist (Kliger and de Vries 1993, 190). The attempted coup in 1991 in Russia resulted in a significant increase in positive attitudes toward religion in general. In 1990/1991, previously hidden and oppressed religious groups and institutions emerged; a euphoria of freedom first appeared; and the Soviet parliament passed the first law concerning freedom of conscience. Religion came back into fashion after seventy years of suppression.

Since 1993, however, this religious fervor has cooled. One reason is that the Russian Orthodox Church and its leaders were accused of collaboration and cooperation with the KGB (the former Soviet secret service). Another reason is that deteriorating living conditions and political situation forced people into a struggle for survival that, many felt, left no time for religion. As a result, Russians, Russian Jews, and Russian Jewish immigrants have expressed a confidence in God's existence, but this may reflect only their emotional and cultural attitude toward religion. A belief in

God's existence is just a philosophical concept that does not necessarily require a person to change his or her lifestyle. It is merely a statement with no social consequences and no obligations.

Believers

The second level refers to those who consider themselves believers. For Russians, "believer" is a deeper, richer term than "belief in God." When a Russian says he is a believer, he means that faith in God has a sacred significance and place in his heart and that he identifies himself as one of the "believers." Although the number of those persons who see themselves "rather believers than not" increased from 1992 to 1994, the rate of those who say they are definitely believers has remained steady and is within a range of 13 to 16 percent (but 20 percent among Jews in Russia). The statement that "I am a believer" entails certain obligations and commitments, which is why a much smaller number of Russians and Jews chose it.

Morality

The third level has to do with religion and morality. The belief that morality goes hand in hand with religion is deeply rooted in the Russian consciousness, literature, and philosophy. According to Dostoyevsky in *The Brothers Karamazov*, "If there is no God, everything is allowed and possible." The Bolsheviks reversed this idea, maintaining that a person can and should be moral without God, which is a concept still strongly held by post-Communist Russian youth: only 11 to 14 percent of the students say that only a believer can be a moral person. Likewise, Russian Jewish immigrants in New York City do not connect religion and morality very closely. Only 10 percent would completely trust "the word of a person with the same religion as me" (AJC 1999).

Religious Practice

On the fourth level are those who say that religion "plays a very important role" in their lives. Such a statement presumes that religion is their lifestyle and everyday practice. Only 4 percent of Jews in Moscow and St. Petersburg and 7 percent of Jewish immigrants in New York and Boston fall into this category.

When religion returned to fashion in Russia in 1991/1992, people did not see much difference between trust in God and religious practice. Although later they did realize that there was a difference, they had become accustomed to an easy religion without an everyday practice.

Conclusions

Most of the recent Jewish immigrants from the former Soviet Union in New York City identify themselves as Jews through ethnicity, memory, culture, literature, a common experience of persecution, and other socio-cultural components, but not through religion. While probably half of them express a belief in God, most do not see a strong connection between their own Jewishness and Judaic religious practices.

While considering themselves Jews, most immigrants from the European part of the former Soviet Union remain "Russians" in terms of cultural and behavioral norms, moral values, and even religious views. As ethnic Russians, they prefer the term *faith*, which implies the idea of a simple belief in God or an inward contemplation of God without necessarily any concomitant lifestyle.

The relationships between Russian Jewish immigrants and their American brothers and sisters are constantly changing. American Jews more often identify themselves along religious lines as a community, and Russian Jews identify themselves through ethnicity and Russian cultural lines. Whereas American Jews are profoundly American, Russian Jewish immigrants are intensely Russian.

NOTES

1. I express my deepest gratitude to Gloria Blumenthal for her discernment of the issues regarding Russian Jewish immigrants' identity that helped me clarify my vision and sharpen this chapter. I also thank Tony Carnes for ideas that he generously shared with me in numerous discussions for this chapter.

2. The numbers of Jews and non-Jews are very hard to estimate because of the various definitions of who is considered to be Jewish. In this chapter, a Jew is a person who has a Jewish mother, has converted to Judaism, or at least considers himself or herself to be Jewish.

3. Except for the "Jews for Jesus" conversion, which most of those converted do not consider as true conversion.

Chapter 11

Religious Diversity and Ethnicity among Latinos

Segundo S. Pantoja

Religion offers Latinos, especially immigrants, a distinct arena in which to forge and maintain their community and ethnic identities. Religion brings together people of diverse national origins and helps them take advantage of opportunities both inside and outside their churches to preserve their heritages. Accordingly, parishes and congregations use "Latino" and "Hispanic" as ecumenical terms to unite diverse nationality groups in worship (Stevens-Arroyo 1995), to share beliefs, rituals, and practices that build communities and comfortable overarching identities.[1]

On the Significance of Labels

The emergence of an identity that reflects the multiple national origins and experiences of the U.S. society of people called Hispanic or Latino is sinuous and conflictive. When asked their race by the 1990 U.S. Census, slightly more than half of Hispanics answered "white"; 40 percent answered "other"; 3 percent answered "black"; and 2 percent said "Asian" (Kosmin and Keysar 1992, 9). The embrace of otherness indicates that many Hispanics feel uncomfortable about being officially framed within the black-white polarity, and their acceptance of an overall identity under the categories "Hispanic" or "Latino" is moving at a slow pace (Oboler 1995).

All types of people commonly designated "Hispanic" prefer their specific national/ethnic identities to any pan-national identity (De la Garza et al. 1992). For instance, Dominicans may be Dominican when with their fellow Dominicans or other Spanish-speaking groups but identify themselves as Hispanic when they need to present a common front to outsiders. As Padilla (1985) revealed about relations between Chicanos and Puerto Ricans in Chicago, pragmatic politics guides the adoption and use of a common Latino identity.

Although Geoffrey Fox's *The Latino Nation* and Earl Shorris's *A Latino People* give the impression that this new identity has been accepted, this claim is premature. Although some signs may point in that direction, each group still clings to its national roots. Nonetheless, the two-thirds of Hispanics born in the United States often grow up in similar circumstances.[2] A look at concrete interactions in specific circumstances may reveal a common identity arising. At the same time, we may see that many of the same factors underlying the rise of a common identity also reaffirm allegiances to national origin and class divisions over any pan-ethnic solidarity.

Research Methods

This chapter uses data gathered over the years by my participant observation in the Hispanic community in New York City. In addition, in 1997, I conducted a survey and in-depth interviews. My sample consisted of 224 adults who answered a sixty-five-question instrument, and I interviewed eighteen of the respondents in depth. The respondents identified themselves as Dominicans (45%), Puerto Ricans (27%), Ecuadorians (7%), Colombians (6%), Mexicans (3%), and other nationalities (12%). Eighty-three percent of the respondents were female and 17 percent were male. Their ages ranged from twenty-two to seventy-one years.[3]

The Larger Context

The United States' and New York City's demographic landscapes are being transformed by Hispanics. The number of Hispanics in the United States has increased by more than 100 percent since the 1970s, so that today one-third of Hispanics are immigrants. About 40 percent are children under nineteen years of age, compared with 28 percent for the general population.

Previously a group composed primarily of Mexicans, Puerto Ricans, and Cubans, today Latinos encompass persons tracing their origins to all the nationalities of Latin America. The U.S. Census projects that from 29 million in 1997, they will reach 96 million in the next fifty years, then about 25 percent of the U.S. population. Some researchers predict that by 2050, only 53 percent of the U.S. population will be non-Hispanic white, down from 74 percent in 1996 (Preston 1996, 96).

According to the U.S. Bureau of the Census, in 1996 Hispanics represented 26.6 percent of the New York City population, making them the city's largest minority (Halfinger 1997). In the boroughs, the proportion of Hispanics ranges from 18 percent in Staten Island to 30 percent in Manhattan and 50 percent in the Bronx (Halfinger 1997, B2). Until the 1970s, the terms "Hispanic" and "Puerto Rican" in New York City were almost synonymous. Since then, other nationality groups have established themselves while Puerto Ricans have dispersed throughout the city, suburbia, nearby states, and Puerto Rico itself. The 1990 U.S. Census counted 896,763 Puerto Ricans out of 1,783,511 Latinos in New York City. While "Hispanics in the New York Region increased by 37 percent, or by 767,000 persons in the 1980–1990 period," Puerto Ricans contributed only 12 percent to the increase (Rodriguez et al. 1995, 2). Dominicans make up the second-largest Latino population in New York City, reaching 495,000 in 1997 and expected to top 700,000 early in the second millennium (Dugger 1998). In descending order of numbers, Dominicans are trailed by Colombians, Ecuadorians, Mexicans, and other nationalities.[4]

Puerto Ricans are still an obligatory point of reference for understanding the institutional, economic, political, and cultural environments of the other Spanish-speaking groups. Puerto Ricans mingle with all the other groups in the tenements, workplaces, ethnic-pride parades, and churches. Also, the Puerto Ricans and Dominicans in New York City have much influence over each other, despite their rivalry and citizenship-status differences.[5] Although Dominicans have a sizable presence in Washington Heights, they increasingly must share housing space with Boricuas (of Puerto Rican ancestry) in neighborhoods long known as "Puerto Rican," such as the Lower East Side in Manhattan, the South Bronx, East New York, and Sunset Park in Brooklyn. Dominicans, famous for their bodegas, bought many of them from retiring Puerto Ricans and Cubans, and in the process, they intermarried and went to houses of worship together (Fitzpatrick and Gurak 1975).[6]

Religious Affiliation: Catholics and Protestants

Religion is noticeably intertwined with Latino culture (Díaz-Stevens and Stevens-Arroyo 1997; Dolan and Hinojosa 1994) and informs their outlook and practices beyond the religious sphere. Moreover, women, who are the main bearers of Latino religious beliefs and practices (Díaz-Stevens 1993) also have the most influence on their children's academic achievement (Zambrana 1995).[7]

Among U.S. Latinos,

> 66% are Roman Catholic and 23% identify with other Christian groups, mainly Protestant denominations. A variety of other religions attract 4% of the Hispanics, while 6% have no religion. . . . Latino Protestant denominations include the various Baptist groups, accounting for 7.4 percent. . . . Pentecostals, Jehovah's Witnesses, and Methodists each account for about 2% of the Hispanic weighted sample. . . . Most of New York's Hispanic Protestants are Puerto Ricans. (Kosmin and Keysar 1992, 5, 10)[8]

Thus, the majority of Latinos still are Catholic, although a growing number are Protestant, especially Evangélicos (or evangelicals). The 1990 National Survey of Religious Identification confirmed this increase in the number of Latino Protestants reported by the General Social Survey (from 16 percent in the early 1970s to 23 percent in the early 1980s). As the rate of Catholic affiliation decreases, the rate of Protestantization grows (Greeley 1988, 1997). Nationally, Catholic affiliation in some groups such as the Puerto Ricans is as low as 60 percent. The highest estimate reaches only 80 percent in the case of immigrant Mexicans (De la Garza et al. 1992). My sample resembles that of the other surveys, with 71 percent indicating a Catholic affiliation. Conservative Protestants (26%) are mostly Seventh-Day Adventists and Pentecostals. Three percent indicate no religious affiliation. Latinos are thus diversifying their institutional allegiances, although their religiosity has deep common cultural roots strongly influenced by a centuries-long shared Catholic past.

The Latinos flocking to Protestant churches often are inactive Catholics. As converts, they are highly committed and have even higher rates of church attendance. In my study, 80 percent of Conservative Protestants reported attending church services once or twice a week, compared with 53 percent of the Catholics. Protestants (76%) more often say grace before meals than do Catholics (36%) and practice "prayer and Bible study" (84% of Protestants to 23% of Catholics).

Historical Continuities

Almost forty years ago, Poblete and O'Dea noted the rapid development of evangelical sects among Puerto Ricans, hypothesizing that

> the formation of sects is one of the known ways out of anomie, and the facts of Puerto Rican life in New York suggest the presence of such a condition among these new arrivals. The sect represents a search for a way out of that condition and is therefore an attempt to redevelop the community in the new urban situation. (1960, 29)

Today, other Spanish-speaking peoples seem to be doing the same. When facing a new and often hostile environment, a common response is to retreat to a church. Perhaps new arrivals to New York do not experience the same degree of anomie as those who came earlier, but they definitely seem to be seeking a sense of community in which religious organizations play an active role. The importance of the churches increases as the Latino family is weakened by its clash with prevailing American values, the need for two breadwinners per household, and the high rate of single-headed households living in poverty.[9]

In New York City, storefront churches, independent or associated like the Assemblies of God, are points of convergence for individuals and families from the many countries of the Caribbean and Central and South America. The evangelical churches that were in place in 1957, when Poblete and O'Dea did their fieldwork, have been joined by many more. Now, heterogeneity in the composition of their membership is the rule rather than the exception. In religious leadership, however, as in politics, the Puerto Ricans still predominate. But because religious leadership in evangelical, especially Pentecostal, churches, is less centralized in the formal structures, the newer groups are generating their own cadres, more often holding posts of higher rank in their churches than Hispanics do in the Catholic Church (Stevens-Arroyo 1995).

In areas where Dominicans predominate, many churches have been established in which the laity as well as the pastors are of the same nationality, even though people from other Latino countries are sprinkled throughout the congregation. The contrast between Catholics and Protestants in this area is obvious. Latinos constitute about 14 percent of U.S. Catholics—and in New York City they account for more than 50 percent—but they are still underrepresented in the clergy—4 percent, or 2,000 out of 52,000 priests. According to Sandoval, for instance, "in the

1990s, Hispanics had only a token number of bishops [20], compared to their proportion of the Catholic population; two hundred native-born Hispanic priests and only fifteen hundred foreign-born Hispanic priests" (Sandoval 1994, 133). In contrast, by 1991 just two of the evangelical branches in which Latinos are active, the Southern Baptist Convention and the Pentecostal denominations, boasted 2,400 and 4,200 Hispanic pastors, respectively (Tapia 1991, 19).

Protestant services are held in Spanish to meet the congregants' needs, even though services in English are more common in Puerto Rican congregations. Owing to a host of reasons, Puerto Ricans are the most bilingual of the Hispanic groups. English was the official language of instruction in Puerto Rico until 1948, and since then it has been on a de facto, if not always a legal, par with Spanish (Carrasquillo 1991; Urciuoli 1991; Zentella 1997). Also, Puerto Ricans have been established in New York since the nineteenth century. In time, though, the newer Hispanic groups also become bilingual, even coming to speak English only. Fifty-seven percent of the Puerto Rican respondents in my study were bilingual, compared with 44 percent of Dominicans and 21 percent of other Latinos. However, despite the rising numbers of bilinguals, respondents often say that they still prefer to attend services in Spanish (see Fitzpatrick 1987).[10]

Compared with Catholics, conservative Protestants have much higher rates of church attendance, as do those who prefer to speak Spanish at home.[11] For the respondents in my study, speaking primarily English or both languages equally at home has an inverse relationship to the rate of church attendance. But as the frequency of church attendance rises, so does the proportion of those who mainly speak Spanish. In addition, intergenerational studies on Latino religious behavior show that church attendance and other indicators of religiosity consistently decrease from the first to the third generation (Cadena 1995).

Because churches offer more than spiritual nourishment, recent immigrants (those who speak mainly Spanish) go to church because they have no other institutional links and they need fellowship and social and psychological help. Evangélicos meet up to seven times a week for religious services and other church-related activities. The community that these people build revolves around common religious beliefs and practices that draw on a common Christian background. The instruments used are often a shared language and the referents provided by similar difficulties that everybody experiences—the aches of the body and the soul and the need of divine and fraternal help to overcome personal troubles. In general, Hispanic evangelicals' experience of the inner city gives substance to their widely shared perception that the U.S. society is besieged by intractable problems. This congruence between belief and reality provides the sociological backdrop for the apocalyptic worldview that many of them have adopted.

Many of the Protestant churches provide a supplement to this common framework rather than compete with the Catholic Church. So far, the Catholic Church has welcomed Spanish-speaking peoples by providing masses in Spanish and more Spanish-speaking priests and helping with their material concerns like housing, immigration, and job training. So, in addition to spiritual nourishment, Latinos find that both Catholic and Protestant churches offer social and cultural benefits as well.

Religion and culture mix to reveal and strengthen unifying threads. For instance, when the feast of Our Lady of Guadalupe was celebrated at Our Lady of Refuge Parish in 1998,[12] Mexicans decorated the church with flowers and balloons in the colors of Mexico's flag, replaced the regular church ensemble with a mariachi band, and treated everyone after the mass to Mexican dishes and dances. Their celebration was enjoyed by all the congregants, who were mostly Dominican and Puerto Rican. The other national-origin groups do the same with their respective patron saints. In this way, the congregants discover that despite their diversity, they all share certain characteristics and concerns that unify them as Hispanics.

Inner-city problems also facilitate a convergence of religious leaders. Recently, after centuries of bitterness and antagonism, New York Latino Protestant and Catholic leaders began a new cooperation emphasizing cultural and nationality similarities rather than denominational differences (Stevens-Arroyo 1995).

Commonalities of Hispanic Catholicism and Protestantism

The inroads made by non-Catholic groups among Latinos is an interesting phenomenon. Some scholars (Figueroa-Deck 1994; Greeley 1988, 1997) believe that Latinos are moving away from the Catholic church. Since there is some indication that those Latinos of low socioeconomic status lean toward conservative Protestantism, the persistence of social immobility among Latinos may mean that they will increasingly affiliate with the evangelical and Pentecostal churches.[13]

Given these developments, will Latinos' Protestantization constitute a real change in religious orientation from traditional beliefs and practices?

Notwithstanding the distinct Catholic and Protestant worldviews, at the root of most Latino Catholicism and Protestantism is a set of beliefs and practices that transcend their temporary organizational manifestations. Figueroa-Deck calls this foundation "the unanalyzed affinity" between popular religiosity and evangelicalism (1994, 421). Because most Hispanics subscribe to a Catholicism far from the rationalized version articulated by theologians and the official creed, they can easily cross over to evangelical forms of Protestantism. Latinos' faith is simple, "quite captivating and graphic, dramatic and emotive," Figueroa-Deck says. "Its main qualities are a concern for an immediate experience of God, a strong orientation toward the transcendent, an implicit belief in miracles, a practical orientation toward healing, and a tendency to personalize or individualize one's relationship with the divine" (Figueroa-Deck 1994, 422). This way of experiencing religion may also enable multiple allegiances to Santeria, Spiritism, and *curanderismo* in conjunction with the Catholic religion or to Catholicism alternating with Protestantism (Rev. Conde-Frazier, personal communication March 1997).

In my observations of churches in areas with a heavy concentration of Latinos, I have also found that Latinos' Catholicism has Pentecostal features that make their assemblies resemble large evangelical churches. Groups of charismatics assume styles of preaching, praising the Lord, and invoking the presence of the Holy Spirit that are closer to Pentecostal services than to the regular Catholic services. Many of these congregants direct their enthusiasm to those sections of the mass that allow for their active participation. In conversations, Catholic charismatics also express their commitment to the Catholic Church. Besides visiting the sick and evangelizing in people's homes, they also participate in parish activities with a social and political content, such as naturalization drives and rallies against abortion clinics and drug dealers in their neighborhood.

Relatively few mass-attending Catholics participate in this charismatic renewal, but they nonetheless are having an impact on the church. Some priests and other groups such as the Cursillistas (another set of hard-core members) perceive the charismatics as coming dangerously close to lowering their probability of remaining in the Catholic fold. An informant referred to them as "people who are more there [in the Pentecostal camp] than here."

Closely following official church directives, Cursillistas orient their spiritual reflections and practices to areas such as church devotions, family, and helping individuals Christianize their environment (Martin

1998). Because Cursillistas and charismatics have similar objectives, charismatics acknowledge the tension between them and the Cursillistas. Indeed, membership in these two movements normally does not overlap.

Others (priests as well as members of the church hierarchy) see charismatics as an invaluable parish resource, for their presence in the works of the church is visible. Thus, although charismatics emphasize conversion and the need to overcome personal sin in ways reminiscent of evangelicals, they also give practical evidence of their commitment to the Catholic Church.

Except for women outnumbering men, the composition of the charismatic group is a demographic cross section of the church. Lay leaders in Manhattan and the Bronx characterize regular Latino participants as having humble origins, mostly working class, and low educational levels. But these characteristics may not be as significant as they seem, given the low socioeconomic status of the majority of Hispanics.[14] The downward social mobility experienced by many Spanish-speaking immigrants means that even educated Latinos may turn to charismatic and evangelical religion for answers to their social dislocation and professional frustration. Furthermore, observers in the Dominican Republic say that the charismatic renewal is so widespread there that the movement has also reached the middle class.

Still, the middle sectors do not express *el calor* (the heat) characteristic of charismatic meetings among the lower social strata. At lower-class churches like Our Lady of Refuge in the Bronx and Our Lady Queen of Sorrows in Manhattan, the faithful are active during the whole service, singing, praising, and responding to the service leaders. The same exuberance is found throughout the poor neighborhoods and countryside of the Dominican Republic. Yet the behavior of the charismatics of middle-class/professional background does not seem to be in the same league as that of people from poorer backgrounds. With the service leader as the protagonist, people remain rather quiet and low key during the meetings, which resemble a regular mass rather than typical lower-class charismatic meetings. Although ethnographic observations point to a correlation between low socioeconomic status and revivalist religious manifestations among Latinos, we must be careful not to fall into an environmental fallacy. For the fact remains that the majority of Latino people share with evangelicals and charismatics a low socioeconomic status without exhibiting the same religious behavior.

Both Catholic charismatic and Protestant evangelical/charismatic religious orientations are organized in ways that allow emotional outpouring. They resemble each other in their intensity of participation (singing, praising, possession), opportunities for lay leadership of religious activities, and reliance on the Bible for reference and guidance. Charismatic prayer circles start by invoking the Holy Spirit and value highly the outward manifestations of the Spirit. Charismatics schedule healing sessions in and out of the church, during which interviewees say they have witnessed the healing of bodies and souls. The similarities of a common social class and culture relativize theological differences between Catholics and Protestants, for example, the question of the centrality of the Virgin Mary. These ways of feeling and expressing transcend particular, temporary forms of religious affiliation. Many go back and forth from one organizational form to another, with Catholics attending evangelical services during the week and mass on Sunday and evangelicals sometimes returning to the Catholic Church.

Conclusion

Religion forges and maintains community and ethnic identity, bringing various nationalities together to negotiate common grounds for preserving their culture and solving common problems. In the church, language, music, and traditional rituals are reenacted and affirmed. Here Latinos recognize one another and provide common values to the younger generations, who learn to share them under the same church roof. Is a pan-Latino identity is possible? So far, that identity is being enacted and appropriated by people as they themselves see and feel the need for it.

NOTES

1. The label "Hispanic" was created in 1978 by the Office of Management and Budget (OMB) for "a person of Mexican, Puerto Rican, Cuban, Central or South American or other Spanish culture or origin, regardless of race." More recently, "Latino" was proposed as "the best label to describe Hispanics since it preserves national origin of the referents as a significant characteristic, it is culturally and racially neutral, and may be the least objectionable of all possible labels" (Marín and Marín 1991, 22). In this chapter, the two terms are used interchangeably (De la Garza et al. 1992).

2. The contrast can be seen in the high percentage of recent immigrants in

the Northeast, especially in New York, compared with the Southwest. My dissertation sample was about 30 percent who were born on the United States mainland and 70 percent immigrants who had lived in the United States between one and forty-five years. Two-thirds had lived in the country for less than twenty years. This distribution coincides with the immigration flows ushered in by the Hart-Cellar Act of 1965.

3. A survey was administered to approximately two thousand Hispanic parents with children enrolled in Catholic, Lutheran, Adventist, and public schools in the Bronx, Queens, Brooklyn, and Manhattan. The instruments were written in both Spanish and English. The sample of parents was obtained in two ways: (1) with the help of school administrators (religious and public), schoolchildren took home the questionnaire and asked their parents to fill it out; and (2) with the assistance of Protestant religious leaders, the questionnaire was distributed to church members who have children in school. Both groups of parents were asked to respond and mail the questionnaire back to the researcher in the supplied self-addressed stamped envelope. The second procedure was used to reach a sufficient number of conservative Protestants who, given their smaller number, would have been difficult to sample through the schools only. All the respondents were asked to mark their willingness to have an in-depth interviews, and about 30 percent agreed.

4. Latinos tend to be homogeneous regarding occupation and income. For instance, a survey by the Gallup organization showed that two-thirds of Latinos reported family incomes under $20,000 a year (D'Antonio et al. 1996, 151). In 1987, "25.8% of Hispanic families had incomes below the poverty line, compared with 11% for the population as a whole" (Marín and Marín 1991, 6). Speaking of Dominicans in New York, Torres and Bonilla reported that "in 20 years (1965–1985) the community has traversed a path toward relative deprivation similar to that lived by Puerto Ricans" (1993, 104). There are, of course, some Latino millionaires, but they are few. Recently, the *Hispanic Business* magazine listed the fifty top Latino millionaires, half of whom are Cubans (March 1997, 18–28).

5. Although politicians care about registered voters, most non-Puerto Rican Hispanics are not registered because they are underage, noncitizens, illegal, or apathic. Moreover, newer immigrant groups have an overriding concern with politics in their home countries. The political parties are, however, beginning to promote Latino politicians. Nationally, Hispanics are Democrats two to one over Republicans (Kosmin and Keysar 1992), and in the last presidential election, 70 percent voted for Clinton.

6. This pattern is not exclusive to Puerto Ricans and Dominicans. As they share more and more spaces and experiences, intermarriage among Latino groups will gain momentum. For instance, mixed couples of Colombians and Dominicans in Queens are becoming commonplace.

7. Women (88%) more often than men (77%) report that religion is very important to them (Cadena 1995, 40).

8. The United States' acquisition of Puerto Rico at the close of the nineteenth century opened the door to U.S. Protestantism as part of the effort to American-ize the island. One century later, the results are so visible that some say that Puerto Ricans on the island may soon be evenly split between Catholics and Protestants, especially the Pentecostals, who started their proselytizing in the sec-ond decade of the twentieth century. This Protestant success made the island into a religious laboratory for evangelizing the rest of the Americas, including the Puerto Ricans in New York City.

9. Coleman and Hoffer say that "religious groups are, of course, only one of the bases of functional community that cuts across generations, but, with the waning of other bases, it is one of the most important, perhaps the most impor-tant, that remains" (1987, 138).

10. The choice of English or Spanish depends on domains of interaction: "[The] use of Spanish was reported primarily in the domain of family, secondar-ily for the domains of friendships and religion, and least of all in those of educa-tion and employment, while the reverse held true for English" (Joshua Fishman, cited in Fitzpatrick 1987, 251).

11. Common cultural roots and the mass media facilitate interaction among members of this imagined community. There are two national Spanish-language TV networks, 233 full-time radio stations, and daily newspapers in several met-ropolitan areas such as New York City, which has *El Diario/La Prensa* and *El Mundo* (Subervi-Velez 1994). Music is another important contributor to a pan-Latino identity.

12. Located in the northwestern Bronx, this parish reflects the borough's changing demographics since the white flight of the 1970s. Presided over by its Irish American but Spanish-speaking pastor, the parish demonstrates the vi-brance that Latinos have injected into Roman Catholicism in New York.

13. Research conducted on non-Latino groups indicates that religion influ-ences educational achievement and attainment. Even after controlling for such variables as class, sex, age, and region of origin, conservative Protestants have consistently shown lower levels of attainment than do Catholics and mainline Protestants (Keysar and Kosmin 1995). In my dissertation sample of 224 Latinos, Catholics tended to cluster more in the brackets "some college" and "college," whereas the reverse was the case for conservative Protestants, who more often clustered in the "grade" and "some high school."

14. A common problem faced by the majority of Latinos is relatively low in-come (annual median family income of $25,000, versus $32,000 for whites; about 30 percent with incomes under the poverty line versus 13 percent for the general population. U.S. Bureau of the Census 1997).

Part IV

Ethnic Diversification

Chapter 12

The Changing Face of Seventh-Day Adventism in Metropolitan New York

Ronald Lawson

No other denomination in New York has a higher proportion of new immigrants than the Seventh-Day Adventists.[1] Over the past thirty years, the church has changed dramatically from a church of primarily Caucasians and African Americans to one that is now 90 percent immigrant. This chapter first explores the changes in metropolitan New York Adventism and then examines the competition to control leadership positions and resources as the racial/ethnic balance altered, asking why such conflict has been especially strong in Adventism.

Although New York may be unusual in having such high proportion of immigrant Adventists, its experience points to a trend. Extensive interviews with Adventist leaders reveal that the cities of Los Angeles, Toronto, Montreal, and Miami also have large immigrant majorities. In recent years, 75 percent of the new members added to the Adventist Church's North American Division (NAD), which includes both the United States and Canada, have been immigrants from developing countries.[2]

Background

Seventh-Day Adventism emerged from the Millerite movement after the "Great Disappointment" of October 22, 1844, when Christ failed to return as William Miller had predicted in his preaching in upstate New York. Adventists were initially so urgently apocalyptic that they thought they had no time to take their message abroad or to create a formal organization. Finally, however, in 1863 they created a centralized church structure and in the 1870s began to send out a stream of foreign missionaries. By the 1920s, the foreign membership total equaled that in North America.

The world membership, which stood at 66,547 in 1900, has had a growth rate averaging 67.9 percent per decade throughout this century, passing 3 million in 1978. A sharp increase in the growth rate starting in the early 1980s, when it rose to 91.4 percent during that decade, brought the membership to 6.6 million in 1990 and more than 9 million in 1996. The bulk of this growth took place in the developing world, where the Adventist membership increased by 995.9 percent between 1960 and 1995. The growth rate in the developed world lagged far behind at 122.9 percent during that same period. As a result, the proportion of the world membership located in North America plunged to only 9.5 percent by 1995.

As the wave of "new" immigrants to the United States gathered strength after 1965,[3] it was inevitable that Adventists would be among them. Indeed, the experience of such converts with upward mobility as a result of the opportunities afforded by Adventist educational institutions in their homelands only whetted their appetites for more opportunities (Lawson 1996c). This, together with the special ties that overseas Adventists felt to the United States because of their experience with American missionaries, meant that the Adventists were especially likely to migrate. Nowhere was this truer than among those mired in the weak economies of the islands of the Caribbean and the countries of Mexico, Colombia, and Guyana.

The Changing Face of Adventism in Metropolitan New York

The extent of this transformation in membership can seen most clearly when the figures for 1945 are used as a baseline, for in that year the Adventist Church in most of the United States was reorganized along racial lines.[4] Until the end of 1944, Adventism was organized geographically, subdividing the nation into local conferences. Although Adventism had grown steadily among African Americans, none of their pastors had been promoted to administrative positions. By the time of World War II, their demands for such opportunities had become so strong that church leaders chose in 1944 to defuse the discontent by creating separate conferences for African American churches which could then elect their own leaders.

TABLE 12.1

Racial/Ethnic Distribution of Seventh-Day Adventist Membership within the Two Conferences in Metropolitan New York, 1996

Race/Ethnicity	GNYC	%	NEC	%	Total	%
West Indians	3,816	28.1	12,306	58.9	16,122	46.8
Hispanics	5,804	42.8	719	3.4	6,523	18.9
Haitians	1,538	11.3	4,346	20.8	5,884	17.1
Afro-Americans	122	0.9	2,639	12.6	2,761	8.0
Caucasians	933	6.9	14	0.1	947	2.7
Africans	391	2.9	277	1.3	668	1.9
Black Central Americans	0	0	572	2.7	572	1.7
Koreans	430	3.2	0	0	430	1.2
Brazilians	232	1.7	1	0.0	233	0.7
Filipinos	146	1.1	24	0.1	170	0.5
Southern Asians	73	0.5	9	0.0	82	0.2
Chinese	75	0.6	0	0	75	0.2
Other	12	0.1	1	0.0	13	0.0
Total	13,572		20,908		34,480	

Until the reorganization, all Adventists in the New York metropolitan area fell under the Greater New York Conference (GNYC), which had 4,499 members at the end of 1944. When the new racially based structure was created at the beginning of 1945, the African American congregations were removed from GNYC and placed in the new Northeastern Conference (NEC), which then elected African American leaders. A total of 1,817 members were transferred from the GNYC to the new NEC,[5] leaving the GNYC with 2,682 members. At that time, the vast majority of GNYC were Caucasians, as the first Hispanic congregation was just organizing.

By the end of June 1996, the official membership of the GNYC in the metropolitan area had increased to 15,164, and that of the NEC, to 29,369. The combined membership stood at 44,533, almost ten times that of fifty-one years earlier. The membership of both conferences, and especially that of the NEC, is exaggerated, however, because missing members remain on the rolls.[6] After excluding them, my estimate of the real membership is 20,870 in the NEC and 13,683 in GNYC, for a total of 34,480 (see table 12.1).

Three Adventist immigrant groups have grown especially quickly, mostly from the Caribbean: English-speaking West Indians, Hispanics, and Haitians.[7] Indeed, Adventism in metropolitan New York has become an immigrant church, and the numbers of the two groups that were dominant in 1945—Caucasians and African Americans—have fallen dramatically. All the English-speaking "white" congregations are now very mixed racially, and only three of the fifty-six English-speaking congregations in the NEC, in which African Americans were previously dominant, now have African American majorities—and all three are small, with memberships of fewer than one hundred.

The Decline of Caucasian and African American Adventists

The decline of the two main "American" Adventist groups has been much more dramatic than the preceding discussion suggests, for earlier, between 1945 and 1970, both groups had grown substantially. Respondents estimate that there were 3,500 Caucasians in the GNYC in 1970 but that there are now fewer than 1,000. In the mid-1970s, the number of African Americans in the metropolitan region of the NEC equaled the number of English-speaking West Indians (interviews), but today they make up barely one-fifth the number of the conference.

Membership growth or decline depends on three factors: natural increase, gains through evangelism and migration, and how these compare with losses from apostasy, deaths, and losses through migration.

Losses

American Adventist youth are stampeding out of the church in New York City. Elsewhere, I have argued that the rate is approaching 75 percent of the youth who grow up as Adventists (Lawson 1996a). But New York has two special problems that exacerbate these losses. First, the network of Adventist colleges funnels many of the youth out of the metropolitan area, with the result that they often do not return. Second, none of the major Adventist institutions—colleges and hospitals—are located in New York (Lawson and Carden 1983). Consequently, Adventist youth have difficulty finding a congregation where they are satisfied intellectually and culturally and where they can talk about the issues on their minds without being regarded as "badventists."

Another source of losses is the "black and white flight"[8] as the ethnic makeup of their congregations has changed, making them feel less comfortable there. Adding to this tendency, the elderly of both groups often move south: retired Caucasians follow the trend to a warmer climate, and older blacks who came from the South choose to return "home" as racial tensions there have eased (interviews). The reverse flow of American Adventists to the New York region is much smaller than the outflow, partly because of an ingrained fear of cities created by church teachings[9] and partly because of the absence of a magnet drawing them there, like church-run institutions.

Furthermore, the number of deaths in both groups now exceeds the number of births because a majority of their members are older. Caucasian members of the NAD, especially New York Caucasians, are now disproportionately elderly, which means that they are no longer reproducing themselves, and the GNYC congregations have very few Caucasian children left. The pattern among Adventist African Americans in New York is similar (interviews). The birthrate of African American and Caucasian Adventists in New York has dropped partly because many of them have moved upward socially (higher social classes have fewer children) and especially because they have aged as a group, as many of their younger generation have left the church or the region.

Gains

Although additions to membership through migration or evangelism can make up for losses and improve the birthrate by adding younger families,[10] there are almost no conversions of Caucasians and African Americans in New York.

Adventists have traditionally used their institutions—schools and hospitals—as their chief means of evangelism. In the United States, however, their schools are now aimed at their own youth for retention rather than evangelism, and their hospitals are now so similar to others and the typical stay in hospital has become so short that they, too, have largely lost their evangelistic function. As their institutions have declined as a means of evangelism, Adventists have placed increasing emphasis on public evangelistic campaigns and seminars and on radio and TV programs.

Adventists have never established any major institutions in metropolitan New York; they have had only some elementary and secondary schools. They have therefore been forced to rely to a greater extent on public evangelism and the media, which received special emphasis in New York during the 1950s. In 1950 a New York City pastor launched *Faith for Today*, a TV program, which was quickly adopted by church headquarters as the official Adventist program. Meanwhile, a crusade in Carnegie Hall by an Adventist evangelist drew audiences as large as four thousand and spurred the purchase of an evangelistic center in Manhattan's theater district in 1956

(Schwarz 1979, 579–591). But these methods have not been as successful among African Americans and Caucasians in metropolitan New York in recent years (interviews).

Why has the Adventist outreach to Americans in the New York region proved to be so ineffective in recent years? African American and Caucasian New Yorkers are becoming more sophisticated, which makes them less responsive to the typically apocalyptic Adventist evangelistic message. New Yorkers are not likely to be drawn by advertisements of traditional Adventist topics and its campaigns in tents. Adventists have been even less successful in the suburbs of New York, and indeed, they have invested relatively little there, realizing that their traditional methods would not be popular.[11]

In part, the reason for this loss of members is that the leaders of the conferences in New York, especially of the GNYC, have often come from outside the region and therefore do not understand it. Moreover, the Caucasian pastors who have served in the city have tended to be of lower quality and have less education, and they are therefore less innovative. In fact, New York City is widely regarded by white Adventist clergy as a place to avoid, since it is seen as a difficult location in which to make a reputation.

The conferences based in metropolitan New York have tended to divert evangelistic resources from African Americans and Caucasians to immigrant groups, mostly because the immigrant pastors are more eager to propose crusades with higher expectations of success. According to church analysts and others interviewed, the most effective means of bringing people to evangelistic meetings is through personal contact; that is, very few attend as a result of impersonal advertising. As Caucasian and African American Adventists have advanced socially, they have often lost touch with the poorer, less educated members of their ethnic groups, who are the ones most likely to respond to the Adventist message, and they are embarrassed by the prospect of attempting to evangelize their better-heeled peers. Some respondents even referred to "the cringe factor:" their fear that peers would react negatively to a presentation aimed at a socially lower-class audience.

Adventist leaders say that African American and Caucasian non-Adventists are highly unlikely to be attracted to evangelistic meetings at which the speaker is from another racial or ethnic group. I have heard several accounts of crusades run by Caucasian or African American evangelists in neighborhoods populated primarily by Americans, to which the Americans present failed to return after the initial meeting because most of the participants were immigrants. Consequently, all those eventually baptized were immigrants. West Indians, however, flock to hear both African American and Caucasian evangelists and feel comfortable in mixed English-speaking churches with either African Americans or Caucasians.

In New York City, the number of Adventists is relatively small and unknown because Adventist congregations are not community churches involved in local issues. Their pastors are moved from congregation to congregation too frequently to allow them to establish a presence in the community, and in metropolitan New York, they rarely live near their churches. Almost all the pastors, regarding themselves as professionals and preferring houses to apartments, have chosen to live in the suburbs. Most of the laity also commute to church, often passing near several other Adventist churches closer to their home en route to their congregations.[12] Consequently, Adventists lack a local presence to attract more members, and their evangelism typically hides the fact that it is Adventist.

Black Adventist churches lost an opportunity to gain visibility when they decided not to join the civil rights struggle. Moreover, unlike many black churches of other denominations, black Adventist churches are not regarded as bulwarks of their communities, and Adventism is not seen as a "black denomination." The churches have thus become even less of a presence, since they are filled with immigrants with alien music and preaching styles.

Typically, both Caucasians and African Americans are reluctant to throw in their lot with mixed congregations. For example, when the Manhattan evangelistic center was sold in the late 1970s, the racially mixed congregation that had been meeting in its auditorium bought a former synagogue in a prosperous section of Manhattan's Upper West Side, hoping thereby to create a strong Caucasian bulwark. However, this segment of its members shrank in the face of increasing numbers of West Indian members from outside the neighborhood. Likewise, when introduced to a West Indian–dominated congregation, African Americans are likely to feel that the West Indians are insufficiently sensitive to their history and struggle and are not even eager to celebrate Black History Month (interviews).

The Growth of Immigrant Groups

Even though Adventism has become an immigrant church in metropolitan New York, it has not drawn equally from all immigrant groups. Three groups in particular—English-speaking West Indians, Hispanics, and Haitians—together now make up almost 83 percent of the total Adventist membership in metropolitan New York City.

Seven factors affect the groups' growth patterns. First, immigrants from those places where Adventist churches are numerous and considered a "standard brand" feel comfortable and seek out Adventist churches.

Second, since Adventism is already strong in the Caribbean, it is not surprising that church members are among those who immigrate to New York. Moreover, Adventists are more inclined to immigrate to America because the church encourages their upward mobility. Caribbean Adventists also feel close ties to the land that sent them their missionaries.

Third, the Adventist Church in New York and especially the members of each ethnic group welcome and help their fellow immigrant Adventists. Although the Adventist Church in New York does not have a comprehensive program to reach out to Adventist immigrants as they arrive, church-related kin and friendship networks help them establish ties to American Adventism. Once immigrants get in touch with an Adventist Church, the social group then usually cements the contact (interviews).

Fourth, the Adventist Church evangelizes new immigrants who are not Adventists. The conferences have increased the resources for the immigrant churches for this purpose. Since new immigrants' networks are shaken just as they face culture shock and alienation in a new society, they are more open to proselytization (Stark and Iannaccone 1993, 257). When they were well acquainted with Adventism "back home," they are likely to view Adventism here more favorably than do Americans, for whom Adventism is usually a peculiar sect. Hispanic and Haitian immigrants are also drawn to Adventism because their crusades are in their neighborhoods and their church services are in their languages. These immigrants also appreciate the close church community of Adventists from their homeland, with members meeting all day on the Sabbath and almost every other day.

Those interviewed agreed that while growth was initially primarily through the immigration of members, evangelism later became an important factor, with the result that the membership among the three numerically predominant immigrant groups is now drawn in approximately equal numbers from the immigration of Adventists and the evangelization of nonmember newcomers.

A fifth factor is fertility. Immigrants tend to be young and to have more children than is typical in America. For example, Hernandez found that 76 percent of the adult Hispanic members in the NAD were forty-one years old or younger (1995, 31).

Sixth, losses alter growth rates. Many children end up leaving the church, so cultural tensions between generations are often high. For example, several pastors told of mediations with the police after the children of immigrants—who had learned from their peers that corporal punishment is illegal and, in New York, is considered to be child abuse—had called the emergency police number after being beaten by their parents, who, in turn, had been taught "back home" that the Bible endorses corporal punishment.

For Hispanics and Haitians, these problems are exacerbated by the language differences between the generations, as the young people are often much more comfortable speaking English. Yet the church has made little attempt to conduct worship services that youth can easily understand. The churches have rationalized that services in their own languages are necessary if they are to attract non-Adventist immigrants. In the last year, however, three Hispanic congregations, finally worrying about losing their offspring, have begun conducting monthly bilingual services for youth. These experiments have been difficult to continue, though, because of the small number of English-speaking Hispanic preachers available (interviews).

The retention of West Indian youth, however, seems to be higher than among Hispanics and Haitians because of the absence of a language problem between generations (interviews), and this may also be a key to the greater growth rate of West Indians.

Seventh, the evangelization of second-generation immigrants may sustain growth. But Adventists have had very little success in this, because the second-generation immigrants have become inaccessible to them for many of the same reasons that Caucasians and African Americans are inaccessible. They have become Americanized and now see the Adventist message as irrelevant. They also have usually established their own strong networks and do not need the Adventist network any longer. In addition, second-generation Hispanics and Haitians rarely speak well the language used in the churches. The Adventists' failure to reach second-generation immigrants shows that church growth rates depend on the flow of immigrants.

The Impact of Racial/Ethnic Diversity on the Adventist Polity

What has been the impact of racial/ethnic diversity on the polity of Adventism in metropolitan New York? The experiences of the two conferences have differed from each other because their racial/ethnic profiles, and therefore the balance of the competing racial/ethnic groups, differ (see table 12.1).

The Northeastern Conference: West Indians Ascendant

The Northeastern Conference has had a clear and increasing West Indian majority for nearly two decades. During this time, it has faced two centers of conflict. As the West Indians gained a majority in the congregations, the competition for leadership positions left a bitterness among the displaced African Americans. The result was "divisiveness and suspicion . . . strife and ill-will." When the West Indians finally gained a majority, they had "almost total control," as the African Americans had had before them (Ashmeade 1991, 16–17, 19).

A West Indian pastor's appeal for the two groups to work together generated a storm, which included the publication of a "critical" review of his book by an African American pastor, who angrily accused the West Indians of organizing to gain power and of neglecting evangelism among African Americans (Creech 1991, 3–5). The tension and conflict were most prominent during the period in which the West Indians were gaining power. It is much less obvious now, however, since the transition has been completed in most congregations. Some congregations that still have a significant minority of African American members have been careful to continue to elect some of them to important positions in order to foster ethnic harmony.

Despite the rapid growth of its West Indian membership to majorities in many congregations, the conference administration has been very slow to employ West Indian pastors. The situation in New York was resolved through the pressure of competition between the conferences. The tension over the paucity of West Indian pastors gave the "white" conference, the GNYC, an opportunity to expand into West Indian communities at a time when it felt its survival was threatened by the decline of its Caucasian membership. Since Adventist West Indians were not used to organizational segregation and did not share the African Americans' bitterness toward Caucasians, a minority of them had already joined GNYC congregations. Realizing that the growth of this community was possible, the GNYC hired West Indian pastors who had migrated in the hope of finding a position in the United States.

This process began tentatively, with one such pastor. When he was successful in attracting Adventist West Indians and in evangelizing others, the conference added more until reaching the current twenty-two. The success of this strategy and its competitive threat forced the NEC to follow suit (interviews). But the West Indian pastors inevitably remained a small minority in the NEC for a considerable time. Their numbers were bolstered, however, when some unemployed immigrant pastors proved themselves by engaging in self-sponsored evangelism and then offering the congregations they had raised up—and themselves—to the conference.

Once the West Indians had achieved a majority of the NEC membership, they found it difficult to achieve the next step, political dominance. One particular African American was well entrenched and could count on support from a cadre of African American pastors. He also had no compunctions about punishing anyone who opposed him. Because the West Indians were reluctant to risk retaliation by trying to replace him, they contented themselves with gradually obtaining some of the lesser positions. By 1982, although they held the positions of both secretary and treasurer of the conference, they still felt neglected by the president (interviews).

The West Indians' political frustration peaked when the NEC's long-term president was succeeded in 1985 by another African American, who was well organized and was supported by visiting Adventist African American luminaries urging his election. The luminaries argued that the conference had been created in order to give African Americans leadership opportunities, so that the position "rightly" belonged to one of them. The campaign also made good use of the West Indian fear of being viewed as "pushy." But this president held office for only one term. He was defeated in 1988 after his insensitive remarks galvanized the opposition, allowing him to be labeled anti–West Indian (interviews).

Although African Americans subsequently felt that they would never again see one of their own elected as president (interviews), the West Indian president's attempt at a fourth three-year term in 1997 was challenged by an African American department director.[13] After the challenger lost, the president then punished those pastors who had supported his rival, by relocating them to much smaller churches far from their homes (interviews).

The Haitians, who in fact make up the second-largest group in the NEC—considerably larger now than the African Americans in the metropolitan area—felt so left out politically that a group of them switched to the GNYC. Haitians have pressed recently for the formation of their own conference.

The Greater New York Conference

The even more diverse Greater New York Conference has faced less overt conflict at the congregational level. In part the reason is that its non-English-speaking segment is larger and such congregations are usually formed as new groups, rather than competing for control of existing structures. When English-speaking West Indians moved into some Caucasian congregations, they were usually welcomed because the latter were already in decline and perhaps having difficulty keeping up with mortgage payments. As the proportion of West Indians in these congregations grew, they took control fairly easily, as those Caucasians who resented the changes usually chose to leave individually rather than fight and the others worked together fairly comfortably with the newcomers.

There was a major conflict in only one congregation, the oldest in Brooklyn, which had originally been mostly Scandinavian in membership but had then, as the neighborhoods changed over the years, become predominantly Italian. When an influx of West Indians eventually resulted in a transfer of leadership, a large segment of the Caucasian minority broke away and formed a new congregation, which has since itself become very diverse.

The GNYC's racial/ethnic diversity has created much tension in conference politics, however. Because the GNYC has no majority group, the Hispanics and West Indians, which have become its two largest segments, have increasingly vied with each other for power and influence as they have grown, while the declining number of Caucasians, who have always regarded the conference as their own, have sought to hold onto power. Caucasians retained the presidency by playing off the two largest groups against each other. The NAD leaders, in turn, saw the retention of a Caucasian president as the best way to avoid civil war in the conference and as essential to Adventism to have any chance of again reaching out to white New Yorkers.

The Hispanic Ministers' Association, formed in the late 1970s, fought for more independence within the conference under the leadership of their elected "Spanish coordinator." In an attempt to placate their demands, a Dominican was appointed secretary-treasurer of the conference in 1980. When he was called to a position higher in the hierarchy in 1988, a Puerto Rican was elected as secretary, which seemed to cement the understanding that that position now belonged to the Hispanics. A Caucasian was chosen as treasurer.

Feeling left out of the decision-making loop, the West Indians organized during the 1980s to gain representation at the conference level. They formed the Black Ministerial Association in 1990, which mobilized the laity behind them for the constituency meeting scheduled for 1991.

The growth of the immigrant groups in the GNYC escalated under the presidency of a multilingual Caucasian (1980–1994) who, as a former missionary, was strongly committed to evangelism. When immigrants were first brought into positions in the conference under his leadership, he gave no indication that he saw either Hispanics or West Indians as future leaders of the conference. Indeed, he was greatly threatened when it became clear, as the 1991 constituency meeting approached, that the Hispanic secretary was planning to challenge him for the presidency.

Consequently, the regional meeting in 1991 was tense and unruly. But neither immigrant group felt ready to pursue the presidency, with the result that the would-be challenge to the president from the secretary failed. With Caucasians holding the positions of both president and treasurer and knowing that this would be the president's final term, competition between Hispanics and West Indians focused on winning the position of secretary. But once he had been reelected, the president prevented his Hispanic challenger from being reelected to his position, in favor of a West Indian. The Hispanic delegates, feeling betrayed, refused to support the nominee. The session became so deadlocked that it was adjourned twice, first for thirty days and then for six months. In the end, the Caucasians, West Indians, and Hispanics got one officer's position each.

In the months preceding the 1994 presidential election, rumors circulated that West Indians were preparing to run for the post. These rumors led to the formation of a Hispanic-Caucasian coalition designed to prevent such an outcome, an effort that was abetted by the national leadership. The Hispanics decided that the ideal candidate would be another bilingual Caucasian who spoke Spanish. However, the new president quickly alienated both groups responsible for his election and created deep tensions between them. He earned the enmity of the Hispanics by altering the formula for dividing funds for evangelism, which had previously favored them. He also removed some of the privileges the Spanish coordinator had previously enjoyed and supported a Caucasian attempt to get rid of the ethnic coordinators. After a bitter struggle, the attempt was defeated. The result rebounded to institutionalizing in the bylaws the status of the ethnic coordinators. The independence of the ethnic groups was also strengthened when the conference's geographic districts were replaced by subconferences based on race. Of course, this new system contributed to racial tensions because it forced the racial groups to compete directly with one another.[14]

The Caucasian pastors also felt shortchanged because their multiethnic congregations lacked political clout, owing to their low membership, even though they sent larger per capita contributions to the conference.[15] They also resented being forced into a leftover, politically weak, "multicultural" subconference.

Despite their victories, the Hispanic pastors remained dissatisfied as well, and they eventually persuaded the GNYC to approve a feasibility study of a plan to create a separate Hispanic conference. They held that this was needed because of their distinct language and their Latin American way of involving the membership much more heavily in church activities. They used the missiological principle that self-governing churches are also self-propagating to argue that a Hispanic conference would be able to focus better on the needs of the Spanish-speaking churches and to foster growth among Hispanics.[16] They also contended that the membership and tithe income of a Hispanic conference would be greater than that of the three existing conferences.[17] A major consideration was creating more administrative positions for their clergy. Some of the better-educated laity in their congregations were upwardly mobile, and the pastors did not want to be left behind.[18] While the Adventist system allows for little variation in salary level, it does define a move from congregational pastor into conference administration as an increase in power and prestige. Consequently, the creation of a separate conference for Hispanics would have the effect of making more room for upward mobility among their clergy.

Furthermore, all the pastors of the Hispanic churches who had been born, trained, and originally pastored in Latin countries and were thus accustomed to a stricter control by administrators claimed that they felt uncomfortable in a structure in which American pastors were independent. Some pastors, though, feared that the future presidents of a Hispanic conference could become dictators like many Latin political leaders.

The views of the majority of Hispanic pastors were also less likely to be shared by those Hispanic pastors (typically Puerto Rican) who had been born or educated on the U.S. mainland. These pastors were now usually stationed at formerly Caucasian English-speaking churches that were part of the "multicultural" group and were attracting increasing numbers of acculturated Hispanics who preferred to worship in English. As one combatant argued, "The very growth of the Latino church raises serious questions about the benefits of raced-based institutions as a major force for church growth" (Hernandez 1995, 50).

The church's higher administration reflexively opposes proposals for additional conferences because they would increase the number of administrative salaries required. Nevertheless, in 1996 the leaders of the Atlantic region were persuaded to appoint Hispanic and Haitian vice-presidents to undercut the protest. The Hispanic pastors saw this as an indication of their power and as proof that their plan would ultimately be realized. As the president of the GNYC struggled to juggle his difficult relations with the various ethnic groups, he adopted the practice of presenting different faces to different audiences. For example, he appeared to Hispanics as supportive of a separate Hispanic conference but then argued against the proposal when he was with other groups. This practice led to turmoil and deep divisions, and ultimately, he alienated all groups.

As the annual GNYC meeting in June 1997 approached, the president of the Hispanic Ministers' Association contacted his West Indian counterpart to create an alliance. The West Indian and Hispanic pastors met together for a communion service, thereby sealing the deal. They agreed to depose the incumbent Caucasian president, nominate their own candidates for the position, and give their joint support to whoever won. The final runoff was between a Hispanic and a West Indian. The Dominican won by two votes, apparently winning the votes of all Hispanics and Caucasians, but not those of the other ethnics and one or two defecting West Indians. The Caucasians were left out of the GNYC's leadership triumvirate for the first time.

The GNYC was the second conference in North America to elect a Hispanic president and the first to elect a foreign-born Hispanic.[19] Less than a month later, the neighboring New Jersey Conference also elected a Hispanic president, a Puerto Rican.[20] The political coup in the GNYC inevitably heightened the tensions among the various ethnic groups. The new president therefore announced that his first priority would be to try to create peace and harmony. But shortly after the election, every Caucasian working in the conference office left. Meanwhile, having had one of their number chosen as president of the GNYC, the Hispanic pastors now found themselves divided over whether they should secede into a separate Hispanic conference or consolidate their gains within the GNYC.

Across the Conferences

The GNYC, hard pressed by a decline of its traditional Caucasian base, trespassed into NEC ethnic "territory" to evangelize West Indians and later accepted a breakaway Haitian congregation, another "black" constituency. In retaliation, the NEC began evangelizing among Hispanics, and its African American pastors accused the West Indians in the "white conference" of being traitors. Today, the conferences continue to mistrust one another, being fully aware of the competition.

In the early 1980s, the president of the Atlantic region recommended that the GNYC merge with the NEC. But both Caucasian and West Indian GNYC pastors argued that the differing cultures of the two conferences made it difficult and unwise to try to meld them: the culture of the "black" conferences supported a much more authoritarian (personal and presidential) leadership than was common in the "white" conferences. The president's recommendation was dropped after it created an uproar of protest in the GNYC. Since that time, the membership of the conference has grown substantially—almost doubling since 1983—but the whole net growth is composed of new immigrants. In 1994, the national Adventist leadership took strong steps to prevent a West Indian from being elected president of the GNYC, for that would have meant that both the two conferences, which had been created to cater to the needs of different racial groups, would have West Indian presidents.

Conclusion

There are two reasons that Adventism in metropolitan New York has experienced greater internal turmoil than other denominations have as a result of the emerging immigrant majority.

First, the proportion of its members who are new immigrants is considerably greater than in any other denomination. Second, because it is centralized and hierarchical, local Adventism has experienced more tensions than it would have if its structure had been congregational. All the racial/ethnic groups have been thrown into a common political competition.[21]

During the last century or so, American Adventism has moved a considerable distance from sect toward denomination (Lawson 1996a). The demographic patterns and declines among Caucasian and African American members in the New York City area are similar to those of mainline denominations. It is the growth from immigration and evangelism among immigrants that continues to make American Adventism's overall demographic profile somewhat different from that of the mainline denominations. Given the American-born Adventists' declining birthrate and the exit of youths, the continued growth of American Adventism will remain dependent on the continued influx of immigrants.

NOTES

1. Some of the material in this chapter has appeared in two journal articles: "From American Church to Immigrant Church: The Changing Face of Seventh-Day Adventism in Metropolitan New York," *Sociology of Religion*, 59, 3 (Fall 1998); and "Internal Political Fallout from the Emergence of an Immigrant Majority: The Impact of the Transformation of the Face of Seventh-Day Adventism in Metropolitan New York," forthcoming, *Review of Religious Research*.

I wish to thank the National Endowment for the Humanities for two fellowships that gave me time to gather data; PSC-CUNY, which helped with travel funds; and the Louisville Institute for a fellowship that gave me time to analyze the data. Metropolitan New York is defined as New York City plus Nassau, Suffolk, Westchester, and Rockland Counties, the four suburban counties located in New York State.

2. This datum was derived from data supplied to me by Monte Sahlin, director of the North American Office of Church Information and Research.

3. The "new immigration" is used to refer to migration to the United States after the passage of the Hart-Cellar Immigration Act of 1965, which initiated a flow of immigrants that was much more ethnically diverse and less European than previously.

4. The research reported here is part of a large study of Seventh-Day Adventism, which has included well over three thousand in-depth interviews with church leaders and laypersons in fifty-five countries in all of the world church. Since I am an Adventist and have lived in Metropolitan New York for twenty-six years, I was well aware of both the demographic changes taking place and the political tensions they created and ultimately decided that these were so dramatic and relevant to my general research theme that they warranted further study.

5. The NEC had a total of 2,228 members, for its territory extended to Boston and Buffalo; however, this chapter is limited to the New York metropolitan area.

6. This is a much more common occurrence today than it would have been fifty years ago.

7. Adventist children are usually baptized around the age of ten or twelve and only then are counted as members. I instructed the church clerks to count the

baptized youth in immigrant families as immigrants, even if they had been born in the United States.

8. For example, some African Americans have moved to churches in suburban New Jersey, where their proportion in the congregations remains higher.

9. Ellen White, an Adventist prophet, portrayed cities as irreligious and unhealthy, warned that they would become centers of persecution during the events that would culminate in the apocalypse, and advocated country living where Adventists could grow their own food.

10. Very few gains are through intermarriage.

11. Tent meetings can still draw an audience of African Americans in the American South.

12. American Adventism has become very diverse, so that its congregations vary not only in racial/ethnic composition but also in style of worship, degree of theological conservatism or openness, social class, and the like.

13. In 1996, the whole conference—which extends beyond metropolitan New York to additional concentrations in such cities as Buffalo, Boston, and Hartford—had fifty African American, thirty West Indian, nineteen Hispanic, and thirteen Haitian pastors (interview).

14. When a similar structural change was introduced recently in the conference centered in Los Angeles, it had the effect there, as it did in New York, of splitting the conference along racial and ethnic lines, especially among the pastors, rather than paying more attention to the congregations (Henson 1997, 21).

15. While their congregations, including seven outside the metropolitan area, sent $3.2 million to the conference in 1995, the Hispanic churches sent $3.8 million, and the West Indian churches, $2.8 million. However, the five Korean congregations, which together submitted $0.6 million, had the highest per capita tithe—$1,422 compared with $935 for the multiethnic congregations, $648 for the Hispanics, $596 for the West Indians, and $228 for the Haitians. (Per capita giving is based on the official membership figures, which include missing members.)

16. The fact that there had been rapid growth among African American Adventists in the United States after they had formed self-governing conferences in 1945 suggested that the principle was effective when applied to the Adventist context.

17. The Atlantic Union consists of New York, New England, and Bermuda. It is subdivided into six conferences.

18. This was so even though most of them had no more than a bachelor's degree and collectively their educational levels were considerably lower than those of the West Indians, who had taken every opportunity to earn higher degrees since their arrival in the United States.

19. From 1991 until 1996, a Mexican American served as president of the Texico conference, which is made up of New Mexico and the Texas Panhandle.

20. Although the president of the Atlantic Union is now African American, both its secretary and the president of Atlantic Union College are West Indians.

21. This is so despite the limits on democracy provided by Adventism's system of "representative government" and the power exercised by its nominating committees, whose membership and deliberations are often manipulated by members of the hierarchy.

Chapter 13

Mormons in New York City

James W. Lucas

This day I have been walking through the most splendid part of the City of New York. The buildings are truly great and wonderful to the astonishment of every beholder and the language of my heart is like this: can the great God, . . . maker of all things . . . splendid be displeased with man for all these great inventions sought out by them? My answer is no, . . . seeing these works are calculated to make men comfortable, wise, and happy.[1]

—Joseph Smith Jr. to his wife, October 13, 1832

Like Joseph Smith, the itinerant laborer from upstate New York who was the first prophet-president of their church, most Mormons in New York City have been transients.

Despite this transience, the number of Mormons in New York City, although still minuscule in relation to the entire population of the city, has grown dramatically in recent years, increasing from 6,500 in 1990 to 17,000 at the end of 1998. This chapter describes these New York City Mormons and discusses some of the issues they confront at the beginning of the twenty-first century.

I use the term "Latter-Day Saint" and its abbreviation "LDS" instead of "Mormon" in deference to the preferred usage of the predominant successor to the church established by Smith in 1830, the Church of Jesus Christ of Latter-Day Saints headquartered in Salt Lake City, Utah.

LDS Church Life

The principal salient characteristic in understanding LDS church life is that there is no clergy. In a church with more than 10 million members, fewer than a hundred men in senior positions are paid for doing what clergymen do, and they all come from lay backgrounds. There are neither seminaries nor career paths toward becoming an LDS clergy. There are not even informal means of remuneration. In describing the LDS Church, therefore, the traditional clergy/laity distinction is basically irrelevant.

This does not mean, however, that the LDS Church is anarchic or democratic. A well-established priesthood hierarchy is in place, headed by a council of twelve apostles and a prophet-president who is deemed not only the successor of Joseph Smith but of St. Peter as well. Indeed, while LDS liturgy reflects the low church Protestant origins of most early Latter-Day Saints, organizationally it is more like Catholicism. Local congregations are organized into diocese-like regional groupings called *stakes* or *districts*, with a clear chain of command leading to the prophet-president. Even the priesthood is restricted to men. But the analogy to Catholicism ends with the fact that all LDS males aged twelve and older are expected to accept ordination in the priesthood.

Without any professional staff, the LDS congregation depends entirely on unpaid, volunteer labor. The congregation functions by breaking its work into numerous part-time assignments called *callings*. Every member is expected to accept at least one calling. In order for there to be callings for everyone, large congregations are divided into new, smaller congregations, even if they must continue to use the same church building. Some of these positions, such as teaching Sunday school, would be common in almost any denomination. Others involve more peculiarly LDS concerns, such as helping members of the congregation prepare family histories so that their ancestors can receive LDS baptism by proxy.

There is no formal instruction for any calling; all training is "on the job." Callings also frequently rotate. Congregational and stake leaders are subject to formal term limits, with the maximum term for the head of a congregation being five years. The highly participatory nature of the LDS congregation is so central to LDS church life that the term used for a Latter-Day Saint in full fellowship is not "practicing" but, rather, "active."

The rotating and nonprofessional nature of LDS church life is perhaps best illustrated in the pulpit. Each Sunday, several different members of the congregation, including women, preach. Every member of

Figure 13.1. Because there is no professional clergy, all members of Mormon congregations are expected to preach and fill other roles. Here an eleven-year-old girl speaks at the principal worship service of a Spanish-language congregation in Manhattan. Courtesy of the collection of James W. Lucas. Photo credit: Jon Moe.

the congregation, no matter how shy or uneducated, is encouraged to take a turn at the pulpit (figure 13.1). It is thought ideal if all members have the same number of turns. For those who have more to say than their turns at preaching allow, at least once a month the pulpit at the principal Sunday service is open to anyone.

Although the priesthood is restricted to men, women can fill most callings and are expected to do so as much as men do. The paradox of a structure that outwardly appears patriarchal but that produces many strong, capable women is not lost on Latter-Day Saints. LDS folk belief explains the restriction of the priesthood to men by viewing women as naturally more spiritual, holding that men need the priesthood responsibilities to enable them to catch up with women. Not surprisingly, LDS feminists have extensively criticized the exclusion of women from the priesthood, but they cannot deny that women have many opportunities for service in the LDS congregation. Indeed, it is generally accepted, at least among rank-and-file Latter-Day Saints, that their all-volunteer congregations would collapse almost instantly without the extensive participation of women.

The final salient feature of LDS church life that is critical to understanding Latter-Day Saints in New York City is that congregations are normally established on a clearly defined geographical basis. Neighbors on opposite sides of a street can be assigned to different congregations but often may meet in the same church building. Congregations in areas such as New York City where the population of Latter-Day Saints is small can often encompass areas with widely varying socioeconomic and ethnic characteristics.

All members are expected to attend their geographically assigned congregation, regardless of whether they find it compatible. Although this aspect of LDS church organization is not often discussed, it is considered vital to the spiritual development of Latter-Day Saints. Members are expected to grapple with local problems rather than leaving for another congregation.

> In the life of the Church, [there] is constant encouragement, even pressure, to grapple with relationships, with other people's ideas and wishes, their feelings and failures, sometimes misinformed or prejudiced notions and to have to make some constructive response; to have leaders and occasionally to be hurt by their weakness and blindness, then to be made a leader and find that you, too, can be weak and blind and unrighteous. (England 1986, 32)

There are exceptions to the geographical definition of congregations. Some accommodate family status. For example, in Manhattan there are congregations for unmarried people and for families with teenagers. But the most significant exception is linguistic. A few months after his 1832 visit to New York City, Joseph Smith produced a new scripture that stated in part that "every man shall hear the fullness of the gospel in his own tongue, and in his own language."[2] The LDS Church and people expend vast resources to comply with this directive. The most visible aspect of this is a language-training program for the more than fifty thousand volunteer missionaries who serve for one to two years in unpaid ministries proselytizing the world for the LDS religion. Another manifestation is the creation of non-English-language congregations. This is of particular importance to a study of Latter-Day Saints in New York City, because more than half of all its LDS congregations are linguistic exceptions to the rule mandating exact geographical boundaries for congregations.

A last point of necessary background is to explain who the Latter-Day Saints are now. The LDS Church was founded in 1830 in upstate New York, and its original adherents were primarily New Englanders by background. By 1900, however, the large majority of Latter-Day Saints were not of American stock but, rather, were converts from Europe who had emigrated to the new LDS Zion in the western United States. These are the "Mormons" one reads about in the history books, who crossed the Great Plains, settled the West, and, most controversially, practiced polygyny until its official abolition in 1890.

Conversion rates declined in the first half of the twentieth century. By the 1950s, most Latter-Day Saints were several generations removed from the nineteenth-century convert pioneers. By that time, their dramatic history and geographical insularity had led them to become a "near-nation" (O'Dea 1957). This near-ethnic unity was enhanced by early policies that encouraged intermarriage among the various emigrant nationalities. Furthermore, the non-English-speaking emigrants were encouraged to learn English and to assimilate into American (or at least Mormon American) culture as rapidly as possible (Embry 1994, 120–121; Jensen 1987). The LDS membership refers to this group as "life" Latter-Day Saints, a term also used in this study.

In 1950, one would not have needed an identifying name for "life LDS" because they constituted substantially all of the Latter-Day Saints. At that time, 50 percent of all Latter-Day Saints lived in Utah, and most of the remainder lived in neighboring states. Beginning in the 1960s, though, and with increasing acceleration in the 1970s and 1980s, the composition of the Latter-Day Saints changed, because of its explosive growth outside the United States, particularly in Latin America. From 1970 to 1995, while the total membership of the LDS Church grew from 2.9 million to 9.3 million, the percentage of Latter-Day Saints in Latin America grew from 5 percent to 32 percent. Accordingly, statisticians at Brigham Young University project that by 2020, 70 percent of all Latter-Day Saints will be in Latin America (Heaton 1992). This growth parallels the rapid expansion of Protestantism in Latin America (Martin 1990). Sociologist Rodney Stark predicted that the LDS Church will emerge in the twenty-first century as the first new major world faith since Muhammad rode out of the desert (Stark 1984).

Latter-Day Saints in New York City

At the end of 1998, LDS Church records indicated that there were 17,000 Latter-Day Saints in New York City, a significant increase from the 6,500 reported in 1990 and the 3,200 reported in 1980.[3] In evaluating these sta-

TABLE 13.1
Numbers of Latter-Day Saints

Borough	Number of Members	Number of Congregations (number of Spanish in parentheses)
Bronx	2,400	6 (4)
Brooklyn	5,100	12 (5)
Manhattan	3,400	9 (2)
Queens	5,400	17 (8)
Staten Island	700	2 (1)

tistics, we must take into account how the LDS Church counts its members. In this, it again resembles the Catholic Church more than the Protestant churches because it counts as members all who have been baptized, regardless of whether they are currently practicing. Since congregational membership is determined by place of residence rather than participation, it is not uncommon for an LDS congregation to show hundreds of members on its records and yet struggle to have fifty to one hundred actually attending services.

The statistics that would give a clearer idea of the actual rates of participation are confidential, but observational and anecdotal evidence leads to the conclusion that 50 percent is the highest reasonable estimate for rates of actual participation, with many congregations significantly lower than that. Another general observation is that the rates of actual participation are inversely proportional to the number of converts in a congregation. The low rates of convert retention and undesirable levels of *inactivity* (as opposed to being *active*, or fully participating) have recently led the LDS Church's senior hierarchy to launch a major effort to retain more converts and to regain the participation of inactive members. Since I was unable to obtain reliable information for estimating more precisely the rates of participation, this study must rely on statistics of record membership as the best available approximation for learning about New Yorkers in the LDS Church.

At the end of 1998, New York City contained forty-six LDS congregations, including twenty-one Spanish-speaking, two using American Sign Language, and one each operating in Chinese and Korean. Table 13.1 shows the distribution by boroughs.

In an interesting parallel to the international shift in LDS Church membership in the same time period, from 1980 to 1998, the proportion of Latter-Day Saints in Manhattan declined from 38 percent to 20 percent, with

TABLE 13.2

Percentages of Latter-Day Saints According to Race/Ethnicity

Borough	White		Black		Hispanic		Asian	
	LDS	General	LDS	General	LDS	General	LDS	General
Bronx	14	22.6	29	30.7	57	43.5	—	2.6
Brooklyn	18	40.1	28	34.7	51	20.1	3	4.6
Manhattan	50	48.9	12	17.6	36	26	2	7.1
Queens	14	48	13	20	66	19.5	5	11.8
Staten Island	62	80	—	7.4	38	8	—	4.3

the "outer" boroughs, principally Brooklyn and Queens, rising by the same proportion.

The LDS Church does not record racial or ethnic data on its membership. Therefore, estimations of the ethnic distribution of Latter-Day Saints in New York City must rely on recorded membership data for non-English-language congregations and approximations obtained by observation and interviews. Using the U.S. Census categories, my best estimates are that LDS New Yorkers are 50 percent Hispanic, 25 percent non-Hispanic white, 20 percent non-Hispanic black, and 5 percent Asian and other. Table 13.2 gives the percentage distributions of these racial and ethnic groups by borough for the Latter-Day Saints and for the general population.[4]

Clearly, in all boroughs, LDS New Yorkers are significantly more often Hispanic than is the general population. There are also many Spanish-language LDS congregations in areas adjacent to New York City, so it is likely that Latter-Day Saints are also disproportionately Hispanic in Westchester, Nassau, and Suffolk Counties in New York and in the urban counties of northern New Jersey. I could not obtain precise information about the origins of these Latino Latter-Day Saints, but the interviewees generally agreed that most of the Spanish-language congregations included members from many different Latin American nations, without any one nationality dominating. The largest group appears to be Dominicans, particularly in Manhattan and the Bronx, followed by Mexicans in Brooklyn. It was not clear, though, whether these figures reflect anything more than the concentrations of those nationalities in the neighborhoods covered by those congregations. For example, a survey of women in one Spanish-language congregation in an area with a large Dominican concentration found that 40 percent of the women were Dominican, although eleven other Latin American nations were also represented in the group.

Another significant characteristic of Hispanic Latter-Day Saints in New York City is that a significant number of them were already members of the LDS Church when they came to the United States. Interviewees' estimates range from 20 to 70 percent. In the survey referred to in the preceding paragraph, one-third of the women had become Latter-Day Saints in their home countries. This phenomenon is worth noting because it appears that these emigrant Latter-Day Saints tend to have experience in filling callings in their home countries and thus help reinforce New York City congregations. One interviewee noted that of the senior leaders in his regional district, all those who had been missionaries had gone to their home countries.

Despite the presence of these emigrant members, a majority of most New York City LDS congregations, both English language and Spanish language, are fairly recent converts. In fact, all the members of some congregations have been Latter-Day Saints for less than five years.

It appears that a majority of the black Latter-Day Saints in New York City also are emigrants. Most of them are from the West Indies, with a number from various African nations as well. In fact, if I had more precise nation-of-origin data on New York Latter-Day Saints and combined all the Dominicans, Puerto Ricans, and Cubans from the Spanish-language congregations with the Jamaicans, Haitians, and other West Indians in the English-language congregations, I believe that we would find that as many LDS New Yorkers were Caribbean in origin as Hispanic in origin. Because extensive LDS proselytizing is newer in the West Indies and Africa, fewer LDS black immigrants were Latter-Day Saints before coming to the United States than is the case with Hispanics.

The opposite is the case for white Latter-Day Saints in New York City, where the largest distinct group is also composed of emigrants to New York City. These are life Latter-Day Saints who have moved to New York City primarily from the major LDS areas of the western United States. Although it is sometimes difficult to distinguish them from other American whites, I estimate that they comprise between 10 percent and 15 percent of all LDS New Yorkers, with the majority residing in Manhattan. This group is significant because with their more extensive experience in filling callings, they tend to occupy a proportion of leadership positions that is larger than their representation among the general LDS membership in New York City.

As with most Christian denominations, the majority of Latter-Day Saints in New York City are women. For example, in Manhattan 58 percent

of adult Latter-Day Saints are women, and 42 percent are men. More strik-
ing figures appear when one compares congregations in which the majority
of the members are converts with those in which the majority are life Latter-Day Saints. The ratio of women to men in the majority convert congregations is 64 percent to 36 percent, whereas it is only 54 percent to 46 percent in the majority life LDS congregations. Observations and interviewers
indicate that the congregations in the other boroughs, most of which are
majority convert, are also disproportionately female.

Numerical data also are not available regarding the family and household status of LDS New Yorkers. Again, both observations and interviewees agree that fewer than half of all Latter-Day Saints in New York City
reside in complete families in which both spouses are LDS. There are
probably as many or more who are single (both with and without children), with women married to non-LDS husbands accounting for the
balance. These proportions contrast with the larger LDS population in
the United States, which the 1990 National Survey of Religious Identification found, at 73 percent of all adults, to be the most married of all the
major religious groups in the United States (Kosmin and Lachman 1991).
Because LDS teaching and church life are very family centered, the presence of large numbers of singles and incomplete families can create organizational dissonance. Not having a large portion of all-LDS families also
deprives such congregations of the practical benefit that such family situations can offer for the household and time management that is necessary for both men and women to fulfill callings.

Economic data were also not readily available for LDS New Yorkers,
but several observations can be made with confidence. First, Latter-Day
Saints in New York City are almost as disparate in economic status as is
the New York City population as a whole, ranging from well-to-do Wall
Street professionals in Manhattan to undocumented immigrants working
in sweatshops in the Bronx. This disparity is probably accentuated by a
thinness in the middle. Civil servants and small-business owners are perhaps underrepresented among LDS New Yorkers.

Issues for the Latter-Day Saints in New York City

The LDS Church is making a substantial commitment of resources to establishing itself in New York City. It maintains at all times a presence of
more than two hundred volunteer full-time missionaries in the city. As of

the end of 1998, the church had built or bought and converted twelve church buildings, and another five were under construction. Most visibly, the church had purchased a large tract of land and was negotiating zoning clearances to build a temple in nearby White Plains, New York. (In LDS parlance, the term *temple* is applied to edifices used for special rituals to which access is limited to active Latter-Day Saints and are distinguished from the normal congregational meeting facilities that are accessible to the general public.)

Convert Retention

Almost all the interviewees perceived the most important issue to be managing the integration of new converts into LDS congregations. This issue concerns the LDS Church's senior hierarchy as well. Although Latter-Day Saints moving to New York City from elsewhere (be it Idaho or Ecuador) have almost tripled the number of LDS New Yorkers in ten years, most of that growth has been from new conversions. A survey conducted in 1997 in a well-established, older, Spanish-language congregation revealed that half of the respondents had become Latter-Day Saints only since 1990.

It is generally accepted in the LDS Church that the most important element in retaining new converts is their social integration into the congregation. For some people, this means considerably altering their social customs. For example, active Latter-Day Saints are expected to avoid tobacco, alcohol, coffee and even tea, recreational drugs, and extramarital sex. Paying tithes and devoting considerable time to serving in callings are further demands. Few have the fortitude to make these life changes without the support of a social network that facilitates and reinforces these norms of behavior. The LDS congregations in New York City have responded with varying degrees of success of supplying such a social network to new converts.

The most successful appear to be the larger Spanish-language congregations. Hispanic LDS leaders tend to ascribe this to the openness and friendliness of the Hispanic peoples and culture, but it would be worthwhile to study the specific dynamics of this process. In all cases, in both English and Spanish congregations, it appears to help materially if a critical mass of experienced, committed members is able and willing to expend the personal energy necessary to absorb new persons into the existing social network. Perhaps the key is for a social network to exist in the first place. Smaller congregations, including Spanish-language ones, appear to struggle more to hold onto their new converts.

Another aspect of the ability of Spanish-language congregations to absorb and retain new converts is a commonality of language and culture. Even if they acquire an adequate working knowledge of English, first-generation emigrants are never as comfortable in English as they are in Spanish. One could perhaps question the importance of commonality of culture, given the internal diversity of most of the Spanish-language LDS congregations. That is, there can be as many cultural differences between an Argentinian and a Dominican as between an English-speaking and a Spanish-speaking culture. Clearly, though, many similarities in the various Latin American cultures can be comforting to a new convert trying to adapt to a new church life and religious culture.

Interestingly, the next most successful congregations are those English-speaking congregations that are also the most diverse. Some English-language congregations in Queens are almost equally divided among various Asians, whites of both local New York and life LDS origin, Hispanics, and American and West Indian blacks. It seems that when no one ethnic group is dominant, the congregation can develop a culture-neutral ethos that facilitates the adoption of an LDS religious identity and lifestyle.

Smaller congregations of all types seem to be less successful at new convert integration, as are those that on the surface appear to be the strongest, usually the congregations in which the majority is life LDS. Although amply supplied with goodwill and experience and, in the younger generations predominating in New York City, free of prejudices, differences in ethnicity and socioeconomic class have made it very difficult for new converts to integrate socially into these congregations. Indeed, even middle-class white American converts can find it difficult to penetrate the cultural insularity of the life Latter-Day Saints.

Institutional impediments to convert retention include the system of full-time proselytizing missionaries, which has generated most of the new converts and operates autonomously from the local congregations. The resulting disconnect in coordination is a source of constant struggle. In addition, the requirements for baptism set by the senior hierarchy are relatively modest in light of the magnitude of the lifestyle change that is supposed to follow baptism into the LDS Church. For example, although the essence of LDS church life is the devotion of considerable time and energy to religious callings, prospective converts are required to have attended only two Sunday services before being baptized, hardly enough exposure to permit them to understand the degree of commitment expected of an active Latter-Day Saint.

Managing Diversity within Congregations

As noted earlier, with the exception of the majority life LDS congregations, all LDS congregations in New York City, both English and Spanish, are quite diverse internally, which seems to be an issue that is not an issue. All the interviewees asserted that the "majority minority" congregations had successfully managed their internal diversity.

One method of addressing possible conflict among different groups that is commonly, if not consciously, used is inherent in the structure of the LDS congregation. With so many callings available, responsibility and prestige can be broadly distributed among the groups in the congregation. Even if one is unhappy that a Salvadoran or a Trinidadian is leading one of the congregation's organizations, one can accept it because a fellow national is probably in some other equally responsible calling. Eventually one learns that the policy of rotating callings generally results in everyone's having plenty of opportunities to try to persuade other unpaid volunteers to do things.

Economic Stress

With a large number of poorer emigrants among the Latter-Day Saints in New York City, economic issues are a concern. The interviewees estimated that about a fifth of the emigrant Latter-Day Saints were undocumented. LDS Church policy does not place any impediments on participation based on emigration status, but it also makes no organized effort to help undocumented members with their residence status.

Life Latter-Day Saints often assume that simply being in the LDS Church will automatically lead to upward economic mobility because of changed personal behaviors. This supposition has never actually been measured, and anecdotal evidence among New York Latter-Day Saints suggests that the process, if it occurs, is not automatic. The enormous growth of the LDS Church in Third World nations promises that this will be a continuing issue for Latter-Day Saints (Lucas and Woodworth 1996).

Gender Balance and Leadership

Again, a large majority of the majority convert congregations are female. While this is not uncommon in most Christian churches, it is a particular problem in a church that requires that the highest congregational leadership positions be held by men. Historically, the LDS Church has addressed the gender imbalance in religiosity by exposing its young men to intensive indoctrination and training through participation in junior levels of the lay priesthood, culminating in two years of service as a full-time missionary, beginning at age nineteen. This missionary service, combined with the assumption of major responsibilities through callings held as an adult, has served to keep LDS men in the church to a greater degree than in many other denominations. The success of this strategy is demonstrated by the relatively equal gender balances (54% women to 46% men) in the majority life LDS congregations in Manhattan. The drawback of this strategy is that it takes at least one generation to implement it. Currently, approximately fifty young male New Yorkers are serving such missions, with most coming from the Spanish-language congregations.

Ethnic Segregation

Although the LDS Church has separate language congregations throughout the world, New York City is probably unique to the extent to which Latter-Day Saints attend congregations that are exceptions to the rule mandating only geographically defined congregations. This is acceptable to the senior hierarchy as long as members can truly function comfortably only in their native language.

Now the emerging tendency is for the English-speaking second generation of Hispanic Latter-Day Saints to remain in the Spanish-language congregations. First-generation Hispanic Latter-Day Saints generally ascribe this to the tradition of strong family bonds in Hispanic culture, a tradition that generally is powerfully reinforced by LDS theology and practice. Younger Hispanic Latter-Day Saints also say that they want to preserve their linguistic and cultural heritage. This desire is also supported by LDS Church policies, which promote foreign-language study and bilingualism as preparation for overseas missionary service.

It is possible that as more English-speaking Hispanics remain in Spanish-language congregations, the LDS Church in New York City will evolve into a church divided along lines that are ethnic rather than linguistic. This will conflict with powerfully held beliefs about what the LDS Church should be. As one of the current twelve apostles explained, "Our members are asked to concentrate their efforts to strengthen our unity—not to glorify our diversity" (Oaks 1999, 8).

This imperative is balanced by the requirement that the LDS gospel be provided to everyone in his or her own language. Other considerations include how best to provide new converts from ethnic minorities with the experience that will permit them to function effectively in the exclusively lay volunteer ministry of LDS church life. If they remain in majority white English-language congregations, they may have plenty of experienced role models but not as many opportunities to fill callings themselves. In small minority congregations, they may receive important callings but lack the training and advice to fill them effectively.

The LDS Church has adopted varying approaches to congregations based on linguistic and ethnic minorities (Embry 1992, 1997, 79–88, 107). In most cases, efforts to establish ethnically separate congregations have eventually foundered because of the congregation's inexperience.

In the end, the LDS Church would probably not tolerate for long the presence of large numbers of congregations segregated on ethnic grounds when there was not a substantial need for services in another language. The issue for the LDS Church in New York City will be how best to proceed away from ethnic segregation. One possibility is that the senior hierarchy might arbitrarily abolish Spanish-language congregations. Since the entire senior hierarchy are life Latter-Day Saints who live in majority LDS (and very majority white) Utah and are mostly monolingual in English, there is a great risk that such a rule would be perceived as culturally insensitive. Such a perception could alienate many Hispanic Latter-Day Saints and seriously reverse or impede the growth of the LDS Church in New York City.

Another possibility is to permit, perhaps with occasional exhortatory encouragement, the gradual evolution that is already taking place. All the English-language congregations outside Manhattan already have a sizable number of Hispanic members. Interviewees also report that many members of the Spanish-language congregations have transferred to the local English-language congregation. The first families to do so have often encountered some ill feelings from their former congregations, but this will likely diminish by the time the tenth family has transferred to the English congregation.

Indeed, it is possible that the LDS Church may be well positioned to negotiate the problem of the second generation in ethnic churches. Researchers have noted a tendency for ethnic, non-English-language churches to lose the second generation as it assimilates to American society (Chai 1998, 300–301; Lee 1996; Mullins 1987). I would suggest that this is a result of emphasizing ethnic concerns over religious ones.

In New York City, every Spanish-language congregation shares a church building with an English-language congregation, thus providing a natural catchment for assimilating members of the second generation who wish to maintain their LDS religious affiliation. Although they are lost to the Spanish-language congregation, they are not lost to the LDS Church. Another factor that would ease this transition is that because of the high overall proportion of Hispanics among New York Latter-Day Saints, such second-generation Hispanics will constitute a large part of the membership of English-language congregations. Given the broad participation in LDS church life, the culture of these Hispanic Latter-Day Saints will be apparent in these congregations, even if the services are conducted in English.

Transience

Almost all LDS New Yorkers come from someplace else. Young life Latter-Day Saint professionals and students move on to other cities in pursuit of their careers or to the suburbs when they have families. Emigrants from Third World countries often feel that the search for economic security that brought them to the United States should also lead them away from the crowded, dirty New York City neighborhoods where they live. There are no clear indications that a large second generation of LDS New Yorkers is choosing to remain and make New York City their families' permanent home. But given New York City's historical role as a portal city, the LDS Church may continue to grow in New York City as a permanent presence with a constantly moving membership.

The future of the LDS Church of New York City has a relevance that extends beyond the state of religion in New York City. The proportions of ethnic groups among LDS New Yorkers are the same that will characterize the entire LDS Church within five to ten years. Whether the Latter-Day Saints of New York City are able to create a truly diverse yet unified church that transcends the cultural near-nation of the western life Latter-Day Saints may well predict whether Mormonism really might become a new major world faith of the twenty-first century.

NOTES

1. Quoted in Dean C. Jessee, ed., *The Personal Writings of Joseph Smith* (Salt Lake City: Deseret Book, 1984), 252–254. Grammar, spelling, and punctuation have been updated.

2. *Doctrine and Covenants*, sec. 90, v. 11 (Salt Lake City: Church of Jesus Christ of Latter-Day Saints, 1981).

3. The figures for 1998 were supplied by the LDS Church, and the figures for 1990 and 1980 came from *Churches and Church Membership* for 1990 and 1980.

4. General population figures are derived from the 1990 U.S. Census and thus are not exactly comparable with my 1998 estimates. Census information comes from *Demographic Profiles: A Portrait of New York City's Community Districts from the 1980 and 1990 Censuses of Population and Housing* (New York: New York City Department of City Planning, 1992).

Chapter 14

Malcolm X and the Future of New York City Islam

Louis A. DeCaro Jr.

New York City is the lodestar of the development of Malcolm X's religious identity and its conflict with the cosmology of the "Black Muslims."[1] The constellation of *The Autobiography of Malcolm X* is centered in New York City and points east to Mecca, the great spiritual ideal that rose for Malcolm in the twilight of his life. Today, the mosque he once led as a "Black Muslim" is home to a leading congregation, part of the growing presence of traditional Sunni Muslims in New York City. Furthermore, while a number of cities were important to Malcolm's religious life, the development of his religious identity was inseparably linked to New York—Harlem, to be precise—and its particular brand of religion.[2]

The roots of the Nation of Islam (or "Black Muslims") were not in New York City but in the Midwest, where the small movement attained institutional stability before 1952, the year when Malcolm came out of prison and began actively expanding the influence of the Nation of Islam leader, Elijah Muhammad. Although a handful of "Black Muslim" congregations existed in various cities, Muhammad had never been very successful in developing his small congregation in New York City, and it was not until Malcolm X assumed the leadership of the mosque there (originally known as Temple no. 7) that it grew. Acting as a kind of traveling evangelist and pastor-at-large, Malcolm X's contribution to the Nation of Islam was significant. By the late 1950s, he expanded the movement from coast to coast and either shored up previously established congregations or founded new ones in major cities and towns with large black populations.

Elijah Muhammad had no impact on New York City, probably because he never really liked the fast-paced, cosmopolitan urban center. As Malcolm's eldest brother, Wilfred Little Shabazz, recalled, New York City was simply "beyond" Muhammad (telephone interview, January 20, 1998). In particular, Muhammad's southern provincialism left him ill suited for work amid the cultural diversity of New York's black population. An African observer of the "Black Muslims" noted that Muhammad had even expressed dissonant feelings about Caribbean blacks.[3] It appears that Muhammad felt more at home in cities where the black population was almost exclusively from the Deep South, such as Washington, D.C., where he had once worked in the early years of his leadership. Certainly, it was clear to his followers that Washington, D.C., not New York City, was highly valued in Muhammad's religious vision. At the time of Malcolm's arrival on the scene, the constellation of the Nation of Islam was centered in Chicago (Muhammad's residence), circled closely by Detroit (the birthplace of the original Nation of Islam), and Washington, D.C.[4] Even though he made invaluable contributions to the movement's growth, Malcolm X inevitably challenged Muhammad's constellation of cities by advancing the position of New York City. Within a decade of his involvement, Washington, D.C., was easily replaced by the brilliance of Malcolm's work in New York City. At first, Elijah Muhammad was pleased that he finally had a minister who could take on such a challenge, especially since New York City was a problem that he had never really solved himself.

Malcolm's "Black Muslim" Universe

Malcolm's love for New York City went beyond its strategic importance. Long before he became a "Black Muslim," Malcolm Little was enamored with New York City. In his earliest memories, New York was a place of wonder, largely because it was home to one of the country's great black populations. In an autobiographical reflection of his first visit as a teenager working on the railroad, Malcolm mentioned that even as a child, he had been aware of Harlem. "Even as far back as Lansing [Michigan], I had been hearing about how fabulous New York was, and especially Harlem," he wrote. "In fact, my father had described Harlem with pride" and showed us pictures of the huge parades by the Harlem followers of Marcus Garvey. Everything he had ever heard about Harlem "was exciting," and it was this attraction that first drew him in 1941 (Malcolm X 1987, 215, 70–71).

As a young hustler, Malcolm bit off as much of the Big Apple as he could chew. In his autobiography, he portrayed himself as a debased young man with no moral or political sensibilities, a youth adrift on an urban sea of despair. Robin Kelley recognizes the stylization of youth in *The Autobiography of Malcolm X* and contends that Malcolm, like many other struggling workers in urban black society, was not without political conviction. In "The Riddle of the Zoot: Malcolm Little and Black Cultural Politics during World War II," Kelley argues that young hustlers like Malcolm expressed their revolutionary sentiment in countercultural behaviors, petty criminality, and the practice of urban "style politics" (as epitomized by the "zoot suit") that flaunt the conventions and attitudes of white society. Kelley concludes that Malcolm "tragically dehistoricized" his story from the real context of the urban black "race rebels" (Kelley 1994, 161–181). Unfortunately, Kelley ignores the religious dimensions and errs by attributing the motivation of Malcolm's autobiography to a stale, inflexible, ideological stance. Since Kelley tends to politicize criminal behaviors, he finds Malcolm's moral retrospective inconvenient to his interpretation of "race rebellion." In so doing, Robin Kelley entirely misses the point of Malcolm's autobiography, which was to enhance the redemptive claims of the Nation of Islam by portraying himself as having been the greatest of sinners saved by the message of "the Honorable Elijah Muhammad."

Young Malcolm came to Harlem with a sense of his parents' heritage as activists on behalf of the black nationalist leader Marcus Garvey. In his *Autobiography*, Malcolm recalls that one of the exciting aspects of New York City was his childhood awareness that it was the place where Garvey reached the height of his success in the United States (DeCaro 1996, 67; Malcolm X 1987, 70). But the Garvey legacy did not draw Malcolm to New York for political or race consciousness reasons. Instead, his early days in Harlem show more evidence of immaturity, waywardness, and moral rebellion than that of a proletarian revolution in an urban setting.

Malcolm's passion for New York City as an "exciting place" is more important to understanding his autobiography. Recalling his sentiments in the 1940s, he wrote that "New York was heaven to me. And Harlem was Seventh Heaven!" Although he later turned away from a life of hustling and petty criminality, his love for New York City was not diminished. When he returned in 1954 as a pious, fundamentalist-oriented "Black Muslim," Malcolm recalled that his ministerial assignment left him feeling a "welter" of indescribable emotions. A little less than a decade after he had left Harlem disillusioned and prison bound, Malcolm X returned to New York City with a new dream to see "Islam . . . grow very big." "And nowhere in America was such a single temple potential available as in New York's five boroughs," Malcolm wrote. "They contained over a million black people" (Malcolm X 1987, 76, 215).

Although Malcolm's passion for New York City was not specifically a product of his family's Garveyite legacy, he instinctively sensed the city's importance as a center of liberation activity. Malcolm saw New York's vast cosmopolitan black population as a representation of the larger African diaspora. Although he continued to work from coast to coast to develop the movement as a whole, the New York Muslims better reflected his more refined administrative and political outlook, as well as his internationalism and interest in the traditional Islamic religion of the East.[5] As the movement grew, Malcolm X was aware that New York City was growing in prominence within the constellation of the Nation of Islam, and he labeled it one of "the major cities" of the movement, third only to Detroit and Chicago (Malcolm X 1987, 224).

As his *Autobiography* shows, in order to plow through the hard soil of indifference toward the Islam that he found in Harlem, Malcolm found ways to reach out to the community, such as using leaflets and scheduling meeting times that would not conflict with Christian church services. Recognizing the preponderance of women in the Christian churches, Malcolm began to include respect for black women in his strong moral rhetoric (Malcolm X 1987, 217–222). The New York congregation grew quickly as a result, although its success was not particularly noted in the heavily politicized and church-oriented community of Harlem.

In 1957, Malcolm's reputation in Harlem grew noticeably after the Nation of Islam stood up against the New York City Police Department in a landmark brutality case, an incident dramatized in Spike Lee's movie *Malcolm X*. The case, which ended up in a successful lawsuit by the victim, gave Malcolm and the Nation of Islam citywide recognition and increased the prestige of Temple no. 7 in the movement. (It also increased the concern of the surveillance community.) During this time, Malcolm launched a newspaper, *Muhammad Speaks*, for the organization. The paper further enhanced the importance of New York City in the Nation of Islam, but it also created problems with Muhammad's jealous family members in Chicago. Increased media attention came in 1959 after Elijah Muhammad, Malcolm X, and the Nation of Islam were featured in a controversial television documentary entitled "The Hate That Hate Produced."[6]

With his newfound notoriety, Malcolm X was pulled into a wider orbit than he had known in the 1950s. Increasingly sought after for interviews, debates, and speaking engagements on campuses across the country, Malcolm became the focus of the media. Muhammad's family resented the attention that Malcolm, instead of Elijah Muhammad, received from the media, but at first Muhammad seems to have recognized the advantage of having such an able, eloquent, and charismatic young man working as his representative. By 1963, Malcolm was working as Muhammad's official national representative while leading the most formidable mosque in the organization.

The constellation of the Nation of Islam had begun to shift in response to Malcolm's success in New York City. He and his New York Muslims became the magnet for controversy and attention while Chicago circled like a moon in orbit, dependent on the light and heat emanating from the East Coast. Although Malcolm frequently conferred with Muhammad in Chicago, Temple no. 7 in New York City was emerging as the model for a progressive, sophisticated, and political "Black Muslim" movement. Malcolm wrote that from the "tiny" congregation he had initially found in New York City, by 1963 he had built "three of the Nation's most powerful and aggressive mosques—Harlem's Seven-A in Manhattan, Corona's Seven-B in Queens, and Mosque Seven-C in Brooklyn" (Malcolm X 1987, 290). Just as his ministry, charisma, and oratory helped Malcolm eclipse Elijah Muhammad as a public figure, his New York Muslims also proved to be far more adept at establishing and running successful businesses than were Muhammad's congregants in Chicago.[7]

Even though he devotedly revolved around Elijah Muhammad, Malcolm's orbit was widening. New York City was an ideal location for his expansive rapport with the Muslim world of the Middle East. As he moved to the farthest point of his orbit there and in Africa, the organizational and religious distance was increasing between New York City and Chicago. Both men made overseas trips to the Muslim world (Malcolm in the summer of 1959 and Muhammad in late 1959 and early 1960), but only Malcolm X seemed genuinely interested in building religious bridges. While Muhammad had had Sunni Muslims as consultants, close collaboration with traditional Muslims seems to have threatened him, apparently because his teachings did not conform to those of the Qur'an.

As Malcolm fought to defend Muhammad and the Nation of Islam from the mounting criticisms of traditional Muslims in the early 1960s, he was actually moving away from the constellation of black Islam. In the face of police and media opposition, Malcolm found solace in his growing solidarity with the Muslim world. His open, enthusiastic interaction with Muslim leaders visiting the United Nations or living in New York contrasted vividly with Elijah Muhammad's guarded provincialism.[8]

Other aspects accentuated Malcolm's widening orbit away from Elijah Muhammad. Having suffered bronchial ailments since 1961, the elderly leader began to winter in Arizona, leaving the impression to many outside the movement that he was fading away. Since Malcolm was acting as the movement's spokesman, the public often mistook him as the heir apparent to Muhammad—something that only exacerbated the heated jealousy of Muhammad's children.[9] At the same time, Malcolm was becoming dissatisfied with what he called the "general nonengagement policy" of the Nation of Islam toward the heightening crisis over civil rights. His concern about the movement's conservative posture was paralleled by religious tensions that heightened with his desire to align himself with the Muslim world.

When conflicts with the police left the Nation of Islam reeling in 1962/1963, Malcolm lost patience with Muhammad's apparent indifference to political action. He was all too aware that blacks were beginning to dub the movement as a "talk only" organization and that his opponents pointed out the absence of the "Black Muslims" from the "frontline struggle" for civil rights (Malcolm X 1987, 289).

The bittersweet struggle of Malcolm's own work was being fleshed out according to a New York City paradigm of spirituality and activism that did not conform to the mind-set of Elijah Muhammad and his family in Chicago. In Malcolm's heart and mind, New York was not simply a major city in the movement; it was now a force pulling him out of the "Black Muslim" orbit—farther and farther from Muhammad, Chicago, and cultic Islam. By basing himself in New York City, Malcolm X was challenging the religious constellation of the Nation of Islam. It now was inevitable that his orbit would collide with that of Muhammad, who continued to maintain his role as the sovereign center of the "Black Muslim" universe.

"Something in Nature Had Failed"

Although the break between Malcolm X and Elijah Muhammad seems inevitable in retrospect, Malcolm was not prepared for the separation. As Malcolm described in his *Autobiography*, the occasion for the break came in late 1963 with Chicago's harsh reaction to his indiscreet remarks in New York City regarding the assassination of President John F. Kennedy.

Muhammad immediately silenced Malcolm. Particularly stunning to Malcolm was the "quick and thorough publicity job" that the "Chicago officials" of the Nation of Islam carried out in announcing his silencing. Malcolm began to realize that Muhammad's family had misrepresented his reaction to Muhammad's discipline by portraying him as a rebel. As his ostensible ninety-day period of silence passed, Malcolm found he could "not evade the obvious strategy and plotting coming out of Chicago to eliminate me from the Nation of Islam . . . if not from this world." Malcolm sensed that Chicago's hostility was so great that he was in mortal danger. But the sense of betrayal he felt was even "worse than death," a personal cataclysm that "felt as though something in nature had failed, like the sun, or the stars" (Malcolm X 1987, 302, 304–305).

If something in nature had failed, it was Elijah Muhammad. As early as 1955, Malcolm heard rumors about Muhammad's adulterous affairs, but he put them out of his mind in disbelief. When they could no longer be ignored, Malcolm approached Muhammad with a plan to interpret the affairs as a kind of fulfillment of biblical prophecy. When Malcolm attempted to explain the sexual indiscretions to other Nation of Islam ministers in light of biblical prophecy, "the Chicago Muslim officials" interpreted his intervention as subversion (Malcolm X 1987, 394–400). Consequently, when he raised a storm of public controversy with his "chickens coming home to roost" remark about the death of the president, the Chicago officials seized the opportunity to silence Malcolm completely.

A World of His Own, a City of His Own

In March 1964, Malcolm announced his separation from the Nation of Islam, though in reality he had been ousted from the movement. Malcolm founded the first of his two independent organizations, the Muslim Mosque, Inc. (the Organization of Afro-American Unity, a nonreligious movement, was founded later in the year), but realized that he first needed to achieve religious authenticity for himself and his new movement. His famous pilgrimage to Mecca in April 1964 demonstrated not only his personal conversion to Islam but also his deliberate quest for official recognition by the leaders of the Muslim world (DeCaro 1996, 194–198; Malcolm X 1987, 315–316).

Malcolm's autobiographical details about his *hajj*, or pilgrimage, make his story one of the great modern religious narratives. His critics, however, often praise only the last chapters of *The Autobiography* without understanding that his life as a whole is a powerful story of spiritual pilgrimage. They fail to see how many aspects of his racial and political analyses extend from the Nation of Islam chapters to the Mecca chapters.

Of course, Malcolm was quite aware that the pilgrimage to Mecca did mark a conversion experience and broadening of his view of the world. Mecca provided an alternative religious universe to Malcolm the Muslim activist, allowing him to reorder his life and worldview for the first time since his departure from the Nation of Islam. In Mecca, Malcolm was able to engage in valuable meditation and retrospective analysis ("I played back for myself the twelve years I had spent with Elijah Muhammad as if it were a motion picture") while taking solace in the "complete human being" experience afforded to him as a black man outside the context of the United States.

If Mecca proved invaluable to his personal religious and social experiences, Malcolm also believed it could serve as a model for a racially depraved society like the United States. He thus returned to the United States presenting Mecca as a model of religious and social redemption. His subsequent, and longer, visit to the "Holy World" of Islam in 1964 both solidified his role as a representative of Islam in the West and affirmed his determination to offer Islam as an alternative to the race-tainted religion of Christianity (Malcolm X 1987, 365).

Nevertheless, Malcolm X was a realist. Despite the lack of U.S.-style Afriphobia among "white Muslims" in the East, the Muslim world also had a history of black enslavement. Malcolm privately questioned the white Muslims' discrimination against African Muslims and women. Furthermore, many prominent Eastern Muslims were unwilling to accept Malcolm even after he achieved good standing in the Muslim world. The sympathetic director-general of the Islamic Centre in Geneva, Switzerland, suggested that Malcolm's antiwhite rhetoric was a psychological compensation for his experience of racism rather than a legitimate response (DeCaro 1996, 254–255).

Malcolm X considered Mecca to be a symbol of an ideal not yet reached. Like all Muslims, Malcolm loved Mecca and gestured toward the Holy World as a religious and spiritual center point in his teaching and motivation as a religious revolutionary. Yet for him, the real center for the current spiritual battle against racism and injustice was New York City. In his *Autobiography*, he wrote that "in New York City . . . I would naturally base any operation" (Malcolm X 1987, 309–310).

Malcolm resisted opportunities and offers to move himself and his family out of New York City, and until the day of his death, he remained committed to Harlem as a base for his life and work. Given his Garveyite background, his preference for New York as an international center, and his devotion to Harlem as a prototype of the black diaspora and as the quintessential black neighborhood, New York City remained the center of Malcolm's religious and political universe. He clearly intended to spread Islam among African Americans from his base in New York's Muslim Mosque, Inc., and to politically unify blacks from the New York headquarters of his Organization of Afro-American Unity. He recognized that New York City was the "natural" center of his universe and that, for Malcolm X, all roads religious and political began and ended there.

This was even the case in his death. The irony of Malcolm's assassination in New York's Audubon Ballroom on February 21, 1965, is that other assassination attempts had been made on his life by the Nation of Islam in cities like Los Angeles and Chicago in early 1965,[10] but Malcolm had been able to escape. Yet when he seems to have accepted the inevitability of death at the hands of his former brethren, perhaps concluding that his death would serve to bring light and expose meaningful truth concerning racism,[11] Malcolm X walked quietly and humbly onto a New York stage to face his assassins. A week later, in the main service of the Nation of Islam's annual conference in Chicago, Elijah Muhammad spoke of Malcolm's departure from the movement in celestial terms. "He had no right to reject me!" the little shaman blurted out in his frail, unimpressive voice. "He was a star, who went astray!"[12]

The Muslim Universe Today

Today Malcolm X is a constellation, and New York City is the center of the Muslim presence in the United States. Most African American mosques feature his picture, and a significant number of leading imams are his former aides and associates. To some degree, Malcolm X is perceived by African American Muslims as a charismatic founder, and the current generation of leaders, as organizational successors to his work.

Traditional Islam in New York City—which has far surpassed the influence of cultic Islam in the black community—actually predates Malcolm X. As far as we know, a white journalist named Alexander Russell Webb, a convert from Presbyterianism, established the first Islamic institution in New York City in 1893, called the American Muslim Brotherhood (Smith 1999, 190). In 1907, immigrants in Brooklyn from Poland, Russia, and Lithuania first founded the American Muhammadan Society and then a mosque that exists today as the Muslim Mosque. The founding of the Islamic Mission of Brooklyn in 1928 may mark the birth of Africa-founded mosques in the United States (Abusharaf 1998). Between 1994 and 1999, the number of mosques in the city increased from 20 to more than 120, a 600 percent increase. Conservatively, there are about 200,000 Muslims in the city, made up of converts from the United States (mainly African American), Africans, South and Southeast Asians, and Middle Easterners (interview with Ihsan Bagby, March 22, 1999). The number of active Muslims, however, is probably much smaller.

The diversity of the Muslim community of New York City is also unique in the United States. While other cities like Los Angeles and Detroit have Muslim populations representing particular ethnic groups, New York City is the main entrepôt of African Muslims, who then spread out over the rest of the country. There are also Muslims from Turkey and Kurdistan, Bosnia, Palestine, Yemen, Pakistan, Bangladesh, and India. One New York Muslim leader jokes, "We have become tabouli!" (a mixed salad).

New York City's denominational diversity is reflected in the presence of Sunni, Shi'ite, Sufi, and Ahmaddiyya Muslims. Along with these Eastern Muslim groups are the Islamic-style sects and cults in the black community, all of whose practices differ widely from one another (see Abusharaf 1998, 247). Most of New York City's Muslims are Sunni (see Mamiya 1995), but there are significant Shi'ite and Sufi centers (figure 14.1). Traditionally, Sunni Muslims do not recognize the Sufi and Ahmaddiyya as authentic Muslims, although in light of the Malcolm X story, they are more hopeful about the Nation of Islam.

Most of the people who convert to Islam are African Americans (who make up about 40% of the city's Muslims, see Smith 1999, xiii), Latinos, and whites. In Manhattan, a Sufi mosque has a fair number of white converts. Many African Americans transferred to Sunni Islam from the Nation of Islam in the 1970s, following the lead of Warith D. Muhammad (né Wallace D. Muhammad) (see Marsh 1984). In the 1970s, even some "first-generation Puerto Ricans . . . entered Islam by affiliation with African American mosques." One convert started PIEDAD (Propagacion islamica para la educacion y devocion de Ala'el divino) and another, Alianza islamicato, to evangelize Latinos. Prisons are active recruiting

Figure 14.1. The Islamic Center of New York, Third Avenue and Ninety-sixth Street. This Sunni Muslim mosque has the largest Muslim congregation in the city. Courtesy of the collection of Tony Carnes.

grounds among African Americans and Latinos, and recently a few members of the "Latin Kings" gang have become Muslims. There is even a Spanish-language mosque in East Harlem.

The most visible mosque in the city is the $17-million Islamic Cultural Center, which demonstrates the role of Middle Eastern money and guidance among New York City's Muslims. The shepherd behind the scenes is the Kuwaiti ambassador to the United Nations. Usually the imam at the mosque is a prominent Muslim scholar from the Middle East. However, the most famous Sunni Muslim leader in the United States is African American, Imam Siraj Wahaj, of the Masjid At-taqwa, at Bedford Avenue and Fulton Street in Brooklyn. Formerly a Baptist and then a Nation of Islam minister, he followed Warith Muhammad into Sunni Islam, the world's most common religious denomination. Wahaj carries on the work of advancing traditional Islam, although he is now independent of Muhammad's organization. Notably, in 1991, Imam Wahaj became the first Muslim to give the opening prayer for the U.S. Congress.

New York City's African American Muslim community is divided between those who follow Warith Muhammad and those who do not, while the rest of the Muslim population usually identify themselves according to national origin and language. Typically, Muslims say that they "are associated" with a mosque or leader, rather than identifying themselves as members. If they do not like a leader, the disagreement is coded indirectly: "That fellow doesn't follow Sunni carefully," or "he is not real knowledgeable." If the disagreement is extreme, some may even question whether a leader is truly Muslim.

At midday on Friday, New York City's Muslims stream into the mosques (*masjids*) for Jum'ah (meaning "gathering" or "Friday") prayers, the main religious service of the week. The incense and oils at the entrance indicate that one is departing the world to enter a sacred space.

Every Friday at the Malcolm Shabazz Mosque at 116th Street and Malcolm X Boulevard in Harlem, congregants spread out in the mosque after taking off their shoes and sit on the green carpet facing Mecca, which is indicated by a plaque (figure 14.2). Women sit in the back with their children, dressed in uniforms, seated in front of them. Then an older man, the muzzerin, attired in fine gray suit, rises to call out the beginning of the service: "Come to the prayer, come to the time of felicity."

Immigrants at several mosques say that since they have come to live in the United States, religion has become more important to them, that it helps them exist in a society from which they sometimes feel disconnected. So mosques here often play a different role than they do in Muslim countries, where most mosques are essentially places for prayer services. In Muslim countries, the state acts at the implementer of an Islamic way of life, while in the United States, the mosque is the social, cultural, and educational center encompassing the Muslim's whole life. As a result, immigrant Muslims have often become much more involved in their religion and far more evangelistic in their orientation. "American Muslims are deeply involved in formulating what it means to be part of the 'umma (community) in the West,' and are in the process of determining the nature and authenticity of an indigenous American Islam" (Smith 1999, xiii; also see Haddad and Esposito 1998; Poston 1992).

As worshipers file into Masjid Malcolm Shabazz, they pass mosque-sponsored stores, clinics, housing, and schools. Imam El Haff Izak-El Mu'eed Pashah explains, "It is a mosque when it encompasses all of life. The whole earth is a mosque" (figure 14.3). For "Black Muslims," the idea of an all-encompassing mosque seems like a throwback to the traditional role of the African American church. Only recently have African American tradition and immigrant religion matched up.

Imam Pashah represents traditional Islam for many African Americans. Reared in the Baptist Church, Pashah tried a number of Christian denominations before converting to Islam. Like his mother, Pashah was a religious seeker who finally found in Islam a satisfactory answer in his search for the divine, as well as a strong moral and ethical code for life. Many African Americans embrace Islam not only as a means of identifying with distant cultural roots in Africa but also because they have found the traditional religion of the black church to be lackluster and its leader-

Figure 14.2. Malik El Shabbaz Mosque, Malcolm X's former headquarters. Courtesy of the collection of Tony Carnes.

Figure 14.3. Imam Izak El Pashah, head of the Malik El Shabbaz (Malcolm X) Mosque, both preaches and gets out the vote from his multiethnic congregation in Harlem. Courtesy of the collection of Tony Carnes.

ship disappointing. Like Malcolm X, modern African American Muslims see Islam as a moral alternative to the jaded institutionalism that prevails in some sections of the black church.

Pashah is quick to note that his daughter served in the U.S. Army during the Persian Gulf War and that his son is in the navy, an indication that African American Muslims see their role with respect to the nation not as dissenting separatists but as proactive citizens with a prophetic message of healing and reform. The political retreat from radicalism and racial dissent that characterizes most African American Muslims has sometimes been compared with the conservative politics of fundamentalist Christians. Perhaps some of this is compensation for the militant, anti-American reputation that black Islam has in popular opinion, due largely to the Nation of Islam's harsh rhetoric and Malcolm X's revolutionary agenda. Elijah Muhammad's son Warith D. Muhammad was notably cooperative with the FBI in the early days of his independence,[13] and his followers have sometimes been criticized for being too politically conservative. As for Pashah and his colleagues, the role of the imam has shifted to resemble the full-time professional clergy of most churches and synagogues in the United States (see Williams 1988, 93). This is a far cry from the "Black Muslim" concept of a religious leader as a radical dissenter and social critic. The conservative, even patriotic, stance of many African American Sunni Muslims may also be a reaction to the "radical fundamentalism" of certain foreign-born Muslim teachers who promote bombings, assassinations, and other forms of social disruption in the name of religious principle. Although these groups are small and few in number, African American Muslims resent the popular notion of a "violent," "terrorist" Islam as much as the rest of the Muslim world does.

Like many African American Muslims, Pashah found his way from Christianity to Islam across the bitter landscape of the Nation of Islam. As a young man resentful of white racism and its systemic limitations, young Pashah found the message of Elijah Muhammad to be a double-edged sword—it gave him both a God and an effective analysis of white supremacy in the United States. "Whites said that black was the devil. Islam said white was the devil. I thought, 'Sounds good to me!' It came from an extreme reverse of white hatred." Those who have moved from the Nation of Islam to Islam tend to see their past involvement in these terms; but without denying the reality of racial injustice, they prefer to speak of Islam as a religion that unifies people of all colors and culture, just as Malcolm X came to believe.

As a member of the Nation of Islam, Pashah was one of Malcolm X's parishioners compelled by the aggressive, businesslike philosophy that made Temple no. 7 excel in the movement. Following Malcolm's lead, young Pashah worked hard as a plumber by day and devoted his evenings and weekends to serving "the Honorable Elijah Muhammad." Having distinguished himself among the brothers, Pashah was promoted by Malcolm himself, first to lead the Nation of Islam's mosque in Brooklyn (no. 7-C) and then the mosque in Corona, Queens (no. 7-B), not far from Malcolm's home.

Malcolm's crisis was also a crisis for the New York Muslims. After Malcolm's ouster, Louis Farrakhan was sent from Boston to lead the New York congregation, and Pashah remained faithful to Elijah Muhammad's teachings. When Muhammad died in 1975 and his son Warith succeeded him, Pashah followed Warith into Sunni Islam. As the new leader of Muhammad's Muslims, not only did Warith convert to Sunni Islam, but he also immediately opened the mosque to white Muslims. The following year he renamed the mosque Masjid Malcolm Shabazz in honor of Malcolm X. Pashah was elected imam in 1994.

Today the congregation of Masjid Malcolm Shabazz is only about 52 percent African American, with 40 percent African immigrants and 5 percent South Asian, according to leaders' estimates. Although some eight thousand claim to be part of the mosque, leaders there say that the allegiance of most is purely symbolic. About four hundred to six hundred people regularly attend Friday noon services.

"Religion is always having an impact on New York City, and the city on us," says Imam Pashah. "On my hajj, I could not identify race from where I stood. They were all wearing white garments. This is the decoration of our faith." It is also a legacy in harmony with Malcolm's lonely sojourn a generation ago. The universe of Masjid Malcolm Shabazz now stably revolves around New York City, with Mecca providing distant, wondrous light.

NOTES

1. While the proper name of Elijah Muhammad's movement was the Nation of Islam, its adherents became popularly known as "Black Muslims," even though they resented the term and insisted on being called simply "Muslims." Traditional Muslims, however, did not want the Nation of Islam to confused or associated with Islam. In this chapter, I have enclosed "Black Muslims" in quotation marks to reinforce the distinction between cultic Islam and traditional Islam that is all too often blurred, especially by writers with religious-sentimental reasons for wanting to see the Nation of Islam as an authentic Muslim movement. See, for example, Moustafa Bayoumi, "Moorish Science: The Secret History of African American Islam," *Transition* (80): 100–119. Also see DeCaro 1996, 155.

2. On the background of the Nation of Islam movement and its relationship to Islam and Christianity, respectively, see DeCaro, 1996, 1998.

3. In fairness to Muhammad, the context of his antagonism to Caribbean blacks was a defense against the criticisms of a black Caribbean Muslim who conducted a campaign to discredit him in the late 1950s and early 1960s. Yet there was

an apparent indifference to black Caribbeans in Muhammad's thinking, which is probably why he never allowed Malcolm X to advance the movement in the black West Indies (see DeCaro 1996, 147–150, 264; Essien-Udom 1963, 314–315).

4. Wilfred Little Shabazz noted that Elijah Muhammad's favorite cities would likely have been Detroit, Chicago, and Washington, D.C.

5. I take issue with Shelby Steele's contention in the *New Republic* that Malcolm X "looked bigger than life because he always lived in small, cultish worlds, and always stood next to small people" (see Steele 1992, 27–31). Actually, Malcolm's presence in the "cultish world" of the Nation of Islam forced it to expand nationally and globally. Even as a "Black Muslim," Malcolm X was inclined toward internationalism, and being a minister in an international city, he made numerous contacts with politicians, writers, students, and representatives from what he glowingly referred to as "the dark world." In the early 1960s, Malcolm was one of the most sought-after campus speakers and was quite capable of holding his own in many panel discussions, debates, and radio and television broadcasts with some of the brightest minds of the day, including the civil rights leaders that Steele would uphold as "big" people. Once independent of the Nation of Islam, Malcolm X earned the official status as a leader in the Muslim world in 1964 and met with many heads of state and was much in demand while touring overseas.

6. As Malcolm reveals, the Muhammad family eventually seized control of *Muhammad Speaks*, moving its editorial office to Chicago. In 1962, Malcolm began to notice that they were using the paper to block coverage of his activities in New York City and elsewhere; see Malcolm X 1987, 238, 292. On "The Hate That Hate Produced" documentary, see Carson 1991, 159–170; DeCaro 1996, 134–135.

7. In 1951, several years before Malcolm's involvement, Hatim Sahib (1951, 241) noted that Elijah Muhammad was "the intellectual of the movement." Shortly before his assassination, Malcolm told a radio interviewer that Muhammad's businesses and supposed black economic empire in Chicago were a farce; see Malcolm X 1992, 201–202.

8. Some Muslims apparently patronized Elijah Muhammad in the hopes of leading the Nation of Islam toward Islam or in order to exploit it for personal reasons. The most notable in this regard was the Pakistani Muslim Abdul Basit Naeem, who used his own Muslim publication to advance the Nation of Islam in the 1950s and who remained loyal to Elijah Muhammad even after Malcolm X embraced traditional Islam (see DeCaro 1996, 137–140, 150–151).

9. When Elijah Muhammad was too ill to attend the Nation of Islam's annual conference in Chicago in February 1963, Malcolm took the helm and consequently was prominent in Chicago-area interviews and broadcasts. Muhammad's family was embittered by Malcolm's celebrity in the absence of the elder, and their jealousy was exacerbated when the *New York Times* reported that Malcolm was overshadowing Muhammad; see New York Office Memorandum, "Malcolm

K. Little," May 16, 1963, 21, in *Malcolm X: FBI Surveillance File* (Wilmington, DE: Scholarly Resources, 1978), reel 2; also Carson 1991, 243.

10. During an interview conducted a few days before his death, Malcolm discussed, though only briefly, assassination attempts made on his life in Los Angeles and Chicago (see Malcolm X 1992, 198–199).

11. The expression is actually Malcolm's closing sentiment on the final page of his *Autobiography*, 1987, 382.

12. Muhammad quoted in Alex Haley's epilogue (Malcolm X 1987, 450).

13. An interview with Warith Muhammad conducted by the FBI on February 15, 1965. Their report notes that Muhammad was "most courteous to the Agents" and would be willing to cooperate in the future (Airtel from SAC, Chicago to FBI Director, February 17, 1965, "Wallace D. Muhammad," in *Malcolm X: FBI Surveillance File* (Wilmington, DE: Scholarly Resources, 1978), reel 2.

Part V

Religion as Therapeutic

Chapter 15

Black Churches as a Therapeutic Institution

Mary B. McRae

I woke up this morning and the devil was trying to keep me home and not to go to church. My feet hurt, but I would come even if I had to use a cane.

—A Baptist woman from Brooklyn

The black churches in New York City function as therapeutic systems that provide healing, spiritual renewal, and interpersonal learning for their congregations (Moore 1991). New York City African Americans often "feel right" when they go to church, echoing the sentiments of the woman who told us, "If I didn't go to church on Sunday morning, I wouldn't feel right about going to the movies, going out."

A black church is a social system with boundaries, a hierarchy, subunits, and cognitive and emotional themes that sustain both the church and its members. The administration, choirs, clubs, and individual members need one another. Each member adapts to the world outside the church using resources from the church. In New York City, African Americans often say that the church's message—that blacks are worthy of respect and honor and that society lacks the honorable qualities of justice and equality—tunes out the feelings of discrimination that members accumulate in daily life.

Historically, black churches in New York City have brought a sense of communal belonging and values that have instilled a sense of responsibility and commitment to family. The black churches have also provided hope to people living under oppressive conditions and have often been the only place in which black people have felt that they could openly express their feelings about the outside world, learn that they were not alone, and be able to assume leadership roles.

Black Churches as Group Therapy

The churches' survival and continuing vitality depend on the emotional and interpersonal satisfaction derived from the worshipers and the ministry.

Cheryl Gilkes (1980) was the first to delineate the role of the black church as a therapeutic community. She identified several practices of the black religious experience as having therapeutic functions: (1) the articulation of suffering, (2) the location of persecutors, (3) a provision of asylum for "acting out," and (4) a validation of experiences. Others have addressed the common purposes of religious and mental health institutions such as helping people live "properly," belief in the healing powers of individuals and communities, and the power of community narrative or the telling of shared stories (Rappaport and Simkins 1991).

Another study found that the service as a whole imparted a sense of group closeness like that found in group psychotherapy and that the black church service "functioned as a community mental health resource for its participants" (Griffith, Young, and Smith 1984, 464).

A Diverse Church with Diverse Emotional Styles

> The church is a body, all the people belong to that body and when we come together, we make up that one body. That's why you need organization, an organization of people doing their part, using their different talents. You [are] supposed to use your talents within the church because the church belongs to God and there is only one God.
>
> —Deacon in a Baptist church

Although outsiders may think that the black church is a monolithic institution, the churches themselves are actually quite diverse in size, the education of their ministers, the emotional style of their worship, and the degree to which they isolate themselves from the external environment.

In 1994 we studied seven black churches: four Baptist, two Episcopal, and one AME church in Manhattan and Brooklyn.[1] Although we did not look at any Pentecostal/charismatic churches, one of the large Baptist churches and the AME church had a Pentecostal flavor. Their sizes ranged from two hundred to three thousand, with two having 2,500 to 3,000 members.

Members of the Baptist churches come from the lower to upper-middle classes, with the middle classes more heavily represented in the Episcopal churches and least in the AME church. None of the churches consisted of only poor people, and most of the ministers were highly educated, with two having Ph.D.s and the rest master's degrees.

All the churches made a point of trying to connect to Sunday service attenders. When entering the sanctuary, greeters would say "Good morning!" and usher the visitor to a seat.

The Episcopal churches were the most conservative, with no shouts, open yelling, "amens!" or standing up and waving of the arms. At one point, though, everyone walked around, shaking hands and exchanging greetings. But while the pastor gave a lecture-style sermon on a single given topic such as how to treat your neighbor, the congregation sat listening silently. Indeed, one of the churches seemed cold and divided into cliques.

In contrast, at the Baptist churches we observed, lecture-style sermons were delivered with more emotion, punctuated by the audience standing and shouting, "Yes, preach it! Tell it! Amen!" At one church, the preacher responded to the audience, jumping up and down a bit to make his points.

At the AME church, a Pentecostal-like emotion ran high. Although the minister was not very demonstrative, he did travel from one side of the stage to the other, occasionally yelling out his points. The people loudly shouted, however.

External Environments and New York City's Black Churches

Many congregants perceive New York City's social environment as unfriendly and often hostile. One woman remarked, "It is difficult to live in the city. You have to deal with aggression every day." She felt that she was not respected at work or even in her own neighborhood. The members of the bigger churches felt empowered to do something about the external environment, while the smaller Baptist churches lacked the resources to help their members with social problems. Their principal extraspiritual contribution was to provide an opportunity for sisterhood among the women. The congregants of one of the small Baptist churches did have political concerns, but without resources and the minister's support, they were unable to offer community services.

Black Churches in New York City Help Their Congregants to Deal with the Outside World

Many congregants see the city's difficulties in racial terms. Black churches mediate and diffuse their participants' anger against the outside world. One of the church members whom we interviewed reflected, "If I were not a Christian, I would be in jail. It is the Christian values that I get in church that give me guidelines." Men, particularly, mention that the church serves as a therapeutic restraint on their outrage against racism in the city.

Congregants also talked about how the churches refuel their emotional and cognitive resources with which to handle the stresses of work. They described the churches as being like gas stations and their lives by Sunday morning as "out of gas." As one congregant explained, "I come to church for refueling. Something to get me through the rest of the week. Something to get me through a very stressful week. . . . I need something to fill me up, and something to reaffirm that I'm doing the right things, and believing the right things."

This process of "refueling" is achieved through a number of means. While the majority identified the church service or the fellowship as the "gas," a smaller group emphasized the emotional release of the music, and still others pointed to the importance of the sermon. Some, of course, mentioned all three church fuels in varying degrees. Those who pointed to the sermon spoke of how they looked to it to tell them something "that would make a difference" in their lives. That is, the church offers this group alternative approaches to their troubles and practical solutions to their daily problems. Refueling in fellowship occurs in the congregants' personal relationships with one another, when other congregants "know their name" and are interested in what "their week was like." Thus they recognize church as a place where others feel the same way. Identity and commonality open the way to "caring."

The churches, of course, have open doors, but sometimes there is no movement out of the doors to the community. Friendly enough inside, some churches find it emotionally difficult to reach out to their surrounding neighborhood. Indeed, many members have moved to the suburbs and come back only to sit and be refueled. Not surprisingly, these members are not very open or available during the week to reach out to the community.

Black clergy can choose either to tackle the problems that affect their congregation or focus on the afterlife. Many black churches have assumed leadership roles in the black civil rights struggle. For example, Pastors Calvin O. Butts of the Abyssinian Baptist Church of Harlem and Floyd Flake of the AME Church in Jamaica, Queens, have assumed political leadership roles outside the church.

Sometimes the churches aggressively intervene in the problems of their neighborhood. One of the Baptist churches we observed had adopted the village concept popularized by Hillary Rodham Clinton and carried out a survey of the neighborhood. It discovered that housing was an urgent problem, and so the church has since become a key leader in the Nehemiah Project to provide affordable, privately owned housing in Brooklyn. Also faced with complaints about drug dealing in the area, the congregation bought out the record shops, barbershop, and dry cleaner from which the drug dealers operated.

Although members support their church's involvement in the outside world, some are nevertheless uneasy with their mixing "the world and the spirit." A few argue that the church should just deal with the Bible and how it helps them conduct their everyday lives. One said, "I don't come because of the social and political stuff. I really just want to deal with the Lord." Still, even these members liked relevant contemporary music and were usually not adamantly opposed to some "worldly" help.

For example, at the two Episcopal and two of the Baptist churches, the pastors presented a message to the congregation that started with Scripture and its exegesis and then applied it to everyday life. In this way, the pastors were trying to get the congregation to face their problems as members of a community.

Although one small Baptist church steered its members mainly toward emotional release, many of the people at the various churches we visited wanted something more. For example, several members of the AME church had come over from a Pentecostal church because they wanted a minister "who had something to say." This church was also involved in the surrounding community.

Opening and Closing the Boundaries of Church

Boundaries distinguish what goes on inside the church from what goes on outside and provide a sense of group identity for the congregation. The churches vary in the degree to which they open their doors to outside resources, influences, and new membership and in how active they are in the world outside the church. In the smaller churches where members are often more closely connected to one another, the boundaries may be less permeable.

All of the churches and particularly the Baptists, have "the Call" on Sunday morning to visitors to be saved and join the church. But generally, potential members interact with people like themselves and come to church if a member of this network invites them. Permeable boundaries allow potential members to examine the church's mission, services, and membership before joining.

Denominational Boundaries Often Determine Church Leadership, Leadership Networks, and Membership

"My family has always been Baptist," one woman declared to us. Her sentiments were widely shared, though perhaps in favor of different denominations. There are, however, some signs of denominational switching in the search for "something different." Several Baptists mentioned that their families had switched from the Baptist to the Episcopal Church in the 1940s and 1950s in order to go to a "less emotional" church. The switches coincided with a move into the middle class. Some Episcopalians also say that they had switched from the Catholic Church because it was "too white."

The reasons given for joining a particular church vary but included the desire to worship with families and friends, the involvement of the church in community organizations, the warmth of the congregation, the music, and the charisma or vision of the minister. The focus on "worldly" and "particular" issues, especially those pertaining to black folk, versus "other worldly" and "universal" issues (Lincoln and Mamiya 1990) may become deciding factors for crossing church boundaries. Congregants from the large, more middle-class churches gave more intellectual reasons for coming to church, and the members from the smaller churches tended to be more emotional. All the reasons for coming to the church were wrapped in a "testimonial style" of "how one was lost but then was found."

Church people perceive the denominations as hierarchically structured by status. Not surprisingly, they perceived the Episcopal churches as more elite. Also, as middle-class professionals return to the large Baptist churches, there is a perception that those churches' status is also rising.

The Therapeutic Church

In our interviews, we found three therapeutic strands that related church members to one another: "church as family," "spiritual renewal," and "interpersonal learning." "Education" also seems important but was not mentioned as often.

The following categories represent the religious experiences described by African Americans in various church settings. "Church as family" includes universality, altruism, the corrective recapitulation of the primary family group, group cohesiveness, and development of socializing techniques. "Spiritual renewal" includes instillation of hope, catharsis, and existential factors. "Interpersonal learning" includes learning about personal relationships and getting feedback on one's behavior. "Education" includes imparting information and sometimes developing socializing techniques and imitative behavior.

From a systems theory perspective, the therapeutic variables may be considered as the conversion process occurring within a system. Both the members and their resources enter the system when they join the church. Once these resources are put into the system, a conversion process must take place before the system can respond. Here, "conversion" describes the process by which entrants come to feel that their values, beliefs, and ideas are reaffirmed or are rightly shaped by the church. In time, members come to think of the church as a place of "refueling." They talk about what they learn from one another and how certain special people in the church touch their lives.

Rose M., a Baptist Church member, recalls how much she trusted and believed in Sylvia S., who was the church clerk and taught her about the faith. One day, Rose was getting ready "to do trouble" when she imagined seeing Sylvia coming around the corner. Rose was afraid that Sylvia would "think bad" of her. Rose needed only a second to turn back into her house, relieved about her decision and, more important, happy that she had passed through a trial of temptation—with a little help. Rose is now the church clerk.

Individuals may regard some churches as more supportive, as providing more opportunities for learning, or as more open to emotional expressiveness than others. Members' experiences of the church thus determine their sense of connectedness and commitment to its growth. Consequently, those churches that provide adequate therapeutic experiences for its members ensure their own survival.

The Church as Family

> I am from the South, and coming to New York was a big transition, especially to be here with limited family. So, family is real important, but family is more than just people you connected to biologically and even that you're connected to in a sense spiritually. I think that when I say family, I mean a working unit because I am connected to all of the people here.
>
> —A Brooklyn Baptist woman

A dominant theme in our interviews is that the members see their black church as a family, a place of sharing and "letting their hair down." Black churches serve as a social network where individuals get help dealing with day-to-day problems, learn that they are not alone in their experiences, and feel accepted.

Most of the research on the black religious experience identifies the black church as a supportive network that provides spiritual assistance, personal assistance, and guidelines for moral behavior and acts as a source of unity (Ellison 1990; McAdoo and Crawford 1990; Taylor and Chatters 1988). Religious involvement also may be positively related to subjective well-being, supportive family ties, effective coping strategies, and life satisfaction (Chatters and Taylor 1994; Ellison and Gay 1990).

"I am the Church Mother," one congregant declared. This bold statement epitomizes the familial feel of the churches. In particular, the Baptist churches provide "church mothers," who are older, respected women. In one case, the "church mother" was the wife of a pastor who had died. Some are assigned this role because they are thought to be very nurturing. This Baptist institution has also migrated to the other churches. In one of the Episcopal churches, a woman told us, "I am the church historian and am called 'the church mother.'" In the AME church, the wife of the minister was called the "church mother."

Many congregants are comforted knowing that their families are rooted in the church's history. Indeed, there is much talk of the generations of ancestors who have been part of the church. One Episcopal woman did not attend church but brought her children on Sundays because "My parents belonged to this church. I am now carrying on the tradition. " Another man brought his mother who had Alzheimer's and stayed out of a sense of historical connectedness. Part of being a member of a functional family is doing things for its members to demonstrate caring. In black churches, this can mean visiting nursing homes, feeding the homeless, or just talking to someone about a problem he or she might be having.

The experience of being strongly identified with a black church and having a sense of getting something from that experience leads members to want to give back to the church and the broader community. On an individual level, giving back can be as simple as providing warmth in the church. One member recalled, "When I first joined the ushers, I was joining because my girlfriend was an usher. But I grew to understand what was going on, how people came in on Sunday morning, and the warmth that you could give them at the door."

The congregants' sense of family extends to a racial fellow-feeling. According to Lincoln and Mamiya (1990), black churches are different from white churches in their religious worldview that combines an African heritage with a unique emphasis on salvation from oppression through conversion to Christianity. Indeed, some of the churches have African themes. Several ministers emphasize the importance of people knowing their origins and traditions, even though they seldom explained how they should find out. A few congregants at one church talked about the church as a village, and the large churches held Kwanza celebrations.

All the congregants identified the death and resurrection of Jesus with the slavery experience of oppression, suffering, humiliation, and death (see Lincoln and Mamiya 1990). They all believed that the struggle of black Americans had created a church-group identity with an intense sense of belonging and that they now could deal with their problems by living like Jesus. A few congregants also compared themselves with Moses and Job.

An important theme in the interviews was that racial pride and comfort brought cohesiveness. Many said that in the black church they could realize their sense of black familyhood. One woman declared, "I can work with white folk because church provides me a feeling that I am not dumb or stupid." Some of the fastest-growing churches espouse a more African-centered ideology (Harris 1997). According to Gilkes (1980), the articulation of suffering supports church members by affirming that they are not alone or imagining their problems, as some white colleagues claim. Locating the persecutor also identifies the problem and implies a resolution. This type of activity occurs constantly in black congregations through structured prayer sessions in which help is sought from the Lord and the congregation every day. Ministers and other church attenders validate their experiences.

The church provides a formal structure of acceptance, offering valuable roles in the church to black people (Eng, Hatch, and Callan 1985).

One Brooklyn Baptist church makes a special effort to engage African American men as heads of their families. This was the only church whose focus group was mostly male. In this church, the pastor openly shared his pain over his absent father and invited men in the congregation to work on their issues with their fathers. The church has also established a men-only Board of Elders. While some observers see this as sexist, the women in the church seem happy enough to have the men engaged in the church, comparing the situation with that of the black family in which men and women share the responsibilities of taking care of the family, with a male at the head of the household.

Since the congregations of most black churches are approximately 70 percent women, this church's ability to engage black men is unique. Indeed, the testimonials from African American men were particularly impressive, since this group has generally been difficult for psychotherapists to recruit into stable therapeutic relationships.

Spiritual Renewal

Black churches provide spiritual renewal, which is felt as a sense of liveliness, comfort, and personal transformation. The presence of the spirit is known when one feels emotionally swept up and senses the presence of God. Although the interviewees often mentioned the inner peace that they felt, it was an intensely personal experience that they did not necessarily want to talk about with someone else. Perhaps the inner peace functions also as a sanctuary away from the outside world.

In black churches, suffering is expressed in singing and in individual testimonials (Griffith et al. 1984). All the churches had choirs and a choir director, and most had several. One church had a gospel choir, a men's choir, an inspirational choir of younger people, and a senior choir. The Baptist churches have a reputation for having good gospel choirs; in fact, among Baptist and AME congregants, a good choir is a standard measure of a church's vitality. When an AME member told us, "The music ministry is not what it used to be," we knew that this was her lead into a tale of church decline.

Spiritual renewal is experienced by disclosing distressing information to the congregation, friends, or the pastor. This usually is done while praying or talking, but sometimes the congregants suddenly feel so connected to what the minister is saying that they feel he is talking about them. This helps a person tell others about his problems and deal with them more objectively. One member stated, "Sometimes I come and my burdens seem almost too hard to bear. But when I get here, and I hear the word, and apply it to my situation, the Lord takes away all of the sin and sorrow. I go home with peace."

Spiritual renewal is a cathartic letting go of tension and built-up feelings, thereby bringing emotional relief. The church is an asylum or safe place for members to act out and work through what ever troubles them by "shoutin'" or "getting happy" (Gilkes 1980). Other members encourage them to "let it all out," providing support and comfort. Interestingly, the congregants talked less about their spiritual struggles with the church and instead focused more on spiritual release. "A place where you can come and vent rather than take it out on your loved ones or other friends, something like that. A place where you can come and just let it all out and find support and affirmation."

The church also provides insight into the meaning of life. When a family member dies or someone is worried about losing a job, the church can provide a sense of purpose. "I was just unemployed recently, and during that time I didn't feel inadequate or incompetent by not having a job because I had a purpose. I had something to do here. I was involved in various ministries that gave me a sense of not only belonging but a sense that I am achieving something and my worth was not based on my profession or my job or income that I was bringing to the household."

In stressful situations, religion can help people come to terms with tragic life events (Hathaway and Pargament 1991). In addition, Ellison and Taylor (1996) found that prayer is widely used as a form of coping by African Americans when confronted with serious personal problems. Because it requires verbalizing one's problems, it may help crystallize and clarify them. Psychologically and physically, this form of spiritual renewal is important, especially for African Americans who suffer from high rates of hypertension and other stress-related diseases. One researcher found that people who were able to talk about their trauma experiences had fewer health problems and that people were more able to divulge information about themselves if they felt that they would be accepted regardless of what they said (Pennebaker 1990). This is also especially important in cities like New York City where stress and racial tensions are common.

Interpersonal Learning as Therapy

In New York City's black churches, when a person receives feedback on her behavior in a mostly caring manner, it leads to "interpersonal learning." One man commented, "It's helping me to come and it's a little frightening, but it's helping me to come into a better understanding of who I am as a man and I say that it's frightening because there's some growth that I'm experiencing as a result of the intentional work that is going on here. And I don't know where it's going. I don't. I'm becoming someone. I don't know. There are things about myself that I am discovering that I didn't know was there, you know, a walk I didn't have before, an attitude that I didn't have before, that at times can be frightening because other people don't understand. And it's not just men, it's also women. And there's a sense of security I have that I never really had before, almost a . . . you know, bring whatever challenge you want kind of attitude."

Interpersonal learning also takes place in structured situations like Sunday school. For example, one Sunday school teacher talked about planting seeds in a boy's mind who said he wanted to be a truck driver, "I planted another thought in his mind. Is there any reason why you don't want to be a doctor, lawyer or a judge? Not saying that a truck driver's not an accepted career, but we want to plant the idea that you don't have to just settle for what's there."

Conclusion

Church involvement for both white and black populations has been consistently related to personal adjustment, happiness or life satisfaction, psychological well-being, lower suicide rates, and fewer depressive symptoms (Ellison 1993; Koenig 1992; Krause 1992; Levin, Chatters, and Taylor 1995; Taylor and Chatters 1991).

The recent growth in the size of black churches indicates a return of African Americans to their indigenous organizations to address their spiritual, physical, social, and emotional needs (Harris 1997; McRae, Carey, and Anderson-Scott 1998). Since the traditions of the black church are an intricate part of the beliefs and feelings of many African Americans, mental health from a Christian perspective may be more acceptable to them. Indeed, the church has been the womb of black culture, nurturing moral values, traditions, ways of being, and ways of thinking about the life and condition of African Americans. It has provided hope and faith that the stresses of life can be resolved. Therapeutic programs that promote positive messages of caring, loving, sharing, transformation, and the meaning of life can be an extension of what seems to be the most powerful part of the black church experience.

NOTE

1. The focus groups, each ranging from five to seventeen people, were formed right after the Sunday service, and one of these focus groups was held after a club meeting on Wednesday night. The participants were mainly professionals or other middle-class people, although each group contained one or more working-class persons. Only in Big Brooklyn Baptist Church 1 were there a significant number of men in the focus group, even outnumbering the number of women.

Chapter 16

Cultural Crossroads in a Flushing Zen Monastery

Leah Davidson

New immigrants from highly structured Asian religious cultures find it difficult to adapt to our pragmatic, Christian, nuclear family–centered values and cultural metaphors. Because such assimilations often take up to three generations to be completed, psychotherapeutic and religious syntheses may help ease the transition. Further, many Asian countries are currently adapting Western psychodynamic and psychoanalytic therapies to existing moral and religious philosophies such as Zen Buddhism and Confucianism (Rhee 1990; Tatara 1994). Western psychoanalysis, however, has been slow to address human differences rather than human similarities.

The newer Western therapies stress the benefits of incorporating meditation and Zen Buddhism into behavior modification and mood stabilization in patients (Rubin 1996), with the combination of psychoanalysis and Confucian Zen Buddhism an example. Given the diversity of peoples found in New York City, the environment is particularly conducive to difficulties stemming from cross-cultural transitions. Because the cultural and religious backgrounds of those seeking help may affect their analysis and treatment, combining different traditions to address these problems and tailor the therapies to the patient's needs sometimes is helpful.

The Therapists

This chapter describes one such psychotherapeutic attempt at combining Korean "Confucian Zen Buddhism," and American psychoanalysis. The therapy was conducted in approximately thirty-five sessions with Dr. K, a

Zen Buddhist master being trained in Western psychotherapy. The patient being treated was a first-generation Korean immigrant.

I, the author of this chapter and the supervisor of the therapy, am a European-born, Jewish American woman with thirty years of psychiatric and cross-cultural experience. Dr. K selected me as the supervisor because I am also a specialist in cross- and transculture and had participated in many discussions with his Korean mentors in psychotherapy in New York and Korea. In addition, because I have a Korean daughter-in-law and two half-Korean grandchildren, he felt that I would understand the patient's background and adjustment to America better than most Westerners would. He also knew that I had some personal experience with meditative practices (those of the Hindu teacher Muktanada) and had learned from my Korean colleagues some of the basic assumptions of Zen Buddhist soteriology (path of salvation) and philosophy of mind.

I am also a Hasidic daughter, although at first I was part of a nonreligious socialist family. My father had been destined to become a Hasidic rabbi but rebelled and joined the socialist movement. His brother was a leader in the "Bund," a Jewish workers' group in New York City. Late in life, my father returned to Hasidism. Whether Hasidic or socialist, a religious sensibility always played a role in my family. I grew up among Hasidic people and, as a child, enjoyed hearing their stories. When I first began to work with Dr. K, I was interested in working with someone who was a Korean Zen Buddhist master, a physician, and a psychotherapist. In fact, the whole concept of remaining who we are while adapting is a very Jewish question.

Combining "Confucian Zen Buddhism" and Western Psychoanalysis

Dr. K's particular "Confucian Zen Buddhism" is a soteriological search for an enlightened understanding. The search is depicted by twelve ox-herding pictures telling a story of a search for a cow, a metaphor for enlightenment. The simple, humble story is reminiscent of the tone of the Yiddish stories that I had heard as a child.

In the 1970s, when Dr. K came to Queens to establish a medical practice, he brought with him a syncretic spirit. He was interested in combining Western psychotherapy with Confucian Zen Buddhist meditation. From his Confucian perspective, he was seeking to create a harmony based on a balance between a community and a religion. Similarly, in my own work I have combined Hasidism, Zen, Catholicism, and Greek mythology.

The search for enlightenment is also called the practice of "Borim," or "training the ox." The three essential elements for this discipline are (1) great faith, (2) great courage, and (3) *koan* (thought-provoking riddles).

J

Dr. K's *zendo?* (a Zen teaching center) in Flushing, Queens, had almost a dozen students. When one of his students had trouble with his Zen search, Dr. K suggested that such free-floating anxiety was best dealt with by Western-style psychotherapy. J thus volunteered to become his patient. In the first psychotherapy session, J stated on his own initiative, "I cannot meditate; my feelings are surfacing."

At the time, J was thirty-four, married, and had a three-year-old son. He worked as a dental technician and was seriously involved with his Zen studies. But he had been unable to make progress for more than a year, so he began psychological treatment with Dr. K.

J's father had recently developed a liver tumor and was slowly dying. J also showed many of the symptoms of abuse and codependence common to children of alcoholics. When drunk, his father would preach Confucian philosophy about "respect for the father" while making his two sons kneel before him. J's psychological defense against this abuse was to "think delightful thoughts" while the father preached. For a long time, J had repressed his hostility, but when it surfaced, it became rage, which he again repressed. But when he then became fearful, he ran away.

This vicious circle represents J's whole life. His interest first in Hindu religion and then in Zen practice was one of his escapes from his painful relationship with his father. At the same time, J wanted to restart like a boy and be loved by his parents. It was for this reason that he volunteered to receive psychotherapy.

Family Relations

Initially, the important difference between J and similar American patients was the Confucian ethical system binding him tightly to his family and to prescribed cultural behaviors. Confucianism teaches subservience to authority, particularly to the father and to traditional cultural patterns of family and social relations. Because this strong bond of authority between parent and child can turn into parental abuse, it might appear that J could be treated simply on the diagnosis of parental abuse and childhood trauma. But his Confucian belief system and cultural investment in obedience and suffering stood in the way of a standard Western psychotherapeutic approach.

Early on, the patient stated that he had a great deal of anger toward his father and also shame regarding his father's alcoholism. He was enraged by the father's use of Confucian teachings to justify familial abuse. In contrast, he revealed that his mother had always given him special treatment when his father was not around. He thus resented the fact that when his father returned, his mother would withdraw the special treatment and give it to his father—for example, in the serving of food—despite his father's frequent physical abuse of his mother when he was drunk.

At the same time, the patient was depressed about his father's illness and complained to the therapist about not being able to please his father. He also expressed guilt about not being able to follow the Buddhist way of "taking care of others." Dr. K understood that the patient was both fighting an internalized negative image of his father and avoiding the issue of his father's impending death. J reported yelling at his three-year-old son and was having a problem being close to his wife. He said he felt like a child when his wife tried to take care of him in the traditional Korean manner, and he also felt burdened by his mother's overprotectiveness and felt that she was still too close to him. His anger and shame made him feel that he was not a good enough son and husband. He stated that he did not "feel like a man."

J's wife wanted to go back to Korea, an outcome that J thought would shame him as a failure in America. He asked Dr. K about his need to achieve work and social status and his own sense of powerlessness to change things. J also stated that he was depressed because when he compared himself with his brother-in-law and other successful relatives, he had not achieved as much materially.

J's wife was Roman Catholic but J was not. Dr. K could mediate this difference somewhat based on his own Christian values and his experience of halfhearted attendance at his own Korean Protestant church.

Authority East and West

J's treatment was based on his relationship with Dr. K as his Zen teacher and psychotherapist. He began with reverence for his mentor and included the relationship of Dr. K as his therapist in this respectful, obedient relationship. On the surface, it might seem that these two functions of the therapist, transferential and reverential, should not be joined. Together, they make the client very dependent on the therapist, making it very difficult for the client to become emotionally independent. The question of whether the therapist can be admired or even revered is important, for after the therapy has been completed, the therapist's influence as an inner guide is always somewhat idealized and comes close to the Asian concept of *sensei* (master).

Dr. K's roles as a Zen master and a psychotherapist contained several paradoxes. For example, during meditation, he trained the patient to suppress intrusive feelings and thoughts, and during Western psychotherapy sessions, he encouraged the patient to express these same feelings and thoughts. Zen discipline relies on silence, and Western psychotherapy relies on verbal communication, with which Asian cultures are less comfortable. Dr. K was also examining his own feelings as he changed roles, a formidable task that was currently evolving for him.

The patient's struggle with these two sets of developmental tools is reflected in his attempt to develop a positive "teacher transference" rather than transfer his negative feelings about his father to the Zen master-therapist. The "teacher transference" can also be regarded as a transitional phenomenon, for it gives the patient a familiar security blanket and a second chance at relating positively to an authority figure in his life while he is expanding his autonomy and creating a hybrid self that spans both cultures. But the patient also had difficulty releasing his anger toward his father without forming a "negative father transference," which is a key method in psychotherapy.

J spent some of the sessions examining his feelings about his therapist in the double role of Zen master and Western therapist. He did not fully understand why "sudden enlightenment," that is, the ability to transcend and grow, could not take care of all his guilt, shame, and anxiety. He resented the fact that he had to engage with Dr. K in Western-style therapy, even though he had volunteered to do this. As Dr. K observed, "Anger is interfering with his meditation."

Along the way, Dr. K was able to clarify for the patient his father's mis-use of Confucian teachings for pathological reasons, and he stressed to J the Confucian concept of harmony in interpersonal relationships by means of quotations from Confucius.

Another method that Dr. K used was focusing on how J's need to be special was affecting his growth. When J began to ask many anxious questions, Dr. K used a paradoxical koan, "You are a person with many questions whose answers you don't know." This intervention seemed to calm and intrigue the patient and to help him continue in his quest. At the same time, Dr. K began examining the patient's dreams for evidence of transference feelings toward himself as a replacement figure for his dying father. He felt that the patient's self-esteem was low and could not improve without an idealized mentor, which he, in his role as Zen master, could be. The following two dreams illustrate this process. J said he dreamed that "I saw my father. He had a red tumor (hemangioma) on his head. He wanted to hide it under a hat. I asked, "What are you hiding? Don't drink any more. You give us problems."

J commented, "I feel sorry for him. He is in the hospital, but maybe he is getting what he deserves. I feel sorry for my mother. I love her."

J's dream continued: "I am going along a road. There is a parked car. I go in front of the car, step onto the hood, then onto the roof, then onto the trunk and back down to the ground. As soon as I came back to the ground, I felt that someone was following me, and [so I] began to run. Another boy ran with me. I asked him, 'Why are you running?' He answered, 'I kissed a girl who is engaged to the son of the president.' We went into a building and on the roof. There was no place to escape. We got the idea of a little child who said, 'There are two suspects running away!' I ignored the child and came out of the building. We went to a lake where John Gotti was sitting on a bench waiting for us. The other boy said, 'I am his son.' Mr. Gotti welcomed me and said, 'You escaped safely, thanks to my help.'"

J commented, "John Gotti feels like my father. My father helped me after my army duty. I worked for my father temporarily. I also felt that John Gotti was you, Dr. K, because of your strength and reliability. The walking over the car reminds me of a student demonstration I attended while in college. A student walked over a car during this demonstration." Dr. K observed, "You have two emotions. You want protection from your father, but you also want to find your own way."

Mother and Son

Dr. K also taught me about the mother–first son bonding in traditional Korean society. According to Confucian tradition, the firstborn has the privilege of carrying on the family lineage and inheriting the family's land, house, and other material items. In return, the son is obligated to take care of his parents when they grow old and to perform the annual memorial ceremonies to the ancestors.

Part of the patient's difficulty was his failure in his own eyes to fulfill his mother's early expectations that he become a doctor or a judge. Since the father was an inadequate husband, the mother had expected her son to make up for his father's defects. As the firstborn son, the patient's sense of being trapped in karmic obligations to his parents, who were irrational authorities and poor role models, increased. In his adolescence, J had recurring dreams of wanting to run away.

J's mother was also an extremely hardworking woman, with four different jobs and four children. This added to J's guilt and shame about his anger and ambivalence about his mother's inability to stop her husband's drinking and his own inadequacy as the firstborn son.

Death of the Father

Shortly after session 7, the patient's father died and the patient had to go through the Zen Buddhist mourning ritual, which lasts for forty-nine days. According to Buddhist tradition, on the forty-ninth day, the soul of the deceased goes before the king of heaven to be sentenced.

After his father's death, J's adolescent dreams of running away resurfaced. The first dream after his father's death indicated both his need to transcend his mourning process and to grow and his reliance on the strength and authority of his Zen Buddhist therapist. He felt much like a young student who was both dependent and defiant at the same time. J recalled his dream: "My father is lying in a wooden box in a tomb. It is located near the house. I looked at him and he seemed alive. I asked him, 'How come you are alive?' He answered, 'I am reborn and healthy. My cancer is gone.' I asked him, 'When you died, how did you feel about death?'"

A month later, J became very anxious in my own work and hung a picture of his father in his room at which he shouted, "Why didn't you listen to me when I told you to stop drinking? Then you would not have died from liver cancer!" J shouted that he felt sorry for him, that he blamed himself and his mother for not protecting the father from his own drinking. He felt nihilistic and empty but tried hard through meditation to restore his calmness.

J felt that his mother's expectations were weighing on him, and he became irritable and disrespectful to both mother and wife. His wife accused him of being like his father.

The Dead Father Lives On

During this approximately three and a half months, Dr. K focused on J's denial of his negative identification with the father and his superficial ideas of enlightenment. But J became overly sensitive to Dr. K's questions and described them as "stupid, like my father's questions." Although he was having more dreams, he was more silent in the sessions. The Eastern koan most useful to him at this time was the concept of *busang*, "everything passes and cannot be relied upon."

Dr. K felt rather burdened by both his patient's negative transferential feelings toward him and his denial and persistent questioning of the need for Western therapy. He therefore undercut J's need for a quick enlightenment by using Zen Buddhist koans. At the same time Dr. K brought out the negative transference and the similarity that the patient was feeling with "the stupid questions" asked by his father.

Agreeing with the patient's wife that her husband was becoming abusive toward the women in his household, Dr. K reminded J that Confucian concepts were designed for healthy people and could become too rigid when mental illness was involved. Thus J's negative identification with his father was beginning to produce some of the same abusive behavior in himself.

J's silences and irritability were indicative of his fear that the therapist would become angry with him and reject him as unacceptable. J became more ambivalent and quiet in sessions and wished to leave his job, even though he did not have another one lined up. He slept poorly and became disrespectful to his in-laws. He talked to his mother about her not resisting his father's violence, and when she told him, "I didn't divorce him because of you," he felt even more guilty.

J reported that his wife was depressed and ashamed because he was disrespectful to her family. He again began to wonder whether he needed

Western-style therapy and felt that he was too anxious to concentrate on his English studies. His emphasis was on suffering, not transcendence.

Although he repeated the koan *bang ha cha*, "let it be," he obtained no relief. He felt trapped by his wife, his mother, and his in-laws. When his wife became more autonomous, he saw this as his fault for being a bad husband. He became more irritable and began to treat her as a sex object. He realized that he expected her to serve him in the same way that his mother had served his father. In the midst of all this, he even asked his in-laws for help in learning computer graphics as a way of making more money. Another preoccupation at this time was obtaining his "green card."

Rejection of the Western Psychotherapist

Despite Dr. K's invitations to J's wife to come to a joint session with her husband, she refused. This made J feel, "What use is Western psychoanalysis?" At this time, he had another significant dream about the double tool of Zen Buddhism and Western therapy: "It is evening. My family and in-laws go out driving with me. I am driving but someone gives me a beer. I am worried about drunken driving. I see a police car, but it passes by. There is a playground, so I park there. I need to urinate. There is a three-story pagoda with a bathroom at the top. I climb up to the bathroom which is dirty and has urine and feces in it. I am not comfortable but I manage to pee."

He interpreted that "the bathroom is Western therapy. The pagoda is a symbol for Eastern culture."

This dream also illustrates J's growing sense of self-assertion and his retaliation for the put-downs by his in-laws was his urinating from a height. His therapist is his "base," the ground floor of the pagoda. J has, in fact, acquired a new tool, the combination of Zen and Western therapy which has enabled him to feel stronger.

A dream from approximately the twenty-fifth session indicates his discomfort with the therapy because he is the only patient in the Zen group undergoing this dual-therapy approach: "I was in an army infantry school getting basic training. There were a couple of soldiers there. I wondered why I was doing this, since I had done it before. I felt mistreated and went to the battalion commander and asked why I was here. He said, 'It is an error in the computer disk. A copy of your discharge will be given you. You can go home, but you have to report yearly for duty.' I asked why, and the commander said, 'The original computer disk was destroyed with your discharge.'"

J felt both resentful and helped by the therapy. The original "disk," that is, his old self, had been changed, but he wanted to be "discharged," with "check-ins" from time to time, an arrangement he actually used later.

Around this time, financial considerations took priority for J. He took a second job, and when an opportunity arose to become involved in a Korean import/export business, he stopped treatment but continued at the Zen center. Before leaving, he told the therapist that he had told no one that he was in Western therapy. He did say that three things had changed for him: "I have become aware of the reasons for my anger, and I can control them better. Dreams of my mother's death have stopped recurring, and dreams of running away have also stopped recurring."

During the period after the death of the patient's father, Dr. K had much empathy for him and also an increased sense of burden. Dr. K emphasized that Zen teaching also means that "talking back to a parent is attacking." But this created a dilemma regarding the expression and nonexpression of feelings in the two philosophies. He bridged this dilemma by stating to the patient that he understood things in Buddhist terms but not in terms of his own feelings. One cannot achieve enlightenment by omitting the pain of self-exploration. "If you go through love and hate, you will see more clearly." He also gave J the koan "What is it?" to help him explore and transcend his feelings. Dr. K felt that his patient's silences and resistance to Western-style psychotherapy were due to confusion between his negative feelings toward his father and (transference) and his current double role of Zen master and therapist.

Pride and Fall

Dr. K also felt that his patient was refusing to recognize how dependent he still wished to be on his mother and wife while protesting that he wanted to be a good son and husband and talking about enlightenment. He was having difficulty accepting his position as a beginner vis-à-vis enlightenment. In addition, he felt that he was splitting the transference into a positive transference toward Dr. K as a Zen master and a negative transference toward Dr. K as his therapist. When offered twice-weekly sessions, he refused.

J also had a great deal of false pride and used both Western psychotherapy and Eastern Buddhist ideas of transcendence to serve his own neuroses. He remembered that when his father was mean to his mother, she would sing to him to "grow faster and be a great man, take care of my enemies." J fantasized how he could become a great man through sudden enlightenment while in reality he was behaving more and more like his brutal father and feeling put down by his in-laws.

J told Dr. K that he thought he could surpass him. Dr. K accepted this as a helpful catharsis of anger. The patient, however, continued to be impatient about achieving buddhahood. Dr. K says that toward the end of J's therapy, "I opened up the issue of his feeling about Western therapy. He wanted me to act as a Zen teacher rather than as an analyst. He intends to come to the Zen center, so he feels that he is not really leaving treatment. Koreans do not have patients for psychotherapy. I tried to make [him] a patient. The patient viewed the treatment as helpful but found it alien. There was a basic mistrust of the therapy, but the patient did stay for thirteen months. He bowed when leaving me after the last session."

The Counselors' Challenges

As the Western psychoanalytic supervisor, I found that I constantly needed to do "cross-referencing," an act of cultural parallelism, to understand and advise on the balancing of therapy and mediation. I felt like the Hasidic rabbis who lived close to their congregations while being intellectually distant. How can the expression of feelings be integrated with the suppression of feelings? Can a therapist be a Zen master? Can a course of treatment run parallel to the path of enlightenment?

Perhaps Dr. K had the greater challenge. He was often frustrated by his double role. His student-patient used Zen-like silences to rebel against Western therapy. But in fact, the silences were a cover for J's very un-Zen-like feelings of guilt, shame, and denial regarding his relationships and his behavior. J was not so much in Zen transcendence as caught in a web of debilitating dependencies and reactions.

J hated and felt ashamed of his dependencies and his anger. But he could not replace them with therapeutic dependencies so that he would not have to face up to his dilemmas and struggle to leave them (which both therapy and Zen call transcendence). J never really liked being in the role of "patient," and he was uncomfortable with Western therapeutic ideas of maturing into autonomy. Neither could he accept a beginner status of Zen enlightenment.

His mother's song, "grow faster and be a great man, take care of my enemies," was a motivating force throughout the therapy. It was the command against which J rebelled while feeling small and helpless. His sense of shame about his own immaturity made him particularly sensitive to being in the double therapy of Zen meditation and Western therapy. In a culturally acceptable way, Dr. K became a role model for his patient combining both therapies. He tried to help him become his own self-affirming authority, telling him, "You are asking me for recognition, but I will not give it to you unless you give it to yourself."

A paradox in the therapy was the patient's denial of his attachment to Dr. K, yet J's dreams were clearly full of feelings about him. I, too, was challenged culturally: was the patient really resistant in the sense of not knowing his feelings, or was he simply seeking a culturally acceptable way of expressing his unacceptable feelings? Could Zen Buddhism enable him to deal with unacceptable feelings? It seemed to me that Zen enabled the patient to escape temporarily from his inner conflict and also allowed him to gain autonomy of choice. The concept of attaining buddhahood is similar to the release of emotional conflict in psychotherapy in its emphasis on and the transcendence of suffering.

Dr. K taught me that the Eastern *dao* (Way) and Western psychoanalysis are similar in that they both explore the search for one's own true self, a search that requires discipline. While both have the goal of attaining a better self, the Zen model seeks transcendent buddhahood with the hope of returning some good to the community. Both practices emphasize the importance of previous experience and the role of memory. But when J realized that there was no sudden enlightenment in Western therapy and that insight is followed by only gradual changes, he began to think about leaving therapy, although he had made some progress. He then stressed that he wanted to be "normalized" like Dr. K's other Zen students because he feared that if he told others about his psychotherapy, he would be perceived as "weak."

Results

After J left therapy, Dr. K felt let down that his experiment had been only partially successful. Dr. K also seemed to be only partly successful in bridging East and West. His patient-disciple fell back to being only a "disciple."

Dr. K followed up with J for two and half years. J continued to meditate at the Zen Buddhist Center, with Dr. K in the Zen teacher role. He was able to work on holding the koan *bang ha cha*, "let it go." Although he often wanted the therapist's attention, he was able to control his need for approval. J returned to his job, earned more money, and then attended dental school. He seemed to have more time for both meditation and family life. At the Zen center, he became an influence on other Zen students. Indeed, his increasing calmness was an incentive for four other students to enter Western therapy with Dr. K. Ironically, J felt that he was achieving the final goal of transcendence by giving to others. Dr. K's experience in combining Zen and psychoanalysis increased, and he is currently working under the supervision of senior Korean psychotherapists.

Eventually, J made friends with another Zen student who was an herbalist, and together, they became more confrontational. One day, J appeared unexpectedly at Dr. K's office. He was very excited and said, "I got enlightened in a dream." The dream was that he had been fighting his father and killed him. This was in keeping with the Zen instruction, "If you meet the Buddha on the way, kill him." J felt that it was a statement about letting go of his hate and anger toward his father, but it was also a competitive statement with regard to Dr. K and a reversal of any reverential "teacher transference" he may have developed up to this point.

Dr. K informed him that this was an important dream but was not enlightenment itself. He explained that true enlightenment was an experience of emptiness and facing the void. J did not understand that he was still not a full initiate and became angry with Dr. K. Subsequently, although J came to the center to listen, he meditated by himself. He and his friend the herbalist seemed to be feeding each other's grandiosity.

After a while, J went back to Korea to see another Zen master who was not highly respected in Korea. He stayed in Korea and continued his import/export business. Dr. K now feels that he should not have terminated J's treatment of Western therapy. My own feelings, in retrospect, are that Dr. K showed much courage and dedication in tackling this difficult synthesis of diverse cultural approaches to the mind.

The patient was able to work through and let go of his rage and grief about the loss of the father. But he was not able to let go of his need to be a great man and to surpass his role models. So far, neither psychotherapy nor Zen Buddhism has enabled him to "let go," as demanded by the koan *bang ha cha*. That is, J was not able to develop fully a bridging "teacher transference," which would have helped him accept and internalize the wisdom of his mentor and to "let go." In sum, he gained neither Zen enlightenment nor therapeutic transcendence.

Ten Ox-Herding Pictures and Psychotherapy

The seventh picture, "Ox forgotten," is the attainment of no inner conflict. The tenth picture, "entering the city with bliss bestowing hands," is giving back to the community.

Until now, Western psychoanalysis has not included the highest religious concepts of Zen Buddhism as represented by the seventh and tenth pictures.[1] In today's New York City, the search for multicultural relevance and deep peace of mind is bringing some seekers to psychoanalytical Confucian Zen Buddhism.

With regard to J's particular cultural cognition, it is difficult to judge whether the cultural prescriptions for his behavior as a son, husband, and father changed. However, if one looks at his dreams and his own statements about change, it becomes apparent that had he been encouraged by his family and peers to stay in "the double treatment," he might have worked through his competitive and grandiose feelings toward his therapist and teacher. This would have resulted in a true "enlightenment." His rigid and self-punitive interpretation of his Korean cultural obligations as a son, husband, and father might then have changed, helping him achieve some of his goals for his life in America.

Many years ago, as a young trainee and a new immigrant myself, I was assigned to train foreign doctors. We seemed to understand one another. Much later, the same thing seems to have happened with Dr. K. A bridge was made between a Hasidic Western daughter and the diverse religions of the world in New York City. As immigrant minds change, so do ours.

NOTE

1. With the exception of the work of C. G. Jung (1967), Erich Fromm (1950), and Harry Stack Sullivan (1940).

Chapter 17

New York Neo-Puritans
Using Counseling to Overcome Stereotypes of Religion

Hannibal Silver

Although New York City seems to be the antithesis of the Bible Belt, every week several thousand New Yorkers gather just around the corner from Bloomingdales at the evangelical Redeemer Presbyterian Church. Redeemer's senior pastor, the Reverend Timothy Keller, says that his church has been careful to counteract the stereotypes of evangelicals with an atmosphere of "emotional warmth" that is "friendly to doubters" (Kirkpatrick 1993, 1). As *New York Times* reporter Edward Lewine observed, "The 47-year old Mr. Keller has managed to make a pull-no-punches Christianity credible to his congregation by packing conservative theology in a non-judgmental style" (1998, 18).

On a Wednesday evening in 1986, Redeemer was just an idea to a dozen people who had gathered at an Upper East Side apartment. As David Balch, a founding leader of the group, recalls, they originally gathered as a task group of people from parachurch ministries to plan the founding of a church and to interview pastoral candidates. Then the assembly became a nurturing group as they began praying and planning for a vision. The members, Balch says, started to share more about their personal lives and ministry hopes and failures in the city. These meetings became a seedbed for a church culture emphasizing both organization and nurture. One of the results was Redeemer Presbyterian Church (RPC), founded in 1989; another was RPC's counseling center, founded in 1992.

From this small group, at an unremarkable address in New York, sprang an evangelical Christian movement that ten years later involves more than four thousand people in Redeemer Presbyterian Church in Manhattan (mostly young professionals of an average age of thirty) and many more in

TABLE 17.1
Who's Who in the Church?

Average Age	30
Marital Status	About 70% single
Residence	
East side	30%
West side	30%
Downtown	15%
Other	25%
Ethnicity	
White	55%
Asian	35%
Other	10%

seventeen other affiliated churches. Redeemer Presbyterian Church continues the sharing of life and faith characteristic of its seedbed small group.

The counseling center also continues Rev. Keller's early counseling sessions over coffee at the Tramway Diner, on Second Avenue and Sixtieth Street. Here, the pastor learned about New Yorkers' struggles and aversion to judgmental religion and came to understand how evangelical Christianity could work in the city.

Redeemer's counseling center is now composed of thirteen mental health professionals who offer individual counseling (about three hundred visits each year with an annual 13% increase) as well as sixteen group sessions. Redeemer counselors draw from different schools of psychology, amplified by a biblical worldview.[1] Without denying the nature/nurture factors in developmental and abnormal psychology, they also acknowledge a spiritual dimension as relevant to the therapeutic process (see table 17.1).

One counselor recalled a lecture by his secular teacher Alfred Byon as an example of the difference between RPC counseling and secular counseling. According to Byon, humans are intelligent monkeys with solutions for every situation. But humans do not know the meaning of life or the wisdom for the long term. But RPC counselors stress that they can offer both meaning and wisdom for the long haul.

In the RPC sessions, counselors explore two windows to the human soul: thoughts and emotions. Their caution against a hasty diagnosis rests on their belief that "the heart is deceitful above all things" (Jeremiah 17:9). For example, before declaring that a client has been a victim of sexual molestation, counselors are advised to help that person retrieve more than repressed memories by searching for external confirmation.

The counselors also use a messianic hope that is linked to an optimistic sense of providence. One counselor suggested, "God is the sovereign of human destiny as the experience of Joseph and Esther illustrate." Messianic images such as the ones found in Isaiah 53 and 61 are regarded as resources to guide the therapeutic process. In addition to insight and personal awareness, the counselors believe that clients need the assurance of hope and redemption.

For example, the counselors believe that client Jennifer's experience points to the significance of messianic hope as a psychological resource. At group sessions, Jennifer spent most of her time crying, and at first she did not say a word. She appeared paralyzed by a sense of mistrust, betrayal, and rejection, and her two basic coping mechanisms were isolation and shame.

After a while, though, she called a counselor to ask, "Are you praying for me?"

Surprised, the counselor said, "Yes."

"Why are you praying for me?" she asked.

The counselor replied, "I was praying on whether I was supposed to be helping you in a counseling relationship." Jennifer then started to come for individual sessions.

At first, Jennifer always studied the floor as if she were being asked to confess a crime, for in her eyes she was guilty and ashamed of the abuse she thought she had provoked. "I feel worthless, like nothing," she said. The counselor listened and shared his confidence that God had redeemed her for a life of hope and reward. Jennifer made remarkable progress. Even in the first six sessions, one could tell that her eyes rose a little more each week. After three months, Jennifer shared enough of the counselor's spiritual optimism to begin to trust people outside the counseling circle. The counselors believe that messianic hope helped Jennifer look beyond the immediate situation and take a chance on life again.

The counselors do admit that "divine providence" can be mysterious. One cautioned, "In a few counseling situations, silence is better than theological insight. Job's counselors were committed to the task of rescuing God from any blame in their clients' predicament; therefore, they chose to judge their client." The counselors try to turn divine silence into a belief in the redemption of any person or situation.

One counselor noted that Job's friends were controlled by the tyranny of the past, a belief that one harvests today what one planted yesterday. The counselor argued,

It is safe to say that no human tragedy is beyond the power of divine re-demption. When confronted with a man blind from birth, the disciples of Jesus reasoned in a similar manner: "Rabbi, who sinned, this man or his parents, that he was born blind?" "Neither this man nor his parents sinned," said Jesus, "but this happened so that the work of God might be displayed in his life." (John 9:2,3)

One client, Robert, came while he was dying of AIDS, saying he wanted to be at peace with God, and at first, that is all the counselor helped him with. During one counseling session, Robert admitted, "Now I have a real life." During Robert's bout with pneumonia, the counselor laid his hands on and anointed Robert in a Christian ritual prayer for healing. The week before Robert died, he wrote his last testament for the counselor: "I am thankful that you were willing to lay your hands on me for anointing." Often, the counselors are surprised that terminally ill clients do not ask God for healing but pray to experience eternity in the here and now as a prelude to life after death.

Redeemer's Via Negativa

Most Protestant denominations have regarded Manhattan as the great graveyard of failed attempts to renew or start churches. Indeed, the first attempt in New York by Redeemer's parent organization, the Presbyterian Church of America, limped along for several years before giving up. Evangelicals have been particularly fearful of Manhattan liberals' sharp hostility to any kind of Christian fundamentalism, as they believe that New York's media elites have created a caricature of evangelicals as walk-ing know-nothing bigots.

But evangelical leaders also believe that the hostile liberal culture will create conformity in any church that it does not crush. Before supporting Redeemer, evangelical leaders had to convince themselves and their sup-porters that they were not creating a vehicle of secularization that would drag everyone in the project down into liberalism. Rev. Keller recalls that his field research in the city left him "awed and stirred by the arrogance, fierce secularity, diversity, power, and spiritual barrenness of NYC in the late 1980s" (Keller 1992, 24).

Tim Keller and his small band were determined to shape a church that would overcome the caricatures of evangelicals circulating among liberal New Yorkers and even city evangelicals themselves. They decided to create a church culture around several core convictions. They envisioned that Redeemer would be (1) a "third way" between moralism and relativism, (2) procity and antisuburban, (3) socially concerned, (4) racially and ethnically integrated supporters of the arts and humanities, and (5) an urban movement, not a lonely outpost for Middle America.

Redeemer Rejects a Number of Stereotypes about Evangelicals

Countering the common caricature of evangelicals as rigid moralists Redeemer emphasizes the "good news" of personal peace and social healing rather than damnation and guilt. RPC counselors counterpoise their approach to fundamentalist "rule solutions." As one counselor pointed out, "The Bible is not a book of rules but a book of wisdom." The underlying assumption is that spiritual redemption means coming to think for oneself in dialogue with God and the Bible.

Redeemer's counselors strive to keep a proper balance between an acknowledgment of the complexity and danger of the human condition and the possibilities of personal redemption. Like RPC as a whole, the counselors say they also reject the simplistic black-and-white fundamentalist approach to personal problems. Counselors say that Christianity does not hinder personal freedom and development. One counselor cites the definition of freedom used by Abraham Heschel in *The Meaning of Shalom* as living in harmony with others, including God. The "rules" are wisdom for harmonious living, not guilt-producing, punishment-driven do's and don'ts.

Redeemer and its counselors often use the metaphor of a "third way" to present themselves as an alternative between the "religious" and the "irreligious." The religious person may say, "I am doing the right things that God commands and others are not," and the irreligious person may say, "I decide what is right and wrong for myself." The counselors argue that both ways are strategies of self-salvation, that both actually keep the self in control. In contrast, they maintain that the gospel defines the root sin as not relying on God as the way out of problems, that what the gospel presents is the "third way" between legalism and moralism, on the one hand, and hedonism and relativism, on the other. Redeemer's counseling center assumes there will be a spiritual conflict but de-emphasizes conflicts against groups of people or cultural and political parties.

The counselors often see people who have been horribly victimized. These clients, however, are often as miserable from their hate and anger at their oppressors as from the original victimization. Using slave and penal metaphors, the counselors depict the clients as being enslaved by not forgiving the people they hate or as being in prison for life behind the bars of their ugly memories and deep-seated anger against their oppressors. One counselor told his client, "Yes, someone has to pay for what was done so you can have release from your anger." The counselor suggested that the death of Christ was Christ's way of substituting himself to receive punishment for the evil doer so that even the evil doer could be forgiven by God and, likewise, by the client.

Redeemer counselors claim that classical Christian faith understood counseling as a war against the lies of the mind and spirit that keep people in bondage to abusive relationships, oppressive environments, addictive habits, and destructive patterns of thinking, feeling, and behavior. This war is won through the liberating power of Truth about God, oneself, and good and evil. To them the slogan "you will know the truth, and the truth will set you free" (John 8:32) sums up their counseling approach.

The counselors mostly agree that belief systems that do not focus on Christian teaching are destructive to their adherents. So counselors sometimes say that low self-esteem means that a person may be neglecting the doctrine that humans were created in the image of God. Or they might counsel the achievement-driven person about defining oneself by success instead of God. In this way, RPC counselors argue, deceitful beliefs create "a false self," a psychological construct similar to the theological one about a "natural man" who lives to the flesh, the world, and the devil. "At Redeemer . . . we treat non-Christians with respect, remembering what it is like to not believe. We consider virtually every public event to be something we do 'before the nations,' and we expect to be 'overheard' by many friends who do not believe or who don't know what they believe" (*Redeemer's Vision Statement*).

Countering a common perception of evangelicals as rejecting those different from them, the center welcomes all people, and some of the center's clients do in fact come from different religious orientations. The center's goal is to provide them with a safe environment from which they can grow into their unique identities. At the same time, Redeemer's counselors see an opportunity for their own growth. One observed, "We have much to learn and much to unlearn about others." Out of one such encounter, a Seventh-Day Adventist joined Redeemer and today leads the counseling center.

In a Calvinist turn, Redeemer counselors embolden themselves and their clients with biblical stories of how God overrules disaster and guilt.

They say that God can turn any turnip into a tulip. And counselors assert that forgiveness is founded on a knowledge that God's sovereign plan means that everything will work out in the end.

Deeply religious people are often perfectionist in spirit and self-condemning in practice. To counter this problem, the counselors use the sense of divine plan to counteract the accusations of a guilty conscience. A few years ago, one of Redeemer counselors was invited to spend the night in a house stricken by tragedy. Tony, young and without a driver's license, had been killed in a highway accident. Tony's parents blamed themselves for his death. One parent said, "If we had been better parents with a more directive discipline, our son would be alive today." Through counseling, the parents came to see that they could use Tony's death to make a more meaningful life for themselves by actively helping other parents with their children.

Redeemer leaders are sensitive to characterizations as "fundamentalist dopes," that is, those people whose ancestors threatened scientists like Galileo, tried evolutionist John Scopes in the early twentieth century, and are said to make up the religious right today. To counter this view, Redeemer's counselors are quick to insist that they do not favor faith and revelation over reason and science:

> We help our clients discover how God relates to his creatures as intelligent beings. Through the use of parables and psalms, history and prophecies, circumstances and trials our Maker wants to reason and dialogue with his creation. The rules of his open forum are only three: the participants will agree to talk, to listen, and to think. Mere Christianity is not for those who don't ask questions for fear of the answers.

Nevertheless, counselors face conflict with clients over what is truly "spiritual." One morning, a troubled woman sat down and asked, "Will you exorcise several demons from my husband?" She reported that her husband was a sweet human being who, under the devil's power, had tried to kill her. As the counselor listened to her story, he was convinced that she was telling the truth about the risk to her life. But rather than exorcisms, the counselor advised her to call the police and seek personal protection. The counselor and client were operating from two different views of spirituality. The client saw her husband as a good man who had become evil under the devil's power, whereas the counselor saw him as a dangerous person in need of treatment.

The counselors believe that people are too complex to be reduced to the purely spiritual. For example, a few people have come to the center claiming oppressions by the devil and the need for exorcism. One person claimed her anorexia was the result of demonic burdens. Another claimed that a satanically driven spouse had tried to murder his partner seven times. RPC counselors discount a sort of quick "magical" exorcism of such problems, although they do not discount satanic spiritual realities.

As one counselor put it, "We might first deal with the anorexic's physical problem of 'no food.'" Then the counselors point to the common problem of identifying with fashion models, suggesting that beauty can fade, leaving behind an undeveloped kindness or wisdom. Counselors say that clients find peace with themselves through a belief in the human as made in the image of God.

The Christian notions of "salvation" and "new birth" are easily misunderstood as meaning the death of self and the surrender to God. After Joanne was sexually abused by her uncle, she spent her life hiding from her shame and pain. But after several group sessions, she began to see a glimmer of a new life. She saw a new identity "in Christ," and it became a tool to redefine herself. Her story was no longer a personal story of shame but a story within Christ's story of rejection and resurrection.

But as Joanne told her counselor, "I still feel like a shadow rather than a visible person. How can I become a real person?" She found Paul's words in his Letter to the Galatians particularly discouraging: "I have been crucified with Christ and I no longer live, but Christ lives in me" (Galatians 2:20). Joanne wondered, "Would I have to remain a shadow for the glory of God?" Joanne was still defining herself in light of the abuse she had suffered. She had abandoned her old bruised self in Christ but had not yet found a new self. While losing herself in Christ instead of shame was a positive step, Joanne needed a new self, too.

Redeemer counselors broadened her scriptural interpretation, telling Joanne that the whole Bible needed to be used to balance out the teaching of any one text like that of Galatians. They also cited Christian apologist C. S. Lewis's conviction that Christ came to this world not to make us Christian but to make us human. They counseled Joanne to be thankful for her personality while letting her relationship with Christ gradually give her new insights about a new self.

The counselors also encounter internal conflicts regarding sexuality. For example, John came to the center struggling with pornography and sexual addiction. His business trips were marked by binges of adult TV and prostitutes. Within himself, John had both delight in Christian principles of personal integrity and also a gripping sexual passion. Guilt and shame plagued him.

Because evangelicals are often assumed to condemn sexuality, John came expecting to undergo a round of condemnation and exhortation followed by a probationary time of "monastic" life. Yet he was neither condemned nor approved. Instead, he was encouraged to seek real intimacy with God in the context of a healing church community (Schaumburg 1992). In counseling and support groups, John was encouraged to replace his inner pattern of vicious cycles of self-accusation, self-hatred, and false intimacy with cycles of forgiveness.

John's final homework assignment surprised him: he was expected to seek and find a woman to marry and to serve her with integrity. The counselors believe that the antidote to sexual addiction is not the avoidance of sex but, rather, true intimacy. This somewhat unusual assignment resulted in a marriage that seems to have remained healthy.

Religion is often a hindrance to recovery from psychological disorders. For example, Helen came for counseling in regard to her relationship with Jay, who was the father of her four children but who refused to marry her on spiritual grounds. Every time he was confronted with the notion of marriage, he would get "more religious" and request more time for prayer and meditation. Helen would also use religion to avoid the pain of her situation. Through counseling, both were encouraged to see faith as a resource for moral decisions rather than as a mechanism of escape and denial.

Many evangelicals arrive at Redeemer battling inner demons of fundamentalism. They feel caught between the freedom of being unconditionally loved by God and the moralism of evangelical piety. They feel called to excellence in their worldly professions but face a church movement that is often parochial or otherworldly. They are, in fact, urban outposts of a suburban and rural religion; they live in New York City, which most evangelicals see as Sodom.

By contradicting these common stereotypes of evangelicals, Redeemer has attracted New Yorkers who would not normally be open to evangelical religion, and the counselors have succeeded in incorporating spirituality and divine wisdom into their therapeutic work.

NOTE

1. The ideas expressed in this chapter are my own and not necessarily those of Redeemer Church. The counseling experiences and names have been changed to protect confidentiality.

Chapter 18

Religion Class at Sing Sing Prison

Victoria Lee Erickson and H. Dean Trulear

The soul is the prison of the body.

—Michel Foucault

For so it is Oh Lord, My God, I measure it but what I measure, I do not know.

—St. Augustine

In the words of Mike, an inmate at Sing Sing State prison, religion classes "are a place of transformation for me." Each year, New York Theological Seminary (NYTS) graduates a growing number of prisoners who, almost miraculously, seldom return to prison. Mike recalls, "It was a great turning point in my rehabilitation. The year at New York Theological Seminary was very important to me to not lose faith and that I could and would be redeemed from that sin of the past. Here I was a student—a person—and not just a convict. This is very important."

During one recent twelve-month period, not one alumnus of NYTS's Masters in Professional Studies (MPS) Program was rearrested, compared with 30 percent in the larger population (O'Connor et al. 1996; O'Connor and Erickson 1997).[1] After twenty-eight months, the comparable rearrest rates were 9 percent for the graduates and 37 percent for the non-MPS ex-offenders. Subsequent program changes that increased students' personal accountability have further reduced recidivism of alumni to almost zero. Although all prison service programs officially try to reduce recidivism, the NYTS program's main goal is simply to create chaplains inside the prison. The results have unexpectedly been much more profound.

Sing Sing Prison and New York Theological Seminary

For more than a century, both Sing Sing and New York Theological Seminary have claimed to seek the personal and social transformation of prison inmates. Under a mandate of the "justice system," Sing Sing Prison was built in 1825 with one thousand cells. Seventy-five years later, shaped by the faith of believers and the mandate of religious traditions, New York Theological Seminary was founded to serve the poor immigrant communities of New York City, and in 1981 NYTS joined with Sing Sing (now Ossining State Correctional Facility) to create the Master's in Professional Studies program for inmates—from all religions—with long sentences who would work in their prison as chaplain's assistants.

Each year, the highly competitive program enrolls an average of ten to fifteen students per class out of seventy-five applications. Each applicant must have a college degree and come highly recommended by NYTS alumni. Later, the students will join this network when they get out of prison. The seminary's program also requires one year of fieldwork and pastoral counseling course work, supervised in a prison setting.[2] All NYTS programs offer traditional and liberation-oriented seminary classes and pastoral counseling, with courses addressing racism, sexism, and classism.

A profile of alumni released from prison indicates that about two-thirds are Christian and that the majority of the non-Christians are Muslim. Sixty-three percent are black, 16 percent are white, and 14 percent are Hispanic. The mean age of the inmate alumnus is forty-four, and he has an average of an eleventh-grade education completed before his incarceration (1996 NYTS Released Alumni Survey).

Because of its commitment to faith, NYTS invests more in the Sing Sing program than is normally expected from New York prison college programs. That is, the seminary expects its senior staff to teach classes and holds them accountable for the students' success. To communicate better with their students, the faculty learn the languages of their student subcultures and discuss with each student not only educational goals but also personal goals.

The seminary has succeeded as a "world reconstruction" program largely because of the inspiration and guidance of its charismatic leader

Bill Webber. With degrees from Harvard, Union Theological Seminary, and Yale, Webber's involvement communicates sacrifice and quality to both the students and the faculty. His charisma is manifested in his deeply emotional identification with the student inmates. Together, they often cry over their stories and share the excitement as inmates' learning rises to unexpected heights. Webber's booming, joyful voice lifts everyone, and his visible struggle with anger against the bureaucracy identifies him with his students. By watching him, the inmate students say they discover how they can change their own emotions from an obstacle into a resource. When Webber hears these comments, he always says, "I don't know anything about that. It's all the students; they have taught me everything I know." This type of comment, of course, lifts the students even higher.

The Faith Vocabulary Shared by Correction Specialists and Seminarians

To explain the motivation to intervene in messy life stories caught in a complicated "justice system," community corrections researchers and practitioners use a spiritual vocabulary, including words like *mission, goodwill, virtue, peace, faith*, and *spirit*. Furthermore, in the seminary-within-the-system, socially conservative, liberal, and radical people are all connected by *faith* that people will respond to human caring. Even though humans are not "indefinitely malleable," corrections personnel and religious people alike have a holy or "secular faith that human nature permits the possibility of wide social cooperation to bring about a just or egalitarian society" (Arneson 1985, 627). For the seminary interventionists, the reclamation of individuals has little to do with a psychological or sociological label (Irvin 1994) and everything to do with the *spiritual* context of building relationships of accountability (Lemert 1993, 243–247).

In "Probation as Good Faith" (1996, 5), Souryal claims that the successful probationist stands between the victim and the perpetrator and, with blind faith, seeks to change a relationship based on the pain of transgression to one based on the equality and potential of all persons. So, for those doing probation work, reconciliation is like a spiritual task. NYTS itself draws from the probation tradition as well as a variety of theological traditions such as the evangelical, conservative, liberal, radical Protestant, and Catholic.

Some feminist traditions that NYTS incorporates also recognize that reconciliation is a voluntary spiritual activity requiring self-denial. The student inmates love to hear the story of Letty M. Russell, who created a "plywood theological school" in a Harlem church. Russell, now a professor at Yale, put a plywood sheet on cinder blocks out on the sidewalk to hold communion and discuss gender reconciliation. Given the success of the NYTS programs, one might even conclude that, for example, a forced "gender peace" using "extra-church" resources delayed genuine reconciliation in many communities (Russell 1993).

Indeed, Emily Greene Balch, a Nobel Peace Prize winner, stated that solutions should be anchored in "disinterested benevolence" (Faver 1991). This benevolence arises when one gives up privilege and sacrifices oneself for the good of all. Balch's sense of justice includes a notion of quiet, friendly self-sacrifice that creates space for hearing all voices (see 1996 NYTS Released Alumni Survey). She exemplifies that uncanny ability that NYTS uses to enter conflicting communities, create a bridge between their stories, and develop a mediating strategy to seek the common good anchored in the parties' moral integrity. At their own cost, liberationist reconciling agents establish a conversation between the victim and the perpetrator that modulates into a story of reconciliation.

A Pedagogy for Transformation

The students' reasons for being in prison are frequently clouded in mystery. Many younger inmates' belief in street morality and lack of older male role models have left them baffled by legal and mainstream social moralities. The experience of prison only intensifies their feelings of powerlessness, ignorance, and despair. When asked what frustrates them, the students cite feelings of being lost. Prison policies seem to reflect "hopelessness and meaninglessness" with little regard for prisoner outcomes. Between Kafkaesque bureaucratic and criminal cruelties, the students worry that they do not have "a spiritual guide" to lead them to a better future.

To start peeling away the bewilderment and powerlessness, the student inmates are asked to think about why they are in prison. Commonly they say, "If you are good on the streets, you get run over"; or "The kids are hungry and they need shoes, so you do what you have to do"; or "My job was the street."

Although these "I-centered" responses locate the moral source of action in the student, they also point a finger at society. In fact, the way that society relates to the "I" creates the "me," a socially defined self. In the MPS program, students learn that new ways of relating require new ways of interpreting the world and self. The teachers help the students sift through "scenarios" to discover how other social actors helped them end up in prison. As a result, the students come to realize that an extensive social conversation is taking place without them. Prodding one another to explain how they arrived in prison, students learn that "recreating the self" is a community project, too.

At first, the students are very guarded about talking about their crimes. But starting on the first day, Webber keeps asking them how it is that they are in prison. Also, as the student inmates talk with one another about the tangled emotions of the sacred texts, they gradually form a cohesive group and help one another confess and analyze their stories. Webber's attention to the students' stories also contrasts with the lack of attention from virtually everyone else. Personal and biblical stories start to come together to help create a new social space for self.

Although all inmates know that they have to talk about their victims if they want to be paroled, the NYTS program seems to create not a bunch of manipulative storytellers but a community with a new self-affirming narrative against a corrupted former self and a hostile society. In the end, each student inmate has a complete narrative legitimated by sacred tradition as well as a new community and identity to present to the larger world. Some, of course, fall back into being street manipulators, but a surprising number emerge with an authentic newness that stands the test of time.

Self-creation is a task that all religious traditions address. But for prisoners, the question often is, how can self-creation take place without violent self-assertion? In a tolerance strategy, all students must read the sacred texts of other peers before analyzing their own story. In the city, the stimuli are so strong that if the students do not first recognize the incongruity of perspectives in prison, they will not be prepared to be challenged on the street about their worldviews. Also, learning to handle religious disagreement without hostility leads to listening to wise counsel and nonviolence.

While reading the sacred texts, the students discover that although there are social boundaries around the text's meaning, these boundaries are broken by narrators coming and going and the loss of historical sequence. In addition, from their own multicultural experiences, the students find out that they know something about a sacred text that was not known to its actors. And as they examine one another's different interpretations, they learn something about themselves and life's many meanings. Sitting around a table, the students find out that knowledge is its own reward, empowering because it is communal and most fun when it is shared, and that it has various meanings. They discover the joy of doing something ancient and the joy of forgiveness arising from their "table talk."

Guided by faculty, the students unpack their life stories and learn to trust one another with them. Students are often for the first time talking to a caring group about sex, lovers, their feelings for their fathers and mothers, and their desires for children. Twenty-four percent of alumni say that the NYTS program brought them good friends who helped them sustain their new social identity. "At NYTS I met . . . fellow sojourners who supported my change," one said. Others talk about their discovery of a "brotherhood" and "a network of friends." The impersonal changes into an intensely social bond leading the inmate out of the "prisoner" identity. In fact, another 13 percent of the alumni specifically referred to this "sense of community" that was "created . . . in the class."

For people of faith, formative stories that craft moral identity are *holy stories*. The students comment on the similarity of their own changing stories and that of the actors in the sacred storybooks (the Bible, Qu'ran, and Torah) who also change their course of direction and plot their way to the end. As the students dare to speak to others across the breaks in their life boundaries, they begin to realize that they also are changing. Along the way, they learn one another's languages and then create another language that they all share.

When Webber realized that this "talk" is critical to the students' success, he added another day each week to his schedule at Sing Sing so that he could "just sit in the classroom and listen to people talk" (interview, December 10, 1997). The relational "I-you" is a third-way alternative to the nonrelational "I-me" and leads to the creation of a new "sense of shared structure" (Buber 1970; Sumedho 1960). Once the students learn how relationships are conversationally and interactionally created, they also learn how to restructure them. Talking and sharing end up being the most profound "soulcraft."

The NYTS program is unique in that it combines theological values with an ethnomethodological perception of the social world. Ethnomethodology is a type of sociology that locates the creation and continuation of the social world in everyday conversations and interactions. It looks at the superstructure of the great big society as riding and arising on the snap and crackle of the small-scale talk and acts of everyday life. Consequently, instead of plugging the students into "the system," NYTS instructors help the students recognize how they themselves in their ordinary conversations and interaction replicate and can change their place in the system and even change the system itself.

Teachers plot normal, natural change in the students as they come to create a "sense of shared structure" (Pfohl 1975). Of course, this change must come from within the student's conversations with his society, home community, and peers so that he feels he "owns" it.

Members of a sociology class begin by reading a familiar sacred story and discussing the meanings given to the story by their various cultural traditions. In one class, the students read I Samuel 28. Traditional commentators say that I Samuel 28:1–25 contains a pivotal event in biblical history. King Saul, the founder of Israel's monarchy, is about to lose the last vestiges of his legitimacy, thereby opening the way to David's monarchy from which is traced all millennial hopes of Judaism and Christianity.

In those days the Philistines gathered their forces for war, to fight against Israel. Now Samuel had died, and all Israel mourned. Saul had expelled the mediums and wizards from the land.

When Saul saw the army of the Philistines, his heart trembled greatly. When Saul inquired of the Lord, the Lord did not answer.

Then Saul said to his servants, "Seek out for me a woman who is a medium, so I inquire of her." His servants said to him, "There is a medium at Endor." So Saul disguised himself and went there, and two men with him. They came by night.

And he said, "Consult a spirit for me and bring up for me the one I name to you." The woman said to him, "Surely you know what Saul has done, how he has cut off the mediums and the wizards from the land. Why then are you laying a snare for my life to bring my death?" But, Saul swore to her by the Lord, "As the Lord lives, no punishment shall come upon you for this thing."

Then the woman said, "Whom shall I bring up for you?" He answered, "Bring up Samuel." When the woman saw Samuel, she cried out, and said to Saul, "Why have you deceived me? You are Saul!" The king said to her, "Have no fear; what do you see?"

Then Samuel said to Saul, "Why have you disturbed me by bringing me up?" Saul answered, "I am in great distress, for the Philistines are warring against me, and God has turned away and answers me no more; so I have summoned you to tell me what to do." Samuel said, "The Lord has torn the kingdom out of your hand, and given it to David. Moreover, the Lord will give Israel along with you into the hands of the Philistines; and tomorrow you and your sons shall be with me."

Immediately Saul fell full length on the ground, filled with fear; and there was no strength in him, for he had eaten nothing. The woman came to Saul and she was terrified, she said to him, "I have taken my life in my hand, and have listened to what you have said to me. Now, therefore, you also listen to your servant; let me set a morsel of bread before you." He refused, and said, "I will not eat."

But his servants, together with the woman, urged him; and he listened. So, he got up and sat on the bed. Now the woman had a fatted calf. She quickly slaughtered it, and baked unleavened cakes. She put them before Saul and his servants, and they ate. Then they arose and went away that night. (Adapted from *The New Oxford Annotated Bible* [New York: Oxford University Press, 1991, 379–380])

Most of the NYTS students know quite a bit about and have particular feelings about this biblical story. Their parents taught it to them, and gospel hymns harmonized it into a cultural refrain. The passage narrates King Saul's consultation of a "profane" source of information—the medium of Endor. (Some translations call her a wizard, witch, or a woman with *a familiar spirit.*) Just as King Saul has inched away from the attacking Philistine army, he is unable to communicate with God, who has also "turned away." But Saul is desperately wondering what will happen to him in life and in death. Like the inmates, he needs help to face his fate and asks for a medium. At this point, most students come up with an interpretation that chastises King Saul for disobeying God and seeking a medium, and so they are not surprised that God kills Saul as punishment.

Using the ethnomethodology taught by one instructor, the students talk about how the Israelites sustained patriarchal structures with "sacred," priestly law, and kingly persecution. Indeed, the outlawed knowledge was available as a subterranean resource in crisis, and the king's soldiers knew exactly where to find it. In fact, they already knew the best of the lot, and so they brought Saul to the medium of Endor.

Humans create stable relationships (social structure) with an ability to interchange places with others to the point that they can understand others' assumptions. At first, they assume similarity, but this assumption is disrupted in the course of interaction. A new common ground is then negotiated. The students observe that both Saul and the woman had to reverse their perspectives. The woman unsettles Saul by revealing that she knows that he is the king and a persecutor of mediums. She wonders whether he might kill her for doing what he asks. But Saul begs her to look at him from another standpoint: he is a desperate man about to die. The medium embraces her enemy and calls up the Israelite prophet Samuel from the dead. The NYTS students commonly respond that the street does not teach people to embrace their enemy nor does it leave much time for understanding the motives of others. But gradually they come to agree that too often, commonsense street wisdom closed them to good advice. Mike observed, "I have not made use of the opportunities to learn how to resist the street."

We "tolerate the utterances of another" because we expect to find a common meaning, something ethnomethodologists call the "et cetera assumption." Typically, the students observe that the woman decided to tolerate Saul and that Saul tolerated his need of her. Then the prophet Samuel grumpily appears from the dead, and all three of them establish a common meaning. In contrast, the students note, the street teaches self-centeredness and a lack of tolerance. Yet the very people that we do not tolerate are those who may hold the keys to our life. One prisoner remarked, "I have not made the right friendships."

Even when disjointed, these conversations continue under the assumption that they all will make sense in the end. The students point out that Samuel explains how Saul's past has shaped the present moment and that Saul has no choice but to live through it, even though this means dying. Samuel gives Saul the meaning for the moment. Society, too, has sentenced the inmate to social death. Prison life threatens death. God offers death as a gate to heaven. Which death will the prisoner live? A student said, "The meaning for this moment is the kind of death we will live."

People attempt to "define the situation," thereby "normalizing the chaos" of their encounter. Students observe that the chaos of the encounter (the woman could be put to death by the man who needs her; Saul knows he is about to die; Samuel is annoyed at being disturbed) is calmed by an agreement that this chaos is expected and normal for the extraordinary situation in which "God has turned away." Students look at the situations of their own lives as extraordinary, in which God has turned away. In their discussions with others in the program, they gain help in finding God again.

We talk to establish the "features" of our interaction. If such talk is restrained, the structuring task will fail. The students see that at first Saul spoke to the medium without giving her public recognition and protection. So she talked back, "I listened to what you said and I risked my life to obey you. Now listen to me." Saul listened.

Likewise, students say, "We have been silenced, and yet we have silenced others." Society stops listening to the prisoner; fellow inmates do not listen except for cruel advantage; and their families are often too fragile to be good listeners. posts. The students admit that they have learned well the lessons of silencing. They ignore their neighbors, silencing them by killing and selling drugs; they ignore their grandmothers who keep offering words of hope and morality.

What "really" exists is glossed over by a common vocabulary that brings into being the everyday world we want. The students observe that when Saul confirms that he will die, he decides on self-murder by refusing to eat. But the woman and his servants "gloss over," or deny, Saul's self-murder wish. They get him up and offer him a Passover-like meal. The woman that Saul persecuted as a "medium" performs the "priestly" blessing of his death. They all want a death for Saul that has integrity. In the meantime, the people have gone around patriarchy and have "ordained a woman."

The students apply this part of the story by saying that they can form the vocabulary they need around a table of people who want what is best for them. At first, it is painful to admit that there is no way around the punishments for their behavior. And it is embarrassing to remember the people they rejected, harassed, and humiliated, many of whom only wanted what was best for them. Now the students come to the point of confessing and seeking so that their wounds may heal and normal talk may resume. For this to happen, society too must confess its rejection and its desire for healing.

After reading feminist gender ethics, the students begin to see the medium of Endor as a rather interesting character. They recognize her as one of the many women who saved them, and they are startled to realize that they had adopted their preachers' patriarchal interpretation of the medium's life. In the face of death, she purposely bridged the chasm between Saul and God. The servants, the oppressed classes, knew that her knowledge was suppressed by elite priests who did not want competition, but they risked their lives to go to her, anyway. When prophets and dreams failed King Saul, her ancient knowledge saved him and his servants.

Comparing the woman of Endor's story with their own, the students talk about being discarded people, "demasculinized/profane" men in a world of powerful, "sacred" white men. They raise all sorts of questions. One or two take over the feminist interpretation advocated by the teacher. Another two or three admit that Saul was wise to deal with the woman of Endor. None argues that Saul should not have dealt with her. Many identify the medium's situation as similar to their own. What does it mean to be a black lover, father, husband in a world that prevents achievement? How do you ever repay your wife for standing by you through your life sentence? Or what does it mean not to know your wife and the mother of your children? What knowledge do I have as a man of color that can save me, my family, and perhaps even my community?

Students learn that by constructing a shared language, they can bridge the borders between their differences. They embrace one another and deconstruct their social boundaries. The language of embrace radically reverses time so that they can start over and build new relationships. Forgiveness is returning to the way their relationships were before they were shattered. Of course, they cannot really go back, but they can change their life in a way that would have prevented the shattering, and sometimes that is enough. This new shared language is the saving language of grace that eventually deters recidivism.

The biblical stories also include episodes of struggle that name the difficulties encountered en route to a transformed life and lifestyle. In particular, Webber reports, inmates use the Exodus narrative to interpret their journey from prison to home. But release from prison is not entry into the Promised Land. Rather, NYTS students see the period of release and transition as the "wilderness," a time of testing, trial, and adjustment that, once successfully accomplished, leads to a "promised land" of productivity, activism, and wholeness. The "wilderness" metaphor provides a realistic integrative scheme for the difficulties of transition back into community.

Learning from the Sociology of Moral Indignation

When labeled as a "criminal," an individual is banished from memory and the commonsense world of responsible actors to out of sight behind bars (Pfohl 1986). When the felons are "socially differentiated," the normal process of creating and maintaining social relationships is interrupted. The prisoners have been put out of the world, and a kind of social silence settles over them. Indeed, the labels *felon, prisoner,* and the like are noise deadeners to these men's voices. To reverse the process of criminal-ization, therefore, the NYTS program tries to create a mirroring process of "moral en-dignation" (literally, "putting moral dignity back into" the inmates).

Intervention into the process of criminal identity formation requires documentation of banishment and silencing. The prisoners need to give a name to what they did. In prison everyone says, "I didn't do it! I'm not so bad!" But the instructors ask, Then how did you get the label *prisoner*? As they describe the process, the inmates acknowledge their responsibility but also see that the labeling is a purely human process that can be re-versed, that social identities can be regained. They also can more persua-sively point out the evils of the culture of incarceration. As Bill Webber argues, often against his own teachers, there should be no prisons and no prisoners. In addition, overcoming a "criminal" identity requires ritualis-tic repair and reentry into the normal process of social relationships. This repair work is collective, and identity is formed in the social interaction with "one another."

Status Degradation Rituals

Incarceration is the ultimate degradation of being labeled "unfit for human contact" that makes possible a future radical transformation of people into rehabilitated members of society with new identities.

Status degradation ceremonies ritualistically replace the old identity as a regular "citizen" with a new "criminal" one. Degradation rituals are a kind of secular "communion" that brings with the denouncing party a re-inforced group solidarity.

Harold Garfinkel found that not only do the following elements create a successful ceremony, but they also tell us how to "render denunciation useless" (1956, 420). The NYTS program reverses the status degradation into a status renewal.

Denunciations require	Status renewals require
1. A denouncer	An announcer
2. A perpetrator	A good citizen
3. An event in which witnesses agree with the denouncer	An announcer with whom witnesses agree

The MPS program displaces the denouncer and declares the inmate to be a valuable member of society. Indeed, the inmate (perpetrator) is given the respectable titles of *student* and *soon-to-be-alumnus*. Through the program and at graduation, the seminary and others witness the student inmate's transformation. One student said it was like being given a new "orientation." Another called it "a new view, a unified sense of self." The positive view of the NYTS alumni by the parole board also gives the students a feeling of rising social status. "It impressed the parole board," Mike observed. "The commission said, 'you have a MPS.'"

After a rigorous admissions process, the student inmate joins a tightly knit group of alumni who affirm his identity while requiring strict accountability. One student concluded that what he got most from the NYTS program was a circle of "caring friends with good morals and spiritual values." Seeing themselves as creators of relationships and nurturers of others gives the alumni a sense of purpose and strength to keep going. Their leadership role teaches them how to hold themselves and others accountable to moral community. Answering to God, friends, and community for what one has done wrong has taught them how to forgive themselves and to seek forgiveness from others.

In a successful degradation, the perpetrator is removed from everyday life into the "out of the ordinary." To counteract this expulsion from ordinary life, the NYTS teachers guide the student inmates through confessions and scriptural exegesis revealing that all normal events are out of the ordinary and unique. Classifications are convenient pigeonholes that ignore the uniqueness of each person. Prisoners leap at the chance to discover the minute details of their degradation. They gradually understand that each prisoner's extraordinariness as a child of God had been hidden by their careless lives and by society's reaction to them.

The student comes to realize that "the me who did that is not me." Forty percent of the students say that of the skills that they learned through the professional training classes, the most important ones were personal skills, particularly the ability to see themselves in a new way. Indeed, they often valued these skills much more than the standard educational skills or the theological knowledge.

Common sense teaches that everyone wants to be loved and to love others. Although the student failed, he is not fundamentally a failure. Theologically, in fallenness there is a place for goodness. Nor would the students be admitted into the program if they were true failures. They come to believe that they will never do anything like their crime again. Ed reflected that what kept him growing was his need to help his peers "to get beyond self-hatred." He is not a profane being but back on the journey toward the Holy. Whether saving crackers for a sick friend or having loving dreams of their children, the inmates are on a moral time track to freedom and dignity. John said that the experience gave him "a better self-image and self-esteem." Indeed, the students recaptured "a genuine feeling" about themselves, "a unified sense of self," as one put it.

MPS alumni are also continually disappointed that the prison system does not recognize their transformation. Equally frustrating is society's continued stereotyping of their identity. A common question is, "How can I change the way people think about me?" (For expanded discussions of how people cope with damaged identities, see Goffman 1963; Gregory 1990; La Capra 1991.)

In criminal justice degradation, the denouncer is identified as someone who knows the criminal. So the NYTS professionals now publicly de-incarcerate and reclaim the person. A denouncer speaks in the name of the values that he supports. Then the NYTS reconciling agent speaks on behalf of "all society" and claims that its students also support these social values. Fundamentally, the students restart as faithful religionists with "roots" in a sacred tradition. Students often feel that they have reentered society as "members," not as "aliens." Albert reflected, "I returned with confidence and faith rather than fear." Another alumnus noted that he had come back to society "as a professional, . . . not just an ex-con."

A denouncer leads the witnesses to experience the distance from the perpetrator. NYTS declares that the student is not an enemy to be feared but a friend and family from whom separation is undesirable. The denounced is then ritualistically separated from the legitimate order and placed outside it and made "strange." In contrast, the student is ritualistically matriculated and graduated, that is, made a legitimate member of a responsible organization. The prison system, parole board, employers, and family all come to see the convict in a different light. Eighty-two percent of the student inmates say that NYTS helped them achieve parole. Another alumnus allowed that his certificate gave him "a credibility and respect by others [that] opened doors for me." Words like *recognition, respect, distinction,* and *acceptance* reflect how going through the NYTS program affected the students "back in society." More than three-fourths believe that their NYTS graduation helped them reenter society. Students return to the community through jobs (78%), community programs (56%), prison ministry (35%), and helping youth (67%).

The steps toward a successful degradation are intended to announce that (1) the old identity was an accident and the new identity was there all along, (2) the rightful identity has been established in the eyes of witnesses, and (3) the old identity is not changed; it is reconstituted. Reconciliation is achieved when the degradation identity as "criminal" is replaced by an ancient honorable one of "child of God" as the student's rightful identity affirmed by witnesses. The inmates want the churches' respect and acknowledgment of their spiritual transformation. Tony asks, "Bring churches into the prison so that they can be properly educated and taught how to forgive us." Students invite everyone to join their religion class for personal and social transformation.

NOTES

1. Portions of this chapter were presented to the annual meeting of the Sociological Practice Association, Alexandria, VA, June 1998. The inmates' names have been changed. Permission to republish portions of this chapter was granted by the *Journal of Offender Rehabilitation.*

2. 1996 NYTS Released Alumni Survey, s-87, from an alumni population of 191, of whom 54 percent were incarcerated, 47 percent have been released, and 7 percent are dead.

Part VI

The Religious Woman

Chapter 19

Latinas in the Barrio

María E. Pérez y González

"Mama Leo," otherwise known as the Reverend Leonicia Rosado Rousseau, is perhaps the first Latina Pentecostal pastor in New York City.[1] Since World War II, she has been a well-known dynamo against gangs and drug addiction, and her Damascus Christian Church in the Bronx has created more than seventy-five churches. Yet many in her church and the Puerto Rican community at first thought that her ministry was "too worldly" and "too social."

Today, quite a few Latinas in ministry are engaged in social actions that are deemed a type of heresy by many in the Protestant/Pentecostal[2] Latino religious community. *Heresy* is not used here in its strict sense of the holding or teaching of erroneous doctrine within the church (Hastings 1963). Rather, church and lay leaders say that these acts are superfluous to the church's mission and tend to stir up conflict. An atmosphere of suspicion surrounds those who do not agree with the traditional church leadership.

Most church leaders and congregants are concerned with the traditional religious life of prayer, Bible study, church attendance, and so forth, and their focus is on the vertical relationship between God and the individual. But some members in Latino churches who believe that one's faith should also be extended to include the horizontal relationship between human beings, with an outward expression of justice to the needy. Moreover, these Latinas are not allowed to use the church building, its name, or resources to realize their vision of what the church should be. Despite the obstacles, our research on Latinas in ministry in New York City reveals that quite often, barrio women engage in acts of heresy as a result of their culture, social location, and particularly their religious beliefs.

287

Background

For six months in 1992/1993, the research project Latinas in Ministry identified 673 Latina women in ministry along the northeast corridor of the United States (Pérez y González 1993, 4–6). Information was also gathered on 250 denominations, local churches, Bible institutes, seminaries, Christian schools, colleges and universities, departments of religion in secular universities, a Christian magazine, and a national organization focusing on Latino theological education.

Since that time, at least 150 more women have been identified, and approximately 98 percent are Protestant/Pentecostal and 2 percent are Roman Catholic.[3] Although not all the women could be categorized according to denomination, since identification was sometimes through a secondary source, most of them belonged to Pentecostal, nondenominational, or interdenominational churches, followed in numbers by Methodists, Baptists, Presbyterians, and Lutherans. Nationwide statistics categorize 35.7 percent of Latino Protestant congregations as Pentecostal, 23.1 percent as Baptist, 13.7 percent as other/miscellaneous, 9.2 percent Pietist/Holiness, 4 percent Lutheran/Episcopal, and 3.8 percent Reformed/Presbyterian (Holland 1993). Taking into account that the northeast corridor of the United States has fewer representatives of certain denominations that are more numerous in other regions of the country, the findings are consistent with nationwide statistics on Latino Protestants.[4]

Since the beginning of this study, the definition of Latinas in ministry has expanded from pastors and ministers; Roman Catholic religious sisters; and students, educators, and administrators of theological institutions to include women in lay leadership positions and community- and church-based service and educational programs. All these women view their work as "Christian ministry," although more often than not they receive little or no remuneration.

Latino Community Statistics

The Latino community represents approximately 10 percent of the United States population, totaling about 27 million persons, with women comprising about 51 percent (U.S. Bureau of the Census 1994). However, Latinos are statistically overrepresented in every 1990 U.S. census category that reflects disadvantage. For example, 31 percent of Latinas and 26 percent of Latinos live in poverty, compared with 16 percent of non-Latina women and 12 percent of non-Latino men. Seventeen percent of the total United States population consists of female-headed households. Among Latinos, 24 percent are households headed by women, of which 48 percent live in poverty, and among non-Latinos, 29 percent of the households are headed by women, of which 32 percent live in poverty (U.S. Bureau of the Census 1990). Because of the economic disparity between women and men, particularly in the Latino community, there is a compelling need for redressing these social ills. Among Latina women, these issues of social justice are an increasingly significant part of church ministry.

The Barrio and Social Justice

The Spanish term *barrio* is commonly used by Latinos to signify community. Consequently, in our study we use the term *barrio* to refer to inner-city areas where the majority of Latinos have made their home.[5] The median household income of some barrios is quite low. For example, in Hunts Point/Longwood, the Bronx, the median household income is only $8,448, with 70 percent of the population living below 125 percent of the poverty level.[6] Because of their poverty and neglect by the government (Haslip-Viera and Baver 1996; López 1980; Rodríguez 1991), barrio women have often tried to compensate by opening their homes to those in greater need. One of the proverbs heard in many Latino homes describes it best, "If there's enough for one, there's enough for all" (*Si hay para uno, hay para todos*).

Latina culture fosters women's sense of social justice by teaching them to attend to the needs of others with whatever resources are available, including being the primary caregivers of their immediate and extended families. In addition, Latina women care for the community at large through *hijas/os de crianza* (nonbiological children whom one raises, usually without any legal papers) and by fulfilling the roles of the *partera* (midwife), *rezadora* (leader of communal prayer), and *curandera* (faith healer; Díaz-Stevens 1994, 250–251). As a result, Latinas' strong sense of social justice, as described by one woman, claims, "Sin is not a matter of disobedience but of not being for others . . . not to care for the children of the community—that is a sin, a crime!" (Isasi-Díaz 1993, 40).

Social Justice and the Soul

In the language of theological discourse, a commitment to social justice takes the form of a holistic ministry in which a church and its members care for the whole person, including his or her social needs and not just the salvation of the soul (Pérez y González 1997). As Fontañez explained,

> The Church in its redemptive concern, has the responsibility of liberating the person from sin, but it also has to try to liberate those structures and institutions where sin originates and flourishes. Love of neighbor does not mean avoiding confrontations, but means trying to liberate the oppressed from the oppressor and the oppressor from the ambition for power and selfishness. (1980, 233–234)[7]

Holistic ministry creates a community of faith that is viewed as a real family institution, called "the Body of Christ." Examples of holistic ministry are educational and social programs for children and adults, food pantries, homeless and domestic-violence shelters, support groups, and the creation of jobs and housing. In regard to social justice, the Roman Catholic Church has a long history of proactive involvement, although Puerto Rican (im)migrants have been underserved (Díaz-Stevens 1993, 87; Fitzpatrick 1987, 125–165; National Conference of Catholic Bishops 1986; Stevens-Arroyo 1980). Nonetheless, Latino Protestant/Pentecostal church leaders in the United States have long preached that the church should deal only with matters of the soul (Villafañe 1992).

As a result, Latino Protestant/Pentecostal church leaders tend to avoid acts of social justice as inappropriate participation in the political arena, explaining, "God will distribute justice in God's own time, not necessarily ours."[8] They often point to the First Amendment to the U.S. Constitution concerning the separation of church and state as a reason for not engaging in social justice or holding people of authority accountable. Furthermore, many Latinos have adopted the Protestant work ethic, which includes valuing oneself and others based on "productivity" in society and the ability to "pull yourself up by your bootstraps."[9] The ethic has also created both a wariness of communally sharing wealth and hardened hearts toward the less fortunate.

Latinas engaging in social justice say that their actions have biblical support in such passages as Isaiah, Jeremiah 22, Hosea 4, Matthew 25, and James 2. Hence, they claim what deeds of social justice are done unto others are deeds done unto God and that an absence of social justice is disdainful regard for others and for God (Tamez 1992). As one writer put it, "Our commitment to the poor and exploited will be the sign of our love for God" (Fontañez 1980, 234).

The Heresy of Social Justice

Still, against the church's resistance to social justice, Latinas engaging in the praxis (critical reflective action) of the gospel teachings are in a sense engaging in heretical acts against the established church order (Collins 1997; Costas 1989, 30–32; González y Pérez 1991, 22–24; Isasi-Díaz 1993 166–185). Indeed, they are occasionally accused by the denominational hierarchy and their fellow congregants of opposing the church's norms and condoning the lifestyles and "wrongdoings" of those they assist.[10]

Today, the almost ninety-year-old Reverend Leoncia Rosado Rousseau, "Mama Leo," fervently continues her pathbreaking pastoring, preaching, and encouraging of other Latinas to follow her example. Yet Rev. Rosado received much resistance from her church owing to her gender and her attempts to eradicate gangs and rehabilitate drug addicts. After immigrating from Puerto Rico to New York City in 1935, Rosado helped her husband-pastor found the Concilio de Iglesias Cristianas Damasco, Inc. (Council of Damascus Christian Churches). After her husband was drafted in World War II, the church called on her to be its minister, making her perhaps the first Latina Pentecostal pastor in New York City. With the authority as pastor, she took the opportunity to do ministry the way she envisioned it for Puerto Ricans living in dire conditions. As historian Sánchez Korrol pointed out, "Until that point, Pentecostalism among the Puerto Ricans in New York had served as a sanctuary from the . . . malaise inherent in the migration experience. It basically shielded the congregants from spiritual contamination by the outside world" (Sánchez Korrol 1990, 328).

Within her denomination, Rosado successfully broadened the emphasis from only spiritual matters to include a social mission for the church as an agent of positive change in the barrio. Accordingly, she established a rehabilitation center for drug addicts and alcoholics in the New York church, as well as other programs throughout the United States and the world (Sánchez Korrol 1990, 328–329). The denomination now has eight churches on the East Coast, each with an average of one hundred members, an additional thirty-nine churches and missions in Ecuador, fourteen in

Mexico, and nineteen in the Caribbean and elsewhere. The denomination also operates a school and an orphanage.

Rev. Rosado's case is an extraordinary one. Usually, Latinas in ministry have had to run their ministries apart from their denominations, mostly because of differences with local church leadership about what the church's mission should be. Consequently, these women have had to venture out on their own or with other like-minded individuals to create their own not-for-profit organizations and funding sources.[11]

Latinas in the Protestant/Pentecostal traditions have organized both for emergency situations with food pantries and the like and for long-term situations like unemployment and poverty. They have done this by providing women and men who are abused, substance abusers, batterers, homeless, and those who have nowhere else to turn with new skills, jobs, support systems, transitional housing, and, in abuse situations, help with court appearances. The help takes place within the scope of spiritual growth for a healthy, productive life. For example, The Gathering Place, founded and directed by the Reverend Elizabeth Gómez,[12] has been dealing with such issues since its inception in 1991. Under the slogan "For where two or three are gathered in My name, there am I in the midst of them," (New KJV 1985, Mathew 18:20), The Gathering Place offers social justice in the barrio by serving as a resource center for their community "through community and church group experience . . . one-on-one pastoral counseling . . . Christian oriented therapy groups. . . . Through the operation of a child care system in order to facilitate working parents" (The Gathering Place brochure).

Bruised Reed Ministry, founded and directed by the Reverend Rosa Caraballo since 1990, also engages in social justice action.[13] Under its slogan "A bruised reed He will not break, A smoking flax He will not extinguish, He will faithfully bring forth justice" (Isaiah 42:3), Bruised Reed Ministry helps Latinos who have tested HIV positive or have AIDS and educates the larger community about the prevention and the physical and spiritual impact of being sick with the HIV/AIDS virus. They provide direct support during all stages of the disease, including funeral services and grief/bereavement support groups to assist widows and orphans. Once again, the focus is on meeting social needs, but with a spiritual foundation. As Bruised Reed advises clients, "Giving hope, planting hope to people who have become hopeless because of HIV disease. We offer services with mercy and grace, and the love of God" (Bruised Reed Ministry brochure).

Angels Unaware/Angeles Inadvertidos, directed by its founder, the Reverend Olga Torres-Simpson, since 1992, aids in the spiritual, mental, physical, social, and emotional development of exceptional Latino children and their families.[14] They preach to the Latino community that strangers, even mentally challenged ones, should be treated with love, for one might be entertaining angels unaware (Hebrews 13:2). The organization also helps the needy obtain government services and provides counseling and referral services. Its education regarding mental retardation challenges the belief that it is a demon-related phenomenon that should be cured by means of exorcism.[15] Families can be bedeviled by constantly bringing their loved ones to be prayed for during healing/liberation services and by being condemned for insufficient faith when the loved one is not "healed" or "liberated." Born out of the founder's personal experience with the lack of services available for Latinos, Torres-Simpson started as a one-person referral service that now has expanded to include an office, a residential home for four adults, programs of recreation and education, and home care for approximately twenty children and five adults. Overall, Angels Unaware serves about 150 persons, predominantly Latino and African American.

Ms. Alexie Torres, one of the few Roman Catholic Latinas in ministry identified in the study,[16] founded and directs Youth Ministries for Peace and Justice. Like most other Latinas in social justice ministry, she established her organization apart from the church. Youth Ministries for Peace and Justice trains young people for proactive leadership through afterschool academic, sociocultural learning programs, emphasizing teamwork through recreational sports, leadership development, and work with gangs against violence. The organization particularly promotes the teaching of Christian values and practices concerning peace and justice among youth.

Conclusion

These social-justice organizations reveal the breadth of needs in the barrios and how they are being met. These initiatives have in common the difficulties that the women leaders and their loved ones experienced in their barrios and churches because the churches did not know how to respond, feared to respond, or did not see a need for these services. Yet based on their religious convictions, these Latinas organized to enable their community to counteract the devastating effects of poverty, predators, illness, and stigmatization. Despite the initial lack of church support, these Latinas maintained their belief that their communities needed both spiritual hope and physical renewal. According to them, their heretical acts of social justice were justified throughout Scripture, nowhere clearer than in the Epistle of James:

> If a brother or sister is naked and lacks daily food, and one of you says to them, "Go in peace; keep warm and eat your fill," and yet you do not supply their bodily needs, what is the good of that? So faith by itself, if it has no works, is dead. (New KJV 1985, James 2:15–17)

The integration of faith and works is the Latinas' praxis of social justice.[17]

That Latina women are organizing to fulfill the basic needs of community members is not new. What is new is that most of these women come from Latino Protestant/Pentecostal churches, many of whose congregants still believe that churches should maintain as much distance as possible from worldly affairs, since they "are not of this world."[18] Yet all the organizations begun by these Latina women have been an extension of their sociocultural religious lives. It is imperative for "women and men to become aware of the extensive contributions in terms of prevention and intervention that [Latina] women have made to society through their unpaid and often unrecognized service in the Church" (Pérez y González 1997, 19–35). Overall, Protestant/Pentecostal Latinas are engaging in the heresy of social justice, despite the many obstacles, by using their culture and religious foundations to promote a healthy spiritual and social environment in their New York City barrios. What remains to be seen is the degree to which their heresy of social justice will affect the Latino Protestant/Pentecostal Church of the twenty-first century and the extent to which the church will follow in those same heretical footsteps toward social justice.

NOTES

1. This chapter is based on a larger project on Protestant/Pentecostal Latinas, entitled Latinas in Ministry: A Pioneering Study on Women Ministers, Educators and Students of Theology, commissioned by the New York City Mission Society (see Pérez y González 1993). A version of this chapter was presented at the 1995 meeting of the Latin American Studies Association, Washington, D.C., Septem-

ber 28–30. I would like to extend my gratitude to my companion, Rev. Dr. Belén González y Pérez, for his contributions to this work.

2. In this chapter, Protestants include Pentecostals and other evangelicals who belong to nondenominational and interdenominational churches, since many tend to identify themselves within this broad-based religious affiliation category, as distinct from being Roman Catholic.

3. When discovered, Roman Catholic women in ministry were included as Latinas in ministry, although the study's data gathering did not target these women.

4. As a result of the 1993 study, the Latinas in Ministry Program was founded by Dr. María E. Pérez y González as part of the New York City Mission Society, under the former executive director, Emilio Bermiss, and currently a program of the Latino Pastoral Action Center located in the Bronx, an affiliate of the New York City Mission Society.

5. Barrios include neighborhoods such as Hunts Point/Longwood, Mott Haven/Melrose, Belmont/East Tremont, and Fordham/University Heights in the Bronx; Bushwick, Sunset Park, Greenpoint/Williamsburg, and East New York/Starrett City in Brooklyn; Washington Heights/Inwood, East (Spanish) Harlem, Morningside Heights/Hamilton, and the Lower East Side (Loisaida)/Chinatown in Manhattan; and Jackson Heights, Elmhurst/Corona, and Woodside/Sunnyside in Queens (Office of Planning and Program Development 1998).

6. For a family of four in 1997, 125 percent of the poverty level meant an income of $20,063 (Office of Planning and Program Development 1998, T-5). Statistical information is based on the New York City Housing and Vacancy Survey, 1996.

7. He was a Puerto Rican Catholic lay leader from the New York Archdiocese who was very active in the Cursillo movement, president of the St. Vincent de Paul Society, and the first chairman of the Hispanic Association of Deacons in the Northeast.

8. Participant observations since 1975 reveal that these beliefs have often been voiced in churches, particularly in Latino Pentecostal churches. They were also raised in 1993 by the participants in the focus groups of the Latinas in Ministry study (see Thomas 1980, 151–152).

9. The Protestant work ethic legitimated individualistic profit seeking as the will of God and helped expand capitalism (Weber 1930).

10. These issues have been raised in discussions by the planning board of the Latinas in Ministry program and in the First Latinas in Ministry Conference in Ossining, New York, October 14–15, 1994, funded by the Lilly Endowment Fund, Inc.

11. Consent to use their actual names was obtained from each of the Latinas featured here. Each organization targets and mainly services Latinos, but they serve anyone who comes to them in need.

12. Although Rev. Gómez identifies herself as Lutheran, her ministry is nondenominational, and she also acknowledges her Pentecostal background.

13. Rev. Caraballo has a Baptist/Pentecostal formation. Her ministry is non-denominational.

14. Rev. Torres-Simpson is Pentecostal, although her ministry is nondenominational. The purpose was translated from the Angeles Inadvertidos brochure.

15. Since 1975, my participant observations in diverse Latino Protestant/Pentecostal churches reveal that mental retardation is mostly handled as a strictly spiritual rather than a biological phenomenon.

16. Ms. Torres, a Roman Catholic who often worships with Pentecostal Protestants, is in her twenties, but the other women, who are Protestants/Pentecostals, are from the baby boom generation. The age differential seems to reflect their socioreligious upbringing (Roman Catholics have a long tradition of social justice).

17. All these Latinas are Puerto Rican with organizations located in the Bronx, New York City. The demographics of the Northeast indicate that the majority of the Latinos are Puerto Rican, ranging from 40 to 69 percent of the Latino populations in each of the states from Massachusetts to Washington, D.C. (U.S. Bureau of the Census 1990). The most detailed information obtained about the autochthonous ministries of Latinas was gathered from New York City, particularly from the Bronx, where the largest group of Puerto Ricans in New York City resides.

18. Derived from Scripture such as 1 Peter 2:11 and John 15:19 that refer to Christians as pilgrims on this earth whose true home is in heaven.

Chapter 20

Orthodox Jewish Women Openly
Studying the Torah

Mareleyn Schneider

For those who think tradition is immutable, the idea of women studying Talmud and other texts in the original is scary and iconoclastic and has the potential to result in social schism.

Although Scripture says, "And you shall teach them [Torah] diligently to your children [male and female]" (Deuteronomy 6:7), traditional teachers have been ambivalent about Jewish women learning Torah. For example, Ben Azzai stated, "A wise man is required to teach his daughter Torah." But Rabbi Eliezer retorted, "Anyone who teaches Torah to his daughter is as though he taught her lechery" (Bialik and Ravnitzky 1992, 636).[1] Johnstone concluded, "Jewish women have traditionally been discouraged from studying the holy Torah or even learning Hebrew" (1988, 181).

Traditionally, Talmud study[2] was a male domain except for unusual cases in which daughters and wives clandestinely learned Talmud in their home and, on rare occasions, in public. Typically, Jewish women read male-authored, translated synopses of Jewish law, custom, and history; attended communal lectures by men on Jewish topics; or were informed about most *halacha* (Jewish law) by their husbands, fathers, brothers, rabbis, or male teachers. Women in New York today, by contrast, have access to a variety of places in which they, with the support of other women, are learning and mastering Talmudic language and logic, examining codes of Jewish law, and adding to the corpus of interpretation of traditional texts.

This chapter, an ethnographic sketch of Jewish women's study groups in New York City, presents a novel picture of Jewish life. It illuminates the involvement and repercussions, expressed in hopes and fears, of women

297

who learn Torah outside the home. It explains to some degree how a woman can now take on one or more new Jewish roles that are gaining both recognition and backlash on both sides of the ocean: a *toenet* (rabbinic court advocate in Israel), a member of a Jewish women's prayer group that reads (chants) from the Torah scrolls, a learner in a women's *bet medrash* (study hall on the Talmud), and a graduate student in Jewish schools of higher education.

What Does It Mean to Be a Traditional Jew?

A tractate in the Talmud asserts that the world endures because of three things: Torah, *avodah*, and *g'me'lat chesed* (Avot 2:2). *Avodah*, denoting service to God, refers to praying in private, participating in synagogue services, and vocalizing one's commitment to Judaism. *G'me'lat chesed*, literally meaning acts of loving kindness to fellow humans, is expressed as giving charity, treating others (in courts, at home, in communities) with justice and compassion, and supporting political freedom.

While all three are key ingredients in Jewish life, Torah "remains primary and preeminent" for the behaviors of its people (Bunim 1964, 38–45). In its strictest sense, the term Torah may signify the Pentateuch, the scroll of parchment calligraphed by a religious scribe with the first five books of the Tanakh (Hebrew scriptures), the Tanakh and Talmud together, and the entire corpus of religious law and learning.

So how does a Jew "do Torah"? Throughout Jewish history, this duty consists of a threefold operation: (1) listening to and thinking seriously about the words, lessons, commandments, and other treasures found in the Tanakh and Talmud; (2) teaching about them; and (3) conducting one's life in accordance with them. It is a lifelong process in which the Torah's words, goals, logic, and messages are examined and reexamined.

Although Orthodox Jews resemble one another to a large degree in their conduct, not all have the same inclination or ability for scriptural studies. Given the demands of active lifestyles, implementing these Torah operations (especially reflecting and teaching) is difficult for many. In response, today's Jewish communities have, as in times past, implemented supplemental or surrogate "doing Torah" activities. For some, commissioning a scribe to produce a handwritten Pentateuch scroll or another holy text, an expensive and time-consuming task, is an example of a life filled with the love of Torah.

Making an effort to tune in and really listen—in the synagogue or any public forum—to the recitation of the weekly portion of Jewish religious works is also actively participating in Torah. Studying *parshas ha'shavuah* (the designated weekly portion from the Pentateuch) on Friday nights with neighbors is a goal that many people pursue. Asking and answering questions about the Torah anywhere is doing Torah. Reviewing rabbinic authorities or even taking infants and little children to houses of study and synagogues where men are engaged in Talmud study is doing Torah.

Working in Jewish settings (such as summer day-camps and nursing homes) in which people may learn and practice Hebrew and Jewish philosophies and commentaries is a choice for some. Maintaining[3] and using a Jewish library of holy books in their own homes is, for many, keeping Torah as well as demonstrating their commitment to being a member of *am ha-sefer* (people of the Book, that is, the Torah).[4] Merely reciting the Shema (three biblical passages proclaiming belief in the unity of God) once in the morning and once in the evening is entering the Torah (Bialik and Ravnitzky 1992, 440). But in contemporary times, studying Tanakh and especially the Talmud in their original tongues has become the mainstay of doing Torah among all segments of the Orthodox Jewish world, including the Hasidism.

Studying Torah

Traditional Jews say that studying all types of Torah texts buttresses the cornerstone of Jewish faith and survival, bestowing esteem and power on individuals and the collectivity (Schiff 1988, 6). It also connects people to God, their rich heritage and ancestors, and their souls: the "ultimate goal is sanctification; and while what is learned may appear to be secular facts, the source of what is learned, which is Torah, and the intent of the ones who do the learning . . . reshape the intellectual act into a religious quest, a holy event" (Neusner 1987, 318–319).

The Zohar (Berachot 1, 184a–184b) contends that Torah study helps people secure worthwhile rewards in this life and rescues them from punishment in the hereafter. In addition, at death, those who studied Torah will find the Torah standing guard over their bodies, breaking through barriers to the souls' destinations, and acting as a defender if the resurrected bodies in the time of the Messiah face any false allegations.

But some people warn that if Torah study is not accomplished *lishmah* (for its own sake), Torah study becomes a deadly poison, or the Torah becomes viewed as a Torah without *chesed* (that is, loving kindness; Ta'anith 7a; Sukkah 49b). In other words, students who think of the ends—and not the means—may not fully concentrate on the words before them. In addition, if students are forced to study because of pressures to do well or to escape punishment, they may turn their resentment outward against the educational process and/or the material, the very things that are supposed to improve their life. When students are not intrinsically motivated, they may decide the readings are disagreeable, corrupt, or ridiculous.

Nonetheless, the most prevalent view is that no matter what the initial motives are for Torah study, the very act of studying will eventually engender an intrinsic desire to continue doing so (Berachot 17a).

Women's Involvement in Studying Torah Lishmah *and for the Sake of Judaism*

In Isaac Bashevis Singer's novel *Yentl the Yeshiva Boy* (1962, 49) a female student who exemplifies Torah study for its own sake (*lishmah*) and delights in debating Talmudic tractates had to disguise herself as a man to continue her Torah study. Avigdor, a Talmud scholar, upon discovering his study partner was really a woman, remarks: "You could have married me." She retorts, "I wanted to study the Gemara and Commentaries with you, not darn your socks."

Besides demonstrating a female's yearning for higher education, this story raises an age-old question for parents: Wouldn't it be best for our daughters to marry, raise children, keep house, perform home-related Jewish rituals, let their husbands support them, and stay far away from any threatening outside obstacles? Wouldn't it be best for our sons, who are physically stronger, to chance the intimidating and often decadent public sphere, to represent the family in communal Jewish rituals that often require travel through inhospitable territory, and to use their business training or academic skills to navigate through the Torah?

Jewish educators, parents, and leaders rebut these questions with histories of Jewish women. Some Jewish commentators assert that the biblical Deborah was not only a judge but also a teacher of Torah to the masses (Judges 4:5) and that the daughters of Zelophechad were wise and lettered (Numbers 27:6–7). Almost two thousand years ago, Ima Shalom, a descendant of famous Torah scholar Hillel and wife of the head of Talmudic academy, inserted her comments into Talmudic discussions and negotiated settlements (Henry and Taitz 1983, 48–58).

Legitimation and Routinization of Torah Study of Women

Although Jewish texts and histories mention these and other women who were Torah scholars, for centuries the cultural norm was that females should not usually preoccupy themselves with Torah study as did their male coreligionists. But about a hundred years ago, notions about women's Jewish education changed.

Until the early twentieth century, most Jewish women received a nominal Jewish education. They were often taught at home, receiving the minimal amount of education necessary to keep a Jewish home and to pray. In early-twentieth-century Europe, Jewish girls began to receive better secular educations and to question traditional values (about their social roles). The renowned scholar Rabbi Israel Meir ha-Kohen, better known as the Chafetz Chaim, ruled that girls should be taught Bible because their religious education should be put on par with the secular studies. In 1918, with his support, Sara Schnirer founded Bais Yaakov, the first network of yeshivas for girls.

More than half a century later, Rabbi J. B. Soloveitchik, the acknowledged leader of modern Orthodoxy, taught one session in a Talmud class in Stern College (the women's college of Yeshiva University in New York) to indicate his approval of Talmud studies for women. Consequently, some yeshiva high schools now offer Talmud classes to girls as part of their regular curriculum. There are also a number of Orthodox institutions of higher Judaic studies for women, in both Israel and the United States (Grossman and Haut 1992, 7–8).[5]

In Hasidic circles, women's education has also been evolving. Culling support from other Hasidic rebbes in recognizing that modern American female students are "taught to probe, to question, and to seek reasons behind the facts" and that "women are commonly exposed to the sophisticated demands of professional involvement in contemporary society," the Lubavitcher Rebbe, Rabbi Menachem M. Schneerson, advised educators to cultivate the females' thinking processes within the Torah's conceptual and value systems (Kaploun 1994, 67–75). Without it, he argued, the Torah could not be perpetuated.

As this century progressed, secular educational paradigms rejected the perception that students are empty receptacles awaiting their teachers' ideas. Furthermore, an unexpected outcome of the midcentury military conflicts was the growth of coeducational colleges and a declining number of gender specific institutions and courses on the high school level, such as home economics, stenography, and typing for girls and shop for boys.

These changes, reinforced by the women's movement, transformed our society's view of sex roles. In the last generation or so, the new view of children and females as competent vehicles has had a quiet, subtle effect on Jewish education. Day schools and yeshivas have modified their courses to use seemingly ingrained superior student abilities. While not advocating coeducation, the Jewish girls' schools reduced the boy-girl curriculum gap by making available more courses on Jewish topics.

Do these adjustments in Jewish schools really mirror the wider society, or are they really props to shore up religious structures against the temptations of the secular world? Although the secular world's values and actions are often viewed with sadness and dread, they are not deemed a real threat because that is really another realm for most of them. Most Orthodox Jewish young women (and men) study their secular subjects in yeshivas or day schools in which "uncomfortable" notions are censored, debunked, or demonstrated acceptable within normative Judaism.

In addition, legendary narratives recount the stories of Jewish women since biblical times who have resisted temptations, unlike their male counterparts. The stories act as barriers against unsolicited, alluring "dangerous" thoughts and actions. When faced with cognitive dissonance between religious and secular models, many Orthodox Jewish women sacrifice the outside world's pleasures and tenets for an ineffable inner peace. And last, because traditional Judaism concentrates more on a way of life than theology, many of its women are willing to forgo some intellectual and emotional pursuits for a preferred goal of unerring religious conduct, including Torah study.

In general, formal Jewish education is now seen as a "maven haven" rather than a "fright flight from the real world." Torah study for women is no longer considered a luxury or a pipe dream; it has become a necessity. Thus, girls and young women in Orthodox Jewish communities are now expected to attend Jewish day schools or yeshivas to learn from traditional texts. Jewish leaders frequently claim that if women are not supported in their study of Torah, then the Jewish nation will suffer.

Studying Torah beyond High School or College

Once past available formal education with new familial or professional responsibilities, do these women continue their Torah study? Do they rely on husbands, fathers, brothers, and rabbis to answer any newly emerging questions? Or do they, using skills they developed in school, find the answers for themselves? More precisely, have Jewish women adopted for life the ideal Torah *lishmah* philosophy?

Women (and occasionally men) involved in three different strategic programs in New York City—each introduced less than twenty years ago—supply the answers. One site is a *baalei teshuvah* (returnees to traditional Judaism) school for women[6] which teaches the necessary skills to be Torah observant Jewish women, generates spirituality in people who are sorely missing it, and does not grant degrees or certificates. Another is a Hasidic seminary that trains young women to be teachers and is a cradle for Jewish educators who extend their reach beyond the school premises. Finally, we look at a modern Orthodox institute that encourages and prepares women for the "serious study of classical Jewish texts" in full-time or part-time, degree or nondegree (or certificate), programs.[7]

Baalei Teshuvah

The administrator of the school for "returning Jews" reports that women who attend classes often remark, "I never heard that" or "I never knew that." For these women, who learn the foundations of Judaism—Chumash (the Pentateuch), *halacha*, the specific weekly Torah portion, Jewish philosophy, and Midrashim—by reading translations in English and attending lectures, the groundwork produces a curiosity about their heritage and texts and a desire for more study.

For most of the women, the sex-segregated classes create a special, welcoming atmosphere for examining the three pillars of Judaism, that is, Torah, *avodah*, and *g'me'lat chesed*. The part-time courses (and occasional daylong or weeklong workshops) not only teach about traditional ritual observances and *Weltanschauung*, but they also inculcate the necessity of explaining, understanding, collaborating, and getting at the root of things—skills to be honed for a lifetime of study at home or in academic settings.

According to an informant, the women feel they are not in a pressure cooker when they are in this milieu. There are no social pressures (be-cause men are absent from this setting), no competitive academic pres-sures (because grades and exams are not part of the experience), no intel-lectual pressures (because obscure and abstruse matters are not de rigueur), and no living-up-to-the-ancestors pressures (because their ear-lier cultural baggage is no longer relevant).

The school is also open to Orthodox Jewish women who wish to con-tinue Torah study with little or no advance text preparation, who would enjoy an occasional peripheral excursion into texts, who want to get ex-cited when they reexamine their heritage, who long to establish connec-tions with other Jewish women with the same religious ideals and behav-iors, or who want Jewish learning adjusted to limited time frames.

Hasidim

Questioned how her graduates and neighbors learn Torah *lishmah*, the dean of the Hasidic girls' high school and seminary advises that the ideal for men in her community is to learn daily three chapters of Maimonides' *Yad ha-Chazakah* (literally meaning "strong hand" and also known as the *Mishneh Torah*, a Hebrew work divided into fourteen books, each em-bodying a separate legal category).[8] The ideal for women, however, allows them a choice: They can pick this larger, more involved text, or they can select the codifier's concise work, *Sefer ha-Mitzvot* (Book of command-ments), which names fourteen principles used to identify and classify the 248 positive ("Do!") and 365 negative ("Don't!") commandments. She believes, considering the exigencies of their life of service,[9] that most of the women use the abridged version. Whatever version is used, the women (and men) follow a printed schedule organized by the commu-nity leaders so that all are studying similar materials on the same days and complete the work within a given time frame.

In which setting(s) do these women study? They have three possible venues, depending on their physical health, the number of young chil-dren at home, the locations available for study,[10] and/or their desire for camaraderie with adult women. Thus, some choose individual study at home at free times during the week, while others prefer group study at their own dwellings (or someone else's) in the evening. Most, however, in addition to the weekday Torah study, attend adult Sabbath classes for women either at houses of worship or in homes.

Another administrator explains the psychological rewards of study and mentions that studying Maimonides' works is just the beginning of Torah study:

> We put much emphasis on education. After we finish school, we motivate ourselves to continue education constantly—whether we are working or not working. This is part of our social structure. Everyone should be learning Torah and other subjects. So we set up classes. I myself have given weekly 1_-hour classes in my home since my children married. We work on our inner selves and our attitudes. I say, have pity on yourselves. Work on yourselves and fix up your own little world. And then you have to worry about the outside world.

What do women discuss in these classes? They study quite a few things: "the Torah portion for the week; their children; philosophical works, especially *chasidus* [what it means to live a Hasidic lifestyle] in the form of the *Tanya* of Rebbe Shneur Zalman of Liadi; *Mishlei* [Proverbs], the *Haftorah* [a chapter from the Prophets read in the synagogue following the weekly Torah portion]; and general topics in *Chumash*."

By studying the scriptural and Hasidic texts, the women reinforce their knowledge and commitment to their religious lifestyle. Although they sometimes use original sources or translations, they prefer to review the work of compilers. They enjoy the works of a burgeoning group of female teachers who collect the traditional commentaries into lucid anthologies called "Torah books." A teacher, known as the "scholar-in-residence," regularly questions her students about their study obligations. The most common response from her students is that it is no simple task.

Considering that today's young women are exposed to so much more than their mothers, do they demand more in terms of studying Mishnah or Talmud? Rarely, because of time constraints and pragmatic concerns. The scholar elaborates, "What many don't realize is that there is so much to learn. I just don't want to sit there for hours nitpicking about where does this *halacha* [Jewish law] come from. If it is told to me in a more general way and it fits into everything I have learned, I am fine with it."

When asked about what changes in continuing Jewish education for women over the last few decades seem most dramatic, she declares:

> What I find now is that people are more interested in studying *kabbalah* [mystical teachings of rabbinic origin] than in learning Talmud. People are intrigued by it. It is mysterious. It talks about celestial beings. It talks about metaphors of things. People are tuning into something more. They see the

world as it is—with its science and technology—but they think there must more. They want to reach out beyond the physical world.

In short, for these women, Torah study is geared to earthly and spiritual forms of practice. Theory, reflection, and disputation have little or no direct impact on their day-to-day actions and desires.

Modern Orthodox

In contrast, the executive director of the modern Orthodox learning center perceives a different set or type of needs and expectations on part of her constituents and the school's founders: "The guiding philosophy here is that women's learning is taken seriously. Women's thinking, women's questions, women's ideas are encouraged. We don't make any demands. We don't have any expectations except that people want to come and learn and engage with the text seriously. It's not like fluffy entertainment."

Some of the classes offered are lectures, but the instructors are flexible. As one teacher says, "In one class, students want to talk; in my other class, students want to listen." Most of the classes, however, are similar to men's yeshivas in which students spend large periods of time in *chevrusa* (partnered preparation, independent learning). They eventually convene for thirty- to ninety-minute discussions and further discourse with the instructor.

In a way, this school of continuing education is like a traditional yeshiva. The approach to learning—*chevrusa* and heavy emphasis on Talmud—matches men's learning. But in some ways, it is not the same: There are no questions that are off limits; there are no answers that are off limits; and there are no conversations that are not allowed. And that is rare, very rare.

The director describes the atmosphere:

> It is really providing the opportunity for women to take ownership of their own learning. . . . They flock here. We have been bursting at the seams. It is a positive, not a patronizing, environment. We are like a *kollel*[11] where women get paid to learn. We have high-quality [male and female][12] teachers, and the texts are so exciting once you start getting into it.

Advertisements in Jewish newspapers and word of mouth have drawn increasing numbers of students to this particular school. The administration, with lofty goals to "build a vibrant Jewish community of committed, active, questioning, and creative members," actively recruits top students from high schools and their own summer high school program. They pay stipends and offer tuition waivers to those women enrolled in full-time programs.

The director, acknowledging some in the Jewish community might find fault with this emphasis on Talmud study, concedes: "There are those who say that men have it wrong also. Nobody should be learning only Talmud." Thus, because they believe all would not agree that Torah study is Talmud study, the school offers such elective classes as Hebrew Bible, liturgy, and Jewish philosophical thought. However, she argues it is important for women to study Talmud. "If women are interested in having a solid foundation that will lead them to more credibility in the community, then you have to play by the rules [studying Talmud] even if some think they are wrong."

For women to broaden their societal roles to outside the home, they have to probe and master the same elaborate codes, logical systems, and linguistic skills that men have claimed as a right, a privilege, and an honor for centuries. Without evidence of their authority and erudition, Jewish women will never be permitted by their traditional communities to engage in public discourse, implement policy, and contribute in new ways to their families and to the rest of the Jewish people. Consequently, the director argues, "Women learning is important for the whole community. It's important for boys to see their mothers learning also. It's important for husbands to be able to talk Torah with their wives and daughters."

Furthermore, the director notes, because of their experiences and attitudes—which do not require keeping feelings and intuition in check—Jewish females learners often ask questions, perceive situations, and suggest alternative approaches to problems differently than do men.

"Teaching helps people become part of the chain of tradition. . . . So, in a certain way, every good Jew is a teacher, whether they know it or not." Historically, when Jewish teachers (in synagogues, schools, or homes) have summoned pupils to commence their studies, they have done so with this petition: "Let's learn." Jewish teachers do not say, "I'm going to begin my lesson" or "tune in." For this group of instructors, it has never been "you" or "I" or "me," but "we" or "us." The teacher and the student are in a symbiotic relationship, each benefiting the other. Teachers soon recognize that in the act of teaching, they are really learning, too.

The Precariousness of Torah Study for Women

Although these women teachers support Torah study as a way to strengthen commitment to the Jewish people, they also acknowledge that advanced study poses some dangers. One of the modern Orthodox teachers mentions the parable of children who crave the latest popular toy: they beg, demand, and dicker. And too often, when the object of their desire is finally given to them, they quickly lose interest. Sooner rather than later, they covet the next latest plaything. Unfortunately, she argues, the same possibility holds true for women who have gained access to Torah study. Some well-intentioned women, weighted down by American values that contradict lasting commitment, start Torah study and then swiftly stop. But Torah study, for Orthodox Jewry, is not a discardable toy, and treating it as such will affect the wider community.

Those who fear and fight social change use this evidence as a fulcrum to push women's roles back to older traditional patterns. Those who appreciate the changes have to control their displeasure at this "betrayal" and create strategies that will make Torah study fresh, beguiling, and manageable. The latter is not an easy job even for those sheltered from the host society's values and determined to be fully dedicated to Torah study. The dean of the Hasidic school observes:

> When you first get hold of a thing that was once denied, it is so precious and so exciting. When it becomes a part of a curriculum, a subject to be studied in school, it means you have to take it. To have a girl feel the Torah is just a course dulls any sensitivity to [that is, appreciation for] learning. So whereas today girls learn more than when you and I were growing up it, something could easily get lost.

Another concern is that some in the Jewish community assert that women who study Torah, and especially Talmud, stimulate alarming role changes in traditional Jewish communal life. As one modern Orthodox teacher admits:

> I do think that learning can cause one to rethink in exactly what way one wants one's commitment to the Jewish people to be reflected. So, in reality, it is possible—even inevitable—as more women learn, with women gaining equal access to the texts, they will want equal access in every area. But if it emerges from authentic learning and authentic interaction, then I think it is an authentic Judaism.

She continues by reminding the listener that no one could have predicted the development of the Hasidim eight hundred years ago. Moreover, when it first emerged, this way of life was deemed a threat by mainstream Jewry. Today, "this path is an authentic and legitimate path [within Orthodox Judaism]."

Conclusion

The continuity and development of Judaism depend on women' learning Torah in its original languages because

> Judaism is based not so much on just belief or just on practice, but on the very act of inquiry, the very act of interacting with this body of Jewish texts. And anyone who studies any subject should look back at what people have thought before. That's why you can't truly understand what Judaism is saying on a really deep level if you don't have access to these texts.

Contemporary Orthodox Jewish women contend that the quality of their religiosity is improved by having direct contact with traditional Jewish texts. These three models of women learning Torah *lishmah*–specializing in different materials, devoting varying amounts of time to study, and employing diversity in methodology and purpose—clearly demonstrate that for Orthodox Jewish women in New York City, religion is much more than belief or observance of the Torah's commandments. Their experiences provide evidence to debunk the popular myth that women are dependent on men in religious matters and that they are simply enablers for men who want to study Torah. These voices illustrate women's own religious commitment and active membership in *am ha-sefer*.

NOTES

1. Some exegetes claim this means that teaching women laws that discuss departures from prescribed sexual behaviors may inspire them to hedonistic and improper conduct.

2. According to tradition, on Mount Sinai, Moses received the Torah in two parts. The written component is known as Tanakh; the oral segment, Mishnah. About the year 200 CE, the leader of the Jews of Israel, Judah ha-Nasi, transcribed the Mishnah. The Talmud, a multivolume collection compiled between the third

and seventh centuries CE, restates (in sequence) a paragraph of the Mishnah, explaining and amplifying it with legends, complicated legal arguments, Tanakh quotations and commentaries, rabbinical and lay attitudes, and other "discussions" by noted scholars. The study of Talmud (also known as the Gemara), the basis for much of Jewish practice and belief, is regarded as an intricate course of study requiring as a prerequisite tenacity and analytical skills.

3. Maintenance is more than general upkeep. Observant Jews kiss their holy books when they close them; do not leave them open when not in use; return these books to their appropriate shelves when they have completed using them; never stack secular books on top of them; never place them on the floor; and make sure closed books are placed face up on a table.

4. The Torah, a portable tome, tangibly connected an exiled people to God, to their homeland, to coreligionists who settled and were later expelled from diverse lands, and to their early history.

5. Ever increasing numbers of young women spend a year studying Talmud and other holy texts in yeshivas after completing high school; some are now spending an additional year after completing college. (For more on the education of Jewish women and literature specifically prepared for Jewish women's enlightenment, see Brayer 1986). And even in ultra-Orthodox circles, girls must be given some sort of Jewish education (Heilman 1992, 35).

6. Baalei teshuvah schools are generally not coeducational.

7. In Orthodox circles, Jewish studies classes are segregated by sex. In these circles, men teach both genders; women, women; and, on rare occasions when the female teacher is celebrated and acclaimed, women teach men, following practices recorded in the Talmud. Occasionally, if a renowned teacher gives a lecture, both sexes might be in the audience; in these cases, however, what is known as separate seating (men sit on one side of the aisle, women on the other) is the norm.

8. If they keep this pace, the work is completed in nine months.

9. Many of these women are active voluntary association members who visit the sick in hospitals and in their homes; provide meals for the indigent, the homebound, and families with newborns; help in wedding preparations and the ensuing seven days of feasts for neighbors, friends, and relatives; and baby-sit for women who are financially obliged to work.

10. Most, but not all, are in a short walking distance from their homes.

11. In yeshivas and seminaries, this is the place where the most intellectually gifted Talmudic male students, the religious virtuosi, engross themselves in full-time Talmud study for a number of years. Jewish communities not only offer stipends and pay tuition, but they also provide housing and other amenities for them and their immediate families. A student who is in a *kollel* has achieved a high status in society.

12. Most of the male teachers hold doctoral and/or rabbinical degrees; a few

are still in rabbinical school. All the women, holders of advanced degrees in Jewish studies or unrelated disciplines, have countless years of learning under their belt. Some were former students at the institute, and most have spent time in Israel learning in women's yeshivas.

Chapter 21

Congregation Beth Simchat Torah
New York's Gay and Lesbian Synagogue

Helaine Harris

It was the Kol Nidre service, the evening prayer service to usher in the holiest day of the year for the Jewish people, Yom Kippur. New York City's Javits Convention Center was filled to capacity with the largest gathering ever of gay and lesbian Jews from throughout the greater New York area, Germany, and even Israel. For some, it was their first time worshiping with the congregation. For others, it was a continuity of their Sabbath and Holy Day tradition—to pray with the only congregation in New York that was founded for the exclusive purpose of serving the gay and lesbian Jews of this city—Congregation Beth Simchat Torah.

The American Synagogue and the Gay Community

The synagogue has historically been the center of American Jews' religious, social, political, and philanthropic life. The synagogue also provides the Jewish community a place to integrate their identities as Americans and Jews. Among its many functions, the synagogue has served as a support system for the family, as many life cycle events are celebrated there. The synagogue is the center of the bat and bar mitzvah rituals, baby-naming ceremonies, anniversary celebrations, circumcisions, and other significant events in a family's life.

Until recently, the gay and lesbian Jewish community has not experienced itself as its own entity, as a community with its own social, family, religious, and educational needs. As the gay and lesbian community strives for legitimacy and public recognition, it has been venturing into mainstream institutions, such as establishing gay and lesbian synagogues across the country. This movement, as described by Shokeid (1995), may suggest the attainment of a new status challenging the "primacy" of the gay and lesbian identity to include a gay and lesbian and Jewish identity as well.

As gays and lesbians "come out of the closet," they no longer accept social and religious isolation. No longer "second-class citizens" in their secular lives, having fought the battle for equality in employment, domestic partnership, housing, adoption, and same-sex marriage rights, they also want full respectability in their religious community.

The creation of Congregation Beth Simchat Torah (CBST) on Bethune Street in the West Beth Artists Complex in Greenwich Village has provided a home for the gay and lesbian Jewish community of New York City (figure 21.1). Since the founding of CBST, at least twenty other gay and lesbian religious institutions have been formed throughout the United States. Gay and lesbian synagogues have also been established in Canada, England, France, Israel, Belgium, the Netherlands, and Australia, and the World Congress of Gay and Lesbian Jewish Organizations was founded in 1980 at its first convention in San Francisco (Maggid 1989).

The first CBST shabbat service took place on February 9, 1973, with ten men in the basement of the Church of the Holy Apostles on Twenty-ninth Street. Jacob Gubbay, an East Indian Jew, advertised the upcoming service in *The Village Voice* (Shokeid 1995). By the end of the second year, members numbered more than one hundred, and the congregation moved to its present location on Bethune Street. For the first few years, a man from an Orthodox background, who had left his community of origin because of his homosexuality, led the newly formed gay and lesbian congregation. Word has it that his warmth, charisma, and "Hasidic style" were popular with the congregants and that they considered him to be their spiritual leader. CBST became a refuge from the city's bars and nightlife and offered an opportunity for gay Jews to participate fully in a Jewish environment that accepted and validated their gay identity.

By 1980, CBST had grown from a small group of male regulars into a gay and lesbian congregation, and it and the Gay and Lesbian Community Center were among the most powerful and influential gay organizations in New York City. By 1991, CBST had more than one thousand members, and over the years, CBST has been an important participant in the Gay Pride Parade, with its own float playing Israeli dance music as it travels down Fifth Avenue.

Figure 21.1. Congregation Beth Simchat Torah, Greenwich Village. Courtesy of the collection of Helaine Harris.

Although it joined with other American Jewish organizations in protesting the treatment of Jews in Russia, as well as in supporting other Jewish causes, CBST has been both rejected by and disappointed with the American Jewish establishment. CBST was in the limelight in 1992 when it was refused permission to participate in the Salute to Israel Parade (Shokeid 1995).

From the time of its inception until 1992, CBST prided itself in being a "lay-led" congregation. The decade of the 1990s, however, brought with it different needs for the congregation. The membership had greatly increased, and most important, the AIDS crisis had created the need for a rabbi to conduct hospital visits, counsel the sick, and perform funerals. But hiring a rabbi was quite a challenge for CBST. Could such a religiously diverse congregation agree on a rabbi who would represent all its members? CBST was not affiliated with any particular branch of Judaism, and its members were concerned about its religious autonomy if they hired a rabbi from a specific sector. Also, because of its growing lesbian population, the rabbi's gender and sexual orientation were important.

In February 1992, Rabbi Sharon Kleinbaum, a Reconstructionist, was appointed as the first rabbi of CBST. She has given the congregation strong leadership and inspiring teaching and has been immensely popular. She frequently describes herself as the "luckiest rabbi in America" (Witchell 1993) because her congregation participates freely and fully in all aspects of synagogue life. Kleinbaum encourages her congregation to live fully and completely as Jews and gay men and lesbians, and by her example of living with her partner and raising two children together, she continuously affirms this philosophy. She has advanced the spirit of renewal and *tikun olam* (healing the world) by encouraging members to participate in the Jewish, gay, and lesbian communities; volunteer in social settings; and take an active and personal role in improving relationships with the non-Jewish world.

Despite hiring a full-time rabbi, CBST remains a mainly volunteer congregation. Since its birth twenty-five years ago, it has become the largest and most active gay and lesbian synagogue in the world. But what is most unusual about this synagogue is its heterogeneity. United only by their sexual orientation, its congregants come from all walks of life and every socioeconomic background and span the geographical area from Staten Island to the Bahamas. The occupations of CBST's members range from blue-collar jobs to professional positions. Its members are taxi drivers, poets, physicians, professors, attorneys, opera singers, therapists, police officers, rabbis, and businessmen. CBST supports a policy of inclusion, turning no one away because of a lack of financial resources.

Of its more than one thousand members, about 60 percent are male, and 40 percent are female. More than three hundred people attend regular Friday-evening Sabbath services. In addition to the variety of adult worship services, about thirty young children participate in a "tot Shabbat" program at CBST. Statistics are not currently available for the numbers of CBST families that have children. Many couples have blended families as the result of a previous heterosexual marriage by either one or both of the partners, and many gay and lesbian couples have their own children. CBST has just begun to request this information on its membership forms, so there should be more information available in the future.

CBST is composed of a president, a vice-president, and other officers who preside over a board of directors. It has a music director, two rabbinical interns, a chorus, and more than twenty committees that are sewing a synagogue AIDS quilt, feeding the Jewish poor, teaching the adult bat mitzvah classes, planning a Martin Luther King Day observance, and much more. CBST publishes a monthly newsletter listing the anniversaries, recent commitment ceremonies, births, deaths, and Yahrzeits (anniversaries of deaths) of its members and their families. CBST offers adult Jewish education four evenings a week, with courses ranging from beginning Talmud to Rabbi Kleinbaum's class on the complex relationship with God. In an unexpectedly large response, more than seventy people attended her first class.

CBST and American Judaism

American congregations usually identify themselves with one of the major branches of Judaism (Reform, Conservative, Orthodox, or Reconstructionist), and their members have a common religious background. CBST is unique, therefore, in its religious pluralism. According to its current president, Yolanda Potasinski, "CBST has created a model for American Jewry as well as for Israel in demonstrating how people from all different walks of Jewish life can live together." Some members of CBST have had little or no Jewish education and come from assimilated Jewish families. Some of them even celebrated the Jewish holiday of Passover for the very first time at CBST. Other members have had the benefit of an extensive Jewish education and have graduated from Orthodox yeshiva high schools and universities. CBST counts among its members a representation of congregants with Hasidic backgrounds as well. In addition, many Jewish members have non-Jewish partners, some of whom are interested in converting to Judaism.

What brings this religiously, philosophically, and socioeconomically divergent group to a gay and lesbian synagogue? What are these gay and lesbian Jews seeking from their affiliation with CBST that they cannot find in a mainstream synagogue? Many gay and lesbian Jews have been rejected by the religious communities of their youth or have had to hide their gay and lesbian identities in order to "fit in." For some, the realization of a gay or lesbian sexual orientation ended their affiliation with anything Jewish. That is, after much struggle and conflict, many sacrificed their Jewish identity in order to live as "out" gay men and lesbians. The two identities, that of gay and Jewish, seemed mutually exclusive.

Rabinowitz (1983) examined the lives of students who regularly participated in a weekly Talmud class at CBST. Although from varied religious Jewish backgrounds, almost all of them had strong Jewish ties as children or teenagers. But most had abandoned their Jewish observances when they "came out" in the gay community. The establishment of CBST has thus allowed many of them to combine both their Jewish and their gay identities and to become an integral part of a Jewish community. Through CBST and within the structure of the American synagogue, New York City's gay and lesbian Jewish community has also gained its own voice as a political entity.

Some gay and lesbian Jews continue to pray in "mainstream" synagogues. Most, however, remain uncomfortable revealing their sexual orientation to fellow members and are thereby excluded from participating fully in the social aspects of the community. Rabinowitz poignantly expressed the particularly unsettling experience of attending an Orthodox synagogue: "When a man is over the age of thirty and still single, people become suspicious" (1983, 437). So some gay Jews choose to pray in large synagogues where they can remain anonymous, thereby avoiding the close scrutiny of others. How does one openly express a sexuality that many consider to be unacceptable? The degree to which that expression is forbidden or, conversely, how it may be embraced is dictated by the response of the particular Jewish denomination.

CBST and the Judaic Denominations

As it is in other religions, the traditional end of the Jewish continuum is the most opposed to gay rights, and so not surprisingly, Orthodox Jews opposed the passage of a gay rights bill in New York City in 1978 (Zwiebel 1985). Around the same time, the Rabbinical Council of America, the main organization of Orthodox rabbis, issued a statement condemning homosexuality as a "corruption of healthy family life." Perhaps the most frequently cited Orthodox opinion on the subject, written by Norman

Lamm, president of Yeshiva University, states: "Homosexuality, whether male or female, is thus considered abominable and can never be legalized in the eyes of Judaism" (1974, 194).

Orthodox Jews consider their position to be rooted in the prohibition by biblical texts like Leviticus 18:22 and 20:13: "You shall not lie with a man as one lies with a woman; it is an abomination . . . they shall be put to death and the fault is theirs alone." However, many liberal Jewish thinkers in the Reform and Reconstructionist movements have argued that if interpreted literally, this passage leaves room for most types of homosexual activity, specifically those in which a man does not pretend that his lover is a woman. It also does not prohibit any kind of sexual relationship between two women. In addition, some scholars believe that this particular prohibition was in response to the ritual practices of pagan cults and has little bearing on modern same-sex relationships.

The Reform movement has supported equal rights for gays and lesbians, both inside and outside the Jewish world. Reform Jews ordain gay and lesbian rabbis and cantors and officiate at same-sex commitment ceremonies. Currently, however, they do not religiously sanctify gay unions (Ain 1998).

The Reconstructionist movement has been in the forefront of a progressive acceptance of gay and lesbian rabbis and has promoted an educational awareness of homosexuality within the Jewish community. In addition, it has been the only established Jewish denomination to equate the holiness of a same-sex union with that of a heterosexual one and to officially sanctify the relationships between gay men and lesbians by allowing their clergy to officially marry same-sex couples within the Jewish religion (Gluck 1993).

The Conservative movement appears to have the most ambivalent attitude toward the rights and roles of gays and lesbians, especially as applied to the Jewish clergy. Although Conservatives support a nondiscrimination policy and full rights for gays and lesbians under the general law, their by-laws oppose the performance of commitment ceremonies for gays and lesbians and the knowing admittance of a gay or lesbian into their rabbinical or cantorial schools (resolutions adopted by the Committee on Jewish Law and Standards of the Rabbinical Assembly in 1990).

Along with the Reconstructionists, the "Renewal movement" has had a strong influence at CBST and on the greater Jewish world. Jewish Renewal seeks to return Judaism to its origins of healing and transformation. Its inclusive and egalitarian approach to Judaism derives in part from the social-change movements of the 1960s and 1970s, the women's movement, and concern about ecology and the environment (Lerner 1995). Among its inspirations, the Jewish Renewal movement counts Abraham Joshua Heschel, a philosopher who himself was active in the Civil Rights movement of the 1960s.

God is seen as a God of transcendence and compassion for the healing of the world, which in Hebrew is called *tikun olam*. Renewal promotes an egalitarian, nonsexist Judaism that supports the emergence of a Jewish feminist consciousness. Not only do women participate as equals in all aspects of religious practice, but women's insights also are viewed as enriching Jewish tradition and enabling a deeper understanding of different attributes of God and Jewish spirituality.

Both the Renewal and Reconstructionist movements recognize diversity in sexual orientation and support an end to homophobia in the Jewish world. They enthusiastically support the community's taking responsibility for its children, whether or not its members are single, married, straight, or gay and whether or not they have their own children. Both favor legitimizing gay and lesbian marriage as a means of strengthening the Jewish family and perpetuating the teachings and practices of Judaism into the next generation (Gluck 1993; Lerner 1995).

Although CBST has remained unaffiliated with any denomination, it has embraced many of the concepts and practices of the Renewal and Reconstructionist movements. Some of these include its innovations in the liturgy, egalitarian philosophy and ritual practices, community/social programs, political involvement, a strong sense of community, and the emphasis of deepening individual spirituality and *tikun olam*.

While enriching the synagogue, the tradition of religious diversity and independence has created some unique challenges as well. Can CBST both remain true to its egalitarian/feminist roots and satisfy those who wish to worship in a traditional manner? If so, then how does a congregation satisfy its members from Orthodox backgrounds, accommodate those from Reform orientations, and continue to extend itself to the assimilated, secular Jews? One approach to this problem has been to create more than six different worship services on the Sabbath. Currently, CBST holds liberal services, lesbian new moon services, traditional services, and learner services, to name just a few. In addition, it offers classes of all kinds, presentations, workshops, and retreats so that those who have chosen to follow the Orthodox interpretation of the laws and not travel on the Sabbath can at least participate in some aspects of CBST. Nonetheless, those who have remained or have become Orthodox have moved to the periphery of the CBST community, as has a small group that was active in founding and leading the congregation in the early years. Being a religiously observant gay and lesbian Jew therefore continues to be a dilemma.

In the fall of 1998, CBST formed an institute for Jewish learning, called the Lehrhaus Judaica, named for the Lehrhaus in Frankfurt, Germany, in 1920, where Jewish learning took place. The CBST's Lehrhaus Judaica is perhaps the first time that gay and lesbian and Jewish studies have been combined. The list of courses includes "Introduction to Hasidism," "Judaism and Homosexuality," "Yiddish Culture," and "Synagogue Skills."

CBST and the "Mainstream" Jewish World

For the first time, in 1998, Hadassah, an international organization of Jewish Women, held a meeting at CBST. This was an important milestone for the synagogue, as it meant the recognition of a mainstream Jewish organization. Among other recent notable gestures of acknowledgment were inclusion in a United Jewish Appeal fund-raising event; the participation of the Reform, Reconstructionist, and Conservative rabbinical seminaries in the CBST rabbinical internship program; and a large grant from the United Jewish Appeal.

In 1998, CBST celebrated its Gay Pride Sabbath service at Congregation Ansche Chesed, a large, established, Conservative synagogue on the Upper West Side of Manhattan. It was the first time that CBST was invited by a Conservative synagogue to celebrate an event. And during the summer of 1999, the CBST chorus participated in the North American Jewish Coral Music Festival for the first time.

At present, CBST struggles with a myriad of issues. As it grows from a small, intimate group to a substantial and influential community, it must renegotiate its philosophies, purpose, leadership, structure, and goals for the future. Some of these issues are concrete ones, such as the need for a larger space, as the present home of CBST is too small to accommodate its membership. Another issue is the struggle to meet the needs of both old and young gays and lesbians. Balancing the needs of the gay and the lesbian members, reconciling the partnership of lay and rabbinical leadership, and attracting new members all are significant challenges. CBST is also concerned with deepening the spiritual growth of the synagogue community as well as increasing its impact on the greater Jewish community and the world. What will CBST's mission statement be for the new millennium? On the basis of what paradigm will it grow? Will it gain the acceptance of the mainstream Jewish community? Some of this synagogue's concerns are unique to a gay and lesbian religious community. Others are not but, rather, reflect the concerns and struggles of many religious institutions in the 1990s.

Very few people are not profoundly touched during their first visit to this synagogue. Many congregants have spoken about how CBST has changed their lives by allowing them to lead a dynamic Jewish life while at the same time allowing their gay and lesbian relationships to be acknowledged and celebrated. According to its members, few, if any, other synagogues celebrate their relationships, participate in gay pride, and afford them the opportunity for an integrated gay or lesbian and Jewish life.

Rabbi Kleinbaum described the "coming-out" process as the most important common denominator of its participants, the single most unifying experience that gays and lesbians share, and one in which the person who goes through it is changed forever. During this process, one asks the difficult questions: Who am I? What am I willing to do in the face of rejection—from my family, friends, job, and so forth? What is my spiritual essence, and what role does my homosexuality play? How can I reconcile my lesbian or gay identity with my Judaism? Reflecting on these issues and participating in a coming-out process is character building and "makes people thirsty for spiritual experiences." To many, Congregation Beth Simchat Torah plays an important role in satisfying that thirst.

Chapter 22

Feminists, Religion, and Ethics in New York City
The Roman Catholic Example

Susan A. Farrell

Women are central to the continued existence of New York City's religions because they not only give birth to the future generations of churches but they also socialize their children into their religious traditions.[1] In addition, women do much of the volunteer work that keep the churches going and the faithful mended. In more recent times, women have also become priests, rabbis, ministers, pastors, and theologians, although in many cases, women are the dissenters "defecting in place," as one study of mainline denominations put it (Winter, Lummis, and Stokes 1995). In other instances, women remain staunch supporters of the status quo, especially in the evangelical, fundamentalist, and orthodox churches (Ammerman 1990; Davidman 1991).

The struggle for equality takes place most often in women's demand for ordination in churches that have clergy. Generally speaking, the more informal and less hierarchical a religious group is, the more likely its female members are to be treated equally (for example, the Quakers; see Brown and Stuard 1989). Even so, in Judaism, women in the Reform and Conservative traditions have become rabbis. Other challenges for women in religion are usually issues of sexuality, family, and equality (Farrell 1991; Weeks 1989). For instance, the more traditional religions discourage women from working, in favor of a more patriarchal family arrangement. Divorce is barely if at all tolerated. On sexual issues, Roman Catholicism represents one of the most extreme positions: no sex outside marriage, no contraception or abortion, and no divorce, although church teachings do support women's rights in civil society. Likewise, the evangelical and fundamentalist Protestant

Christian traditions tend to support traditional gender roles in the family and society and are less tolerant of women working outside the home. New religious movements also represent a broad spectrum. New Age religions and Wiccan practices treat women as equal, superior, or separate from men, but other new religious movements, such as Promise Keepers, reinforce traditional gender roles.

Women usually become theologians through the social-activist movements that emerged in the 1960s and through their experience of gender inequality and sexual dilemmas such as pregnancy and abortion. Deeply affected by the social activism of the 1960s and 1970s, feminist theologians and ethicists. saw their movement as a natural development of its liberationist and ecstatic themes. Opposition to the Vietnam War and the breaking of traditional taboos renewed the concern about ethics. As one feminist ethicist remembered, "I just slid from the peace movement into feminism." The path to feminist ethics often traveled from early childhood religiosity to social activism to feminism. Thus, the ethics of feminist theologians has always predominated over abstract discussions of God, salvation, and heaven. Instead, feminist ethicists build more on people's real experiences, dilemmas, and decisions than do their traditionalist colleagues, who decry subjectivity and praise the deduction of abstract principles (see Andolsen, Gudorf, and Pellauer 1985; Farrell 1991; Lake 1986). Feminist ethics "emerged as a reaction against traditional, male-dominated modes of doing ethics as it became clear to . . . women, and to some men, that those modes refused to acknowledge the reality and the value of people whose experience differs from the typical white, middle- to upper-strata man" (Daly 1994, xiii).

The two main areas that have driven feminist ethics are sexuality and equality. Religious feminist discourse in New York City has often centered on abortion, an issue directly related to female bodies and lives. Although abortion and birth control are forbidden to Roman Catholics, New York City's Catholic feminists have argued that traditional Catholic ethics were formulated by mostly celibate males as if sexuality and its consequences were disembodied notions.

Roman Catholic Women in New York City

Women's participation in Roman Catholicism has been primarily in women's religious orders. These orders founded many of New York City's parochial schools and city hospitals, such as Cabrini, but since the 1960s, there has been a precipitous decline in the number of commitments to women's and men's religious orders, as well as to the priesthood in general (see Ebaugh 1993; Schoenherr and Young 1993). For example, the number of Daughters of Wisdom, who used to staff the high schools of Lady of Wisdom Academy in South Ozone Park, Christ the King in Middle Village, and Good Samaritan Hospital on Long Island, has fallen in the United States from 500 in the 1970s to just over 140 nuns today. In the 1960s, St. John's Prep in Astoria, Queens, had about ninety teachers, mostly nuns and priests. But by 1980, only three Sisters of Mercy and one Josephite remained. Indeed, some hospitals and schools closed or were taken over by others. Currently, the religious teaching personnel in the New York Archdiocese are 8 priests, 65 brothers, and 255 sisters. Brooklyn has 26 priests, 63 brothers, and 357 sisters teaching in the schools. Hundreds of lay women and men have picked up the slack: New York has 4,414 lay teachers and Brooklyn has 3,228, and especially in the grammar schools, the majority are women (*Official Catholic Directory* 1999).

Most parishes could not operate without the voluntary labor of women as lay teachers of the catechism (basic church doctrine) and as Eucharistic ministers for the sick and dying. Rosary-Altar Societies raise funds to maintain and decorate the churches and schools, for example, for FISH programs[2] for the sick and the elderly. Although New York has more priests than do other parts of the country (Wallace 1992), women still hold many positions because of the shortage. For instance, both the New York and Brooklyn Dioceses have women vicars.[3]

Catholic women have always been committed to parish and community life, if not always to the letter of church law (D'Antonio et al. 1996; Wallace 1992). For example, although membership data are not broken down by gender, spokesperson Frank D. Rosa estimates that of the Brooklyn Diocese's 1,625,547 Catholics, three-quarters are probably women (see *Official Catholic Directory* 1999). Despite their very poor pay ($14,000 to $15,000/year) and low appreciation by the hierarchy, women fill numerous administrative jobs in the church. In addition, women hold these offices without the status and power of ordination, so the church's bureaucratic structure remains patriarchal as well as hierarchical. Power is vested in the bishop by the pope, and this includes organizational authority and power as well as spiritual power, an example of Max Weber's perception that organized churches are hierocracies. According to Weber: "A 'hierocratic organization' is an organization which enforces its order through psychic coercion by distributing or denying religious benefits. . . . A compulsory hierocratic organization will be called 'church' insofar as its administrative staff claims a monopoly of the legitimate use of hierocratic coercion" (1978, 54).

In the Roman Catholic Church, religious benefits, that is, grace, come mainly through the administration of the sacraments, preferably by an ordained priest. A small minority of Roman Catholic men therefore determine the dispensation of the sacraments and the graces that accompany them and, ultimately, salvation, which all Catholics are supposed to desire. The New York and Brooklyn Dioceses are merely local manifestations of the general situation.

New York City Catholic feminists have not targeted a specific member of the hierarchy for their anger. Rather, as one feminist ethicist put it, "The opponent is the Catholic Church, its hierarchy in general." Gay and lesbian feminist ethicists cite John Cardinal O'Connor for his lack of support for gay and lesbian Catholics and Bishop Thomas V. Daily of Brooklyn for his monthly demonstrations at a Queens abortion clinic. But most feminist ethicists prefer to talk about a faceless generalized opponent or criticize the Vatican rather than any specific person.

Vatican II emboldened liberalizers to open up the church while conservatives, hierarchically obedient, hesitated to shut things down. Called in the early 1960s by Pope John XXIII, Vatican II liberalized doctrinal restraints, reduced the scope of the hierarchy's authority, and increased the number of lay roles (D'Antonio et al. 1989; Elizondo and Greinacher 1980; Kennelly 1989; Kolbenschlag 1987; Seidler and Meyer 1989; Wallace 1988, 1992; Weaver 1985). Because the conservatives were slow to react, they lost the initiative. In 1975, feminists formed the Women's Ordination Conference in Chicago, a center of support for Vatican II. In 1974, Mary Lynch called together thirty-one acquaintances at the Catholic Theological Union in Chicago and asked whether it was time to raise the issue of the ordination of women in the Catholic Church. A task force grew out of this assembly, and the first conference, Women in Future Priesthood Now—A Call for Action, was held (Foley 1976). Conferences have played an important role among feminist ethicists in New York and elsewhere. Even though feminist theologians and ethicists were organized at the grassroots level here in New York, they also needed to come together nationally and even internationally so as not to feel out of touch with one another and their leaders.

In 1976, church conservatives slowed down the momentum toward a married priesthood and women's ordination. The Vatican issued the Declaration on the Ordination of Women to the Priesthood, which stated that women should not be ordained because they could not "image" Christ. The declaration's deliberate ambiguity about how males "image" Christ became a point of attack by Catholic feminists. The Vatican's attempt to smother the issues only encouraged progressives to fight back. The feminist response was much more vigorous than their response to the 1968 papal encyclical against abortion and contraception, and they established a network of conferences, organizations, support groups, and publications.

By the summer of 1978, opponents of the conservatives' Vatican declaration organized the first feminist theology conference, sponsored by St. John's University and held at the Immaculate Conception Seminary in Douglaston, Queens, a huge, almost empty training center for young men entering the priesthood. The irony of more than fifty women discussing women's ordination in buildings with urinals in all the bathrooms took the conference from an intellectual plane to a tangible sense of revolution. This was the first place that women in the United States formally organized to discuss women's rights and issues in the church. Some of the now well-known names in feminist theology were present, including Elisabeth Schüssler Fiorenza (see Fiorenza 1983, 1992, 1993).

Picking up the momentum from this theology conference, a second women's ordination conference followed very quickly in Baltimore. Then, the following summer, a liberation theology conference was held at Archbishop Molloy Retreat House at the Passionist Monastery in Jamaica, Queens. Again, there was a strong feminist presence: Elisabeth Schüssler Fiorenza, Rosemary Radford Ruether, Mary Hunt, Dianne Neu, Ada Marie Isasi Díaz, Beverly Harrison, and numerous other feminist theologians and ethicists.

A few years later, Mary Hunt and Dianne Neu founded the Women's Alliance for Theology, Ethics, and Ritual (WATER), a grassroots organization for the transformation of Catholic theology, ethics, and spirituality. WATER also became a founding organizational member of Women-Church.

At that time, New York was in the forefront of Roman Catholic feminist theology events, largely due to the work of two women: one Roman Catholic, Mary Buckley, a professor of liberation and feminist theology at St. John's University, and her close friend Beverly Harrison, a professor of Christian ethics at Union Theological Seminary.

The Roman Catholic Feminist Activist Tradition
in New York City

Mary Buckley became active in the 1930s as a founding member of the Grail, a lay social-action group similar to Catholic Workers. She organized the first feminist theology conference, which was held in Queens, and the next one, in Grailville, Ohio. Buckley also became the mentor of many feminist ethicists, such as the noted author Elisabeth Schüssler.[4]

At the first feminist theology conference, Buckley (1978) raised the contradiction of baptizing women but denying them ordination. She asserted that if women could not image Christ, as stated by the Vatican in the Declaration on the Ordination of Women to the Priesthood, then in essence, they were beyond redemption. Coming so soon after the Vatican declaration, Buckley's paper had a large impact at the conference, spurring participants to extend their challenges to the Vatican.

As a founding member of the Association for the Rights of Catholics in the Church (ARCC), Buckley signed a 1984 *New York Times* ad asserting the diversity of opinion on abortion. Many feminist ethicists still talk about this ad as a "watershed moment." The church hierarchy's severe, swift reaction forced Catholic Church employees to choose among leaving the church, joining extrachurch institutions, or remaining quiet. Up to this moment, many supporters thought that dialogue was still possible. Instead, the church hierarchy hounded people out of jobs and religious communities. Under pressure, some people recanted but often could not keep their positions.

Along with many others, especially religious sisters and priests, Buckley was the target of punitive measures from the organized church. She was denied promotion to full professor at St. John's University but continued to teach there along with Father Paul Surlis, another liberal moral theologian, training many people in an alternative ethical tradition within Roman Catholicism.

Fordham University, the other major Roman Catholic campus in New York, was less militant (on both sides) than St. John's but also produced a number of activist scholars. Indeed, sociologist Father Joseph Fitzpatrick was a key mentor to the city's social activists. Through his teaching, writing, and moral support, he encouraged women in theology. Also at Fordham, Madeleine Boucher was one of the first feminist theologians and wrote one of the first responses (1977) to the Vatican declaration on the ordination of women.

Local Activism

In 1978, Manhattan and Long Island chapters of the Women's Ordination Conference (WOC) were established. In Manhattan, the Women's Ordination Conference was founded by sisters at the Intercommunity Center for Justice and Peace in Greenwich Village. The center itself had been founded by the Leadership Conference for Women Religious, one of the main national organizations for nuns, to promote issues like women's ordination. In Brooklyn, because Catholic feminists wanted to tackle more than just ordination, they founded the Catholic Women's Office but remained affiliated with the WOC. The Brooklyn group also differed in that of its sixty to seventy-five members, almost two-thirds were nuns, mostly from the Sisters of Mercy and the Congregation of St. Joseph.

After the *New York Times* ad on abortion and the resulting crackdown on outspoken Catholics, Frances Kissling of Washington, D.C., founded Catholics for a Free Choice (CFFC) as a support group for prochoice Catholics and an avenue for social change in the church and society. Eileen Moran, a former director of a shelter for abused women, helped established CFFC in New York, which also lobbies state and city authorities for women's right to choose and access to family planning and contraception.

According to interviews with members from both groups, New York City has both advantages and disadvantages for organizing. On one hand, usually large numbers of people can be mobilized very quickly. Hot topics such as abortion and gay rights often hit public consciousness in New York before most other areas of the country. Furthermore, as a media center, New York activities usually gain some coverage. Important people visit New York, thereby supplying opportunities for focused demonstrations or marches. New York City also has a dense network of foundations that provide money and places to meet.

Some disadvantages were apparent as well: Cardinal O'Connor's good ties with the media means that the hard questions raised by activists are often filtered out of interviews. Although quick mobilization is possible, some activists feel that New Yorkers are overcommitted, thereby making it difficult to get members to act. Also, since most members of CFFC are women, child-care arrangements affect how much they can do. In this regard, class issues can also cause conflict. Working-class women often have less flexible working hours and thus cannot participate as much in daytime demonstrations, and they like to reserve the evening hours for their family.

Activist Catholic groups often join other groups with sympathetic goals, such as DIGNITY (Gay and Lesbian Catholics) or CORPUS (married priests) when demonstrations are planned for church organizational sites. DIGNITY, which may currently be the strongest group in New York City, attracts various groups of activists under the assumption that sexual issues are interconnected. Feminist groups and liberationist movements in the Roman Catholic Church recently came together under an umbrella organization called Women-Church, a coalition that helps assemble various activists around an issue, a process that the organization calls *convergence.*

Feminist Ethics in New York City

In addition to supporting, training, and mentoring women students in theology and ministry, Mary Buckley was also a pioneer in feminist ethics. Together with Beverly Harrison, Buckley sought an alternative to traditional ethics that was centered on women and included an economic analysis. After Buckley retired from teaching several years ago, Harrison continued to pursue this project with her students at Union Theological Seminary and through many conferences until she also retired, in 1998. Harrison held the first endowed chair in Christian ethics named for a woman and filled by a woman.

Auburn Theological Seminary has sponsored many conferences on feminism, feminist theology, and feminist ethics. Indeed, Auburn is the first seminary to be headed by a woman, Barbara Wheeler. In 1994, Dr. Wheeler initiated the Women's Multifaith Programs. Starting as an informal gathering of women from New York City churches, synagogues, and mosques, its planning committee now "sponsors and develops educational programs that promote understanding, respect, and appreciation for the similarities and differences among religious traditions" (Working Mission Statement 1997). The newest item that they have added is the annual Lives of Commitment Awards Breakfast which honors three women whose public commitments are religiously motivated—"a 'sung' hero, an unsung hero, and a young person" (informational brochure).

Most recently, Dr. Wheeler sponsored several lectures and conferences, including the Women's Multifaith Lecture, with Karen Armstrong, author of *A History of God* (1994). Other programs include lectures on women mystics, the question of St. Paul's misogyny and anti-Semitism, and women's voices in Islam today. Lectures entitled "Prayerfully Pro-Choice:

'How' and 'Why' Guides for Religious Leaders" are meant to help clergy, theology students, and laypersons of all religious traditions think through options regarding childbearing and reproductive choice.

Auburn Theological Seminary has also held conferences to advance feminism within major Protestant denominations. One of these conferences was led by Delores Williams, a student of Beverly Harrison, who in 1980 organized a group to analyze Alice Walker's *The Color Purple*. She explained (1993) that African American women, prevented until recently from engaging in academic work, often expressed their theology and ethics in their fiction. Now a Union Theological Seminary professor, Williams was one of the first women of color to challenge white Christian feminists, leading to widespread discomfort. At first, feminist theology meetings were attended mostly by white, college-educated women. Now, besides Williams, other African American theologians and ethicists find their homes at Temple (Katie Cannon 1988, 1995, a member of the Mudflower Collective) and Boston's Episcopal Divinity School (Joan Martin).

Another place for women to come together on issues of sexism, racism, and classism is the National Council of Churches headquarters near Union Theological Seminary. In particular, the council provides a meeting place for feminists from mainline Protestant, Orthodox Christian, and Metropolitan (a gay and lesbian denomination) churches. Theology in the Americas, a very important ecumenical group based at the National Council of Churches in Manhattan, has worked with many feminist theologians to begin a multicultural theology reflecting a theology of liberation.[5] In Latin America, this group educated peasants using Paulo Freire's *Pedagogy of the Oppressed* (1970), while here it brought together Western and Latin American liberation theologians such as Gustavo Gutierrez (1973).

Another group that grew out of the work at Union is the Mudflower Collective. This is an interracial, interreligious coalition of students from Union and the Episcopal Divinity School in Boston formed in the 1980s "to do ethics" with the radical feminist notion that "the personal is the political." This group represents the very opposite of how traditional ethics and theology are formulated in an abstract, context-free manner with little relationship to people's lived experiences.

With several other feminist ethicists in the New York and Boston area, Beverly Harrison founded the Northeast Feminist Ethics Consultation in 1976. Since then, the group and its individual members have produced many seminal works. One of them, Beverly Harrison's construction of feminist ethics, puts women at the center of moral decision making. She argues that the economic dimension of moral decision making also needs to be understood in the ways it often restricts women's choices (Harrison 1983, 1985). For example, the economic dependency of women in the family affects their senses of self and ethical options (1985, 218).

In the area of sexual ethics, Beverly Harrison's work greatly influenced other feminist ethicists' explorations of intimacy, desire, sexual practices, abortion, contraception, and procreative technologies. Her book *Our Right to Choose* (1983) traces the history of beliefs on abortion in the Christian tradition from biblical to modern times to expose the contradictions in the Roman Catholic Church's assertion that its teaching on abortion has always been the same. Harrison's collection of essays in *Making the Connections* (edited by a former student, Carol Robb) constructs feminist ethics as a challenge to ethics as an academic discipline and to Christian church policies on sexual issues (1985). Her basic criticism of traditional Christian ethics is that too often it assumes "that 'disinterestedness' and 'detachment' are basic preconditions for responsible moral action. And in the dominant ethical tradition, moral rationality too often is *disembodied* rationality" (1985, 13).

The Future

Future feminist activists and ethicists coming out of the myriad religious traditions in New York City can look to Mary Buckley, Beverly Harrison, the local chapters of WOC and CFFC, and other social and human rights groups for inspiration as they continue to live in New York City with "a passion for justice" (Harrison 1985, 263). Feminist ethics has turned to community and relationships as its foundation, and it has established women as moral agents capable of making their own choices, even if they make mistakes. It also understands that those choices are made in reference to a particular community, family, neighborhood, ethnicity, class, and workplace. This understanding underscores the basic quality of feminist ethics: constant recreation in the crucible of the diversity of women's experiences (see Bell 1993, 55). As new religions and ethnicities bloom in New York, feminist ethics will be recreated, offering new, perhaps unexpected, paths for moral lives.

NOTES

1. For an overview of religion in America, region by region, see Kosmin and Lachman 1993. In addition, the following are just a few of the many books and articles on American women and religion: Ruether and Keller's encyclopedic *Women & Religion in America*, a four-volume series, the last of which was published in 1996; and Janet Wilson James, ed., *Women in American Religion*, 1978.

2. FISH is not an acronym but refers to the secret sign by which early Christians made themselves know to each other.

3. A vicar is the highest administrator of a diocese but does not oversee spiritual matters, which only a priest can do.

4. Now Schüssler Fiorenza, her work, along with Rosemary Radford Ruether's, is the best known of that of the Roman Catholic feminist theologians.

5. Jualynne Dodson reminded me of this important role during a presentation made at the Society for the Scientific Study of Religion in San Diego, CA, November 1997.

Chapter 23

Gender, Community, and Change among the Rastafari of New York City

Tricia Redeker Hepner and Randal L. Hepner

The Rastafari movement is strength for women—any woman—I don't care if you're black, white, Chinese, I don't care what you are. It gives you a certain strength. A lot of things that women outside of the culture might think of or view negatively, once you're a Rasta for some time and overstand things then you get to appreciate them. Rasta is power!

—Sister Makeda

New York City[1] is the largest "Caribbean city" anywhere in the world and likely claims the largest Rastafarian population outside Jamaica.[2] The sights and *wordsounds* of Rastafari in the city echo the movement's *livity* (lifeway) in many parts of the world while also representing new trends in the movement's organization and institutionalization. Only recently have ethnographers begun examining New York City as central and historically significant to the rise of a Rastafari transnational social field. New York City has also been the site for local innovations in Rastafari belief, practice, and community building.

The growth of Rastafari has created the need for greater community institutions in New York, such as churches, political associations, and community and day-care centers. While Rastafari remains an organizationally diffuse sociocultural and religious movement, the trend toward institutionalization may well foreshadow future developments in the movement globally as well as in Jamaica (for the growth and development of Rastafari and Rasta churches and organizations in North America, see Hepner 1998c).

As we show in this chapter, Rastafari represents a transnational movement in transition. The emergence of a significant and multiethnic Rasta population has raised aspects of traditional (Jamaican) Rastafari practice for discussion and debate (for standard works on Rastafari history, doctrine, and practice, see Barrett 1988; Campbell 1987; Owens 1976). Issues relating to women's roles in the community and family have been central to the emergence of a Rastafari *livity* (a way of being in the world) that challenges many commonly held stereotypes about the movement's male-identified character. Although patriarchy and sexism remain as prevalent in Rastafari as in other cultural and religious communities the world over, Rastafari women are finally being recognized as leaders in their communities and, using Rastafari as the source of their empowerment, have articulated powerful critiques of the movement's patriarchal and androcentric elements.

Historical Background

The crowning of Emperor Haile Selassie I on November 30, 1930, in Ethiopia was followed by a strange new doctrine resounding throughout the infamous shantytowns of Kingston, Jamaica. Gathering inspiration from the great nationalist leader Marcus Garvey, fiery, bearded men from the poorest strata of this colonial island claimed that the Bible foretold the imminent redemption and restoration of Africans residing in an evil European Babylon to the promised land of Zion. Through the coming of a black messiah, New World Africans would regain the identity and history stolen from them by slavery, colonialism, racism, and other-worldly mission Christianity. Moreover, this black messiah had clearly appeared, they preached, in the royal figure of Ras Tafari Makonnen, known to the world as Emperor Haile Selassie I of Ethiopia, crowned King of Kings, Lord of Lords, Conquering Lion of the Tribe of Judah, Elect of God, and Light of this World.

Since its inception as both a new religious movement and a social and political philosophy advocating black liberation, Rastafari has spread throughout the world to become one of the fastest-growing popular and grassroots religious cultures today. Carried abroad on the wings of reggae music and the migration of Jamaican and other Caribbean peoples, Rastafari since the 1960s has penetrated every continent, attracting followers from disparate cultural, ethnic, and national backgrounds (see Cashmore 1979, 1984; Savishinsky 1994a, b, and c; Van Dijk 1998, 178–198; Yawney 1994b). Rastafari's incisive yet malleable symbols and messages have inspired and transformed individuals and communities throughout the world. Among these are the universally recognizable and often fierce appearance of dreadlocks; the use of the Ethiopian colors of red, gold, and green; the plaintive one-drop of reggae rhythms; and the ritual use of *ganja* (marijuana, or the "holy weed of wisdom"). Rastafari has dramatically articulated and enacted resistance against the forces of modernity and postmodernity threatening the planet and the human rights, dignity, and freedom of all people. They have affirmed the centrality of Africa as both the mother of humanity and the origin of the people who see themselves as biblical Israelites enslaved in a foreign land.

While the Rastafari movement continues to locate its origins in Jamaica, and Jamaican forms of Rastafari continue to represent the "tradition" or ideal, Rastafari has both matured and changed as it has traveled throughout the world. In this chapter, we examine two facets of change among transnational Rastafari communities in New York City: the burgeoning organization and institutionalization of the movement into discrete "mansions," that is, religious-political formations and churches; and the tensions, contradictions, and changes that have arisen between Rastafari women and men as they confront the traditional elements of sexism within Rastafari itself. Despite widespread pigeonholing of the movement for its patriarchal beginnings and marginalization of women, our ethnography among Rastafarians in New York City has revealed a far more complex negotiation of gender roles and the development of a "womanist" consciousness among many Rasta women. The carving out of new roles, particularly the reconfiguring of motherhood as a locus of power for women, has been both facilitated and solidified by the increasing influence of Rastafari organizations and institutions.

Many people in the movement view Rastafari as a way of being in the world, a *livity*, that avoids and subverts the influences of a corrupt, racist, and out-of-control society committed to the relentless pursuit of power, human and environmental exploitation, and mindless individual consumerism. Rastas almost universally exhibit an anarchistic attitude toward formal societal organizations and a distrust of leadership claims that carries over to movement-sponsored organizations and leaders.

Consequently, the majority of Rastafarians in New York, as in Jamaica, are not affiliated with any of the established or newly emergent Rasta churches, political associations, or community centers. Instead, small networks of "reasoning" circles provide the principal forms of interaction and socialization for the masses of the grassroots movement.

For a small number of people, Rastafari appears as merely an affected youth subcultural "style," a cloak designed to dress up a personal sense of alienation while projecting a defiant attitude toward Babylon (the establishment). But for a growing number of brothers and sisters deepening their faith or socializing a new generation of Rasta youth, identification with an organized house of worship has become more acceptable and widespread. These brothers and sisters form the most highly active and involved enthusiasts in the movement, although in other respects they are fairly representative of New York Rastafari. In the following pages, we engage the voices and experiences of several such Rasta women and men to illustrate the complexity and changing character of the Rastafari community and gender roles. None are leaders or spokespersons for the broader movement, yet each embodies the ideas and interests of growing numbers of their fellow communicants.

Rastafari Misunderstood

In both Jamaica and New York City, the Rastafari movement has traditionally been characterized as "acephalous" (literally, "headless," that is, leaderless) owing to its organizational diffusion and doctrinal heterogeneity. Despite this decentralized character and the variation in belief and practice among Rastafarians at home and abroad, many researchers have tended to concentrate on the typical forms of Rastafari belief and practice—that is, its original Jamaican forms—as if they were relatively monolithic and unchanging over time. This tendency probably stems from the fact that until recently, the major task facing researchers has simply been decoding the movement's primary symbols, beliefs, practices, and linguistic configurations. Only in the past few years have some scholars suggested that Rastafari is increasing in diversity on several different levels. In New York City in particular, we have observed a chorus of Rasta voices contesting various aspects of "traditional" belief and practice, especially regarding women's issues and gender relations. We have also observed the growth and development of distinct Rastafari organizations and churches, or "mansions,"[3] which compete for the allegiance of the larger, unorganized movement.

Researchers are now beginning to discern a more "polycephalous" (multileader) aspect in the movement. Discrete congregations, institutions, and leaderships have appeared, each trying to advance its own unique "Rastology" and to recruit from the newly converted and expanding ranks of the institutionally unaffiliated. Themes of tension and change as Rastas in Jamaica and New York City renegotiate aspects of traditional Rastafari must therefore be central to analyses if researchers are to account for the increasingly active, dynamic, multiethnic, and transnational movement.

Perhaps the most misunderstood, contested, and underresearched issue in Rastafarian studies is gender and the role of Rasta women and families. Like many other aspects of Rastafari, however, ideas about sex and gender reveal a great deal of diversity, contradiction, and change. The notion that Rastafari beliefs about women's "nature," roles, and place in the movement have remained static for nearly seven decades and across continents is implausible and contradicts our research findings and experience. In this chapter, we explore the development of what might be called "Rasta-Womanism" among sisters, and the transformation of Rasta women's traditionally undervalued roles as mothers or female companions to Rasta men into empowered, central figures in congregations and organizations in New York City.

The Problem of Understanding in Scholarly Accounts of Rastafari

Just as Rastafari itself exhibits doctrinal heterogeneity and organizational diffusion in general, attitudes toward gender relations are equally diverse. It is no longer possible to generalize about Rasta views of gender as the movement is being changed by the differing perspectives of both private individuals and public organizations. In the past, Rastafari was described almost uniformly by outside researchers as a patriarchal faith or movement in which women play a subordinate role (see Kitzinger 1966, 1969), although the new scholarship has begun to address women and Rastafari more specifically. That Rastafari has been gendered from its inception is not contested, but most researchers to date have all but excluded Rasta women's own experiences and perspectives. Equally significant has been the assumption that Rasta men all view women's roles in the same way. Recent work by Rastafari women themselves and that by Chevannes and Yawney promise new attention to changing gender relations in Rastafari (see Chevannes 1994; Rowe 1998; Tafari-Ama 1998; Yawney 1994a and b). For the most part, however, the diverse and evolving views present in Rasta voices have not been examined.

Written sources on Rastafari gender relations actually document the academic tendency toward a static conception of Rastafari practice. Chevannes notes that "the place of all females is below males, regardless of age" (1994, 176), while Yawney criticizes some Rastafari women for having a "false consciousness" about sexism in the movement. Yawney, however, also points out an instructive paradox:

> Male dominance is built into the basic nature of Rastafari in such a way as to constitute its central contradiction. If Rastafari shares with the social system to which it is so opposed a fundamental oppression of women, how can it represent in the final analysis a genuine alternative social form? (1994a, 67)

Yawney's recognition that sexism and patriarchy in the context of a radical movement aimed at primarily black—but increasingly a more broadly conceived human—liberation indeed constitutes a central contradiction is astute and overdue. Moreover, it is not difficult to find Rasta sisters who express similar sentiments. Empress Modupe, a Haitian American mother of twelve, a schoolteacher, and an activist in the Ethiopian World Federation in Brooklyn for some twenty years, argues,

> Sexism *is* a major contradiction in the movement, and within the movement you will find a lot of contradictions. But that stems from how Rasta as a movement began. It began not with gender issues, but with race issues. It was mostly men in the movement, so in a lot of ways this sexism came when they . . . viewed Babylon as a female. Ya mon! It's still the same— Babylon, the mother harlot, Queen Elizabeth as the oppressor—a lot of that energy related to the female principle. The sexism inna Rasta is from this colonial upbringing, and it's one that we can do away with, it's one that's really harmful to the movement. The sexism is really from ignorance, and how we can eliminate it is through education.

Like the Empress, many other Rasta women readily acknowledge the existence of sexist and patriarchal elements in Rastafari. Yet for researchers, assessing and analyzing this dilemma proves problematic, for a variety of reasons. First, researchers informed by Western feminist discourse may find themselves blinded by their own assumptions. Much of this discourse proves alienating and insufficient vis-à-vis the experiences of black and Caribbean women. Moreover, in its quest to expose women's oppression, Western feminism often fails to acknowledge the ways that women actually resist and subvert their subordination. Such an approach, moreover, labels Rastafari as sexist or patriarchal, thus perpetuating the problem by legitimating, rather than critiquing, the attitude both inside and outside the Rasta community that women are only second-class actors in the movement. Rastafari women (and men), the majority of whom are of African descent, have almost uniformly rejected "feminism," which they usually equate with white, middle-class women's concerns. Recoiling from the term itself, Rastafari women choose to address their roles in the movement from perspectives akin to those found in *Black Feminist Thought* (Collins 1991), *Third World Feminism* (Mohanty, Russo, and Torres 1991) and "Womanism" (Walker 1983, xi–xii). The use of these terms, however, is not common, and most Rastafari women express a prowoman stance through Rastafari itself.

Second, many scholars fail to notice that patriarchy and sexism are not inherent features of Rastafari but, rather, a product of the specific Jamaican developments that contributed to its rise in the early 1930s. However, in the past thirty years, Rastafari has transcended its island home and now is influenced by the cultural environments of North America, Europe, and elsewhere. Moreover, Rastafari increasingly finds a following among people of non-Caribbean and, to a lesser extent, non-African descent. The adoption of Rastafari as a way of life or *livity* among these groups interrupts traditional Jamaican cultural specificities and releases a new dynamism. As in the case of gender, the impact of migration, cultural, and environmental change on Rastafari has not been adequately addressed.

Third, the emergence of sizable Rastafarian institutions—churches, political associations, and community centers—in New York both reflects and contributes to the growing diversity in Rastafari and the changing roles of Rasta women. These various groups, among them the Twelve Tribes of Israel, the Ethiopian Orthodox Church (EOC), the Church of Haile Selassie I (CHSI), the Nyabinghi Order of Divine Theocracy, the Ethiopian World Federation (EWF), and the Ifetayo Cultural Arts Facility, each embody unique versions of Jamaican Rastafari. Consequently, we can see a range of beliefs and practices ranging from the most traditional among the Nyabinghi Order, to some of the more progressive among the Twelve Tribes. Such variations also correspond to different mansions and group theologies; for example, the Church of Haile Selassie I exhibits a newly emergent "Rasta fundamentalism" (Hepner 1998c) yet also emphasizes the importance of monogamy, the Rasta family, and the central role of Rasta women in the life of the congregation. In contrast, the Nyabinghi Order retains the "ancient" laws of Rastafari, such as the often extreme segregation of men and women; strict observance of the "Ital" diet with its taboo on meat, alcohol, and cigarettes; and the traditional calendrical ritual gatherings known as *binghis* or *groundations*, featuring drumming, chanting, and sacramental ganja smoking.[4] At Twelve Tribes social events, however, one can observe brothers and sisters mingling, dancing, eating dishes containing chicken, drinking bottled beer, or smoking cigarettes.

These mansions differ not only (sometimes sharply) in certain practices but also in terms of their "Rastologies." Some institutions stress religious worship with their own unique liturgies (Twelve Tribes, EOC, CHSI), while others function primarily as political associations (EWF, IEWF), or community centers and educational institutions (Ifetayo). Given such a high incidence of heterogeneity both within and across congregations, it is not surprising that Rasta views of a variety of issues should also be heterogeneous. A virtual kaleidoscope of both old and new Rasta ways becomes visible. The multiple ideologies, beliefs, and practices make it increasingly difficult to generalize about issues such as gender, race, or traditional conceptions of diet and worship. More important, however, this constant shifting of ideas, in addition to the institutional support offered to individuals with shared views, has in many ways benefited women and contributed to their burgeoning centrality and vocality in the movement.

Thus, Rastafari as a multifaceted and multidimensional movement has become more complex over the last decade or so. The challenge now facing Rastas and researchers alike is identifying a consistent pattern by which to characterize a growing number of culturally and doctrinally disparate followers. At this stage, it may be most accurate to describe the movement as diverse and in transition. In regard to male-female issues as well as questions about the Rasta family, however, we must have an account of the origin of women's roles (particularly as mothers) in the Jamaican context. The historical, sociocultural, economic, and religious foundations of Jamaican Rastafari are central to an accurate analysis of gender change and contradiction.

Roots of Rastafari Gender Relations

The most important factors influencing Jamaican—and Rastafarian—male attitudes toward women are the legacies of slavery, colonialism, and the continuing structures of neocolonialism and cultural imperialism; biblical narratives and stipulations relating to female "nature"; and traditional Jamaican folk beliefs about the dangers inherent in female biology and the necessity of male control over women. As Empress Modupe pointed out, sexism in Rastafari is partly a product of the colonial experience. An early concern with race and the specificity of the Jamaican slave encounter affected the ability of the first Rasta men to see how forms of gender, race, and class oppression affect one another. They focused their resistance on issues of racial and economic inequality without recognizing the gendered character of these inequalities. Instead of creating new ideas about women's roles consistent with the emancipatory impulses of Rastafari ideology, the definition of women's place in the movement more closely resembles the model imposed by European capitalist patriarchy. As Terisa Turner noted,

> The Garveyist "male deal" derived from a colonial idealization of the family promoted during the abolition of slavery. . . . A product of rigorous socialization, the capitalist male deal is a tacit, assumed, "natural" agreement that all men will have a special type of power in relationship to women. In general, this takes the form of patriarch in a nuclear family in which men are heads of the household. (1994, 20, 29)

While the colonial experience created the conditions for the rise of Rastafari as a resistance movement, the effects of slavery, colonialism, and its white, male ideas about power and privilege also created conditions in which male power required the subordination of women. R. W. Connell adds:

> As the world capitalist order becomes more complete, as more local production systems are linked in to global markets and local labor brought into wage systems, local versions of Western patriarchal institutions are installed. . . . In a white supremacist context massive unemployment and urban poverty now powerfully interact with institutional racism in the shaping of black masculinity. (1995, 80, 199)

As Rastafari grew out of class resistance to colonial and neocolonial ideals and structures, it conflated the reclamation of black identity with male identity. The subordination of women helped compensate for male powerlessness. In Rastafari, it is also the central paradox of the movement:

the oppression of women remains fundamental to the functioning of the same system that Rastafari strives to subvert. Faye Harrison argues, "Sexual and gender inequality represents an essential and integral feature of social relations and cultural constructions in Jamaica, where for the past four hundred years colonial and imperialist exploitation has governed the development of economic, political, and socio-cultural patterns and structures" (1991, 98).

The Bible represents another source of women's subordination in traditional Rastafari. Male and female Rastas alike are typically avid Bible readers, using a unique scriptural interpretation that highlights themes of African and human liberation. However, a text as open to multiple readings as the Bible can also be used to circumscribe roles for women and cast on them negative images of female "nature." As Rasta author Maureen Rowe observed, "It was significant that the first female in the Bible was unfavorably mentioned. This was interpreted as a clear warning against the potential evil in the female" (1980, 13). Indeed, a narrow scriptural interpretation supports the notion that woman has from the beginning shown weakness in her moral and spiritual character. By necessity, then, she requires the guidance of a man to lead her into Rastafari and spiritual "upliftment" (enlightenment). The idea that a woman may become Rasta only through a Rastaman is one of the most common and recounted myths of the movement. Yet many sisters increasingly challenge such notions, arguing that the "living word of inspiration" available to all Rasta people creates a fundamental equality between men and women, that biblical interpretation must be tempered by individual inspiration and decision.

Sister Makeda, a Rasta of Eritrean and Nigerian heritage, mother of seven, and African dance instructor, explains why varied interpretations are the central issue:

> Rasta itself don't have too many laws—the laws are based on the Bible, that's God's laws and we're just following them. I don't too much respect people who make up their own laws and try to live by them, because you must live the Ten Commandments before you live any of that other stuff. We all know those are God's commandments, but some Rastas do get off into certain things, half-true and half-incorrect. People have so many different interpretations of the Bible, they'll take a verse and preach it the way they want to.

The Bible is also the source of Rasta dress codes for women and ideas about the menstrual cycle's being a dangerous time of uncleanliness and pollution. Deuteronomy 22:5 posits that women must wear only skirts and dresses; I Corinthians 11:5 states that women must cover their heads while worshiping; and Leviticus 15:19 charges that a woman is unclean for seven days during her menstrual cycle. In Jamaican Rastafari, this often translates into a taboo on any male contact, no matter how casual, with a menstruating woman, including forbidding women to cook food for men during their cycle. Moreover, Elisa Sobo (1993, 117) reports that in Jamaican society, "Few citizens are uninfluenced by the [Christian] church." While Rastafari has rejected Eurocentric Christianity and reconfigured many of its core symbols and values, it nonetheless originated in a society deeply influenced by the aggressive proselytizing of conservative mission churches.

The attribution of negative characteristics to women does not come from the Bible alone, however. Some Rasta practices and beliefs can also be traced to rural Jamaican folk traditions. Sobo points out that among rural Jamaicans, "traditionally, menstruating women do not cook and are considered 'unclean.' This is due to more than mere hygienic fears: menstrual blood provides the most potent means of 'compellance.'" Jamaican men, she claims, "have deep concerns about being poisoned and controlled because, according to cultural ideals, they hold money and others seek it. They are particularly concerned about being taken advantage of by women." Yet she notes that because Jamaican female expressions of power are curtailed, women must manipulate men and can "fix" many things by themselves. Women prepare the food men eat and men hold the coveted money, and so "men have reason to fear women's power" (1993, 228–229). Clearly, there are connections between rural Jamaican folk traditions and Rastafari. While many Rasta men may not possess the "coveted money" of Sobo's account, many do claim primary access to spirituality and also interpret women's power (usually biological) as dangerous to their own.

Traditional Rastafari ideas about women thus may be the result of historically contingent and culturally specific Jamaican developments. At one time, it may have been relevant to speak of male domination as being "built into the basic nature of Rastafari," yet Rasta discourse about gender has become rife with contradictions and tensions.

Changing Conceptions of Gender

Today, Rastafari women and men in New York City do not speak about gender with a single voice. Both Rasta women and men have begun to seriously address the question of gender both as members of distinct communities and as individuals. Common themes that appear in Rastafari discourse about gender include the role of individual agency, the impact of cultural background, the effect of living in New York City on the practicality of certain Rasta traditions, and the specifics of separate institutions regarding male and female roles.

The Ifetayo Cultural Arts Facility in East Flatbush, Brooklyn, is a center for Rasta and other artists, activists, and cultural specialists. There, one of its teachers, Sister Faybiene Miranda, eloquently promotes in poem and song a progressive consciousness about Rastafari women and global liberation. Performing her poem "I Am That I Am" (1987) for a room of silent and spellbound observers, Faybiene challenges stereotypes of modest, submissive Rastafari women with her calf-length dreadlocks swinging unwrapped behind her, brushing the back of her blue jeans:

> I am not your Venus de Milo
> Perfectly sculptured from marble to be
> carefully pedestal placed
> My name is not Eve, I offer you no temptation
> I am not your concubine by night
> Transformed to memory by day
> I am not the milk you thirst for
> Now dry in your mother's breast
> Nor could you call me queen
> For I have no dominion over beast, earth or man
> I am not a receptacle for the seed
> You indiscriminately cast in the wind
> I ask no sacrifice of lamb's blood
> for the stain would be mine
> Do not cast gold trinkets at my feet
> They do not shine for me
> I am no slave to a promise written in ink
> Where there is no master there are no chains
> to be broken
> Bondage is no glory
> I am woman
> Bone of your bones, flesh of your flesh
> When I lay sleeping in your rib
> You called me no name
> I AM THAT I AM. . . .

Faybiene also understands traditional Rasta beliefs and practices and how her own twenty-five years of experience in the movement has given her certain perspectives:

> We have to look at what truth is. Is there *a* truth? Is there a *common* truth? Or are there *versions* of the truth? I think intellectually I have seen all the doctrines and traditions about what a Rasta woman is supposed to be, how she's supposed to dress, who she's supposed to see, what she's suppose to think, whether or not she should use birth control, whether she should be married. All these things are part of the whole socialization of women's roles in society. It's not anything different than anything else women have gone through in any society!

Faybiene grounds her conception of Rastafari in a broader spiritual commitment to human liberation and racial and gender equality. Rastafari women, she rightly argues, are no more afflicted by patriarchy than are other working-class women of color throughout the world.

Faybiene's individual choices and growing up in North America have affected her experience as a Rastafari woman. Living in Jamaica during her early twenties also informed and deepened her commitment to Rastafari:

> For me, Rastafari was an empowerment from day one. . . . My first introduction to Rastafari was really amongst a lot of brothers in Jamaica. Let there be no misinterpretation of Rastafari—there were still the same kinds of rules about what you should do. But [with] all the men up to that point in my life, I felt just as strong and as powerful as them. I never really felt manipulated. I felt very much at home making decisions for myself.

Faybiene's approach also addresses more general issues relating to the discontinuity between ideal and real experience.

Sister Makeda explores the discrepancy between the ideal and the real in male-female relationships, observing that among Rastafari,

> as far as gender traditions, it all depends on the couple. I can only go by my relationship. My kingman doesn't ask me, "Are you menstruating?" Apparently, it's of no concern to him. And I know the Bible says it's unclean, but it all depends on the individual. . . . He's never said to me, "Makeda, are you unclean at this time?"

Cultural background and environment affect the way that one implements Rastafari traditions. Makeda admits, "The ideal is to follow tradition, but different Rastas might live like Jamaicans, some people might live like Trinidadians, some people might want to go straight back to the root of things in Africa, Egypt, Ethiopia." As an American Rasta of African parentage who has made repeated trips to Jamaica over the years, Makeda, too, shows an awareness of traditional Jamaican behavior. "Definitely in Jamaica, the Jamaican Rastas are very strict with their relationships. That's why I'm surprised at my kingman, because he's Jamaican." She notes that her kingman does not always respond in a consistently traditional way.

Indeed, some Rasta men's stated views or behavior challenges the notion that patriarchy or sexism is either an inherent feature of Rastafari or one practiced by all Rastas. Brother Andre, a Trinidadian Rasta and member of the Queens-based Twelve Tribes of Israel, points out:

> In everything, sometimes you have to bend. In the Catholic Church right now, they're bending rules, rules that are two hundred or three hundred years old. They're bending to accommodate the times. You have to somewhere along the line give in. You have brothers who want the separation between men and women, but the separation of man and woman is not really necessary.

For Makeda and Andre, gender roles necessarily reflect individual decisions and the impact of living in different environments. For Brother Andre, the presence of families is setting a new agenda, "With Rastafari, we need to be a family, because in the family unit comes strength."

Andre's views of menstruation also contradict the traditional taboos on female biology; like Makeda, he too believes that considering menstruation unclean is more a personal than a spiritual matter In fact, he says that the woman's cycle could be seen as a sign of power: "The woman has a seven-day cycle. That's seven days of power! It's a rejuvenation for women at that time . . . but whether you interpret it as powerful or polluting depends on the individual."

Many Rasta men remain traditional while acknowledging a role for personal choice and the realities of different times and environments. Jah Lloyd, a longtime Chinese-Jamaican Rasta, recent immigrant, and member of the Nyabinghi Order, believes that Rastafari must maintain the "ancient" practices. He insists that women and men are inherently different due to biological differences but still allows that they have equally important roles to play in the movement. He sees Western feminism as associated with neocolonialism:

With women's liberation me look 'pon it like how Babylon deal with women's liberation is not how I-n-I see the liberation of women. How Babylon sees it, woman is 'pon an equal footing with man, that means if a woman want to play the same role as a man, she can. And that no really work out because Jah no set it out to work so.

Yet he still allows a type of equality between genders: "But equality is not really the issue. Both man and women have equal worth in the sight of Jah, but at the same time a man is a man and a woman is a woman. There's equality but there's also a difference."

Jah Lloyd also supports the biblical guidelines for women's "modest" attire (for example, long skirts or dresses, and head wraps), an aspect of Rastafari often labeled sexist by outsiders. Yet his reasoning shows that he supports such codes not so that he can control a woman but so that she can be seen as a human being and not as a sexual object:

In the Nyabinghi house, everyone know we're supposed to attire a certain way. A woman should dress modestly and not wear dem cut-away t'ings, exposive garments that cause a certain t'ing to come into a man's mind. Cause that mek a man see other t'ings than the person. But if a man see you dress in a cultureway and carry yourself in culture, he automatically give you respect.

Although one might see the dress code as a curtailment of a woman's freedom, Jah Lloyd's position emphasizes that it is a matter of respect, a value deeply embedded in Rasta consciousness.

Four years after arriving in the United States, Jah Lloyd also sees how certain Rasta traditions cannot be carried over into life in New York City. Speaking about the taboo on menstruation, he appeals to changing times,

It's an ancient tradition and I-man don't really oppose it. Me support it, but it is not like the olden days. You still have to deal with a women, regardless if she 'pon her cycle. T'ings are not like in the days when those t'ings were laid down. T'ings change.

Jah Lloyd also recognizes that North American urban life demands a different approach than that in Jamaica does.

In a situation now where it's only Rasta that deal with and support this certain principle we find ourself caught up with people who don't deal with that at all and we still have to move amongst dem. Maybe we can only keep it in the home or whatever. Everyone dat play the part judge it by dem own self.

As Jah Lloyd makes new choices concerning gender issues, his understanding is guided by the Nyabinghi house, as it cautiously preserves tradition and its influence while addressing the needs of the newly transplanted and rapidly growing Rasta communities of North America.[5]

Despite the diversity in Rasta discourse about gender, a patriarchal current still threatens women's struggle for self-determination and freedom. Bongo Iyah, a Jamaican Rasta and former priest-in-training at one of the Rastafari churches, is frank about his views.

> Mon cyaan't have too much contact with woman, because woman's nature weakens mon's connection to Jah. I-mon never look a woman in the eye, because she may want to have relations, and relations are strictly for procreation, not recreation. Sex does not please Jah if it is not for procreation, and it drain I-mon's spiritual energy. I-mon don't have sex unless for procreation, seen?

Bongo Iyah admits, however, that this attitude has met resistance. Recalling a relationship with a young female college student, he says,

> I-mon want the dawta to give me child, but she say she want to go an' finish her education. I-mon don't see that her education could be more important than having pickney. So one day when she was giving a little I-mon go and take a lot, and now she don't want to see me no more.

Bongo Iyah has made trouble with other Rastas as well. His former church preaches a strong message of monogamy, intra-Rasta couples, and the central role of women in the church and family. Bongo Iyah had a falling-out with the church when he was told that he could involve only one of his "wives" and her children in church activities. Apparently, Bongo Iyah's understanding of gender relations in the movement also entails polygamy—a practice that is widely debated in those currents of Rastafari in which it has not yet been completely abandoned.

Rastafari in New York City does not consist of a single set of beliefs and practices inherited from Jamaica from the 1930s but, rather, a chorus of voices. Rasta's highly variable views of gender establishes a sense of unpredictability among and between brothers and sisters as they renegotiate their roles. This tension and negotiation heighten as many sisters move toward a prowoman consciousness, or what we are calling here "Rasta womanism." Following Alice Walker (1983), we use the term *womanism* in place of *feminism* to refer to those sentiments shared by women who continue to struggle for their equal rights as women, though not at the expense of their relationships with men or the fulfillment they derive from motherhood.

Because Rastafari remains a movement of resistance against forces of oppression and inequality worldwide, its foundation has long been ripe for "feminist ferment" (Turner 1994, 10). Both Rasta men and women, however, dislike the term *feminism*, because for them it evokes privileged white women's concerns and often locates women's oppression in motherhood and child rearing. Even the term *sexism* causes communication problems between Rasta men and women, as Empress Modupe explained: "Most Rastas don't see themselves as being sexist. The term 'sexism' is, to them, a European term. Most Rasta brethren that I speak with, including my own kingman, will tell me, 'I don't really see that I am subjugating you. This is your rightful place!'"

As black feminist scholar Patricia Hill Collins pointed out, however, resistance is not as much about theory as it is about "the interdependence of thought and action" and everyday acts of defiance (Collins 1991, 28). Furthermore, bell hooks argues that feminism is neither an identity nor a role but, rather, a consciousness that one develops and advocates (hooks 1984, 26). For Rastafari women, resistance, self-determination, and the struggle for freedom, justice, and equality are key components of Rastafari consciousness and practice. Just as Rastafari in general has reconfigured meanings drawn from previously oppressive traditions like those of mission Christianity into new reservoirs of empowerment, so too have Rastafari women reconfigured the meaning of practices that many Western feminists have disparaged as oppressive. In true Rasta fashion, sisters have remade these in the image of their own human and female worth.

Rastafari women accord enormous value to motherhood and the raising of new generations of Rastafari men and women, female-centered networks, and the growing incidence of leadership space for women in formal Rastafari institutions. Whereas the notion of the Rasta woman as valuable only as a "vessel" for the Rasta man's seed was once seen as the primary indicator of women's second-class status in the movement, women have transformed their role as mothers into responsibility for the growth and reproduction of Rastafari itself. Rasta men have come to understand that the only way to ensure that their children will be raised as Rastafari is to have them with a Rasta woman. Rasta women, too, have realized that they can teach their children that women are not secondary actors in the movement. As Empress Modupe asserted:

> I don't really have any hope for this generation of Rastaman. I see it in the future, in the youth-dem coming up right now. My daughters and sons will

make a difference because they've seen the struggles of their mothers and fathers, and they're more advantaged than we were when we came into Rasta. My hope is in the youth, not in trying to change the brethren.

Rasta women also find support in female-centered networks, formal and informal institutions encompassing an array of activities ranging from cooperative economic ventures to educational classes. While tension still exists between sisters who view their roles in the movement differently, more Rastafari women are reaching out to one another. Sister Faybiene works to bridge the divisions among women to overcome their devalued status:

> I see myself as a Rastafari women in the broadest context. And I see so much pain and so much hurt and so much misunderstanding dividing women trodding along this course, that I wanted to have a forum, some kind of gathering of a lot of sisters to begin to address what it is that has prevented us from recognizing ourselves as positive.

Gatherings such as Faybiene's, emblematic of the many newly emerging and informal networks of Rasta sisters throughout New York, allow women the opportunity to meet in one another's homes, organize their own reasonings, and articulate a prowoman Rasta consciousness. Makeda, too, emphasizes the importance of solidarity among women. Her family itself is a veritable network of women—she and her six daughters perform African dances in schools and shopping malls and run a doll-making and jewelry business out of their home. On the topic of gender separation, she confesses, "I don't have a problem with men and women being separate for *some* things. It can be a good thing because you get to chat with the sistren."

Women's networks can also be found in formal Rasta organizations and churches, where Rasta women have emerged as individuals and leaders with specific concerns. In the Brooklyn-based Church of Haile Selassie I, for example, the Daughters of Zion women's group meets on Saturdays to discuss women's issues and family concerns and to plan events for the entire congregation. This is an active and growing church that aspires to lead the larger Rastafari movement, which it views as hopelessly mired in factionalism and an outworn traditionalism. In an August 1994 official church newsletter addressed to the broader Rastafari movement, Sister Sonya, a Jamaican immigrant and mother of five, wrote:

> Rastawoman, the time is now to stop calling yourself a Rastawoman. That name represents a colonial name given to the woman of a Rastaman. We

the Daughters of Zion realize this name represents a domiciled conception which only undermines the socio-religious development of the daughters and subjects them to medieval practice. . . . Today we the Daughters of Zion need to take an active part in the development of the Rastafarian community. We should follow the footsteps of our woman ancestors like the Queen of Sheba, and Empress Menen of Ethiopia, and Sarah. . . . Our children need an example to follow. Let us be that example for them and the future generation of daughters to come. (CHSI Daughters of Zion Document 1994)

In this church, several women hold positions of leadership, even in the political wing, the Imperial Ethiopian World Federation (IEWF), whose local president in the mid-1990s was Sister Bernadette, a forceful and artic-ulate Guyanese immigrant and mother of six. So central has the institu-tional structure and "temple worship" of the CHSI and IEWF become to her faith and *livity* that she cannot conceive of any other Rasta group providing leadership for the increasing number of Rasta sisters. She exclaims:

> You can tell the true Israel from temple worship. Wherever Israel is gath-ered, Israelites are in the temple at worship, which is no ganja smoking and drumming kind of thing. True temple worship requires order and author-ity. Only the priest can officiate. Temple worship is a must if I-n-I are to carry this movement into the twenty-first century. And no Nyabinghi, Twelve Tribes, Federation [EWF], or Orthodox [EOC] can do that. Only the Church of Haile Selassie I and the Imperial Ethiopian World Federa-tion can lead Rasta in this crucial time!

Sister Bernadette's testimony reveals a sectarian propensity among some of the most active members of organizations competing for the leadership of the larger movement. Frequently, it results in an inability to form alliances with other Rasta groups and a propensity to assume that one's own group represents the "true Rastafari." Despite this, there can be little doubt that the sisters of the CHSI and IEWF have created their own institutions that allow them to exercise considerable influence over its largely male and conservative leadership.

Conclusion

The globalization of the Rastafari movement has created a diverse con-stituency out of which have come debates about gender identity and community organization. Among Rastas living in New York City, there is a growing need for community-building organizations and institutions that address the concerns of Rasta women and families. No longer can the reggae dance hall and "smoking yard" provide the principal forms of interaction in a movement attempting to socialize a vast and growing second generation. And no longer can the patriarchal norms of traditional Jamaican Rastafari accommodate a multiethnic, transnational movement.

To meet these challenges, Rastafarian women and men have elaborated new strategies, created new networks, and revitalized old institutions. The congregational thrust of many new Rasta organizations in New York City provides a more routinized, local, face-to-face form of association that represents an innovative renegotiation of the movement's institutionally anarchic past. In addition to standardized forms of worship, these congregations provide an array of services, including Sunday school classes, biblical reasonings, band and choir rehearsals, "Rastological counseling," day-care centers, political education, Ital cooking workshops, and African history and language instruction. Such institutions create new contexts for community involvement and leadership.

The emergence of Rasta womanist voices and activism is central to the community-building character and institutionalization of contemporary North American Rastafari. It is doubtful that groups like the CHSI and Ifetayo could provide the kinds of services and activities they do without the enthusiastic participation of the sisters. To ensure that participation, Rasta mansions have had to rethink and modify traditional attitudes and practices, as well as create new spaces for female participation and leadership.

Rastafari views on gender still remain complex, diverse, and highly contested. Simultaneously shaping and shaped by the growing institutionalization of the movement as well as its transnational spread, Rastafarians no longer (if they ever did) speak with a single voice on gender roles and issues. While one does not have to look hard to find remnants of outdated androcentric and even misogynist currents in Rastafari, the activism of Rasta sisters now and in the future will ensure that such currents become a fading note in the chorus of new voices punctuating the movement of Jah people. International reggae star and Twelve Tribes member Sister Carol echoes the voices of so many Rasta sisters in her anthem "Shackles":

> Take these shackles away, Lord
> A long time I want to be free

From out of Babylon slavery, hunger, and thirst,
Hate and misery
Why do the heathen dem rage and fight against
a woman like me
Who must struggle so hard just to keep on mine
my four pickney....
I just want to live and be an independent woman
Because Jah is my light and my salvation
Selassie-I know I no fear no one....

NOTES

1. This chapter is based on research on Rastafari in Jamaica and New York City (see Hepner 1998c; Redeker 1996). Randal Hepner would like to thank the New Ethnic and Immigrant Congregations Project (NEICP) and Research Institute for the Study of Man (RISM) for research grants that enabled his fieldwork in both Jamaica and New York City.

2. For a variety of reasons, Rastafarians are typically reluctant to participate in census surveys. After thirty years of intense scrutiny by researchers, therefore, we still have no accurate numerical account of the movement in Jamaica, let alone that in New York City. In the mid-1980s, the New York Police Department estimated that there were approximately ten thousand Rastas living in New York City in the late 1970s. But it did not indicate how it arrived at this figure. More recently, the 1989/1990 City University of New York–sponsored National Survey of Religious Identification (NSRI) estimated a national population of fourteen thousand Rastas (see Kosmin and Lachman 1991). The NSRI's projections, however, are woefully low, for even a conservative estimate of New York City's population alone would exceed the NSRI's entire national projection.

3. The Rastafarian practice of referring to their larger churches, political associations, and community organizations as "mansions" and "houses" is proof-texted in John 14:2: "In my Father's house are many mansions." Smaller and less formal associations are referred to as "camps" and "yards." It should be noted that few, if any, Rastafarian churches resemble anything like a real mansion.

4. For a discussion of the role of the Nyabinghi Order as one of the oldest and most traditional of the Rastafari mansions, see Homiak 1985.

5. The rules for Nyabinghi women are laid down in the widely reproduced and distributed "Ancient Order of the Nyabinghi Guidelines" (1993), which functions as a creed and guide to Nyabinghi practice. Produced by the Nyabinghi Order Council of Elders, the guidelines are not for sale but can be obtained at local Nyabinghi houses or by writing to Order of the Nyabinghi, PO Box 21, Granville PO, Montego Bay, St. James, Jamaica.

Part VII

Politics in the Kingdom

Chapter 24

Voices of the Black Religious Community of Brooklyn, New York

Clarence Taylor

Some historians have argued that cold-war hysteria and political repression marginalized black left radicals like Paul Robeson and W. E. B. Du Bois (Marable 1983, 204–206; 1991, 27–28), thereby removing a serious progressive force that might have moved black America to a left-of-center politics. Consequently, a narrow black nationalism rose to fill the void (Horne 1993, 442–443). Radical leadership was diverted into essentialist views of race like that espoused by the Nation of Islam. The black radical voice then was misshaped into an upside-down version of white supremacy and obscured the cross-racial impact of class inequalities. McCarthyism reinforced the trend by making it un-American to criticize business decisions or class inequalities in the United States (Sugrue 1996, 7).

For the most part, Afro-Christianity has not been a focus of scholars searching for alternative left voices. But a closer look at Brooklyn, New York, strongly suggests that political ideological debate was not absent in the black church community, for it took at least three ideological positions. Afro-Christian liberalism, closely associated with New Deal liberalism, was one of the most popular ideological positions among the black clergy of Brooklyn, embraced by pastors of some of the largest churches. A small but significant contingent of black Christian radicals made up another ideological group, and the third group consisted of black Pentecostals. Until recently, scholars for the most part ignored black Pentecostalism's political inclinations during the cold war. The ministers, joined by their parishioners, were quite visible, however, in the political ideological debate.

Afro-Christian Liberalism

Afro-Christian liberals were the most prominent ideological group among Brooklyn's black clergy. Crossing denominational lines and attracting some of the most celebrated ministers in the country, this group included the Reverends Gardner C. Taylor of Concord Baptist Church, Sandy F. Ray of Cornerstone Baptist Church, John Coleman of Saint Philip's Protestant Episcopal Church, William Orlando Carrington of the First African Methodist Episcopal Zion Church, and George Thomas of Brown Memorial Baptist Church.

In order to legitimize their positions to whites as well as to blacks, this group of pastors closely allied themselves to the white power structure. That is, to the black community, the pastors delivered the goodies, and to the white leaders, they delivered black votes. The *Amsterdam News*, one of the country's largest black weeklies, called Gardner Taylor the "unofficial Democratic chieftain in Bedford-Stuyvesant." Taylor's political allies included such notables as Brooklyn borough president John Cashmere and the mayor of New York, Robert Wagner (Taylor 1994, 18).

While Taylor was arguable the most politically influential black pastor of Brooklyn, other ministers also had political connections. In 1941, the mayor of New York appointed the Reverend John Coleman to the New York Board of Higher Education. In 1949, the Reverend Boise Dentm, pastor of Tabernacle Baptist Church in Brownsville, Brooklyn, was selected to head the Republican campaign for Brooklyn's borough president. The Reverend Benjamin Lowery of Zion Baptist Church headed a ministers' and citizens' committee to reelect New York's Republican governor, Thomas Dewey, and the Reverend George Thomas of Brown Memorial Baptist Church was selected by the Republican Party to run for Congress. In fact, the Reverend Sandy Ray of Cornerstone Baptist Church was so closely allied with the Republican Party that he was referred to as "Mr. Republican." Serving in the Ohio state legislature before coming to Brooklyn, Ray campaigned for Republican candidates and even developed a close friendship with Nelson Rockefeller, governor of New York from 1958 to 1974 (Taylor 1994, 116–118).

These prominent black pastors with close ties to the politically powerful were not just seeking political accommodation. They also saw themselves as ambassadors of their race. Using their influence to improve the black community, they argued that their closeness to officials and politicians was for the purpose of winning concessions for the community. As power brokers, these men did not call for an alliance with the black working class but, rather, attempted to win favor with the Democratic and Republican Parties, which decided the distribution of state resources and services.

The tactic of ambassadorship for the race was neither new nor limited to the black ministerial class of Brooklyn (Gaines 1996; Gilmore 1993). Indeed, the black elite in various black communities at the turn of the century adopted the same approach. Although the New Deal had helped give a political voice to African Americans, the New Deal actually institutionalized this tactic.

Although most Afro-Christian liberals in Brooklyn were affiliated with the Republican Party, they nevertheless embraced New Deal liberalism because it helped the poor and fit their belief in a New Deal–type state. Their affiliation with Republicans on both the local and state levels, however, never deterred their faith that the role of government was to assist the disadvantaged, many of whom were members of the churches they led. Consequently, Afro-Christian liberals supported the New Deal expansion of the state as a means of relieving poverty.

So, despite their mostly Republican affiliation, the Afro-Christian liberals were advocates of the social gospel that the church should serve social needs like poverty, racism, and hunger. Sandy Ray remembers that his upbringing influenced his views. His parents' brand of moderate to liberal Republicanism was mixed with NAACP meetings. They identified with the Republicans not because they respected the memory of Lincoln but because they believed that the party was allowing them access in order to win concessions for the black community. In return, the Republican politicians saw votes in a Democratic city, so they selected blacks for assembly seats in 1936, long before the Democrats did.

Because black ministers could influence voting, both Republican and Democratic politicians sought them out. In fact, it was not unusual to see prominent Republicans on a Sunday morning at Cornerstone Baptist or other black churches in Brooklyn, whose pastors headed churches with thousands of members.

While Afro-Christian liberals viewed the New Deal state as the best avenue to address black grievances, they did not rely only on government to help the poor. They also were concerned with reconstructing a new civic culture for the black community that stressed moral and social uplift. Since the formation of African American communities, black elites have insisted that blacks adopt Victorian virtues like good moral character and a strong work ethic in order to be successful citizens. By the cold war, the black middle class and clergy were still attempting to shape the poor into "respectable human beings." Hence, the home and family remained an important focus.

In this regard, a popular family event was scouting. By the 1940s, dozens of Brooklyn's black churches had established scouting programs. Furthermore, scouting was not just a children's affair but reinforced family bonds. Parents provided adult role models as scoutmasters, den mothers, advisers, and other leaders. Their activities emphasized the importance of the family and responsible citizenship, and the brochures of their churches emphasized "family nights" and the importance of the nuclear family. This type of voluntarism addressed plaguing problems like juvenile delinquency (Taylor 1994, 133–135). During the post–World War II period, one of the big issues in Brooklyn churches was finding an alternative to street life for their children. Through scouting, the churches created a formula of good wholesome fun, making children productive while encouraging the continuous involvement of their parents.

Because Afro-Christian liberals adopted an ambassadorship type of politics and an advocacy of a civic culture, they distrusted militant protest and radical politics. Instead, they wanted to rely on civic organizations and their leaders to bring about change on a one-on-one basis. Some Brooklyn liberals joined other black clergy to support cold-war liberalism. In the summer of 1953, eight AME ministers issued a statement proclaiming their cause and denouncing Senator Joseph McCarthy's assertion that Protestants were the largest body supporting American Communist fronts. The AME ministers stated, "Such political onslaught is the same process used by the leaders of Communism to rid the nation of God and to destroy the faith of the humble believers." True friends of democracy were those fighting for equality. The eight declared that McCarthy's statement was a vile attack on "religion and the faith upon which this nation is founded" (Taylor 1994, 133–135).

Sandy Ray adopted the approach of identifying their cause with God, country, and other Brooklyn black ministers. At a National Baptist Convention, Ray claimed that "we have not, and shall not commit our convention to any foreign or subversive ideology. The justification for our fight is within the framework of our constitution and our accepted Christian principles." Ray also defended Protestant ministers against McCarthy's attack by denying any links between the clergy and Communism. "Neither the Negro Protestant clergy nor laymen have given any support to Communism" (*Amsterdam News*, August 22, 1953).

Afro-Christian liberals' distrust of the left was apparent in their refusal to support militant grassroots action. Some black militant pastors complained that prominent fellow clergy refused to join them in working with the grass roots (Maines 1987, 53; Taylor 1994, 1997). The Reverend Milton Galamison, a radical black Presbyterian minister, accused the liberals of red-baiting and avoiding the Bedford-Stuyvesant Health Council's struggle for a hospital in Bedford-Stuyvesant because they believed that it was Communist controlled. When he was president of the Brooklyn branch of the NAACP, Galamison also complained that some prominent black clergy were red-baiting the more militant members of the civil rights group (Taylor 1997, 37, 68–72).

Although in July 1963, many prominent black pastors did help protestors at the Downstate Medical Center construction site against the lack of blacks and Puerto Ricans hired as construction workers, they relied more on their political contacts than on the ordinary people taking part in the demonstrations. Years later, Taylor bragged how important his close association with Mayor Wagner was, noting that he had city hall remove a police captain who had mistreated him. During the two-week protest against the building trade union and the State of New York that were building the medical center, Sandy Ray, Gardner Taylor, Benjamin Lowery, and other well-known ministers contacted Governor Rockefeller to work out an agreement to end the demonstrations. The militant Brooklyn chapter of the Congress of Racial Equality, which had initiated the protest, was not invited. The ministers and the governor reached an agreement that included promises from the state to enforce already existing antidiscrimination laws and to set up hiring halls in black and Puerto Rican areas (Taylor 1994, 139–163; interview with Gardner C. Taylor, October 1, 1988).[1]

Black Christian Radicals

Left of the Afro-Christian liberals were the black Christian radicals. Although consisting of just a few pastors, this group, united by their common beliefs, was extremely vocal and gained citywide notoriety. Unlike the Afro-Christian liberals' penchant for negotiation, the black Christian radicals identified with grassroots and militant action. Rather than individual transformation, they believed that in order to enact structural changes, they needed organizations from outside the traditional structures. Because these pastors did not believe that the state would address class concerns on its own, they maintained that the people and powerful institutions who allocated resources and services had to be coerced to help the working class. The black Christian radicals were not afraid to associate publicly with leftist forces. Like Afro-Christian liberals, they called for an intrusive role for government in eradicating poverty. However, while Afro-Christian liberals viewed the New Deal state as ideal, black Christian radicals called for even greater economic and structural changes. Their vision was a state that went far beyond just assisting the poor. A few ministers radically criticized capitalism and called for a redistribution of the wealth.

George Frazier Miller of the St. Augustine Protestant Episcopal Church was a member of the Socialist Party and had been active in the women's suffrage movement. Viewing opponents of suffrage and equality for women as "he-men," Frazier's involvement in the suffrage movement led to his socialism. But because he was unwilling to associate with the mainstream political parties, Miller ran for Congress as a Socialist Party candidate. Miller's activities included editing A. Phillip's socialist journal *The Messenger*. Miller opposed war and refused to fly the American flag outside St. Augustine during World War I. He blamed the Great Depression on capitalist greed, warning that a great upheaval would erupt if the wealth were not distributed more fairly. "Revolution is in the air" and "if the masters of industry are not wise enough to share profits with the workers, they may themselves be responsible for the impending dangers, and they might as well expect any kind of outbreak." Miller died in 1943, never renouncing the left or socialism (*Amsterdam News*, December 2, 1931, February 29, 1936; *New York Age*, December 2, 1943; Taylor 1994, 122–123).

Theophilus Alcantara of St. Simon African Orthodox Church also participated in leftist politics. A founding member of the left-wing American Labor Party, he ran as its candidate for the New York State Assembly in the 1930s and 1940s. He also became very critical of the black clergy who surprised him by undermining his candidacy in favor of his status quo opponent. Lashing out at their groveling, he said that black ministers of Brooklyn were into patronage up to the tops of their heads. He never forgot their opposition, although he later renounced the American Labor Party. Alcantara kept his militant leanings and joined the campaign to free members of the American Communist Party jailed under the Smith Act. He also became a central figure in the fight for better housing for the poor and worked with various grassroots organizations (*Amsterdam News*, April 29, 1944; Taylor 1994, 125–127).

The Reverend Thomas Harten of Holy Trinity Baptist Church was unique among Brooklyn's Baptist ministers in his support for leftist street protests. On several occasions, Harten participated in militant street protests against police brutality, and in 1925, he became head of the local chapter of the National Equal Rights League, organized by William Monroe Trotter. He also became head of a group called the Afro-Protective League, which protested police brutality and lynching.

Harten was able to draw thousands of people to his church to protest injustice. Sunday attendance ranged between 500 and 2,100, depending on what Harten was involved in. He denounced President Franklin D. Roosevelt as not having the best interest of blacks at heart. He was an early supporter of the Scottsboro Nine, who were accused of rape by two prostitutes (who later recanted their stories), and called for an alliance with the American Communist Party. Although in the 1930s, Harten curtailed his militant activity to concentrate on church matters, he remained critical of the Democratic and Republican Parties and called for an independent black candidate for the New York Assembly. "We must endorse our own man. That will prevent the political leaders from endorsing one of us who would be a Negro handkerchief head Uncle Tom political pigeon." Like Alcantara, Harten also supported the struggle to free jailed communists in the 1950s (Taylor 1994, 123–124).

Unlike some of the radicals whose activities had waned by the late 1940s, Milton Galamison's career as a militant activist pastor was just beginning during the cold war. Born in 1923, he was twenty-five when he became pastor of Siloam Presbyterian Church in 1948. By the 1950s, judged by his activities, associations and sermons, Galamison had become the most radical black minister in Brooklyn. In his sermons, he blamed imperialism, class exploitation, and racism for the underdevelopment of blacks. Capitalism had failed to end hunger. For Galamison, the drumbeat of militarism was governed by the clinking coins of greed.

Galamison felt politically connected to radicals and defended communists and other leftists against red-baiting. In one sermon, he argued that Marxism stressed human dignity and that socialism and "Russian Communism" were attempts at winning respect for humanity. Soon after the Cuban revolution, Galamison became the only New York City black pastor to visit the island, praising the revolution after he returned (Taylor 1994, 128, 1997, 26–37).

Galamison worked more than any other Brooklyn pastor with the leftist forces. In the 1950s, he became allies with Annie Stein, a member of the Communist Party, and other militants active in the Brooklyn NAACP. Annie Stein herself was born in Brooklyn of Russian socialist parents. In high school, she became a Communist, which led her to City University of New York, where she met her husband, Arthur. In 1933, after joining the New Deal stream into Washington, D.C., they became labor organizers for the CIO. During this time, Stein met Galamison, whom she later joined in Brooklyn when she and her husband became targets of anti-Communist criticism. While her husband organized the local Progressive Party, Annie threw herself into the civil rights struggles in which Galamison was involved. In one famous incident, they joined in a struggle to desegregate Brooklyn's restaurants.

Before she left Washington, Stein was instructed by the Communist head of the local civil rights movement to join the Brooklyn PTA, at the time a very important force for school integration in Brooklyn. So Stein joined and helped the PTA and the NAACP integrate PS 258, a school right across the street from Galamison. After she was red-baited in the NAACP, she asked for Galamison's support. The movement was advantageous for Galamison because he was just beginning to develop his militancy. He told Stein that he would support her (Taylor 1997, 55–65).

Complaining that the NAACP was too moderate in the fight for desegregation, in 1960 Galamison organized the Parents Workshop for Equality in New York, an independent grassroots organization for school integration. It became the most militant advocate of school integration. In February 1964, the Parents Workshop helped organize a citywide boycott for integration. In one of the nation's biggest such events, more than 460,000 students stayed home to coerce the board to produce a plan and timetable for integration. With the support of almost all the liberal and militant black pastors, freedom schools were set up in many churches to aid the boycott. Although the movement failed, the struggle prepared Galamison for a fight over community control of schools a few years later (Taylor 1997, 91–104, 121–145).

Black Christian radicals argued that the Bible dealt with social justice, combining the premodern text with modern ideology to address class exploitation, racism, and other social evils. In particular, George Frazier Miller and Milton Galamison blended Western Enlightenment doctrines with the Bible. Declaring, "I look upon the whole teaching of Christ as Socialist," Miller explained that "Christ was fundamentally a revolutionist, revolutionizing society from one in which the powerful suppressed the poor for their own enrichment to one where all could live abundantly." "The savior," the Socialist pastor claimed, "was not only interested in moral righteousness but also in social and economic righteousness."

Galamison also praised Marxism and the Russian and Cuban revolutions, although he was not an advocate of a workers' state. Instead, he argued for a harmonious community based on Christian principles. Connecting social activism to religion, he contended that Christ was a revolutionary and that it was the duty of true Christians to address the social sins of society using the Bible as a blueprint.

It was natural for Miller and Galamison to turn to ideas of the modern period. Both had been exposed to modern Western thought while in prominent universities. Miller received his bachelor's degree from Howard University and studied philosophy at New York University. Galamison received his bachelor's degree from Lincoln University where he studied Kant, Marx, and Bertrand Russell. Both also belonged to predominantly white denominations that favored rationality and opposed reaching God through experience (*Amsterdam* News, February 29, 1936; Taylor 1997, 35–38).

Black nationalism shaped others outside the black Christian radical group, like Pastor Alcantara. Because of his experience with British colonialism in his native Guyana, Alcantara found the African Orthodox Church (AOC) attractive. Founded by George Alexander McGuire, a follower of Marcus Garvey, the African Orthodox Church rejected the whiteness in Christianity and reenvisioned God in a black image. However, Alcantara, like the other followers of the AOC, also embraced the Anglican worldview in addition to a black nationalist approach. Unlike an African sacred cosmos in which one reaches God through experience, the AOC's followers reach God through the Enlightenment principles of reason and the written word. Hence, Alcantara came out of a Western as well as a black nationalist tradition (Gilroy 1993; Taylor 1994, 125–126).

We know little about Thomas Harten's early life and education, although his sermons note that he relied on an Afro-American tradition of folk religion. His sermons were described as ecstatic. The black press reported that the pastor's delivery was so emotional that on Sunday, one would see both men and women fainting at Holy Trinity. What is certain is that Harten came out of an African American religious tradition that had at its core a sense of social justice. Labeling this sense of social justice the Afro-American jeremiad, David Howard-Pitney says its rhetoric offers a religious critique of America's racial practices while optimistically declaring its potential for radical social change and leaving racial hatred behind (Howard-Pitney 1990, 5–56).

Black Pentecostals

While Afro-Christian liberals put their faith in the liberal state and a mixed economy, and black Christian radicals advocated an alternative society in which all forms of social justice would be eradicated, black Pentecostals relied on premodern notions to analyze present conditions and propose solutions to end black oppression. They put their faith in a fundamentalist political vision, relying on an "unadulterated, pure Christianity."

Unlike the radicals who modernized biblical narratives, the Pentecostals stressed a strict interpretation of the Bible. They did not extend the boundaries of Christian doctrine to modernity or even Enlightenment ideals. Rather, their ideal society predated modernity and was based on biblical social relations. Their assertion that "you are in the world and not of the world" meant that believers had to be only concerned with spiritual well-being.

For Pentecostals, the Bible's narratives are paradigmatic acts that one relives. By reenacting them, the narratives are brought to life in the current age, thereby creating social harmony. Directed by the Spirit, they receive "gifts" from God to demonstrate his power. These include the gifts of "speaking in tongues," "interpreting tongues," and "healing the sick." Spelled out in the Bible is the correct behavior for Christians and their relationship with God. Because he is in constant communion with God, all of a believer's time should be sacred time, which he should spend as much as possible among other believers, even attending church four or more times a week for services lasting well into the night.

Early scholars of black Pentecostalism argue that the notion of "otherworldliness," a key doctrine of this religious group, is apolitical. For example, Gary Marx contends that Pentecostals are one of the least politically active religious groups in America. However, more recently, Hans Baer, Merrell Singer (Taylor 1994, 53–65), C. Eric Lincoln, and Lawrence Mamiya have noted that many black Pentecostal ministers have been active in mainstream politics. Indeed, in Brooklyn in the last half of the twentieth century, black Pentecostal leaders and parishioners contributed an important political voice.

Dozens of black Pentecostal churches were created in Brooklyn in the

1940s and 1950s by the black working class. Members of these congregations offered a political critique of a society that set up barriers to exclude black people. They were neither right nor left on the political scale but created a space that redefined the political dialogue and allowed for alternative action to conventional politics. The Pentecostals believed that they were enacting the Kingdom of God that challenges the distasteful powers that be. They made a "political space" for an alternative Kingdom politics and offered a critical political analysis based on how they saw the world. Consequently, they argued that "man-made" doctrines could not offer a social solution to the plight of people during the cold war.

For example, U. L. Corbett, a founder of the Church of God in Christ on the Hill, the second-oldest church in Brooklyn,[2] argued that both communism and the "American system" were evil. One had to "walk and talk on the name of the Lord" in order to find peace.

Samuel Gibson, who joined the Deliverance Evangelistic Center in the 1950s, also noted that the "pleasures of the world" were rejected by the "saints." Following his friend Orturo Skinner (1924–1975), the center's dynamic founder, Gibson maintained that God would take care of the problems that the politicians were trying to fix, that people should instead find their way through this evil world with the true doctrine of the Word of God.

Maritcha Harvey, a member of the Bedford-Stuyvesant Beulah Church of our Lord Jesus Christ of the Apostolic Faith, argued that in the 1940s and 1950s, the members of her church were faithful only to holiness and no other system. Harvey, who is a daughter of founder Peter Bridges, hates the conventional way that politics is carried out. Thoroughly familiar with both politics and politicians, she has concluded that politics is "of the world," a designation of doom.

Followers of Pentecostalism did not ignore the cold-war debate but created a unique rhetoric for it. They argued that only a strict interpretation of the Bible would liberate people from eventual doom and destruction, actually a far cry from being apolitical. For them, "walking and talking in the name of the Lord" was the only sure political solution to transform the world. So their remedy was an attempt to redefine politics by offering another alternative vision, a "politics of the Kingdom." Instead of focusing on the material, they contended that one could find peace, joy, and harmony only by focusing on the spiritual.

They used the common phrase "in the world but not of the world" for the society that denied blacks access to material wealth. Their strategy was to attack the criteria used to measure success and to offer an alternative

model attainable by poor people saving their souls for the everlasting Kingdom. Accusations that Pentecostals were apolitical was a functionalist approach that judges them by an outsider's interpretation, not by their own
words (Taylor 1994, 53–65).

Today's Political Boundaries in Brooklyn Churches

An important legacy of Brooklyn's black religious community in the early
and middle twentieth century is the creation of a politics of activism and
opposition to the status quo. This community's black religious leaders
created models for leading the next generation of black clergy. The Reverends Herbert Daughtry and Al Sharpton are two of the best examples.

Like their earlier counterparts, both leaders have dedicated their lives
to challenging conditions that keep black people from sharing in the
American dream. During the 1970s and 1980s in New York, the rapid de-
terioration of minority communities, sensational cases of police brutality, and rising racial tensions brought both Daughtry and Sharpton into
the spotlight with their rhetoric of past progressives and struggles. They
have done what cultural critic Kobena Mercer calls "democratic equiva-
lencies," appropriating the goals and language of democratic movements
for use in the present age.

Like earlier black Christian radicals, Daughtry and Sharpton relied on
grassroots struggles to force government officials to act on police mis-
conduct and provide assistance to the poor. In part, they practiced a class
politics by struggling for racial economic justice. For example, both were
active in the Operation Breadbasket boycott to force the supermarket
chain A&P to hire and promote more African Americans. Daughtry also
helped organize Concerned Citizens to use boycotts to force Fulton Street
department stores to support a federal investigation into the killing of a
black youth by a New York City white police officer. Likewise, the pastor
led the black United Front in campaigns against police brutality. Daughtry and Sharpton also have waged campaigns to force the city government to provide summer jobs for black teens.

Sharpton has become the leading figure in New York against police
brutality. Despite his defense of false rape accusations by Tawana Brawley
against Dutchess County law enforcement officers, he still receives support because of his defiance of the power structure and his ability to portray himself as the man who is willing to "say it like it is."

Clear symbols of Sharpton's defiance have been his language and image. It is hard to miss his voice, in a perfect black preacher style learned from his Pentecostal roots. The loud raspy articulation, with a crescendo reaching higher and louder as he moves through his narrative, is used to bring his audience to a state in which they can experience his words. It is not so important what he says but how he says it. This style of oratory relies heavily on an antiphonal structure, measuring its success or failure by applause and shouts from his audience. In a setting that blurs the boundaries between religion and politics, he is successful because he is able to make his audience, like those at a good old-time revival, become one. At times they are filled with the spirit of righteous indignation, and at other times, jubilant over his victory declarations.

In his early career as an activist, Sharpton's class politics were reflected in his clothing. He disregarded suits and ties in favor of jumpsuits and sneakers to identify with the young and the working class. While the suit represented establishment politics and the system, the jumpsuit sent the message that he did not care about the proper and conventional. Sharpton's cultural politics particularly appeals to those most likely to be disenchanted with the political system.

Until recently, Sharpton was a Pentecostal minister, and Daughtry remains a pastor of a Pentecostal church. But unlike many Pentecostal leaders of the past, who cautioned that blacks should not be involved in the world, they reflect a growing trend among Pentecostal leaders to become more active in politics. Consequently, they are more reliant on Afro-Christian liberalism and black Christian radicalism than earlier Pentecostals were.

Has Sharpton Clarified His Politics?

Sharpton says he has left his "impulsive" emotionalism of the 1980s for a serious identification with forces building a progressive coalition for helping blacks and poor New Yorkers. The activist minister has noted that his change came after a stabbing in 1991 in Bensonhurst, Brooklyn:

> I was hit two inches from my heart, and I realized, all of a sudden, I could die doing the work I was doing. I began to question how I wanted to be remembered. I was getting older. I was thirty-eight. I was a husband and a father. My generation was assuming leadership in the community and I realized I had to start thinking about the generation that was coming along

after mine. What were the adults, and me in particular, preparing for them? What would we leave? (Sharpton and Walton 1996, 23)

Like the Apostle Paul's Damascus Road experience of God that changed him from prosecutor of Christians to a devout follower of Christ and Malcolm X's trip to Mecca that made him aware that the Nation of Islam's version of Islam was tainted with racism and was not "true" Islam, Sharpton's stabbing was an act that moved him from "a man who was blind but now could see." Like Martin Luther King Jr., who often cited his near death by a stabbing by a deranged woman, Sharpton uses his brush with death to declare that he has been politically born again.

Sharpton has made some cosmetic changes over the last few years. Those close to him have tried hard to reshape his image. Wilbert Tatum, publisher of the *Amsterdam News* and a loyal friend, presents the minister in his paper as a family man, a respected member of the community, and he has included a number of photographs in the newspaper of Sharpton with his wife and children.

To add to his new image as a responsible leader, Sharpton changed religions, from Pentecostal to Baptist. This was not a trivial event. Although he claimed that he changed denominations because of spiritual reasons, he probably realized that if he wanted greater influence, he would have to travel in Baptist circles. Because some of the most politically powerful ministers are Baptists, Sharpton wanted to become part of their circle. Since his conversion, he has moved closer to Jesse Jackson and is now the national director of the ministers division of Jackson's Rainbow Coalition. Sharpton was the leading spokesperson for black New Jersey ministers who challenged campaign strategist Ed Rollins's claim that he bribed black ministers during the 1992 gubernatorial race. Sharpton is also associated with ministers of the National Baptist Convention and the Progressive Baptist Convention, two of the largest black organizations in America.

After 1992, Sharpton severed his ties with Lenora Fulani and the extremist New Alliance Party. Instead, he has attended conferences sponsored by the Congressional Black Caucus and the Black Leadership Conference and has participated in forums with black notables such as Harvard University philosophy professor Cornel West and Columbia University historian Manning Marable. Sharpton's new image seems to be enhancing his political significance. The success of his campaign to change his image is also measured in his electoral and political accomplishments. Since his run for the Senate in 1992, he has received a great deal of favorable press for his transformation. Indeed, both the *New York Times* and *Newsday* portrayed Sharpton as a responsible candidate, a voice of reason in the Democratic Senate primary of 1992 who stuck to the issues while avoiding personal attacks.

For many people, Sharpton's success in 1992 made him a legitimate and important political leader, and he is no longer routinely portrayed as a "rabble rouser." *New York Magazine*'s "What's Right with New York?" listed the political moderation of Al Sharpton and his growth into a statesman. In addition, *Emerge*, the *New Yorker*, and other magazines have carried positive stories about Sharpton. During the 1992 Senate run, Harvard University professor Cornel West wrote glowingly of Sharpton in the *New York Daily News*. In 1993, *Sixty Minutes* host Mike Wallace spoke of the new Al Sharpton who was moderating his views. Sharpton tells his audiences that even Dan Rather has remarked that the pastor had come a long way (Sharpton and Walton 1996, 226–228, 253–254).

With the help of the media, Sharpton has made himself more accept-able to the general public. In many ways, he has become a symbol of the meaning of race and democracy in the post–cold war United States. His success is due in part to what historian Ben Keppel so aptly labeled the "deracialization of the Horatio Alger Myth." Anyone can move from being a poor person—in Sharpton's case, from a rabble-rouser and an out-of-control opportunist—to an almost gentle, dependable role model who espouses basic American values.

As Sharpton tells his story,

> That's where I differ from some, in that I will acknowledge that there are many reasons for black people to give up on life and stop trying. I had sev-eral myself, my daddy left us, we were on welfare and in the projects, the whole bit, but that was no reason for me not to try, that was no excuse just to hand white folks what they wanted, which was me on the sidelines if not in the gutter. White racism did brutalize and even distort black people. What that means is that a black person should strive harder, have a higher moral code. (Sharpton and Walton 1996, 53)

For Sharpton, the struggle for equality should now include individual initiative along with protest. In part, his appeal goes back to black liber-als' call for social and moral uplift. Sharpton's new direction was appar-ent at the funeral of a twenty-two-year-old black man gunned down by a white police officer on his way to visit his mother on Christmas Day. The officer claimed that the unarmed man looked like a roof shooter in the Canarsie section of Brooklyn. Sharpton spoke as expected of the rampant police abuse of blacks and Latinos, but he also called on blacks to take the moral high ground and stop the killing in their communities.

Part of the new image package is the assertion that "the Rev." is left of center. In his runs for the Senate and for mayor, Sharpton claimed to be a progressive candidate building a broad movement for the poor. Influenced by Jesse Jackson, Sharpton has called for full employment, adequate housing, justice for the poor, and reform of the criminal justice system. He has attacked corporate welfare and special tax breaks and protested the layoff of unionized hospital workers. Sharpton advocates the investment of pension funds into infrastructure repair in the city. In constructing a rainbow coalition for New York, he speaks to women, gay and lesbian, and labor groups.

The flamboyant minister still engages in class politics by appealing to the black working class. When noting the divide between the middle class and the poor, Sharpton says that middle-class blacks are terrified that he will upset their peace with the white power structure. But Sharpton does not allow his class analysis to overshadow the significance of race. When it comes to the greatest evil for blacks, race supersedes class. "I've seen the wealthiest, most famous, most successful blacks face the same circumstances as a poor man from Queens. So if any black person thinks they're transcending this, they're only fooling themselves." According to Sharpton, white racism knows no class boundaries: the white middle-class suburban homeowner is just as racist as the white working-class truck driver in Howard Beach. "Eddie Murphy's kid could be killed as quick as Pernell." His analysis of the dominance of race over class is an attempt to go beyond class politics and build stronger support among black middle class (Sharpton and Walton 1996, 53).

Sharpton has masterfully portrayed himself as the underdog representing those the system has left out. Depicting himself as the voice of the people and using the collective term "we" instead of "I," he represents his success as the "people's victory." According to the minister, his victories are not self-interested but are reflections of the masses challenging the establishment. Shortly after the 1997 Democratic mayoral primary, when it was expected that there would be a runoff between him and the Manhattan borough president, Ruth Messinger, he announced to his supporters: "We will be heard in September." To the enthusiastic crowd, he declared: "They would write stories and act like we weren't even in the race. But we didn't go by what they thought of us. We went by what we thought of ourselves! They always tell us what we can't do, but we end up doing it" (Strickland 1997, 1).

The Reverend seems to be other taking steps in a progressive direction. He distanced himself from Alton Maddox and C. Vernon Mason during the slander suit brought by Police Officer Steven Pagones. Whereas Mason and Maddox attempted to prove that the former prosecutor raped Brawley, Sharpton narrowed his defense to whether there was proof that he deliberately lied when he accused Pagones of rape. More important, he has associated with people building a progressive coalition of labor, racial minorities, and feminist groups. For example, Professor Manning Marable was a speaker at Sharpton's National Network Action, where he called for universal health care, full employment, and an end to police brutality and criticized Louis Farrakhan's conservative politics and economic program. This was significant because in the past, Sharpton was a public supporter of Farrakhan. However, Sharpton has also voiced disapproval of narrow black nationalism, claiming that its supporters are "copping out" of society. He asserts that he is a "Pan-Africanist" in the "Du Bois interpretation of the term" (Sharpton and Walton 1996, 216–217, 246–247).

Sharpton's move from protest to politics has more to do with remaining legitimate than contemplating a legacy. To maintain support and gain new followers, he knows he must deliver the goods. Providing people with only a chance to vent their anger at rallies will lead to early retirement for any protest leader, or at least move them to the political basement with the protest relics.

From Gardner Taylor to Al Sharpton, the black religious community has been an important feature of the black left in New York. Even when the leftist forces were silenced by repression, the black religious community remained a center of ideological debate. To be sure, the black religious community was not unified but diversified. Indeed, it is this diversity that has put this community at the center and not at the margins of politics.

NOTES

1. Although Galamison participated in the protest and was one of the ministers who signed the agreement with Rockefeller, he would state that it was a betrayal of the protestors.

2. The oldest is the First Church of God in Christ.

Chapter 25

The Greek Orthodox Church and Identity Politics

Anna Karpathakis

Accusations of "Thief!" "Liar!" "Monster!" and "Dictator!" echo through the Byzantine domes of today's Greek Orthodox churches in New York City.

What is really happening in New York City's Greek Orthodox churches? To answer that question, like all questions about Greek Orthodoxy, one must look at its history.

Greek immigrants to the United States created their religious institutions with three goals in mind: (1) to transmit the Greek Orthodox religion to the American-born generations; (2) to transmit Greek secular politics, culture, history, and language to the American-born generations; and (3) to help new Greek immigrants adjust to American society and its institutions. The conflicts over the identity of the Greek Orthodox Church[1] in the United States in the late twentieth century may be traced to these original goals.

This chapter examines the identity politics and conflicts confronting the United States' Greek Orthodox Church on the international, national, and local parish levels. The principal issue on all levels is whether the church will remain a Greek immigrant and Greek American Orthodox church or whether it will become an American Orthodox church without an "ethnic" foundation.

A Brief History of the Greek Orthodox Church in the United States

In 1891,[2] New York City got its own first Greek Orthodox church, the Holy Trinity Cathedral in the Wall Street area of Manhattan, which fell under the jurisdiction of the Patriarchate of Constantinople (now Istanbul), Turkey.[3] By 1922, there were 140 Greek Orthodox congregations in the United States, and by 1929, nearly 200. Each church was created independently by immigrants who later sent to Greece for a priest (Konstantellos 1982; Moskos 1989). Because it was increasingly persecuted by Turkish nationalists, the Constantinople Patriarchate in 1908 formally placed the Greek Orthodox Church in the United States under the jurisdiction of the Church of Greece.

The Greek Orthodox parishes nonetheless remained independent of the Russian Orthodox Archdiocese of America, only seldom requesting services from the Russians (Fitzgerald 1995). At the same time, according to church law, the presence of Russian bishops in the United States prevented the Constantinople Patriarchate and the Church of Greece from sending additional bishops to serve the Greek Orthodox community. Until the early 1920s, therefore, the Greek Orthodox parishes were run by lay trustees. Then, after the Russian Revolution of 1917, the trustees asked Greece to send bishops.

In 1918, the first Greek Orthodox bishops, Meletios and Alexander, visited the United States. Meletios came so that Greek liberals could gain control of the U.S. churches before the Monarchists arrived.[4] To do this, Meletios created a synodic trusteeship,[5] with Bishop Alexander as his representative. When they arrived, the local parishes were literally torn apart over Greek national politics, personality clashes, and charges of financial embezzlement. Acting as the canonical archbishop of Athens with Alexander as his auxiliary bishop, Meletios organized the feuding parishes under one jurisdiction and created the first Clergy-Laity Congress in September 1921. Perhaps the congress's single most important decision was to fold all the Greek Orthodox parishes into the Greek Orthodox Archdiocese of North and South America (GOANSA). To ensure its success, Meletios established the first Greek Orthodox seminary in Astoria, New York,[6] and launched the weekly journal *Ecclesiastical Herald*.

Because Greek immigrants still looked to their home (Greece) church for clerical guidance and help in maintaining their churches in the United States, this relationship exposed their churches to Greece's turbulent politics. Consequently, the Patriarchate in Constantinople and the Church of Greece, divided over both personal and national issues (reflecting the struggle for power between the monarchy and the republicans), entered into a fierce competition for control of the church in the Americas.

Meletios (a democratic republican) was removed from his position in the Greek church in the summer of 1921 by the Monarchists who gained control of the Church of Greece. He fled from Greece, taking sanctuary in Trinity Church, New York. Early in 1922, he was elected to the Ecumenical Patriarchate in Constantinople, turned over the church in the Americas to the jurisdiction of the Patriarchate in Istanbul, and named Alexander the archbishop of GOANSA. In response, in 1922, Athens sent an exarch[7] to the United States to lead the church, which had the effect of dividing the parishes between Alexander and the Athens representative. Then in 1923, a Monarchist bishop arrived, further dividing the church by establishing the Autocephalous (that is, self-governing, independent) Greek Orthodox Church of the United States and Canada (which ceased to exist in the United States in the 1930s).

Even though Archbishop Alexander tried to organize his parishes under GOANSA, he was primarily concerned with helping victims of poverty, persecution, and natural disasters. But his successor, Archbishop Athenagoras, who arrived from Istanbul in 1931, succeeded in bringing the majority of the parishes into GOANSA. Athenagoras also drafted a new constitution, replaced the synodic system with a centralized bureaucracy, and created two additional dioceses, for a total of five (New York, Boston, Chicago, San Francisco, and Charlotte, North Carolina). Now bishops were no longer the autonomous heads of dioceses but became auxiliaries to the archbishop. Whereas Alexander had allowed the U.S. church to be decentralized and independent, Athenagoras believed that a decentralized church meant its eventual Americanization, something that he wanted to prevent.

Archbishop Iakovos from the Istanbul Patriarchate arrived in New York in 1959 and was the leader of the church until his retirement in June 1996. During Iakovos's tenure, the church grew when a new wave of immigrants began arriving in the late 1960s, most settling in New York City. In the 1970s, the parishes in Brooklyn and Queens doubled in size, and in the 1980s, the suburban churches experienced similarly unprecedented growth. By 1966, there were 368 parishes under the archdiocese (Counelis 1989), and by 1996, nearly 540 (Archdiocese Yearbook, 1996). The 1996 *Archdiocese Yearbook* listed 50 Greek Orthodox parishes in New York City and its suburbs and exurbs (24 parishes in the five boroughs, 13 in Nassau and Suffolk Counties, and 13 in Yonkers, Westchester, and Orange Counties). The parishes varied in size from as small as a few dozen family memberships in the early immigrant enclave of Washington Heights to as large as 2,600 family memberships in Flushing, Queens.

Iakovos left behind him a complex legacy regarding the church's relations with both its homeland and the mother churches in Istanbul and Greece. Although Iakovos engaged American national politicians on behalf of Greek concerns (see, for example, Karpathakis 1999), during his tenure an Americanization movement, the Orthodox Christian Laity (OCL), gained power in the church's higher echelons. Greek newspapers accused Iakovos of working with the OCL to create a Pan-American Orthodox Patriarchate (or a Pan-Orthodox American Patriarchate) that would break with the Patriarchate in Istanbul and the Church of Greece and eliminate the church's "ethnic" foundation.

When Iakovos announced his support for U.S. presidential candidate George Bush over the Greek American Michael Dukakis, the *New York Times* reported that "fundamentalists" had acquired power in the higher echelons of the Greek Orthodox Church. Indeed, Iakovos had surrounded himself with self-styled fundamentalists, many of whom were non-Greeks converted from Protestant denominations. In 1994, Iakovos joined Orthodox clergy and laity at a conference in Ligonier, Pennsylvania, to compose a statement proclaiming that although they recognized the spiritual leadership of the Patriarchate as the mother church, the Orthodox Church of the Americas was no longer a diaspora church but, rather, an American-born and -maintained church. Soon after this meeting, the Patriarchate of Istanbul asked the eighty-five-year-old Iakovos to retire.

The Istanbul Patriarchate looked at the Americanizers' activities according to its own experiences of ethnic politics. From the Patriarchate's perspective, late-twentieth-century international identity politics was threatening its position as the symbolic leader of Eastern Orthodoxy. First, after the fall of the Soviet bloc, Archbishop Alexii of the Russian Orthodox Church claimed control of the ethnic Orthodox churches in the newly independent states of the Eastern bloc. Since Orthodoxy had originally developed along ethnic lines, Alexii constituted a threat to the traditional ethnic autonomy and balance of power.

Second, the Istanbul Patriarchate's very survival was threatened by Turkish governmental policies and the growing Turkish Muslim fundamentalist movement. For example, in December 1997, the Patriarchate was again bombed by Muslim fundamentalists, seriously injuring one cleric and destroying the roof of one of the buildings. In addition, because the Greek population of Istanbul had shrunk, the Patriarchate was in financial straits. The Greek Orthodox Churches of the United States, the richest of all the churches under the Patriarchate, were therefore a much needed resource. The Patriarchate thus regarded the Americanizers, who were preoccupied with their own status interests and identity politics, as an internal threat at a time when unity was crucial to the church's survival in Turkey.

Iakovos did rely heavily on OCL activists and indeed may not have paid enough attention at first to the Istanbul Patriarchate's own problems, that the mother church was not ready to cut its ties with the church in the United States or that the immigrants themselves were not yet ready to abolish the ethnic aspect of their church.

Soon after Iakovos's retirement, the Patriarchate reorganized the GOANSA into smaller regional units, thereby diluting the power of the U.S. church. That is, the Greek Orthodox Archdiocese of the United States is now only one archdiocese among several. The political reasons for this restructuring were evident to all. Although the U.S. church is only one of many members, its wealth and size enabled it to dominate GOANSA The new archdioceses, however, have been limited in size and power so as to prevent any single cleric from acquiring the power that Iakovos had. This organizational restructuring was also intended to minimize the impact of a "runaway" church if the U.S. church decided to join other ethnic churches to create a Pan-Orthodox Patriarchate of the Americas, for the churches in Canada, Mexico, and Central and South America would remain under the jurisdiction of the Istanbul Patriarchate.

Finally, the organizational restructuring of the church was a symbolic blow to the Americanizers. By the early 1990s, the Americanizers' criticisms of the Orthodox Church and its ethnic foundation had become quite bold and even anti-Greek. As one journalist remarked during an interview, "[The Patriarchate] in effect told them not to get too haughty because when it comes down to it Orthodoxy, even Christianity, exists because of the Greeks. To be honest, I am glad they were told, you can't kick Greeks out because you don't want us around."

Recent Politics

In 1996, Metropolitan Spyridon of Italy was elected by the Patriarchate as the next archbishop of the Greek Orthodox Church of the United States, and both critics and supporters claimed that his election was politically motivated to appease the various factions. Spyridon was born in Ohio, received his theological education at the Patriarchate's Halkis Seminary in Turkey, worked in the Patriarchate at Istanbul, and later became the Patriarchate's liaison to the Vatican. Spyridon was the first American-born archbishop to lead the church in the United States, and he also was loyal to the Patriarchate in Istanbul.

In a sermon in September 1997, Spyridon spoke of the need to reopen the theological seminary in Halkis, which had been closed in 1971 in accordance with a law placing religious studies in Turkey into public institutions. This suggestion was a complete reversal of the Americanizers' proposals. Also that fall, Spyridon hosted Ecumenical Patriarch Bartholomaio's visit to the United States and even arranged a meeting with President Bill Clinton. In fact, through Spyridon, Bartholomaio raised $20 million for maintenance work on churches in Istanbul. Finally, during the Christmas 1997 holidays, Spyridon announced that English would become the "preferred" language of Greek Orthodoxy in the United States.

Despite these accomplishments, Spyridon was widely opposed by all levels of the church hierarchy and was accused of having an authoritarian style leadership and even of covering up a sex scandal in the Hellenic College of Boston. He eventually resigned in the summer of 1999 and was replaced by Metropolitan Demetrios of Vresthenis, a Greek diocese in the Peloponese region. Born in Greece, Demetrios had lived in the United States for a few years where he attended seminary and also taught at the Hellenic College in Boston and at Harvard University as a visiting scholar. Having lived in both countries, Demetrios is said to be familiar with the politics of both Greece and the Greek immigrant community in the United States.

Just as his predecessors had to do, Demetrios must negotiate with two seemingly contradictory forces: first, the Americanizers who demand the creation of an "American" church and, second, a vulnerable Istanbul Patriarchate that needs the Greek Orthodox Church of the United States for its survival. In the end, Demetrios may try to create a culturally and "ethnically" "American" Greek Orthodox Church under the auspices of the Patriarchate of Constantinople. Should he choose to define the Greek Orthodox Church even symbolically as "American," he will undoubtedly cross the immigrant activists of New York City as well as the Church of Greece.

Demographics, Politics, and Affairs

The Greek Orthodox churches of New York City and its suburbs and exurbs are split between those inner-city parishes whose members are mainly aging immigrants and the suburban and exurban churches whose members are younger and economically more successful. Although most of the founders of the older parishes have died by now, many of the founders of the newer parishes are still alive and often still active in the church. The founders of all the parishes in the seven churches considered in this chapter are immigrants who came to the United States before 1965.[8]

Soon after arriving in a town or neighborhood, these pre-1965 immigrants formed committees and donated their time, energy, and money to establish a parish. The committees rented worship space, usually in basements of Protestant churches, and hired part-time priests to lead the Sunday service. These committees—typically made up of small coffee shop, diner, and construction company owners and, occasionally, working-class families—donated supplies and money to organize bingo games, parties, and dances to raise capital to buy property. They later held Greek festivals on the church property to attract non-Greek residents. A few years after they had bought the land, the committees had usually raised enough money to begin constructing the church building. If possible, the construction bid was awarded to one of the parishioners who was willing to work for cost, and the construction crews often consisted of men parishioners who donated their labor. As one seventy-two-year-old woman described it, "There were twenty of us and we did it all. We worked hard, donated our time, emotions, money, our blood and sweat, but in the final outcome, we built a church that is the envy of the town because we did it ourselves. What did we have? Nothing. But look at what we made." Equipped with little formal education, this group literally fumbled its way through their church's creation.

Occasionally, the children of these immigrant founders followed their parents in contributing their own time and money in maintaining the church their parents helped create. But those parishes with a history of conflict were less likely to recruit the children of the founders as active volunteers and leaders. In the most contentious parish in my sample, only one man whose father was among the founders was a member of the parish board. Conversely, in the least contentious parish, a number of the founders' children were on track to be the parish's future lay leaders.

Between 1967 and 1980, nearly 200,000 new Greek immigrants arrived in the United States, most wanting to enter and participate in the church. Those who arrived as adults are likely still living in the original immigrant communities of Astoria and Brooklyn. But those in the one-and-a-half generation who became part of the college-educated middle class or small-business owners have usually moved out of these immigrant communities to the city's suburbs and exurbs, often into towns where the pre-1965 immigrants moved in the 1970s. These new suburbanites enter positions of power in their new, middle-class parishes, the men on the parish board and the women on committees and in the "volunteer pool" carrying out many of the church's daily tasks.

Those pre-1965 immigrants who are middle-class—professionals and their children and grandchildren—are not part of the original founders' groups but, rather, joined the church once it had been built and established. Unlike the majority of the Greek immigrants to the United States, these immigrants came from middle-class families in Greece and practice only a "symbolic ethnicity" (Gans 1994).

A numerically small but important group are the converts to Greek Orthodoxy. In earlier times, Greek Americans left the church after intermarrying, but this has changed in the past two decades with the increase in number of adult baptisms, interethnic marriages, and baptisms of infants with parents of different religions. In one of the parishes in my sample, with a membership of nearly five hundred families, the number of baptisms of infants of parents of different religions increased from three to six each year for the first five years of the 1990s. In another parish, with a membership of approximately 170 families in the mid-1990s, the church baptized eight children of parents of different religions, compared with only four in the previous five years.

Converts from other Christian (primarily Protestant) denominations have little numerical importance in New York City's Greek Orthodox churches. In only one parish in my sample did a convert sit on the parish board. Nonetheless, these converts play a significant symbolic role in the church's Americanization conflicts. At a time when the number of Greek immigrants was decreasing, the converts and the children of intermarriages symbolized for the Americanizers the church's future in the United States. The Americanizers' main antagonists were the pre-1965 immigrant church founders and the post-1965 immigrants and their children, with the Greek and American-born children of the post-1965 immigrants often acting as the "buffer" between the two groups.

The OCL

The nearly 200,000 new Greek immigrants in the 1970s wanted to participate in the local churches beyond just attending services, and they demanded that the church take a stand in Greece's political affairs. The U.S. church did in fact take an active role in Greece's politics, especially after Turkey's 1974 invasion of Cyprus. But the immigrants' demand that the church get involved in Greek politics was opposed by some of the earlier immigrants and their American-born children and grandchildren who were anxious to shed their ethnicity and "blend in" with the "rest of America."

This "blending in" entailed a selective "Americanization" of immigrant institutions. According to the Americanizers, the church should leave politics behind and instead focus on spiritual matters. In effect, the Americanizers wanted the church to be redefined from a church made up of the faithful living in the here and now and sharing their humanity through their relations with one another and with God (see Ware 1996) into a church concerned with individual spirituality (a Protestant theme). That is, they wanted a nonactivist church, a church removed from controversial worldly concerns.

After Turkey invaded Cyprus in 1974 and occupied 37 percent of the island, the new immigrants demanded that their church actively support the territorial sovereignty of Greece and Cyprus. The more assimilated, born in America, interpreted this as the church once again entering ethnic politics. In addition, the high rate of intermarriage between the American-born children of Greek immigrants and non-Greeks meant that in certain areas of the country, the number of non-Greek parishioners had increased.

The OCL's (Orthodox Christian Laity) current political and theological positions are rooted in events of the 1970s and 1980s. Beginning their work informally and limiting it to individual parishes in the suburbs of those cities with large numbers of new immigrants, the Americanizers later centralized their activities in a national movement, the Orthodox Christian Laity. Denied access to the archdiocese's official newspaper, the OCL created its own monthly newsletter, *The Forum,* in 1987 and edited a book in 1993 that presented its platform and demands.

The OCL is critical of the church for losing members because of its involvement in ethnic affairs, and it has called for a "spiritual renewal" of the church, whose main concern should be the "religious education" and "spiritual concerns of the faithful." The OCL made eighty-one recommendations for the church to follow in its administration as well as for its dispensation of sacraments and for the liturgy. Among the recommendations is the creation of autonomous Orthodox jurisdictions without reference to ethnic identities. The OCL also wants a reevaluation of women's history in the church and the evangelization of the Orthodox faith among the heterodox. Taking their cues from American Protestant evangelical traditions, the Americanizers and the OCL argue that the "good news" of the Orthodox faith, representing the "purest" of all the Christian faiths, must be spread to those born outside the faith. In fact, the OCL is redefining the Greek Orthodox Church as an evangelizing church and in this way hopes to increase the number of non-Greeks in the church, thereby turning the demographics in their favor.

The OCL's leaders are primarily from the middle- and upper-middle-class suburban and exurban parishes of New York and Chicago (that is, the two cities with the most new immigrants since 1965). These are also the cities in which the social and economic contrasts between the descendants of the earlier immigrants and the recent immigrants are the greatest. The OCL, however, receives much support from parishes in southern cities like Houston which received a significant number of immigrants before 1965 and whose members are now second- and third-generation Americans and often are married to non-Greeks.

Conflicts on the Parish Level

The Americanizers and the immigrants are fiercely competing for power. Indeed, the competition between the "immigrants" and the "Americanizers" is so intense that it has spilled over into the parishioners' personal and work lives.

The Truly Faithful

The Americanizers offer a moral argument to boost their cause. They accuse the immigrants of not knowing their faith, using the derogatory term "cradle Orthodox" to refer to those born in the faith who are assumed to "never read up on what the history of anything is." The Americanizers argue, however, that "converts" or those who choose to join or stay in the church as adults, that is, the "Americans," do take the time to study the history, the rituals, and the theology of Orthodoxy. According to the Americanizers, the immigrants are less educated, less sophisticated, and less worldly than they are. More important, however, is the idea that it is the Americanizers who are the true faithful because they "witness" their faith on a daily basis (through reading and research), whereas the "cradle Orthodox" take their religion for granted and do not study it. As one woman explained,

> Most of these people don't even know what they believe in. So how can you believe something you do not know? How can you say I believe in this if you do not know what it is you believe in? Did you know that a baptysm [*sic*] is really that there is a difference between baptysm and chrismation? Most Greeks don't even know that.

For the Americanizers, if the church should rightfully be run by those most knowledgeable in the religion, then clearly the "cradle Orthodox," that is, the immigrants, are occupying positions that ethically and morally do not belong to them but rightfully belong to the "truly faithful," that is, the "Americans."

Charges of Embezzlement and Mismanagement

The Americanizers also have accused the immigrants of embezzling church funds, and the immigrants' lack of formal training in management and bookkeeping makes them especially vulnerable to such charges. Furthermore, the immigrants' reliance on volunteer labor, donations, and items or services purchased at cost means that they must be flexible in their bookkeeping of the parish's expenses. Their informal style has become a point of contention with the college-educated Americanizers who are used to more formal management styles.

Immigrants often find themselves on the defensive, having to fight against unofficial charges and gossip of embezzlement, cheating, and conspiracies. Moreover, they often feel unable to defend themselves against such charges. While some have turned to civil authorities for help, primarily—but rarely—through civil lawsuits, most immigrants lack the resources for lengthy trials. One man who was charged with embezzling more than $100,000 of church funds resigned his post on the council because he could not afford to fight the lawsuit. After he resigned, the charges against him were dropped. Immigrants gathered around him to offer support, and one claimed, "If he did it, they would have gone ahead with the lawsuit. But they just wanted him out, and as soon as he left, they dropped the charges. These people are immoral; I don't even know what word to use to describe them."

Boycotting as a Strategy of Undercutting Power

Even parish programs and projects may acquire political significance and be "boycotted" by members of the "opposing camp." In one parish, the immigrants set up a small souvenir shop to attract extra cash from visitors, but the Americanizers will not patronize it. And when the Americanizers in this parish decided to change the way the annual bake sale was run, the immigrants refused to participate.

All the parishes offer part-time Greek-language instruction for the children, and some offer such courses for non-Greek spouses, but Americanizers do not enroll in these courses. Indeed, the language courses are a hotly contested issue for the OCL, which argues that the programs detract from the church's spiritual functions and force it to act as an ethnic institution. But for the immigrants, their religion, language, and culture are intertwined, and any attempt to separate them is seen as altering the foundation of the religion itself.

The Personal Dimension

Political conflicts take on personal dimensions, and often meetings become shouting matches between immigrants and the "Americans." During one heated parish meeting, a Greek immigrant woman with well-known health problems fainted. Her husband claimed that "the only doctor in the room pretended like nothing happened. People came around to try to revive my wife, and the doctor walked out of the room. What a monster! He should have read his Hippocratic oath more carefully." Being in the "opposing camp," the woman claimed that this doctor "felt I did not deserve his medical attention. How can a doctor do this? Is his hatred for us [immigrants] that deep?"

Sometimes parishioners' relationships with one another are based on whether one is an "American" or an "immigrant." Even socializing and seating decisions in church events may be made according to whether one is an "American" or an "immigrant." During one Mother's Day celebration, the Greek speakers are seated away from the English speakers. One group of Greek speakers are talking about their relatives in Greece, and just a few feet away, the English speakers are talking about their retired relatives in Florida. On one side of the room, the discussion is about the children's upcoming visit to Greece, and just a few feet away, the discussion is about an upcoming vacation to the Caribbean.

The Priest's Role

The priest's own political interests and alliances greatly determine how the competing groups will present their demands in the parish and the kind of confrontational or negotiating relations that will emerge. The only parish in which we observed the priest take sides in the conflicts between the Americanizers and the immigrants was also the one with the fiercest conflicts between these two groups. Early on, the American-born and -trained priest angered the immigrants because in an attempt to defend his mistakes during the service, he told a number of immigrants that "this is America. Things change and we have to get used to it." One immigrant woman responded, "Father, if these were issues unrelated to the rituals, I would say fine. [But] it's the readings from the Bible. We can help you learn these terms in Greek. We can help you learn Greek. It will take time, but we can do it. But please don't tell us that the Bible and the epistles change here also. I've been living in this country for fifty years; it's the first time any priest has told me such a thing. Others, yes, but priests, no."

The Americanizers are on the offensive to change the ethnic character of the parish, and the immigrants are on the defensive to maintain the parish as an ethnoreligious institution. The immigrants' position was best articulated by a fifty-five-year-old immigrant owner of a small coffee shop who was one of the parish's original founders: "We created this church, and now the Americans come in and want to take it from us. It's our church. We don't tell them not to come in. But they tell us to hand them the keys and leave. It's our church. What do you tell these people? Making things worse is that these people are Greek, but they say they're not Greek."

The Americanizers' position was summed up by an American-born woman of mixed ancestry (Greek and Russian) who is married to someone of a different religion and is raising her sons in two different churches: "Religion, God, has nothing to do with ethnicity. I came to this church because this is the only place where I felt like I also belong. It's familiar, it's home. But they don't want me because I'm not Greek."

Conclusion

A little over a century after its creation, the Greek Orthodox Church in the United States, and New York City in particular, is riddled with identity conflicts. At issue is whether the church will remain an immigrant and ethnically identified church or will shed its ethnic and immigrant background and declare itself an American Orthodox Church.

NOTES

1. Orthodox Christianity is organized into seven regionally and ethnically based Patriarchates. Each Patriarchate is headed by a patriarch who appoints missionaries and authorizes the expansion of jurisdictions in mission areas. His power, however, is subject to the synod, which is the occasional meeting of all the archbishops and bishops of the Constantinople Patriarchate. Furthermore, each church can decide whether to place itself under the Patriarchate's authority. Below the patriarch are the archbishops, the metropolitans, the bishops, and the priests.

2. The first Greek Orthodox Church in the United States was established in 1862 in Galveston, Texas.

3. The Istanbul Patriarchate is symbolically prestigious because it represents the lost glory of the Constantinian Roman Empire. But it is numerically tiny, with only about two thousand adherents in Turkey. Its struggle to find new sources of funds thus forced Istanbul to establish churches in the United States and Canada.

4. The Liberals in Greece supported a democratic republican form of government without a king, and the Monarchists wanted to retain the kingship. Both parties competed for power within the Greek Orthodox Church.

5. A synod is the meeting of all the bishops in a certain area, and a synodic trusteeship is a group of clerics and laity who are responsible for running certain of the church's affairs.

6. Located on Newtown Road and Crescent Street, currently the site where the archdiocese-run Hellenic Cultural Center stands.

7. An office midway between that of archbishop and bishop, often acting as an archbishop for a foreign land.

8. My sample consisted of seven churches, four in New York City, two in the suburbs, and one in the exurbs, for a total of five thousand members.

Conclusion: New York City's Religions
Issues of Race, Class, Gender, and Immigration

Anna Karpathakis

Two major visions of the centrality and primacy of religion form the bases of the chapters in the volume. There is the view that religion "possesses" a primacy of its own and belongs alongside the economy and politics as a "mega" institution, largely independent of lesser institutions. Religion impacts both the lesser institutions and institutions of its own import (e.g., economy, politics). There is the contrasting view that religion, as an ideological structure, is one of the many social institutions and exists only in relation to social space and time. To understand religion in its full complexity we must place it within a historical context. Religion thus becomes a dynamic institution, transformed by and transformative of other social institutions.

The latter view guides the next few pages. The questions regarding the ways in which religion structures and is structured by other social institutions are many. The issues raised in the next few pages emerge from the papers collected in the volume and are reflective of my own interests in immigration, race, gender, and politics.

The religious dynamics of New York City in the early twenty-first century are complex. Whereas at the beginning of the twentieth century, religious diversity meant a diversity of Christian denominations, today's diversity encompasses all manner of religions. Previously marginalized religious groups are now well integrated into the city's established religious and political establishments, and newer arrivals are striving for the same type of legitimacy. In addition, people from the same religion are arriving from many different countries. Immigrants bring with them the religions of Western missionaries; others leave their countries as members of religious minorities; and still others leave home as members of religious majorities only to find themselves one of the many smaller groups in New York. Still others discover and create their religious faiths and traditions after arriving in the city.

New York is one of the world's financial and trade centers and is also a magnet for immigrants from Third World countries who provide inexpensive labor for the city's service economy. As a consequence, New Yorkers have become more diverse ethnically and racially and less European white. In 1990, Hispanics made up 24 percent of the city's population; they now account for 29 percent. African Americans now make up 26 percent (up from 25%) of the city's population, whites 35 percent (down from 43%), and Asians 10 percent (up from 7%). The traditional black-white dichotomy or one-drop rule of American race history has thus been replaced by a more fluid and complex racial hierarchy. In these new racial conceptualizations, American "blacks" are at the bottom, and "black" immigrants from the Caribbean and Africa occupy a higher place in the city's racial classification.

These changing racial structures are further complicated by class differences. For example, many Jamaican, Indian, and Korean immigrants with high levels of formal education earn middle-class incomes that are not consistent with their position in the city's racial hierarchy. Colombian immigrants in Queens have created a highly livable enclave, but Dominican immigrants in Manhattan tend to reside in unpleasant neighborhoods characterized by high unemployment, low-paying jobs, and high poverty rates. Finally, although the black middle class is expanding, the number of poor blacks is growing as well.

The city's new service economy has paradoxically raised both income and poverty, reflecting the kinds of low-paying, unstable jobs that a service economy creates for new immigrants, women, and minority groups. The per capita income for New York State's metropolitan regions, including New York City, steadily rose in the 1990s, reaching $31,214 in 1997. But at the same time, the poverty rate of the same regions increased to 15.9 percent in 1995 (the last year for which this information is available), up from 13.4 percent in 1980 and 13.0 percent in 1990.

Religious institutions also vary widely in their available resources and structures. Whereas some have available to them multimillion-dollar annual funds supporting clergy on enviable salaries, others must struggle on shoestring budgets to serve the poor. One church on Northern Boulevard that serves Greek immigrants recently purchased land worth more than $1 million for a community center. A Korean immigrant church just one mile west plans to relocate to a larger building in a "nicer" part of the town. Two miles farther west, a church for middle- and working-class African Americans is housed in a modest brick structure that it owns. Another two blocks west, Pentecostal-style church serving Latino immigrants rents a small storefront space for a few hundred dollars a month.

New York City's gender structures and ideologies have changed as well. The new service economy and the women's movement have led to more women than men completing high school and college. At the same time, women still earn only a fraction of what men earn, and women also make up a larger proportion of the poor than do men. Although new ideologies of gender equality have helped women become more active participants in their religious group, they rarely hold important positions of power in these institutions. Of the nearly thirty clergy working in the nine churches and synagogues on a five-mile stretch of Northern Boulevard, only two are women.

Changes in the city's racial/ethnic, class, and gender structures and in the ways in which they interact with religious ideologies and their social structures contribute to the city's transformation. Although this phenomenon is not new, the remarkable resurgence of religious activity in a city with such complex social structures is new.

Immigrants, Race, and Religions

Soon after they arrive, immigrants learn that Americans are more tolerant of religious diversity than they are of ethnic diversity. Accordingly, immigrants use religion as a socially tolerated means through which they can construct their own culture and identity. That is, religious institutions are a public forum for immigrants in which they can create group narratives and histories for the next generation. Through their religious institutions, they also define their group in relation to other groups in the larger social structure. In this sense, then, religious institutions serve different functions for immigrants than they do for white middle-class American Catholics and Protestants.

For example, highly educated professional Hindu immigrants to New York subscribe to a fundamentalist religious faith even while they are assimilating into the city's institutions. In addition, Hindu immigrants use religion partly to distinguish themselves from American blacks. Similarly, the Greek Orthodox Church has created a Hellenic "white" identity in an attempt to retain the American-born children of Greeks.

Class and race intersect in immigrants' construction of their ethnoreligious identity. Greek working-class immigrants are flattered by the Greek Orthodox Church's definition of them as Hellenes and accept the "white" Hellenic identity when their frame of reference is "America," for it is an identity that adds prestige to their social status as restaurant owners and workers. Working-class immigrants who arrived after 1965, however, reject this "racial" identity when their frame of reference is Greece because this identity was constructed by the right-wing military dictatorship of 1967–1974.

Conversion, Race, and Immigration Status

Religious conversions in the city are taking the faithful across racial boundaries as whites join traditionally "minority" religions and minorities join traditionally "white" religions. Religious virtuosos, disenchanted with the religions they were raised in, cross racial and ethno-religious boundaries in search of a religion better suited to their own spiritual needs. One source of ideological and structural change in the city's religions is the converts themselves.

For instance, African Americans who convert to Yoruba are redefining the religion to reflect more closely their own spiritual needs, arising from their experiences with the United States' racial politics and religious history. The Yoruba religion is also attracting Italian and Jewish Americans in Brooklyn. In the case of Jewish Americans, this means a simultaneous racial and religious crossing, given Yoruba's syncretism with Christian traditions.

To justify their "right" to belong to a particular religious institution, converts study their new faith and group, sometimes gaining an expertise in the religion. Often they return to particular theologies and rituals in the group's early history and follow these faithfully. As a result, converts are less likely to question patriarchal structures, whereas Greek Orthodox "cradle" feminists, for example, argue that the early church was less patriarchal than the post-Constantine church is. They are concerned that converts from conservative Protestant denominations are selectively reconstructing the church's history and theology to suit their own conservative ideologies and prolife politics. Furthermore, they fear that these converts are defining these politics as theological. In the meantime, because they are white, "American," college educated, articulate, and conversant with Greek Orthodoxy's theological and social histories, these converted Protestants have been able to capture the ear of the church hierarchy. Then as the converts acquire more power in the institution, they demand that it be "Americanized," which leads to multitude of theological and organizational conflicts.

The experiences of *immigrant* converts, however, are quite different. Immigrant converts create their own parishes or congregations to defuse conflicts (both racial and linguistic) with the white membership and hierarchy. Seventh-Day Adventists and the Church of Latter Day Saints are two faiths in which immigrant converts have created congregations based on language (that is, race). Similarly, Russian Jews who rediscover their Jewish faith when they arrive in New York are creating their own synagogues and community centers in Brighton Beach and trying to remain independent of American Jews. But Russian Jewish immigrants and their children who move out of the immigrant enclave and into other areas of the city or its suburbs may join synagogues established by American Jews, that is, "blend in" with American Jews. Conversely, even after advancing socially and moving away from their original neighborhood, black Seventh-Day Adventists and Mormons return to their ethnicity- or language-based congregation rather than attend a "white" congregation closer to home. Whereas in one case, a common race and religion would seem to supersede cultural and linguistic differences between American and Russian Jews, in the other case, race has remained a predominant factor in the religious participation of immigrant converts.

Gender and Religion

New York City is a religiously competitive environment in which the faithful are always perceived to be "in danger of" being converted. To combat this danger, religious groups mobilize all their resources, including the labor of their women members, the groups' moral gatekeepers. In order to pass on their religious traditions to the next generation, women must be familiar with them, and so women are being called to assume more active roles in the church. Orthodox Jewish women take Torah classes; Greek Orthodox women take Bible classes; Hindu women prepare prayers and maintain shrines; and Latina Pentecostals reach out to the poor in their communities. In this way, women create a "reserve army of labor" for their religious groups and are responsible for carrying out the unpaid daily tasks required to maintain a group- or community-based religion.

Various ideologies have been created to guide women's religious participation. Because their religions are so racially and ethnically diverse, Catholic and Protestant feminist ethicists have had to incorporate antiracialist ideologies into their religions and to address class inequalities. Jewish gays and lesbians are demanding spiritual equality from the larger Jewish community. Eastern Orthodox feminists, however, have been silent on these issues. Because they are largely a homogeneous group of white and middle-class professionals, Eastern Orthodox feminists have not needed to address issues of class and race.

The kinds of gender demands on their religious group that these women make or fail to make are determined by the group's record of opportunities for and limitations on women. Greek Orthodox feminists are calling for women to enter the deaconate, a position that was open to women in the early church. Rasta women are taking the lead in establishing and maintaining the institutions essential to the reproduction of their group. In other words, Rasta women are assuming the role that new immigrant women in this country have historically taken to maintain their group identity and culture.

The position of these women and their religions in New York City's race, class, gender and cultural hierarchies determines how they construct gender ideologies. Although Rasta, Mormon, Hindu, Pentecostal, Orthodox Jewish, and Eastern Orthodox women try to satisfy their group's spiritual needs and maintain their identities, they have made no gender-specific demands or appear to be altering their group's gender structures. Rather, because they regard their group and culture as endangered, their preservation supersedes all other issues, including gender inequality. The women in these groups thus have assumed the responsibility of keeping their group's culture alive and passing it on to later generations. Indeed, these women's roles are celebrated by scholars who view women's increased religious participation as a revolution in gender relations.

Recently, Eastern Orthodox theologians held a conference on the relationship of the medical, mental, and religious fields. In the book produced from this conference, the authors adopted some elements of the mental health and medical sciences but ignored any new scientific understandings of gender and sexuality that might "feminize" the patriarchal theology and church structures. Clearly, in this case, the need to return to the fold those wayward faithful who have rejected a religious view of the world defined by patriarchy and heterosexuality has not eclipsed the need to maintain the church's patriarchal structures. The group's one lone feminist was all but ignored. And so while New York City is the place where Protestant and Catholic feminist ethicists find a receptive audience and have won some of the demands of their church, Eastern Orthodoxy seems to be continuing to lose its cradle Orthodox "feminists."

These changes have by no means stopped; the issues remain unresolved; and the contributors to *New York Glory* hope that this book will contribute to the exploration of religion's changing relationship to politics, to immigration and assimilation, race, gender, and sexual inequalities, and to the local, national, and even global economy.

Bibliography

Abusharaf, Rogaia Mustafa. 1998. Structural adaptations in an immigrant Muslim congregation in New York. In R. Stephen Warner and Judith G. Wittner, eds., *Gatherings in Diaspora: Religious Communities and the New Immigration.* Philadelphia: Temple University Press.

Ain, S. 1998. Reform divided over gay unions. *The Jewish Week*, April 24, 1–2.

Alpert, R. 1989. In God's image: Coming to terms with Leviticus. In C. Balka and A. Rose, eds., *Twice Blessed: On Being Lesbian, Gay and Jewish.* Boston: Beacon Press.

Alpert, R. 1997. Troubling texts from the Torah. In R. Alpert, *Like Bread on the Seder Plate.* New York: Columbia University Press.

American Jewish Committee (AJC). 1997. 1997 Survey of American Jewish Opinion. New York: American Jewish Committee.

American Jewish Committee. 1998. 1998 Survey of American Jewish Opinion. New York: American Jewish Committee.

American Jewish Committee. 1999. Portrait of Russian-Jewish immigrants in New York at the turn of the century. New York: American Jewish Committee, October.

Ammerman, Nancy T. 1987. *Bible Believers: Fundamentalists in the Modern World.* New Brunswick, NJ: Rutgers University Press.

Ammerman, Nancy T. 1990. *Baptist Battles: Social Change and Religious Conflict in the Southern Baptist Convention.* New Brunswick, NJ: Rutgers University Press.

Ammerman, Nancy T. 1996. Spiritually vital Episcopalian congregations. Study commissioned by the grants program of Trinity Church, November 22.

Ammerman, Nancy T. 1997a. *Congregation and Community.* New Brunswick, NJ: Rutgers University Press.

Ammerman, Nancy T. 1997b. Spiritual journeys in the American mainstream. *Congregations: The Alban Journal* 23, 1 (January/February): 16–32.

Andolsen, Barbara Hilkert, Christine E. Gudorf, and Mary D. Pellauer, eds. 1985. *Women's Consciousness, Women's Conscience.* San Francisco: Harper & Row.

Andreassi, Anthony D. 1999. A parish for the people of all nations: A history of the Church of the Holy Family, Turtle Bay, New York City, 1924–1999. Unpublished manuscript, Washington, DC.

Arian, Asher, Arthur S. Goldberg, John Mollenkopf, and Edward T. Rogowsky. 1991. *Changing New York City Politics.* New York: Routledge.

Armstrong, Karen. 1994. *A History of God: The 4000-Year Quest of Judaism, Christianity and Islam.* New York: Knopf.

Arneson, Richard J. 1985. Marxism and secular faith. *American Political Science Review* 79: 627–640.

Ashmeade, Roy W. 1991. *African American–West Indian: Friend or Foe?* Jamaica, NY: Claremont.

Balka, C., and A. Rose, eds. 1989. *Twice Blessed: On Being Lesbian, Gay and Jewish.* Boston: Beacon Press.

Bancroft, Nancy. 1985. Women in the cutback economy: Ethics, ideology, and class. In Barbara H. Andolsen, Christine E. Gudorf, and Mary D. Pellauer, eds., *Women's Consciousness, Women's Conscience.* San Francisco: Harper & Row.

Barboza, Steven. 1994. *American Jihad: Islam after Malcolm X.* New York: Image/ Doubleday.

Barkan, Elliot R. 1995. Race, religion, and nationality in American society: A model of ethnicity—From contact to assimilation. *Journal of American Ethnic History* 14 (Winter): 38–101.

Barna, George. 1999. *African-Americans and Their Faith.* Oxnard, CA: Barna Institute.

Barrett, Leonard. 1988. *The Rastafarians: Sounds of Cultural Dissonance.* Boston: Beacon Press.

Barry, Dan. 1999. Poll in NY finds many think police are biased. *New York Times,* March 16, A1.

Bascom, William. 1944. *The Sociological Role of the Yoruba Cult-Group.* Washington, DC: American Anthropological Association.

Bastide, Roger. 1960. *The African Religions of Brazil: Towards a Sociology of Interpenetration of Civilizations.* Baltimore: John Hopkins University Press.

Bastide, Roger. 1971. *The African Religions of Brazil: Toward a Sociology of the Interpenetration of Civilizations.* Trans. Helen Sebba. Baltimore: Johns Hopkins University Press.

Beier, Ulli. 1975. *The Return of the Gods. The Sacred Art of Suzanne Wenger.* Cambridge: Cambridge University Press.

Bell, Daniel. 1978. *The Cultural Contradictions of Capitalism.* New York: Basic Books.

Bell, Linda A. 1993. *Rethinking Ethics in the Midst of Violence: A Feminist Approach to Freedom.* Lanham, MD: Rowman & Littlefield.

Bellah, R. N., R. Madsen, W. M. Sullivan, A. Swidler, and S. M. Tipton. 1985. *Habits of the Heart: Individualism and Commitment in American Life.* Berkeley and Los Angeles: University of California Press.

Berger, Peter. 1967. *The Scared Canopy.* Garden City, NY: Doubleday.

Berger, Peter. 1982. From the crisis of religion to the crisis of secularity. In Mary Douglas and Steve Tipton, eds., *Religion in America.* Boston: Beacon Press.

Berger, Peter, ed. 1999. *The Desecularization of the World: Resurgent Religion and World Politics.* Grand Rapids, MI: Eerdmans/Ethics and Public Policy Center.

Berger, Peter, and Thomas Luckman. 1966. *The Social Construction of Reality.* Garden City, NY: Doubleday.

Beynon, Erdman Doane. 1938. The voodoo cult among Negro migrants in Detroit. *American Journal of Sociology*, May, 894–907.

Bialik, Hayim Nahman, and Yeshoshua Hana Ravnitzky, eds. 1992. *The Book of Legends (Sefer Ha-Aggadah): Legends from the Talmud and Midrash.* Trans. William G. Braude. New York: Schocken Books.

Bialor, Perry A. 1994. Don't call us Russians. Struggling for identity and survival: The Bukharian Jews of Queens. *New York Times*, August 7, A8.

Billingsley, Andrew, and C. H. Caldwell. 1994. The social relevance of the contemporary black church. *National Journal of Sociology* 8: 1–23.

Binder, Frederick M., and David M. Reimers. 1995. *All the Nations under Heaven: An Ethnic and Racial History of New York City.* New York: Columbia University Press.

Blumenthal, Gloria S. 1998. The Jewish dimension of refugee resettlement: Welcoming and integrating the stranger. *Journal of Jewish Communal Service* 75 (Fall): 28.

Bogue, Donald. 1985. *The Population of the United States: Historical Trends and Future Projections.* New York: Free Press.

Boucher, Madeleine I. 1977. Women and the apostolic community. In Leonard Swidler and Arlene Swidler, eds., *Women Priests: A Catholic Commentary on the Vatican Declaration.* New York: Paulist Press.

Bovin, Alexander. 1996. Interview with Alexander Bovin. *Alef,* October 3–10, 13.

Brandon, George Edward. 1983. The dead sell memories. An anthropological study of Santeria in New York City. Ph.D. diss., Rutgers University.

Brann, Henry Walter. 1944. Max Weber and the United States. *Southwestern Social Science Quarterly* 25, 1 (June): 18–30.

Brasher, Brenda E. 1998. *Fundamentalism and Female Power.* New Brunswick, NJ: Rutgers University Press.

Brayer, Menachem M. 1986. *The Jewish Woman in Rabbinic Literature: A Psychohistorical Perspective.* Hoboken, NJ: Ktav.

Brown, D., and J. Engler. 1986. The stages of mindfulness in meditation.. In K. Wilbur, J. Engler, and D. Brown, eds., *Transformation of Consciousness.* Boston: Shambala Press.

Brown, Elisabeth Potts, and Susan Mosher Stuard, eds. 1989. *Witnesses for Change: Quaker Women over Three Centuries.* New Brunswick, NJ: Rutgers University Press.

Brown, J. C., and C. R. Bohn. 1989. *Christianity, Patriarchy, and Abuse: A Feminist Critique.* New York: Pilgrim Press.

Brown, Mary Elizabeth. 1992a. *From Italian Villages to Greenwich Village: Our Lady of Pompei, 1892–1992.* New York: Center for Migration Studies.

Brown, Mary Elizabeth. 1992b. Italian immigrant clergy and an exception to the rule: The Reverend Antonio Demo, Our Lady of Pompei, Greenwich Village, 1899–1933. *Church History* 42, 1: 41–59.

Brown, Mary Elizabeth. 1995. *Churches, Communities, and Children: Italian Immigrants in the Archdiocese of New York, 1880–1950.* New York: Center for Migration Studies.

Brown, Mary Elizabeth. 1997. Competing to care: Immigrant aid societies for Italians in New York Harbor in the 1920s. *Mid-America* 71: 137–151.

Brueggemann, Walter. 1989. The legitimacy of a sectarian hermeneutic: 2 Kings 18–19. In Mary Boys, ed., *Education for Citizenship and Discipleship.* New York: Pilgrim Press.

Brusco, Elizabeth E. 1995. *The Reformation of Machismo: Evangelical Conversion and Gender in Colombia.* Austin: University of Texas Press.

Brym, Robert J., with Rosalina Ryvkina. 1994. *The Jews of Moscow, Kiev and Minsk: Identity, Anti-Semitism, Emigration.* New York: New York University Press.

Buber, Martin. 1970. *I-Thou.* Trans. Walter Kaufmann. New York: Scribner.

Buckley, Mary I. 1978. Jesus, representative of humanity: What is not assumed is not redeemed. Paper presented at the Feminist Theology Conference, St. John's University, Jamaica, NY, July 8–14.

Bunim, Irving M. 1964. *Ethics from Sinai.* Vol. 1. New York: Philipp Feldheim.

Cabrera, Lydia. 1970. *Koeko iyawo aprende novicia.* Miami: Ediciones universal.

Cadena, Gilbert R. 1995. Religious ethnic identity: A socio-religious portrait of Latinos and Latinas in the Catholic Church. In A. M. Stevens-Arroyo and Gilbert R. Cadena, eds., *Old Masks, New Faces.* New York: Bildner Center.

Caldwell, C. H., A. D. Greene, and A. Billingsley. 1992. The black church as a family support system: Instrumental and expressive functions. *National Journal of Sociology* 6: 21–40.

Campbell. Horace. 1987. *Rasta and Resistance: From Marcus Garvey to Walter Rodney.* Trenton, NJ: Africa World Press.

Candeloro, Dominic. 1994. The role of the Scalabrini fathers in the Chicago Italian American community. In Harral Landry, ed., *They See the Past More Clearly: The Enrichment of the Italian Heritage, 1890–1990.* Proceedings of the American Italian Historical Association, twenty-third annual conference, A Century of Italian Immigration, 1890–1990. Austin, TX: Nortex Press.

Cannon, Katie G. 1988. *Black Womanist Ethics.* Atlanta: Scholars Press.

Cannon, Katie G. 1995. *Katie's Canon: Womanism and the Soul of the Black Community.* New York: Continuum.

Cannon, Katie G., et al. 1985. *God's Fierce Whimsy: Christian Feminism and Theological Education.* New York: Pilgrim Press.

Carle, Robert, and Louis DeCaro, eds. 1997. *Signs of Hope in the City.* Valley Forge, PA: Judson Press.

Carlson, Tucker. 1992. That old-time religion. Why black men are returning to church. *Policy Review,* Summer, 14–21.

Carnes, Tony. 1995. Anti-Semitism in Russia, 1992–1995. Paper presented to the American Association for the Sociology of Religion, Washington, DC, August.

Carnes, Tony. 1996a. *The Bible Institutes of New York City.* A report of the New York Christian Higher Education Consortium by International Research Institute on Values Changes, funded by the PEW Charitable Trust.

Carnes, Tony. 1996b. Decent people in moral mazes—New Russian entrepreneurs in Moscow, 1992–1996. Paper presented to the annual meeting of the Eastern Sociological Society, Boston, March 28.

Carnes, Tony. 1996c. 1996 NYC–NJ Pastors Survey. New York: New York Christian Higher Education Consortium, International Research Institute on Values Changes.

Carnes, Tony. 1997. Methodology of the survey of African-American theological certificate students. New York: International Research Institute on Values Changes (November).

Carnes, Tony. 1999. The Christians of New York City. In Robert Carle and Lou DeCaro, eds., *Signs of Hope.* Baltimore: Judson Press.

Carrasquillo, Angela. 1991. *Hispanic Children and Youth in the United States.* New York: Garland.

Carroll, Jack, and Wade Clark Roof. 1993. *Beyond Establishment.* Louisville: John Knox Press.

Carson, Clayborne. 1991. *Malcolm X: The FBI File.* New York: Carroll & Graf.

Carter, R. A. 1926. What the Negro church has done. *Journal of Negro History,* January, 1–10.

Casanova, José. 1994. *Public Religions in the Modern World.* Chicago: University of Chicago Press.

Cashmore, Ernest. 1979. *Rastaman: The Rastafarian Movement in England.* London: Allen & Unwin.

Cashmore, Ernest. 1984. *The Rastafarians.* London: Minority Rights Groups.

Chai, Karen J. 1998. Competing for the second generation: English language ministry at a Korean Protestant church. In R. Stephen Warner and Judith G. Wittner, eds., *Gatherings in Diaspora: Religious Communities and the New Immigration.* Philadelphia: Temple University Press.

Chalfont, H., and H. B. Calvicanti. 1994. Collective life as the ground of implicit religion. *Sociology of Religion,* Winter, 452–453.

Chatters, L. M., and R. J. Taylor. 1994. Religious involvement among older African-Americans. In J. S. Levin, ed., *Religion in Aging and Health: Theoretical Foundations and Methodological Frontiers.* Thousand Oaks, CA: Sage.

Chertok, Shimon. 1995. Poslednii vsplesk repatriatzii (The last wave of repatriation). *Novoye russkoye slovo* (Russian daily), February 24, 11.

Chevannes, Barry. 1994. *Rastafari: Roots and Ideology.* Syracuse, NY: Syracuse University Press.

Child, Irwin, L. 1943. *Italian or American? The Second Generation in Conflict.* New Haven, CT: Yale University Press.

Chirban, John T., ed. 1996. *Personhood, Orthodox Christianity and the Connection between Body, Mind and Soul.* Westport, CT: Bergin & Garvey.

Christiano, Kevin J. 1987. *Religious Diversity and Cultural Change: American Cities, 1890–1906.* Cambridge: Cambridge University Press.

CHSI Daughters of Zion Document. 1994. Pamphlet no. 1, August 10.

Cimino, Richard P. 1997. *Against the Stream: The Adoption of Traditional Christian Faiths by Young Adults.* Lanham, MD: University Press of America.

Clapp, Steven. 1966. A reporter at large. African theological archministry. Unpublished ms., Schomburg Collection, New York.

Clegg, Claude Andrew III. 1997. *An Original Man: The Life and Times of Elijah Muhammad.* New York: St. Martin's Press. 1997.

Cloud, Henry, and Robert Townsend. 1997. *Safe People.* Grand Rapids, MI: Zondervan.

Coleman, James, and Thomas Hoffer. 1987. *Public and Private Schools: The Impact of Communities.* New York: Basic Books.

Coll, Jorge, 1989. *Una iglesia pionera: Ensayo historico sobre la parroquia de San Benito de Palermo, en la ciudad de Nueva York EE.UU. de America.* New York: Privately published.

Collins, Denis E. 1997. *Paulo Freire: His Life, Works, and Thought.* New York: Paulist Press.

Collins, Patricia Hill. 1991. *Black Feminist Thought: Knowledge, Consciousness, and the Politics of Empowerment.* New York: Routledge.

Colman, J. Barry. 1953. *The Catholic Church and German Americans.* Milwaukee: Bruce.

Cone, James. 1975. *God of the Oppressed.* New York: Seabury Press.

Connell, R. W. 1995. *Masculinities.* Berkeley and Los Angeles: University of California Press.

Costas, Orlando E. 1989. *Liberating News: A Theology of Contextual Evangelization.* Grand Rapids, MI: Eerdmans.

Counelis, James S. 1989. Greek Orthodox Church statistics of the United States, 1949–1989: Some ecclesiastical and social patterns. *Journal of the Hellenic Diaspora* 16: 1–4.

Creech, Charles E. 1991. A critical review of the book *African American–West Indian: Friend or Foe? Historical and Contemporary Perspectives* 3, 1: 1–20.

Cros Sandoval, Mercedes. 1975. *La Religion afro-cubana.* Madrid: Playor.

Crouch, Stanley. 1997. Now let me tell you about my crisis. *New York Daily News*, November 19, 20.

Cruise, Harold. 1984. *The Crisis of the Negro Intellectual.* New York: Quill.

D'Agostino, Peter R. 1993. Missionaries in Babylon: The adaptation of Italian priests to Chicago's church, 1870–1940. Th.D. diss., University of Chicago Divinity School.

D'Agostino, Peter R. 1994. Italian ethnicity and religious priests in the American church: The Servites, 1870–1940. *Catholic Historical Review* 80, 4: 714–740.

D'Agostino, Peter R. 1997. The Scalabrini father, the Italian emigrant church, and ethnic nationalism in America. *Religion and American Culture: A Journal of Interpretation* 7: 121–159.

Daly, Lois K. 1994. *Feminist Theological Ethics: A Reader.* Louisville: Westminster–John Knox Press.

Dan, Richard. 1999. *New York Times* poll finds that fewer than a quarter of all New Yorkers believe that police treat blacks and whites evenly. *New York Times*, March 16, A1, A6.

D'Antonio, William V., et al. 1989. *American Catholic Laity.* Kansas City, MO: Sheed & Ward.

D'Antonio, William V., et al. 1996. *Laity American and Catholic: Transforming the Church.* New York: Fordham University Press.

Dao, James. 1999. Immigrant diversity slows traditional political climb. *New York Times*, December 28, 1, B11.

Davidman, Lynn. 1991. *Tradition in a Rootless World: Women Turn to Orthodox Judaism.* Berkeley and Los Angeles: University of California Press.

Davis, James A. 1983. *General Social Surveys, 1972–1983: Cumulative Codebook.* Chicago: NORC.

DeCaro, Louis A. Jr. 1996. *On the Side of My People: A Religious Life of Malcolm X.* New York: New York University Press.

DeCaro, Louis A. Jr. 1998. *Malcolm and the Cross: The Black Muslims and the White Man's Religion.* New York: New York University Press.

De la Garza, Rodolfo, et al. 1992. *Latino Voices: Mexican, Puerto Rican and Cuban Perspectives on American Politics.* Boulder, CO: Westview Press.

Deren, Maya. 1953. *Divine Horsemen. The Living Gods of Haiti.* London: Thames and Hudson.

Díaz-Stephens, Ana Maria. 1993. *Oxcart Catholicism on Fifth Avenue: The Impact of the Puerto Rican Migration upon the Archdiocese of New York.* South Bend, IN: University of Notre Dame Press.

Díaz-Stevens, Ana María. 1994. Latinas and the church. In Jay P. Dolan and Allan Figueroa-Deck, eds., *Hispanic Catholic Culture in the United States: Issues and Concerns.* South Bend, IN: University of Notre Dame Press.

Díaz-Stevens, Ana María, and Anthony M. Stevens-Arroyo. 1997. *Recognizing the*

Latino Resurgence in U.S. Religion: The Emmaus Paradigm. Boulder, CO: Westview Press.

Dinnerstein, Leonard, and David M. Reimers. 1982. *Ethnic Americans: A History of Immigration and Assimilation.* New York: Harper & Row.

Dinsome, C. 1998 J. Gay synagogue marks 25 year journey. *New York Blade,* January 30, 1.

Dizard, J. 1970. Black identity, social class and black power. *Psychiatry* 33: 195–202.

Dolan, Jay P. 1975. *The Immigrant Church: New York's Irish and German Catholics, 1815–1865.* Baltimore: Johns Hopkins University Press.

Dolan, Jay P., and Gilberto M. Hinojosa. 1994. *Mexican Americans and the Catholic Church, 1900–1965.* South Bend, IN: University of Notre Dame Press.

Douglas, Mary. 1966. *Purity and Danger.* Harmondsworth, England: Penguin Books.

Doyle, Ruth Narita, and Thomas M. McDonald. 1996. Catholic response to changing institutions. Paper presented to the annual meeting of the American Association of Religion, Philadelphia, August 8.

Duany, Jorge. 1985. Ethnicity in the Spanish Caribbean: Notes on the consolidation of Creole entity in Cuba and Puerto Rico, 1762–1868. In Stephen Glazier, ed., *Caribbean Ethnicity Revisited: A Special Issue of Ethnic Groups. International Periodical of Ethnic Studies.* New York: Gordon and Breach Science Publishers.

Dubrovskaya, Nina. 1995. Yehat—ne Yehat. *Novoye russkoye slovo* (Russian daily), July 25, 9.

Dugger, Celia W. 1998. Among young of immigrants, outlook rises. *New York Times,* March 21, A1, A11.

Duin, Julia. 1992. "New" Orthodox attract evangelicals. *Christianity Today,* May 18, 50–51.

Dunstan, John. 1993. Soviet schools, atheism and religion. In S. P. Ramet, ed., *Religious Policy in the Soviet Union.* Cambridge: Cambridge University Press.

Ebaugh, Helen Rose Fuchs. 1993. *Women in the Vanishing Cloister: Organizational Decline in Catholic Religious Orders in the United States.* New Brunswick, NJ: Rutgers University Press.

Ebaugh, Helen Rose Fuchs. 1999. What's new about immigrant religion? Talk to Research on Immigrant Religion Project. New School University, New York, November 17.

Edwards, Jonathan. 1984. *Religious Affections.* Portland, OR: Multnomah Press.

Elizondo, Virgil, and Norbert Greinacher, eds. 1980. *Women in a Man's Church.* New York: Seabury Press.

Ellis, John Tracy. 1956. *Documents of American Catholic History.* Milwaukee: Bruce.

Ellison, C. G. 1990. Family ties, friendships, and subjective well-being among black Americans. *Journal of Marriage and the Family* 52: 298–310.

Ellison, C. G. 1993. Religious involvement and self-perception among black Americans. *Social Forces* 71: 1027–1055.

Ellison, C. G., and D. A. Gay. 1990. Region, religious commitment, and life satisfaction among black Americans. *Sociological Quarterly* 30: 123–147.

Ellison, C. G., and D. E. Sherkat. 1990. Patterns of religious mobility among black Americans. *Sociological Quarterly* 31: 551–568.

Ellison, C. G., and R. J. Taylor. 1996. Turning to prayer: Social and situational antecedents of religious coping among African-Americans. *Review of Religious Research* 38: 111–131.

Embry, Jessie L. 1992. Ethnic groups and the LDS Church. *Dialogue: A Journal of Mormon Thought* 25, 4: 81–98.

Embry, Jessie L. 1994. *Black Saints in a White Church: Contemporary African American Mormons*. Salt Lake City: Signature Books.

Embry, Jessie L. 1997. *"In His Own Language": Mormon Spanish Speaking Congregations in the United States*. Provo, UT: Charles Redd Center for Western Studies, Brigham Young University.

Emerging Trends. 1987a. Princeton, NJ: Princeton University Religion Research Center, February.

Emerging Trends. 1987b. Princeton, NJ: Princeton University Religion Research Center, May.

Emerging Trends.1988. Princeton, NJ: Princeton University Religion Research Center, January.

Emerging Trends. 1997. Princeton, NJ: Princeton University Religion Research Center, November.

Eng, E., J. Hatch, and A. Callan. 1985. Institutionalizing social support through the church and into the community. *Health Education Quarterly* 12: 81–92.

England, Eugene. 1986. Why the church is as true as the Gospel. *Sunstone* 10, 10: 30–36.

Essien-Udom, E. U. 1963. *Black Nationalism: A Search for an Identity in America*. Chicago: University of Chicago Press.

Fareed, Nu'man. 1992. *The Muslim Population in the U.S.* New York: American Muslim Council.

Farley, Margaret A. 1977. New patterns of relationship: Beginnings of a moral revolution. In W. Burkhardt, ed., *Woman: New Dimensions*. New York: Paulist Press.

Farrell, Susan A. 1991. "It's our church, too!" Women's position in the Catholic Church today. In Judith Lorber and Susan A. Farrell, eds., *The Social Construction of Gender*. Newbury Park, CA: Sage.

Farrell, Susan A. 1992. Sexuality, gender, and ethics: The social construction of feminist ethics in the Roman Catholic Church. Ph.D. diss., City University of New York.

Farrell, Susan A. 1996. Women-church and egalitarianism: Revisioning "In Christ there are no more distinctions between male and female." In Georgie Ann Weatherby and Susan A. Farrell, eds., *The Power of Gender in Religion*. New York: McGraw-Hill.

Fauset, Arthur Huff. 1944. *Black Gods of the Metropolis. Negro Religious Cults in the Urban North*. Philadelphia: University of Pennsylvania Press.

Faver, Catherine A. 1991. Creative apostle of reconciliation: The spirituality and social philosophy of Emily Greene Balch. *Women's Studies* 18: 335–351.

Feher, Shoshanah. 1998. From the rivers of Babylon to the valleys of Los Angeles: The exodus and adaptation of Iranian Jews. In R. Stephen Warner and Judith G. Wittner, eds., *Gatherings in Diaspora: Religious Communities and the New Immigration*. Philadelphia: Temple University Press.

Feldbran, S. 1980. *From Sarah to Sarah*. Brooklyn: Eishes Chayil Books.

Feldstein, Donald. 1995/1996. The Jewish federations: The first hundred years. *Journal of Jewish Communal Service* 72 (Fall/Winter): 5.

Femminella, Francis, X. 1961. The impact of Italian migration and American Catholicism. *American Catholic Sociological Review* 12: 233–241.

Figueroa-Deck, Allan. 1994. The challenge of evangelical/Pentecostal Christianity to Hispanic Catholicism. In J. P. Dolan and A. Figueroa–Deck, eds., *Hispanic Catholic Culture in the U.S.* South Bend, IN: University of Notre Dame Press.

Fiorenza, Elisabeth Schüssler. 1983. *In Memory of Her: A Feminist Theological Reconstruction of Christian Origins*. New York: Crossroad.

Fiorenza, Elisabeth Schüssler. 1992. *But She Said: Feminist Practices of Biblical Interpretation*. Boston: Beacon Press.

Fiorenza, Elisabeth Schüssler. 1993. *Discipleship of Equal: A Critical Feminist Ekklesia-logy of Liberation*. New York: Crossroad.

Fischer, Claude S. 1982. *To Dwell among Friends. Personal Networks in Town and City*. Chicago: University of Chicago Press.

Fitzgerald, Thomas. 1995. *The Orthodox Church*. Westport, CT: Greenwood Press.

Fitzpatrick, Joseph P. 1987. *One Church Many Cultures: The Challenge of Diversity*. Kansas City, MO: Sheed & Ward.

Fitzpatrick, Joseph P., and Douglas T. Gurak. 1975. *Hispanic Intermarriage in New York City*. New York: Hispanic Research Center, Fordham University.

Flake, Floyd, and Donna Marie Williams. 1999. *The Way of the Bootstrapper*. San Francisco: HarperSanFrancisco.

Flynn, Kevin. 1999. Two polar views of police and race at U.S. hearing. *New York Times*, May 27, B1.

Foley, Nadine. 1976. Who are these women? In Anne Marie Gardiner, ed., *Women and the Catholic Priesthood: An Expanded Vision—Proceedings of the Detroit Ordination Conference*. New York: Paulist Press.

Fontañez, Luis. 1980. The theology of social justice. In Antonio M. Stevens-Arroyo, ed., *Prophets Denied Honor: An Anthology on the Hispanic Church in the U.S.* New York: Orbis Books.

Fordham, Signithia. 1988. Racelessness as a factor in black students' school success: Pragmatic strategy or Pyrrhic victory? *Harvard Educational Review* 58 (February): 54–84.

Foreman, Jonathan. 1997. Bombay on the Hudson. *City* 7 (Summer): 3.

Fortune, Marie. 1983. *Sexual Violence, the Unmentionable Sin: An Ethical and Pastoral Perspective.* New York: Pilgrim Press.

Frazier, E. Franklin. 1974. *The Negro Church in America.* New York: Schocken Books.

Frazier, Thomas R. 1967. An analysis of social science writing on American Negro religion. Ph.D. diss., Columbia University.

Freedman, R., P. K. Whelpton, and Arthur A. Campbell. 1959. *Family Planning, Sterility and Population Growth.* New York: McGraw-Hill.

Freedman, Samuel. 1996. Crossing the border. *CommonQuest* 1 (Spring): 12–21.

Freire, Paulo. 1970. *The Pedagogy of the Oppressed.* New York: Herder and Herder.

Friedman, Anita. 1995. The great welfare debate of 1995: Ten top changes in Jewish family life and their social policy implications. *Journal of Jewish Communal Service* 71 (Summer): 298.

Fromm, Erich, D. T. Suzuki, and R. Day Martino. 1960. *Zen-Buddhism and Psychoanalysis.* New York: Harper & Row.

Fukuyama, Francis. 1995. *Trust.* New York: Free Press.

Gaines, Kevin. 1996. *Uplifting the Race: Black Leadership, Politics, and Culture in the Twentieth Century.* Chapel Hill: University of North Carolina Press.

Gallup, George Jr., and Jim Castelli. 1989. *The People's Religion: American Faith in the 90's.* New York: Macmillan.

Galperin, Misha. 1996. Redeeming the captive. Twenty-five years of successful resettlement and acculturation of new Americans. *Journal of Jewish Communal Service* 72 (Summer): 229.

Gambera, Giacomo. 1994. *A Migrant Missionary Story: The Autobiography of Giacomo Gambera.* New York: Center for Migration Studies.

Gamm, Gerald. 1999. *Urban Exodus. Why the Jews Left Boston and the Catholics Stayed.* Cambridge, MA: Harvard University Press.

Gans, Herbert J. 1994. Symbolic ethnicity and symbolic religiosity: Towards a comparison of ethnic and religious acculturation. *Ethnic and Racial Studies* 17 (October): 577–592.

Garfinkel, Harold. 1956. Conditions of successful degradation ceremonies. *American Journal of Sociology* 61: 420–424.

Gaustad, Edwin S. 1976. *Historical Atlas of Religion in America.* New York: Harper & Row.

Geertz, Clifford. 1968. *Islam Observed: Religious Development in Morocco and Indonesia* Chicago: University of Chicago Press.

Gellner, Ernest. 1994. *Conditions and Liberty: Civil Society and Its Rituals.* London: Hamish Hamilton.

General Conference of Seventh-Day Adventists. 1961. *98th Annual Statistical Report—1960.* Takoma Park, MD: U.S. Office of Archives and Statistics.

General Conference of Seventh-Day Adventists. 1996. *133rd Annual Statistical Report—1995.* Silver Spring, MD: U.S. Office of Archives and Statistics.

Genovese, Eugene. 1975. *Roll, Jordan Roll: The World the Slaves Made.* New York: Pantheon Books.

Gibson, James L. 1994. Understanding of anti-Semitism in Russia: An analysis of the politics of anti-Jewish attitudes. *Slavic Review* 53 (Fall): 796–797.

Gibson, James L., and Raymond M. Duch. 1992. Anti-Semitic attitudes of the mass public: Estimates and explanations based on a survey of the Moscow Oblast. *Public Opinion Quarterly* 56: 1–28.

Giddens, Anthony. 1990. *The Consequences of Modernity.* Cambridge, MA: Polity Press.

Giddens, Anthony. 1991. *Modernity and Self-Identity. Self and Society in the Late Modern Age.* Stanford, CA: Stanford University Press.

Gilbreath, Edward. 1999. Redeeming fire. *Christianity Today*, December 6, 38–42.

Gilkes, C. T. 1980. The black church as a therapeutic community: Suggested areas for research into the black religious experience. *Journal of Interdenominational Theological Center* 8: 29–44.

Gillette, Howard Jr., and Alan M. Kraut. 1986. The evolution of Washington's Italian-American community, 1890–World War II. *Journal of American Ethnic History*, Fall, xvi, 1–27.

Gilmore, Glenda Elizabeth. 1993. *Gender and Jim Crow: Women and the Politics of White Supremacy in North Carolina, 1896–1920.* Cambridge, MA: Harvard University Press.

Gilroy, Paul. 1993. *The Black Atlantic: Modernity and Double Consciousness.* Cambridge, MA: Harvard University Press.

Glasgow, Douglas G. 1981. *The Black Underclass.* New York: Vintage Books.

Glastris, Paul. 1996. A mixed blessing for the new Russia. *U.S. News & World Report*, June 24, 47.

Glazer, Nathan. 1957. *American Judaism.* Chicago: University of Chicago Press.

Glazer, Nathan. 1969. A new look at the melting pot. *The Public Interest*, special issue: *Focus on New York* 16 (Summer): 181.

Glazer, Nathan, and Daniel P. Moynihan. 1963. *Beyond the Melting Pot: The Negroes, Puerto Ricans, Jews, Italians and Irish of New York City.* Cambridge, MA: MIT Press.

Gleason, Philip. 1987. *Keeping the Faith: American Catholicism Past and Present.* South Bend, IN: University of Notre Dame Press.

Glenmary Research Center. 1982. *Churches and Church Membership in the United States 1980: An Enumeration by Region, State and County Based on Data Reported by 111 Church Bodies.* Atlanta: Glenmary Research Center.

Glenmary Research Center. 1992. *Churches and Church Membership in the United*

States 1990: An Enumeration by Region, State and County Based on Data Reported by 133 Church Groupings. Atlanta: Glenmary Research Center.

Glock, Charles Y. 1959. The religious revival in America. In Jane C. Zahn, ed., *Religion and the Face of America.* Berkeley and Los Angeles: University of California Press.

Gluck, R., ed. 1993. *Homosexuality and Judaism: A Reconstructionist Workshop Series.* Wynote, PA: Reconstructionist Press.

Goffman, Erving. 1963. *Stigma: Notes on the Management of Spoiled Identity.* New York: Simon & Schuster.

Gold, Steven J. 1994. Soviet Jews in the United States. In *American Jewish Year Book 1994.* New York: American Jewish Committee.

Goldman, Peter. 1979. *The Death and Life of Malcolm X.* Urbana-Champaign: University of Illinois Press.

Gonzalez, Robert, and Michael LaVelle. 1988. *The Hispanic Catholic in the U.S.* New York: Northeastern Pastoral Center.

Gonzalez-Whippler, Migene. 1983. Pancho Mora: Babalawo supreme and oracle of Orunla. *Latin New York* 6 (September): 27–28.

González y Pérez, Belén. 1991. A reading of Orlando E. Costas on the theology of contextual evangelization: A Galilean perspective. M.A.R. thesis, Lutheran Theological Seminary at Gettysburg.

Good, Dorothy. 1955. Questions on religion in the United States Census. *Population Index* 25: 3–16.

Gordon, David. 1974. The Jesus people: Identity synthesis. *Urban Life and Culture* 3, 2: 159–178.

Greek Orthodox Archdiocese of North and South America. 1996. *Yearbook.* New York: Greek Orthodox Archdiocese of North and South America.

Greeley, Andrew M. 1961. The impact of Italian migration and American Catholicism. *American Catholic Sociological Review* 22: 320–345.

Greeley, Andrew. 1974. *Ethnicity in the United States.* New York: Wiley.

Greeley, Andrew. 1988. Defection among Hispanics. *America,* July 30, 61–62.

Greeley, Andrew. 1997. Defection among Hispanics. *America,* September 27, 12–13.

Gregory, Henry C. 1990. Incarceration and rehabilitation: A challenge to the African American church. In Gayraud Wilmore, ed., *Black Men in Prison: The Response of the African American Church.* Atlanta: ITC Press.

Gregory, Stephen. 1986. Santeria in New York City: A study in cultural resistance. Ph.D. diss., New School for Social Research.

Griffith, E. H., J. L. Young, and D. L. Smith. 1984. An analysis of the therapeutic elements in a black church service. *Hospital and Community Psychiatry* 35: 464–469.

Grossman, Susan, and Rivka Haut. 1992. *Daughters of the King: Women and the Synagogue.* Philadelphia: Jewish Publication Society.

Gudkov, Lev, and Aleksei Levinson. 1994. Attitudes toward Jews. *Sociological Research*, March/April, 64.

Guroian, Viguen. 1995. Dancing alone: Out of step with Orthodoxy. *Christian Century*, June 7–14, 608–610.

Gutierrez, Gustavo. 1973. *A Theology of Liberation: History, Politics and Salvation.* Trans. and ed. Sister Caridad Inda and John Eagleson. New York: Orbis Books.

Haddad, Yvonne Yazbeck, and J. L. Esposito, eds. 1998. *Muslims on the Americanization Path?* Atlanta: Scholars Press.

Halfinger, David M. 1997. Immigrants continue to reshape the city. *New York Times*, December 1, B2.

Hammond, Phillip E. 1988. Religion and the persistence of identity. *Journal for the Scientific Study of Religion* 27 (March): 1–11.

Hanley, William A. 1988. *Golden Jubilee of Saint Philip Neri Church, 1898–1948.* New York: Privately published.

Hargrove, Barbara. 1979. *The Sociology of Religion: Classical and Contemporary Approaches.* 2d ed. Arlington Heights, IL: Harlan Davidson.

Harris, H. R. 1997. Growing in glory. *Emerge*, April, 49–53.

Harris, James H. 1987. *Black Ministers and Laity in the Urban Church: An Analysis of Political and Social Expectations.* New York: University Press of America.

Harrison, Beverly. 1983. *Our Right to Choose: Toward a New Ethic of Abortion.* Boston: Beacon Press.

Harrison, Beverly. 1985. *Making the Connections: Essays in Feminist Social Ethics.* Boston: Beacon Press.

Harrison, Faye. 1991. Women in Jamaica's urban informal economy: Insights from a Kingston slum. In Chandra Mohanty, Ann Russo, and Lourdes Torres, eds., *Third World Women and the Politics of Feminism.* Bloomington: Indiana University Press.

Harrison, Michael. 1974. Preparation for life in the spirit: The process of initial commitment to a religious movement. *Urban Life and Culture* 2: 387–414.

Haslip-Viera, Gabriel, and Sherrie L. Baver, eds. 1996. *Latinos in New York: Communities in Transition.* South Bend, IN: University of Notre Dame Press.

Hastings, James, ed. 1963. *Dictionary of the Bible.* New York: Scribner.

Hathaway, W. L., and K. I. Pargament. 1991. The religious dimensions of coping: Implications for prevention and promotion. *Prevention in Human Services* 9: 65–92.

Heaton, Tim B. 1992. Vital statistics. In Daniel H. Ludow, gen. ed., *Encyclopedia of Mormonism.* New York: Macmillan.

Hefner, Robert W. 1998. Multiple modernities: Christianity, Islam and Hinduism in a globalizing age. *Annual Review of Anthropology* 27: 83–104.

Heilman, Samuel. 1984. *The Gate behind the Wall: A Pilgrimage to Jerusalem.* New York: Summit Books.

Heilman, Samuel. 1992. *Defenders of the Faith: Inside Ultra-Orthodox Jewry.* New York: Schocken Books.

Helmreich, William B. 1982. *The World of the Yeshiva: An Intimate Portrait of Orthodox Jewry.* New York: Free Press.

Henry, Sondra, and Emily Taitz. 1983. *Written out of History: Our Jewish Foremothers.* 2d rev. ed. Fresh Meadows, NY: Biblio Press.

Henson, Mitchell F. 1997. Mysterious unity in Christ's blood. *Adventist Today* 5 (July): 20–21.

Hepner, Randal L. 1998a. Chanting down Babylon in the belly of the beast: The Rastafari movement in metropolitan USA. In Samuel Murrell et al., eds., *Chanting down Babylon: Arastafari Reader.* Philadelphia: Temple University Press.

Hepner, Randal L. 1998b. The house that Rasta built: Church-building and fundamentalism among New York Rastafarians. In R. Stephen Warner and Judith G. Wittner, eds., *Gatherings in Diaspora: Religious Communities and the New Immigration.* Philadelphia: Temple University Press.

Hepner, Randal L. 1998c. Movement of Jah people—Race, class, and religion among the Rastafari of Jamaica and New York. Ph.D. diss., New School for Social Research.

Herberg, Will. 1955. *Protestant, Catholic, Jew: An Essay in American Religious Sociology.* Garden City, NY: Doubleday.

Hernandez, Edwin I. 1995. "The Browning of American Adventism." *Spectrum* 25 (December): 29–50.

Herskovits, Melville. 1941. *The Myth of the Negro Past.* Boston: Beacon Press.

Heyward, Carter. 1984. *Our Passion for Justice: Images of Power, Sexuality, and Liberation.* New York: Pilgrim Press.

Hill, Kent R. 1989. *The Puzzle of the Soviet Church.* Portland, OR: Multnomah Press.

Hirschman, Charles, Josh De Wind, and Phillip Kasinitz, eds. 1999. *The Handbook of International Migration: The American* Experience. New York: Russell Sage Foundation.

Hispanic Research Center. 1995. Hispanic voting patterns. New York: Fordham University Press.

Holland, Clifton L. 1993. Hispanic Protestant congregations in USA by denominational families. IDEA/Church Growth Studies Program, October 12.

Homiak, John. 1985. The "ancient of days"—Seated black eldership, oral tradition, and ritual in Rastafari culture. Ph.D. diss., Brandeis University.

hooks, bell. 1984. *Feminist Theory: From Margin to Center.* Boston: South End Press.

Hopko, Thomas. 1986. Editorial in *The Orthodox Church*, February.

Horne, Gerald. 1993. Myth and the making of Malcolm X. *American Historical Review* 98 (April): 2.

Howard-Pitney, David. 1990. *The Afro-American Jeremiad: Appeals for Social Justice in America*. Philadelphia: Temple University Press.

Howe, Irving. 1976. *World of Our Fathers*. New York: Simon & Schuster.

Hunt, Carl M. 1979. *Oyotunji Village. The Yoruba Movement in America*. Washington, DC: University Press of America.

Hunt, Mary E. 1991. *Fierce Tenderness: A Feminist Theory of Friendship*. New York: Crossroad.

Hurh, Won Woo, and Kwang Chung Kim. 1990. Religious participation of Korean immigrants in the U.S. *Journal for the Scientific Study of Religion* 99 (March): 1180–1211.

International Center for Migration, Ethnicity and Citizenship (ICMEC). 1999. *Religion and Immigrant Incorporation in New York*. New York: New School University. (A typescript).

Irvin, Dale T. 1994. *Hearing Many Voices: Dialogue and Diversity in the Ecumenical Movement*. Lanham, MD: University Press of America.

Isasi-Díaz, Ada María. 1993. *En la luchai/In the Struggle: A Hispanic Women's Liberation Theology*. Minneapolis: Augsburg Fortress Press.

Jackson, James S. 1991. Methodological approach. In James S. Jackson, ed., *Life in Black America*. Newbury Park, CA: Sage.

Jackson, James S., Linda M. Chatters, and Robert Joseph Taylor, eds. 1993. *Aging in Black America*. Newbury Park, CA: Sage.

Jacobs, Jane. 1961. *Death and Life of Great American Cities*. New York: Random House.

Jacobson, Simon, ed. 1995. *Toward a Meaningful Life: The Wisdom of the Rebbe (Menachem Mendel Schneerson)*. New York: Morrow.

Jacquet, Constant H. Jr. 1990. *Yearbook of American and Canadian Churches*. Nashville: Abingdon Press.

Jagger, Alison M. 1989. Feminist ethics: Some issues for the nineties. *Journal of Social Philosophy* 20: 91–108.

James, Edward. 1970. Introduction to *Shango de Ima. A Yoruba Mystery Play*, by Pepe Carril. Engl. adaptation with a preface by Susan Sherman and introduction by Jerome Rothenberg and Edward James. New York: Doubleday.

Jensen, Richard L. 1987. Mother tongue: Use of non-English languages in the Church of Jesus Christ of Latter-Day Saints in the United States, 1850–1983. In Davis Bitton and Maureen Ursenbach Beecher, eds., *New Views of Mormon History: A Collection of Essays in Honor of Leonard J. Arrington*. Salt Lake City: University of Utah Press.

Johnstone, Ronald L. 1988. *Religion in Society: A Sociology of Religion*. 3d ed. Englewood Cliffs, NJ: Prentice-Hall.

Jones, Linda [pseudonym]. 1976. I don't vote. *New York Times*, June 14, A-35.

Jones, William R. 1973. Is God a white racist? New York: Doubleday.

Joselit, Jenna W. 1990. *New York's Jewish Jews: The Orthodox Community in the In-terwar Years*. Bloomington: Indiana University Press.

Kadushin, Charles. 1966. The friends and supporters of psychotherapy: On social circles in urban life. *American Sociological Review* 31 (December): 786–802.

Kang, J. G. 1995. *Eastern Tao and Western Psychoanalysis. Psychotherapy East and West*. Seoul: Korean Academy of Psychotherapists.

Kantowicz, Edward R. 1983. *Corporation Sole: Cardinal Munderlein and Chicago Catholicism*. South Bend, IN: University of Notre Dame Press.

Kaplan, R. Aryeh. 1984. *Sabbath Day of Eternity*. New York: Shad.

Kaploun, Uri, ed. 1987. *Lessons in Tanya: The Tanya of R. Shneur Zalman of Liadi*. Trans. Levy Wineberg. New York: Kehot Publication Society.

Kaploun, Uri, ed. 1994. *A Partner in the Dynamic of Creation: Womanhood in the Teachings of the Lubavitchter Rebbe, Rabbi Menachem M. Schneerson*. New York: Sichos in English.

Karpathakis, Anna. 1999. Home society politics and immigrant political incorpo-ration: The case of Greek immigrants in New York City. *International Migra-tion Review* 33, 125: 55–78.

Keller, Timothy. 1988. Puritan resources for biblical counseling. *Journal of Pas-toral Practice* 9: 3.

Keller, Timothy. 1992. An evangelical mission in a secular city. In Lyle E. Schaller, ed., *Center City Churches. The New Urban Frontier*. Nashville: Abingdon Press.

Kelley, Robin D. G. 1994. *Race Rebels: Culture, Politics, and the Black Working Class*. New York: Free Press.

Kennelly, Karen, ed. 1989. *American Catholic Women*. New York: Macmillan.

Keysar, Ariela, and Barry Kosmin. 1995. The impact of religious identification on differences in educational attainment among American women in 1990. *Jour-nal for the Scientific Study of Religion* 34, 1: 48–62.

Kilker, Ernest. 1999. Crossing the color line into the next millennium: The multi-racial debate. Paper presented to Columbia University Seminar on Contents and Methods in the Social Sciences, New York, October 12.

Kim, Kwang Chung, and Shin Kim. 1996. Ethnic meanings of Korean immigrant churches. Paper presented to the sixth North Park College Korean Sympo-sium, Chicago, October 12.

Kimmelman, R. 1994. Homosexuality and family centered Judaism. *Tikkun* 9, 4: 53–57.

Kirkpatrick, Melanie. 1993. Jesus in New York: A church yuppies can have faith in. *Wall Street Journal*, July 8, 1.

Kitzinger, Shelia. 1966. The Rastafarian brethren of Jamaica. *Comparative Studies in Society and History* 9 (October): 423–451.

Kitzinger, Shelia. 1969. Protest and mysticism: The Rastafari cult in Jamaica. *Journal for the Scientific Study of Religion* 8: 112–134.

Kivisto, Peter A. 1993. Religion and the new immigrants. In William H. Swatos Jr., ed., *A Future for Religion? New Paradigms for Social Analysis.* Newbury Park, CA: Sage.

Klein, Joe. 1999. In God they trust. *New Yorker,* July 5, 48–66.

Kliger, Samuel. 1996. What Russian immigrants in United States feared in Russia. Paper presented at the annual meeting of the American Association for Advancement of Slavic Studies, Boston, November 14–17.

Kliger, Samuel. 1999. The future belongs to me: Russian students and their religious views. In Vladimir Shlapentokh and Christopher Vanderpool, eds., *The New Elite in Post-Communist World.* College Station: Texas A&M University Press.

Kliger, Samuel, and Tony Carnes. 1994. Religious and moral values in Russia: Surveys from 1990–1994. Paper presented at the annual meeting of the American Association for the Sociology of Religion, Los Angeles, August 4.

Kliger, Samuel, and Paul de Vries. 1993. The Ten Commandments in Soviet people's consciousness. In S. P. Ramet, ed., *Religious Policy in the Soviet Union.* Cambridge: Cambridge University Press.

Koenig, H. G. 1992. Religion and mental health in later life. In J. F. Schumacher, ed., *Religion and Mental Health.* New York: Oxford University Press.

Kolbenschlag, Madonna, ed. 1987. *Women in the Church I.* Washington, DC: Pastoral Press.

Konstantelos, Demetrios J. 1982. *Understanding the Greek Orthodox Church: Its Faith, History and Practice.* New York: Seabury Press.

Kosmin, Barry A. 1990a. The class of 1979: The "acculturation" of Jewish immigrants from the Soviet Union. New York: North American Jewish Data Bank, CUNY Graduate School and University Center.

Kosmin, Barry A. 1990b. Research Report: The National Survey of Religious Identification, 1980–1990. New York: CUNY Graduate School and University Center.

Kosmin, Barry A., and Ariela Keysar. 1992. *Party Political Preferences of U.S. Hispanics: The Varying Impact of Religion, Social Class and Demographic Factors.* New York: Berman Institute at the Graduate School of the City University of New York.

Kosmin, Barry A., and Seymour Lachman 1991. *Research Report—The National Survey of Religious Identification.* New York: City University of New York Press.

Kosmin, Barry A., and Seymour Lachman. 1993. *One Nation under God: Religion in Contemporary American Society.* New York: Harmony Books.

Krause, N. 1992. Stress, religiosity, and psychological well-being among older blacks. *Journal of Aging and Health* 4: 412–439.

Kuralt, Charles. 1996. *Charles Kuralt's America.* New York: Putnam.

Kurien, Prema. 1998. Becoming American by becoming Hindu: Indian Americans take their place in the multicultural table. In R. Stephen Warner and Judith G. Wittner, eds., *Gatherings in Diaspora: Religious Communities and the New Immigration.* Philadelphia: Temple University Press.

Kurien, Prema. 1999. Gendered ethnicity: Creating a Hindu Indian identity in the U.S. *American Behavioral Scientist* 42 (January): 10–29.

La Capra, Dominick. 1991. *The Bounds of Race: Perspectives on Hegemony and Resistance.* Ithaca, NY: Cornell University Press.

La Guida del Clero. Italiano di New York. 1915. *Il Carroccio* II.

La Gumina, Salvatore, J. 1988. *From Steerage to Suburbs: Long Island Italians.* New York: Center for Migration Studies.

Lake, Randall A. 1986. The metaethical framework of anti-abortion rhetoric. *Signs* 11: 478–499.

Lamm, Norman. 1974. Judaism and the modern attitude toward homosexuality. *Encyclopedia Judaica Year Book.* Jerusalem: Keter.

Lane, Robert E., 1959. *Political Life.* Glencoe, IL: Free Press.

Lawrence, Beverly Hall. 1996. *Reviving the Spirit.* New York: Grove Press.

Lawson, Ronald. 1996a. Broadening the boundaries of church-sect theory: Insights from the evolution of the mission churches and international structure of Seventh-Day Adventism. Paper presented to the annual meeting of the American Sociological Association, New York City, August.

Lawson, Ronald. 1996b. Church and state at home and abroad: The evolution of Seventh-Day Adventist relations with governments. *Journal of the American Academy of Religion* 64, 2: 279–311.

Lawson, Ronald. 1996c. The patterns, sources, and implications of rapid church growth within international Seventh-Day Adventism: Applying and testing Stark's revised general model. Paper presented to the annual meeting of the Society for the Scientific Study of Religion, Nashville, November.

Lawson, Ronald. 1998. From American church to immigrant church: The changing face of Seventh-Day Adventism in metropolitan New York. *Sociology of Religion* 59: 329–341.

Lawson, Ronald, and Maren Lockwood Carden. 1983. Ghettoization and the erosion of a distinct way of life: The Seventh-Day Adventist experience. Paper presented to the annual meeting of the Society for the Scientific Study of Religion, Knoxville, TN, November.

Lee, Helen. 1996. Silent exodus. *Christianity Today*, August 12, 51–52.

Lehmann, Hartmut, and Guenther Roth, eds. 1995. *Weber's Protestant Ethic.* Cambridge: Cambridge University Press.

Lemert, Charles. 1993. *Social Theory: The Multicultural and Classic Readings.* Boulder, CO: Westview Press.

Lerner, Michael. 1995. *Jewish Renewal.* New York: Harper Perennial.

Levado, Y. Family values: A response to Reuven Kimelman. *Tikkun* 9: 57–60.

Levin, J. S., L. M. Chatters, and R. J. Taylor. 1995. Religious effects on health status and life satisfaction among black Americans. *Journal of Gerontology: Social Sciences* 50B: S154–S163.

Lewine, Edward. 1998. Making new Christians. *New York Times*, January 25, 18.

Lewis, Richard. 1996. *Black Cop: The Real Deal.* Shippensburg, PA: Destiny Image.

Lieberson, Stanley, and Mary Waters. 1985. Recent social trends: Ethnic mixtures in the United States. *Sociology and Social Research* 70: 43–52.

Light, Ivan, and Cathie Lee. 1997. And just who do you think you aren't. *Society* 34 (September/October): 29–30.

Lincoln, C. Eric, and Mamiya, L. H. 1990. *The Black Church in the African American Experience.* Durham, NC: Duke University Press.

Lipset, S. M., et al. 1954. The psychology of voting. In G. Lindzey, ed., *Handbook of Social Psychology.* Cambridge, MA: Addison-Wesley.

Livezey, Lowell, ed. 2000. *Public Religion and Urban Transformation.* New York: New York University Press.

Lofland, John, and Rodney Stark. 1965. Becoming a world-saver: A theory of conversion to a deviant perspective. *American Sociological Review* 30: 862–875.

López, Adalberto, ed. 1980. *The Puerto Ricans: Their History, Culture, and Society.* Cambridge, MA: Schenkman.

Lucas, James W., and Warner P. Woodworth. 1996. *Working toward Zion: Principles of the United Order for the Modern World.* Salt Lake City: Aspen Books.

Lyman, Stanford M. 1972. *The Black American in Sociological Thought.* New York: Capricorn Books.

Lyman, Stanford M. 1992. *Militarism, Imperialism, and Racial Accommodation.* Fayetteville: University of Arkansas Press.

Lyman, Stanford M. 1994. *Color, Culture, Civilization.* Urbana-Champaign: University of Illinois Press.

Lyman, Stanford M., and Marvin Scott.1970. *A Sociology of the Absurd.* Pacific Palisades, CA: Goodyear.

Lynch, Bernard J. 1888. The Italians in New York. *The Catholic World* 47: 67–73.

MacFarquhar, Neil. 1999. Police get good ratings from most, but not all, New Yorkers. *New York Times,* June 5, B3.

Maggid, A. 1989. Joining together: Building a worldwide movement. In C. Balka and A. Rose, eds., *Twice Blessed: On Being Lesbian, Gay and Jewish.* Boston: Beacon Press.

Maines, Andrew Michael. 1987. *Southern Civil Religions in Conflict: Black and White Baptists and Civil Rights.* Athens: University of Georgia Press.

Malcolm X. 1987. *The Autobiography of Malcolm X.* New York: Ballantine Books.

Malcolm X. 1992. *February 1965: The Final Speeches.* Ed. Steve Clark. New York: Pathfinder Press.

Malony, H. Newton, and Samuel Southard. 1992. *Handbook of Religious Conversion.* Birmingham, AL: Religious Education Press.

Mamiya, Lawrence. 1995. A historical overview of African American Sunni Muslim movements, 1929 to 1975. Paper presented to the Islam in America Conference, DePaul University, Chicago, October 12.

Manes, Andrew Michael. 1987. *Southern Civil Religions in Conflict: Black and White Baptists and Civil Rights*. Athens: University of Georgia Press.

Marable, Manning. 1983. *How Capitalism Underdeveloped Black America*. Boston: South End Press.

Marable, Manning. 1991. *Race, Reform and Rebellion: The Second Reconstruction in Black American, 1945–1990*. Jackson: University Press of Mississippi.

Marín, Gerardo, and Barbara VanOss Marín. 1991. *Research with Hispanic Populations*. Applied Social Research Methods Series. Vol. 23. Newbury Park, CA: Sage.

Mark, Jonathan. 1997. Woman takes giant step in Orthodox community. *Jewish Week*, December 19, 1, 22.

Markowitz, Fran. 1993. *A Community in Spite of Itself*. Washington, DC: Smithsonian Institution Press.

Marks, Morton. 1974. Uncovering ritual structures in Afro-American music. In Irving I. Zaretsky and Mark P. Leone, eds., *Religious Movements in Contemporary America*. Princeton, NJ: Princeton University Press.

Marsden, George. 1994. *The Soul of the American University*. New York: Oxford University Press.

Marsh, Clifton E. 1984. *From Black Muslims to Muslims: The Transition from Separation to Islam. 1930–1980*. Metuchen, NJ: Scarecrow Press.

Martin, David. 1990. *Tongues of Fire: The Explosion of Protestantism in Latin America*. Oxford: Blackwell.

Martin, Julia. 1998. Cursillo marks 40th anniversary. *Catholic New York*, April 30, 23.

Martin, William. 1993. *Billy Graham*. New York: Free Press.

Marx, Gary. 1969. *Protest and Prejudice*. Rev. ed. New York: Harper & Row.

Mason, John, and Gary Edwards. 1985. *Black Gods—Orisha Studies in the New World*. Brooklyn: Yoruba Theological Archministry.

Matt, H. 1983. Sin, crime, sickness or alternative life style: A Jewish approach to homosexuality. *Judaism* 27: 13–24.

Mays, Benjamin, and Joseph Nicholson. 1969. *The Negro's Church*. New York: Russell and Russell.

McAdoo, H. P., and V. Crawford. 1990. The black church and family support programs. *Prevention in Human Services* 9: 193–203.

McGreevy, John T. 1996. *Parish Boundaries. The Catholic Encounter with Race in the Twentieth Century Urban North*. Chicago: University of Chicago Press.

McGuire, Meredith. 1977. Testimony as a commitment mechanism in Catholic Pentecostal prayer groups. *Journal for the Scientific Study of Religion* 16, 2:165–168.

McRae, M. B., P. M. Carey, and R. Anderson-Scott. 1998. Black churches as therapeutic systems: A group process perspective. *Health Education & Behavior* 25, 6: 778–789.

Mehta, Amit. 1997. Aldous Huxley and the third generations. Paper presented at the second National Asian Indian American Conference, Rutgers University, New Brunswick, NJ, April.

Melvani, Lavina. 1995. What are over 200,000 Guyanese Hindus Doing in New York State? *Hinduism Today*, August, 10–12.

Milhaven, Annie Lally, ed. 1987. *The Inside Stories: 13 Valiant Women Challenging the Church*. Mystic, CT: Twenty-third Publications.

Miller, John. 1999. Religion and immigration in Los Angeles. Paper presented at the New Immigrant Religion Project Seminar, The New University, New York City, December 15.

Miller, Kelly. 1968. *Radicals and Conservatives and Other Essays on the Negro in America*. New York: Schocken Books.

Miranda, Faybiene. 1987. I am that I am. In Millard Faristzaddi, ed., *Itations of Jamaica and I Rastafari*. Miami: Judah Anbesa International.

Mitchel, Henry. 1970. *Black Preaching*. Philadelphia: Lippincott.

Mohanty, Chandra, Ann Russo, and Lourdes Torres, eds. 1991. *Third World Women and the Politics of Feminism*. Bloomington: Indiana University Press.

Moore, T. 1991. The African-American church: A source of empowerment, mutual help, and social change. *Prevention in the Human Services* 10: 147–167.

Moskos, Charles. 1989. *Greek Americans: Struggle and Success*. New Brunswick, NJ: Transaction Books.

Moss, Michael, Anthony Townsend, and Emanuel Tobier. 1997. Immigration is transforming NYC. New York: Taub Urban Research Center, http://urban.nyu .edu/research/immigrants.

Muhammad, Elijah. 1957. The supreme wisdom: Solution to the so-called Negroes' problem. Report of the Nation of Islam. Newport News, VA: National Newport News and Commentator.

Mullins, Mark R. 1987. The life-cycle of ethnic churches in sociological perspective. *Japanese Journal of Religious Studies* 14, 4: 321–334.

Murphy, Joseph M. 1981. Ritual systems in Cuban Santeria. Ph.D. diss., Temple University.

Murphy, Joseph M. 1994. *Working the Spirit. Ceremonies of the African Diaspora*. Boston: Beacon Press.

Murrell, N. Samuel, William D. Spencer, and Adrian Anthony McFarlane, eds. 1998. *Chanting down Babylon: A Rastafari Reader*. Philadelphia: Temple University Press.

Nakamura, Hajime. 1964. *Ways of Thinking of Eastern Peoples: India, China, Tibet, Japan*. Rev. Engl. trans. and ed. Philip P. Wiener. Honolulu: East-West Center, University of Hawai'i Press.

National Center for Health Statistics. 1995. *National Survey of Family Growth*. Washington, DC: National Center for Health Statistics, U.S. Department of Health, Education, and Welfare.

National Conference of Catholic Bishops. 1986. Economic justice for all: Pastoral letter on Catholic social teaching and the U.S. economy. Washington, DC: U.S. Catholic Conference.

National Opinion Research Center. 1990. General Social Survey, 1990. Chicago: National Opinion Research Center.

National Opinion Research Center. 1996. General Social Survey, 1996. Chicago: National Opinion Research Center.

Neidert, Lisa J., and Reynolds Farley. 1985. Assimilation in the United States: An analysis of ethnic and generation differences in status and achievement. *American Sociological Review* 50: 840–850.

Nelsen, Hart M. 1988. Unchurched black Americans: Patterns of religiosity and affiliation. *Review of Religious Research* 29 (June): 398–412.

Neshei uBnos Chabad (Lubavitch). 1979. *Return to Roots.* London: Stamford Hill.

Neuhaus, Richard John. 1984. *The Naked Public Square.* Grand Rapids, MI: Eerdmans.

Neusner, Jacob. 1987. *Death and Birth of Judaism: The Impact of Christianity, Secularism and Holocaust on Jewish Faith.* New York: Basic Books.

New York City Department of City Planning. 1999. *Report on the Newest New Yorkers.* New York: New York City Department of City Planning, October.

New York City Department of Planning. 1996. *The Newest New Yorkers, 1990–1994: An Analysis of Immigration to New York City in the Early 1990s.* New York: New York City Department of Planning.

New York Office Memorandum (NY Office). 1978. Malcolm K. Little. May 16, 1963. 21. In *Malcolm X: FBI Surveillance File.* Wilmington, DE: Scholarly Resources, reel 2.

Nimbark, Ashakant. 1997. New but old, warm but cold: A critique of Indian-American media. Paper presented at the second National Asian Indian Conference, November 10, Chicago.

Northrop, F. S. C. 1949. *The Meeting of East and West.* New York: Macmillan.

Nyabinghi Order Council of Elders. 1993. *Ancient Order of the Nyabinghi Guidelines.* Montego Bay, Jamaica: Order of the Nyabinghi.

Oaks, Dallin H. 1999. Weightier matters. *Clark Memorandum,* Spring, 3–9.

Oboler, Suzanne. 1995. *Ethnic Labels, Latino Lives.* Minneapolis: University of Minnesota Press.

O'Connor, Thomas, et al. 1996. The impact of the New York Masters in Professional Studies Program on Recidivism: An exploratory study. Prepared for Dr. Earl Moore, Division of Ministerial Services, New York Department of Correction, April 16.

O'Connor, Thomas, and Victoria Erickson. 1997. Theology and community corrections in a prison setting. *Community Corrections Report,* July/August, 67–68, 75.

O'Dea, Thomas 1957. *The Mormons.* Chicago: University of Chicago Press.

Office of Pastoral Research of the Archdiocese of New York. 1982. *Hispanics in*

New York: Religious, Cultural and Social Experiences. 2 vols. New York: Office of Pastoral Research.

Office of Planning and Program Development. 1998. *Community District Profile: Brooklyn Neighborhood Development Area (NDA) 7.* New York: New York City Department of Youth and Community Development, April.

Official Catholic Directory. 1999. New Providence, NJ: P. J. Kenedy & Sons.

Onion, Amanda. 1996. Goy story. *The New Republic,* January 8 and 15, 31.

Orsi, Robert A. 1996. *Thank You, St. Jude: Women's Devotion to the Patron Saint of Hopeless Causes.* New Haven, CT: Yale University Press.

Orsi, Robert A. 1999. *Gods of the City.* Bloomington: Indiana University Press.

Ostling, Richard N. 1993. One nation under God: Not without conflict. An unprecedented variety of faiths blooms across the land. *Time,* special issue, Fall.

Ostling, Richard N., and Joan K. Ostling. 1999. *Mormon America.* San Francisco: HarperSanFrancisco.

Owens, Joseph. 1976. *Dread: The Rastafarians of Jamaica.* Kingston: Sangster's Books.

Padilla, Felix M. 1985. *Latino Ethnic Consciousness: The Case of Mexican Americans and Puerto Ricans in Chicago.* Notre Dame, IN: University of Notre Dame Press.

Pannell, Bill. 1995. *The Coming Race Wars?* Downers Grove, IL: Intervarsity Press.

Paris, Peter J. 1985. *The Social Teaching of the Black Churches.* Philadelphia: Fortress Press.

Patrinacos, Nicon D. 1982. The role of the church in the evolving Greek American community. In Harry J. Psomiades and Alice Scourby, eds., *The Greek American Community in Transition.* New York: Pella Publishers.

Pelton, Robert D. 1980. *The Trickster in West Africa. A Study of Mythic Irony and Sacred Delight.* Berkeley and Los Angeles: University of California Press.

Penn, Mark J., and Douglas E. Schoen. 1995. A tale of four cities. The 1995 *New York* poll. *New York Magazine,* August 21, 25–31.

Pennebaker, J. W. 1990. *Opening Up: Healing Power of Confiding in Others.* New York: Morrow.

Pérez y González, María Elizabeth. 1993. *Latinas in Ministry: A Pioneering Study on Women Ministers, Educators and Students of Theology.* New York: New York City Mission Society.

Pérez y González, María Elizabeth. 1997. Latina women in a traditionally male-dominated institution—The church. *Latino Studies Journal* 8 (Fall): 19–35.

Pfohl, Stephen J. 1975. Social role analysis: The ethnomethodological critique. *Social Science Research* 59, 3: 243–265.

Pfohl, Stephen J. 1986. Criminological displacements: A sociological deconstruction. *Social Problems* 33, 6: S94–S113.

Pier, McKenzie, and Louis A DeCaro. 1999. A reformation in Brooklyn. The story of Bay Ridge Christian Center. In Robert D. Carle and Louis A. DeCaro Jr., eds., *Signs of Hope. Ministries of Community Renewal.* 2d ed. Valley Forge, PA: Judson Press.

Plaskow, J. 1994. Lesbian and gay rights; asking the right questions. *Tikkun* 9, 2: 31–32.

Playor, S. A. 1995. Afro-Cuban religion in perspective. In Anthony M. Stevens-Arroyo and Andres 1. Perez y Mena, eds., *Enigmatic Powers. Syncretism with African and Indigenous Peoples' Religions among Latinos.* New York: Bildner Center for Western Hemisphere Studies of the Graduate School and University Center of the City University of New York.

Poblete, Renato, and Thomas F. O'Dea. 1960. Anomie and the quest for community: The formation of sects among Puerto Ricans of New York. *American Catholic Sociological Review* 21, 1: 18–36.

Pope, Barbara Corrado. 1990. The origins of southern Italian Good Friday processions. In Paola A. Sensi Isolani and Anthony Julian Tamburri, eds., *Italian Americans Celebrate Life: The Arts and Popular Culture: Selected Essays from the Twenty-second Annual Conference of the American Italian Historical Association . . . 1989.* New York: American Italian Historical Association.

Portes, Alejandro. 1994. Introduction to *The New Second Generation,* special issue of *International Migration Review* 28, 4: 632–864.

Portes, Alejandro, and Ruben Rumbaut. 1996. *Immigrant America.* Berkeley and Los Angeles: University of California Press.

Posen, Sheldon I., Joseph Sciorra, and Martha Cooper. 1983. Brooklyn's dancing tower. *Natural History,* June, xcii, 30.

Poston, Larry. 1992. *Islamic Da'wah in the West: Muslim Missionary Activity and the Dynamics of Conversion to Islam.* New York: Oxford University Press.

Powilson, David. 1995. *Power Encounters—Reclaiming Spiritual Warfare.* Grand Rapids, MI: Baker Book House.

Preston, Samuel H. 1996. Children will pay. *New York Times Magazine,* September 29, 96–97.

Primeggia, Salvatore, and Joseph A. Varacalli. 1996. The sacred and profane among Italian American Catholics: The Giglio feast. *International Journal of Politics, Culture and Society* 9, 3: 424–425.

Protestant Council of the City of New York. 1952. *Protestant Directory of Metropolitan New York (1950–1952).* New York: Protestant Council of the City of New York.

Rabey, Steve. 1996. Hurting helpers. Will the Christian counseling movement live up to its promise? *Christianity Today,* August 29, 76.

Rabinowitz, H. 1983. Talmud class in a gay synagogue. *Judaism* 32, 4: 437–439.

Radzikhovsky, Leonid. 1996. Yevreiskoye schast'e (Jewish Luck). *Novoye russkoye slovo* (Russian daily), January 17, 6.

Rappaport, J., and R. Simkins. 1991. Healing and empowering through community narrative. *Prevention in Human Service* 10: 29–50.

Ravitch, Diane, et al., eds. 2000. *City Schools.* Baltimore: John Hopkins University Press.

Raymond, Janice. 1986. *A Passion for Friends.* Boston: Beacon Press.

Record, Wilson. 1951. *The Negro and the American Communist Party.* Chapel Hill: University of North Carolina Press.

Redeker, Tricia M. 1996. Fighting against ism and schism: Changing gender relations in the Rastafari movement. B.A. thesis, Barnard College.

Reed, Adolph L. Jr. 1986. *The Jesse Jackson Phenomenon.* New Haven, CT: Yale University Press.

Reese, Laura A., and R. E. Brown. 1995. The effects of religious messages on racial identity and system blame among African-Americans. *Journal of Politics* 57 (February): 24–43.

Rhee, D. S. 1990. The tao, psychoanalysis and existential thought. In G. A. Fava and H. Freyberger, eds., *Psychotherapy and Psychosomatics.* Basel: S. Karger.

Rodríguez, Clara E. 1991. *Puerto Ricans: Born in the U.S.A.* Boulder, CO: Westview Press.

Rodriguez, Orlando, et al. 1995. *Nuestra America en Nueva York: The New Immigrant Hispanic Populations in New York City.* Hispanic Research Center Report Series. New York: Fordham University Press.

Rollman, Hans. 1993. "Meet Me in St. Louis" Troeltsch and Weber in America. In Hartmut Lehmann and Guenther Roth, eds., *Weber's "Protestant Ethic."* Cambridge: Cambridge University Press.

Roof, Wade Clark. 1993. *A Generation of Seekers: The Spiritual Journeys of the Baby Boom Generation.* San Francisco: Harper & Row.

Roof, Wade Clark, and William McKinney. 1987. *American Mainline Religion: Its Changing Shape and Future.* New Brunswick, NJ: Rutgers University Press.

Rosenthal, Eric. 1975. The equivalence of United States census data for persons of Russian stock or descent with American Jews: An evaluation. *Demography* 12: 275–290.

Rossi, Vincent. 1996. Eleventh-hour laborers. *The Christian Activist,* March, 1–10.

Rowe, Maureen. 1980. The woman in Rastafari. *Caribbean Quarterly* 26, 4: 13.

Rowe, Maureen. 1998. Gender and family relations in Rastafari: A personal perspective. In Samuel Murrell et al., eds., *Chanting down Babylon: Arastafari Reader.* Philadelphia: Temple University Press.

Rubin, J. B. 1996. *Psychoanalysis and Buddhism. Towards an Integration.* New York: Plenum Press.

Ruether, Rosemary Radford. 1974. *Religion and Sexism: Images of Woman in the Jewish and Christian Traditions.* New York: Simon & Schuster.

Ruether, Rosemary Radford. 1975. *New Woman New Earth: Sexist Ideologies & Human Liberation.* New York: Seabury Press.

Ruether, Rosemary Radford. 1977. Home and work: Women's roles and the transformation of values. In W. Burkhardt, ed., *Woman: New Dimensions*. New York: Paulist Press.

Ruether, Rosemary Radford. 1992. *Gaia and God: An Ecofeminist Theology of Earth Healing*. San Francisco: HarperSanFrancisco.

Ruether, Rosemary Radford, and Rosemary Skinner Keller, eds. 1981, 1983, 1990, 1996. *Women and Religion in America*. 4 vols. New York: Harper & Row.

Ruether, Rosemary Radford, and Eleanor McLaughlin, eds. 1979. *Women of Spirit: Female Leadership in the Jewish and Christian Traditions*. New York: Simon & Schuster.

Russell, Letty M. 1993. *Church in the Round: Feminist Interpretation of the Church*. Louisville: Westminster–John Knox Press.

Sahib, Hatim. 1951. The Nation of Islam. Master's thesis, University of Chicago.

Sahlin, Monte. 1997. Information drawn from surveys of church members. Los Angeles: Office of Church Information and Research, North American Division of Seventh-Day Adventists.

Saint Joseph Church. 1977. *Saint Joseph Church Fiftieth Anniversary, 1925–1975*. New York: Park.

Saltonstall, Dave, and Richard T. Pienciak. 1998. Faces to watch in 1998: Due to go places. *New York Daily News*, January 4, City Central Section, 44.

Sánchez Korrol, Virginia. 1990. In search of unconventional women: Histories of Puerto Rican women in religious vocations before mid-century. In Ellen Carol DuBois and Vicki L. Ruíz, eds., *Unequal Sisters: A Multicultural Reader in U.S. Women's History*. New York: Routledge.

Sandoval, Moises. 1994. The organization of a Hispanic church. In J. P. Dolan and A. Figueroa-Deck, eds., *Hispanic Catholic Culture in the U.S.* South Bend, IN: University of Notre Dame Press.

Sanjek, Roger. 1998. *The Future of Us All*. Ithaca, NY: Cornell University Press.

Savishinsky, Neil. 1994a. The Baye-Faal of Senegambia: Muslim Rastas in the promised land? *Africa* 64: 211–219.

Savishinsky, Neil. 1994b. Rastafari in the promised land: The spread of a Jamaican socio-religious movement. *African Studies Review* 37: 19–50.

Savishinsky, Neil. 1994c. Transnational popular culture and the global spread of the Rastafarian movement. *New West Indian Guide* 68: 261–279.

Schaumburg, Harry W. 1992. *False Intimacy*. Colorado Springs, CO: Navpress.

Schiff, Alvin I. 1988. *Contemporary Jewish Education: Issachar American Style*. Dallas: Rossel Books.

Schoenherr, Richard A., and Lawrence A. Young. 1993. *Full Pews & Empty Altars: Demographics of the Priest Shortage in United States Catholic Dioceses*. Madison: University of Wisconsin Press.

Schwartz, B. D. 1988. The Jewish view of homosexuality. In H. Brod, ed., *A Mensch among Men: Explorations in Jewish Masculinity*. Freedom, CA: Freedom Crossing Press.

Schwarz, R. W. 1979. *Lightbearers to the Remnant.* Mountain View, CA: Pacific Press.

Schweder, R. 1991. *Thinking through Cultures.* Cambridge, MA: Harvard University Press.

Scott, Rebecca J. 1985. *Slave Emancipation in Cuba: The Transition to Free Labor, 1860–1899.* Princeton, NJ: Princeton University Press.

Seidler, John, and Katherine Meyer. 1989. *Conflict and Change in the Catholic Church.* New Brunswick, NJ: Rutgers University Press.

Seltser, Barry J., with Donald E. Miller. 1995. The Concept of Dignity. *Homeless Families: The Struggle for Dignity.* Urbana-Champaign: University of Illinois Press.

Sengupta, Somini. 1999. A snapshot of world faiths: On one Queens block, many prayers are spoken. *New York Times*, November 7, 133–37.

Sennett, Richard. 1980. *Authority.* New York: Vintage Books.

Sfekas, Stephen J., and George E. Matsoukas, eds. 1993. *Project for Orthodox Renewal.* Chicago: Orthodox Christian Laity.

Shanks, Hershel. 1996. Can Jewish life be revived in the former Soviet Union? *Moment*, February, 51.

Shapiro, Paul. 1996. Jewish identity and Protestant ethics. Paper presented at Columbia University Seminar on Contents and Methods in Social Sciences, New York, February 14.

Shapiro, Vladimir, and Valeryi Chervyakov. 1992. Results of the poll among delegates of the First Congress of the Federation of Jewish Communities and Organizations in Russia (VAAD of Russia), Nizhny Novgorod, Moscow, April.

Shapiro, Vladimir, and Valeryi Chervyakov. 1993. *What Does It Mean: "To Be a Jew?"* (Linear distribution of survey results in Moscow and St. Petersburg). Moscow: Jewish Research Center.

Sharpton, Al, and Anthony Walton. 1996. *Go and Tell Pharaoh: The Autobiography of Al Sharpton.* Garden City, NY: Doubleday.

Shin, Eui Hang, and Hyang Park. 1988. An analysis of causes of schism in ethnic churches: The case of Korean-American churches. *Sociological Analysis* 49 (Fall): 234–248.

Shipman, Andrew J. 1916. Our Italian Greek Catholics. In Conde B. Pallen, ed., *A Memorial of Andrew J. Shipman: His Life and Writings.* New York: Encyclopedia Press.

Shokeid, M. 1995. *A Gay Synagogue in New York.* New York: Columbia University Press.

Simmel, Georg. 1955. *Conflict and the Web of Group Affiliations.* Trans. Kurt Wolff and Reinhard Bendix. New York: Free Press.

Simon, Rita J., Julian Simon, and Jim Schwartz. 1982. *The Soviet Jews Adjustment to the United States.* New York: Council of Jewish Federations.

Singer, Isaac Bashevis. 1962. *Yentl the Yeshiva Boy.* New York: Farrar, Straus & Giroux.

Singer, Merrell. 1992. *African-American Religion in the Twentieth Century: Varieties of Protest and Accommodation.* Knoxville: University of Tennessee Press.

Smith, Jane I. 1999. *Islam in America.* New York: Columbia University Press.

Smith, John Talbot. 1905. *The Catholic Church in New York: A History of the New York Diocese from Its Establishment in 1808 to the Present Time.* New York: Locke and Hall.

Smith, Robert C. 1996. *We Have No Leaders. African Americans in the Post–Civil Rights Era.* Albany: State University of New York Press.

Snider, Elizabeth Soloway. 1994. Russian Jews find religion—Only it's Christianity. *Moment,* August, 37.

Snow, D. A., and R. Machalek. 1984. The sociology of conversion. *Annual Review of Sociology* 10: 167–190.

Sobo, Elisa Janine. 1993. *One Blood: The Jamaican Body.* Albany: State University of New York Press.

Sommers, Christian Hoff. 1994. *Who Stole Feminism?* New York: Simon & Schuster.

Son, Minho. 1994. Towards the successful movement of the English-speaking ministry within the Korean immigrant church. Paper presented to Katalyst, Sandy Cove, MD, March 21–24.

Souryal, Sam S. 1996. Probation as good faith. *Federal Probation* 60, 4: 5–10.

St. Anthony of Padua Church, 1967. *St. Anthony of Padua Church, New York City.* New York: Custombook.

Stanley, Alessandra. 1997. Success may be bad for Jews as old Russian bias surfaces. *New York Times,* April 15, A1.

Stark, Rodney 1984. The rise of a new world faith. *Review of Religious Research* 26: 18–27.

Stark, Rodney, and Laurence R. Iannaccone. 1993. Rational choice propositions about religious movements. *Religion and the Social Order* 3A: 241–261.

Steele, Shelby. 1991. Race-holding. In Shelby Steele, ed., *The Content of Our Character.* New York: HarperPerennial.

Steele, Shelby. 1992. Malcolm Little. *The New Republic,* December 21, 6–8.

Stevens-Arroyo, Anthony M. 1980. Puerto Rican struggles in the Catholic Church. In Clara E. Rodríguez, Virginia Sánchez-Korrol, and José Oscar Alers, eds., *The Puerto Rican Struggle: Essays on Survival in the U.S.* New York: Puerto Rican Migration Research Consortium.

Stevens-Arroyo, Anthony M. 1995. *Discovering Latino Religion.* New York: Bildner Center Books.

Stevens-Arroyo, Anthony M., and Gilbert R. Cadena. 1995. *Old Masks, New Faces: Religion and Latino Identities.* New York: Bildner Center for Western Hemisphere Studies, Graduate Center of the City University of New York.

Stevens-Arroyo, Anthony M., and Anna Maria Díaz-Stevens. 1994. *An Enduring Flame: Studies on Latino Popular Religiosity.* New York: Bildner Center for Western Hemisphere Studies, Graduate Center of the City University of New York.

Stevens-Arroyo, Anthony M., and Segundo Pantoja. 1995. *Discovering Latino Religion: A Comprehensive Social Science Bibliography*. New York: Bildner Center for Western Hemisphere Studies, Graduate Center of the City University of New York.

Stevens-Arroyo, Anthony M., and Andres I. Perez y Mena, eds. 1995. *Enigmatic Powers. Syncretism with African and Indigenous Peoples' Religions among Latinos*. Program for the Analysis of Religion among Latinos PARAL Series. Vol. 3. New York: Bildner Center for Western Hemisphere Studies of the Graduate School and University Center of the City University of New York.

Stevenson, Robert L. 1999. The challenges and contributions facing the black church in Los Angeles: The legacy of the black church. Los Angeles: Religion and Civic Culture On-Line, August, www.usc.edu/dept/LAS/religion_online/opinion/99_08_stevenson.html.

Strassfeld, Sharon, and Michael Strassfeld, eds. 1976. *The Second Jewish Catalog: Sources and Resources*. Philadelphia: Jewish Publication Society.

Strickland, Lula. 1997. Sharpton ties up vote in the NY primary. *The Black World Today*, December 14, 1. www.tbt.com\articles\usa\usa63.html.

Stuhlmueller, Carroll, ed. 1978. *Women and Priesthood: Future Directions*. Collegeville, MN: Liturgical Press.

Subervi-Velez, Federico. 1994. El papel de los medios de comunicacion colectiva en la diversidad cultural. In Daniel Mato, ed., *Teoria y politica de la construccion de identidades y diferencias en America Latina y el Caribe*. Caracas: Editorial nueva sociedad.

Sugrue, Thomas J. 1996. *The Origins of the Urban Crisis: Race and Inequality in Postwar Detroit*. Princeton, NJ: Princeton University Press.

Sullivan, Harry S. 1940. *Collected Works*. New York: Norton.

Sumedho, Ajahn. 1960. Being patient without inability to forgive. *The Middle Way: A Journal of Buddhist Society* 71: 83–88.

Swanstrom, Edward E. 1962. Introduction to *The Church's Magna Charta for Migrants*, by Giulivo Tessarolo. Staten Island: St. Charles Seminary.

Sykes, Gresham M., and David Matza. 1957. Techniques of neutralization. *American Sociological Review* 5 (December): 667 ff.

Tabory, Ephraim. 1992. Russian migration to Israel. *Journal of Jewish Communal Service* 68 (Spring): 273.

Tabory, Ephraim. 1995. The future of the Jewish community in the republics of the former Soviet Union. *Journal of Jewish Communal Service* 71 (Winter/Spring): 188–189.

Tafari-Ama, Imani M. 1994. Rastawoman as rebel: Case studies in Jamaica. In Samuel Murrell et al., eds., *Chanting down Babylon: Arastafari Reader*. Philadelphia: Temple University Press.

Tafari-Ama, Imani M. 1998. Rasta woman as rebel. In N. Samuel Murrell,

William D. Spencer, and Adrian Anthony McFarlane, eds., *Chanting down Babylon: A Rastafari Reader*. Philadelphia: Temple University Press.

Taketomo, Y. 1989. An American-Japanese transcultural psychoanalysis and the issue of teacher transference. *Journal of the American Academy of Psychoanalysis* 17, 3: 427–450.

Tamez, Elsa. 1992. *The Scandalous Message of James: Faith without Works Is Dead*. New York: Crossroad.

Tapia, Andrés T. 1991. Viva los evangélicos. *Christianity Today*, October 28, 1–10.

Tapia, Andrés T. 1996. Soul searching. How is the black church responding to the urban crisis? *Christianity Today*, March, 16–22.

Tapia, Andrés T. 1997. After the hugs, what? The next step for racial reconciliation will be harder. *Christianity Today*, February 3, 2.

Tatara, M. 1994. Belief and religious sentiments in Japanese as revealed in their dreams. Hiroshima, Japan: Hiroshima Forum for Psychology, Hiroshima University.

Taylor, Clarence. 1994. *The Black Churches of Brooklyn*. New York: Columbia University Press.

Taylor, Clarence. 1997. *Knocking at Our Own Door: Milton A. Galamison and the Struggle to Integrate New York City Schools*. New York: Columbia University Press.

Taylor, Robert J. 1988. Correlates of religious non-involvement among black Americans. *Review of Religious Research* 30: 126–139.

Taylor, R. J., and L. M. Chatters. 1988. Church members as a source of informal social support. *Review of Religious Research* 30: 193–203.

Taylor, R. J., and L. M. Chatters. 1991. Religious life of black Americans. In J. S. Jackson, ed., *Life in Black America*. Newbury Park, CA: Sage.

Thomas, Piri. 1980. The Pentecostals. In Antonio M. Stevens-Arroyo, ed., *Prophets Denied Honor: An Anthology on the Hispanic Church in the U.S.* New York: Orbis Books.

Tiger, Lionel, and Joseph Shepher. 1975. *Women in the Kibbutz*. New York: Harcourt Brace Jovanovich.

Tolts, Mark. 1992. Jewish marriages in the USSR: A demographic analysis. *East European Jewish Affairs* 22, 2: 9.

Torres, Andres, and Frank Bonilla. 1993. Decline within decline: The New York perspective. In R. Morales and Frank Bonilla, eds., *Latinos in a Changing U.S. Economy*. Newbury Park, CA: Sage.

Transfiguration Church. 1977. *Transfiguration Church: A Church of Immigrants, 1927–1977*. New York: Privately published.

Trulear, Harold Dean. 1983. An analysis of the formative roles of ideational and social structures in the development of Afro-American religion. Ph.D. diss., Drew University.

Turner, Terisa, ed. 1994. *Arise Ye Mighty People: Gender, Class, and Race in Popular Struggles*. Trenton, NJ: Africa World Press.

Turner, Victor. 1968. *The Forest of Symbols, Aspects of Ndembu Ritual*. Ithaca, NY: Cornell University Press.

Turner, Victor. 1975a. *The Drums of Affliction: A Study of Religious Processes among the Ndembu of Zambia*. Oxford: Oxford University Press.

Turner, Victor. 1975b. *Revelation and Divination in Ndembu Ritual*. Ithaca, NY: Cornell University Press.

Unchurched American . . . 10 Years Later, The. 1989. Princeton, NJ: Princeton University Religion Center.

U.S. Bureau of the Census. 1958. *Current Population Survey*. Washington DC: U.S. Government Printing Office.

U.S. Bureau of the Census. 1990. *Current Population Survey*. Washington DC: U.S. Government Printing Office.

U.S. Bureau of the Census. 1994. *Current Population Census Reports*. Washington DC: U.S. Government Printing Office, March.

U.S. Bureau of the Census. 1997. *Current Population Survey*. Washington DC: U.S. Government Printing Office.

Urciuoli, Bonnie. 1991. The political topography of Spanish and English. *American Ethnologist*, May 18, 295–310.

Vainstein, Yaacov. 1990. *The Cycle of Jewish Life*. Jerusalem: Publishing Division of the Torah Education Department of the World Zionist Organization.

Van Dijk, Frank Jan. 1998. Chanting down Babylon Outernational: The Rise of Rastafari in Europe, the Caribbean, and the Pacific. In Samuel Murrell et al., eds., *Chanting down Babylon: Arastafari Reader*. Philadelphia: Temple University Press.

Vecoli, Rudolph, J. 1969. Prelates and peasants: Italian immigrants and the Catholic Church. *Journal of Social History* 2: 217–267.

Vecsey, George. 1976. Preaching and politics on weekly agenda for Baptist ministers. *New York Times*, November 6, 83.

Villafañe, Eldín. 1992. *Liberating Spirit: Toward an Hispanic American Pentecostal Social Ethic*. Lanham, MD: University Press of America.

Vitz, Paul. 1994. *Psychology as Religion. The Cult of Self-Worship*. Grand Rapids, MI: Eerdmans.

Vitz, Paul. 1999. *Faith of the Fatherless. The Psychology of Atheism*. New York: Spence.

Walker, Alice, 1983. *In Search of Our Mother's Gardens*. New York: Harcourt Brace.

Wallace, Ruth A. 1988. Catholic women and the creation of a new social reality. *Gender & Society* 2: 24–38.

Wallace, Ruth A. 1992. *They Call Her Pastor*. Albany: State University of New York Press.

Ward, Naomi, et al. 1994. Black churches in Atlanta reach out to the community. *National Journal of Sociology* 8 (Summer/Winter): 49–74.

Ware, Caroline. 1994. *Greenwich Village, 1920–1930*. Berkeley and Los Angeles: University of California Press.

Ware, Kallistos. 1996. In the image of likeness: The uniqueness of the human person. In John T. Chirban, ed., *Personhood Orthodox Christianity and the Connection between Body, Mind and Soul*. Westport, CT: Bergin & Garvey.

Warner, R. Stephen. 1993. Work in progress toward a new paradigm for the sociological study of religion in the United States. *American Journal of Sociology* 98 (March): 1044–1093.

Warner, R. Stephen. 1994. The place of the congregation in the American religious configuration. In James P. Wind and James W. Lewis, eds., *American Congregations*. Vol 2: *Perspectives in the Study of Congregations*. Chicago: University of Chicago Press.

Warner, R. Stephen. 1999a. Religion: Discursive boundaries and ritual bridges. Paper presented to the annual meeting of the Association for the Sociology of Religion, Chicago, August.

Warner, R. Stephen. 1999b. What have we learned about new immigrant religion? Lecture presented to Research on Immigrant Religion Project. The New School University, New York, October 12.

Warner, R. Stephen, and Judith G. Wittner, eds. 1998. *Gatherings in Diaspora: Religious Communities and the New Immigration*. Philadelphia: Temple University Press.

Warner, Steve. 1988. *New Wine in Old Wineskins*. Berkeley and Los Angeles: University of California Press.

Washington, Joseph. 1973. *Black Sects and Cults*. Garden City, NY: Doubleday.

Weaver, Lloyd. 1986. Notes on orisha worship in an urban setting: The New York example. Paper presented to he Third International Conference on Orisha Tradition (A), University of Ife, Ile Ife, Nigeria, July 1–6.

Weaver, Mary Jo. 1985. *New Catholic Women: A Contemporary Challenge to Traditional Religious Authority*. San Francisco: Harper & Row.

Weber. Marianne. 1975. *Max Weber: A Biography*. Trans. and ed. Harry Zohn. New York: Wiley.

Weber, Max. 1930. *The Protestant Ethic and the Spirit of Capitalism*. London: Allen & Unwin.

Weber, Max. 1973. Religious rejections of the world and their directions. In Hans Gerth and C. W. Mills, eds., *From Max Weber*. Oxford: Oxford University Press.

Weber, Max. 1976. *The Protestant Ethic and the Spirit of Capitalism*. New York: Scribner.

Weber, Max. 1978. *Economy and Society*. Vols. 1 and 2. Ed. and trans. G. Roth and C. Wittich. Berkeley and Los Angeles: University of California Press.

Weeks, Jeffrey. 1989. *Sexuality and Its Discontents*. London: Routledge.

Weiler, N. Sue. 1992. Religion, ethnicity, and the development of private homes for the aged. *Journal of American Ethnic History* 12, 1: 64–90.

Weinbaum, Batya. 1983. *Pictures of Patriarchy*. Boston: South End Press.

Weiser, Benjamin, and Susan Sachs. 1998. U.S. sees Brooklyn link to world terror network. *New York Times*, October 22, A1, A8.

Welch, Edward T. 1991. *Counselor's Guide to the Brain and Its Disorders*. Grand Rapids, MI: Zondervan.

Welch, Michael R. 1978. The unchurched black religious non-affiliates. *Journal for the Scientific Study of Religion* 17 (September): 289–293.

Wells, David F. 1993. *No Place for Truth or Whatever Happened to Evangelical Theology?* Grand Rapids, MI: Eerdmans.

Wells, David F. 1994. *God in the Wasteland*. Grand Rapids, MI: Eerdmans.

Wertheim, Aaron. 1992. *Law and Custom in Hasidism*. Trans. Shmuel Himelstein. Hoboken, NJ: Ktav.

Whelpton, P. K., A. A. Campbell, and J. E. Patterson. 1966. *Fertility and Family Planning in the United States*. Princeton, NJ: Princeton University Press.

Williams, Delores S. 1993. *Sisters in the Wilderness: The Challenge of Womanist God Talk*. Maryknoll, NY: Orbis Press.

Williams, Raymond Brady. 1988. *Religions of Immigrants from India and Pakistan: New Threads in the American Tapestry*. Cambridge: Cambridge University Press.

Wilmore, Gayraud. 1973. *Black Religion and Black Radicalism*. Garden City, NY: Doubleday.

Wilson, William Julius. 1987. *The Truly Disadvantaged: The Inner City, the Underclass, and Public Policy*. Chicago: University of Chicago Press.

Winter, Miriam Therese, Adair Lummis, and Allison Stokes. 1995. *Defecting in Place: Women Claiming Responsibility for Their Own Spiritual Lives*. New York: Crossroad.

Wirth, Louis. 1938. Urbanism as a way of life. *American Journal of Sociology* 44: 1–24.

Witchell, A. 1993. "Luckiest rabbi in America" holds faith amid the hate. *New York Times*, May 5, C1, C12.

Wittberg, Patricia. 1996. *Pathways to Re-creating Religious Communities*. Mahway, NJ: Paulist Press.

Wood, James W. 1895. *100 Years of the African Methodist Episcopal Zion Church; or, the Centennial of African Methodism*. New York: AME Zion Book Concern.

Wuthnow, Robert. 1976. *The Consciousness Reformation*. Berkeley and Los Angeles: University of California Press.

Wuthnow, Robert. 1988. *The Restructuring of American Religion: Society and Faith since World War II*. Princeton, NJ: Princeton University Press.

Wuthnow, Robert. 1989. *The Struggle for America's Soul: Evangelicals, Liberals, and Secularism*. Grand Rapids, MI: Eerdmans.

Wuthnow, Robert. 1998. *After Heaven. Spirituality in America since the 1950s.* Berkeley and Los Angeles: University of California Press.

Yang, Fenggang. 1998. Tenacious unity in a contentious community: Cultural and religious Dynamics in a Chinese Christian church. In R. Stephen Warner and Judith G. Wittner, eds., *Gatherings in Diaspora: Religious Communities and the New Immigration.* Philadelphia: Temple University Press.

Yang, Fenggang. 1999. *Chinese Christians in America.* University Park: Pennsylvania State University Press.

Yawney, Carol. 1994a. Moving with the Dawtas of Rastafari: From myth to reality. In Teresa Turner, ed., *Arise Ye Mighty People: Gender, Race and Class in Popular Struggles.* Trenton, NJ: Africa World Press.

Yawney, Carol. 1994b. Rasta mek a trod: Symbolic ambiguity in a globalizing religion. In Teresa Turner, ed., *Arise Ye Mighty People: Gender, Race and Class in Popular Struggles.* Trenton, NJ: Africa World Press.

Yoo, David. 1996. For those who have eyes to see: Religious sightings in Asian America. *Amerasia Journal* 22 (Spring): xiii–xxii.

Yost, F. Donald. 1995. Changes ahead? The numbers say "Yes"! *Dialogue* 7, 2: 28–29.

Zambrana, Ruth E., ed. 1995. *Understanding Latino Families: Scholarship, policy and practice.* Thousand Oaks, CA: Sage.

Zentella, Ana Celia. 1997. *Growing up Bilingual: Puerto Rican Children in New York.* Malden, MA: Blackwell.

Zerubavel, Eviatar. 1991. *The Fine Line.* New York: Free Press.

Zuesse, Evan M. 1979. *Ritual Cosmos: The Sanctification of Life in African Religions.* Athens: Ohio University Press.

Zwiebel, C. D. 1985. Fighting city hall: When gay rights collide with religious rights. *Jewish Observer*, March, 28–31.

Contributors

Mary Elizabeth Brown divides her time between teaching at Marymount Manhattan College and Pace University, processing archival material for the Center for Migration Studies, and writing parish history. Her most recent publications are *Shapers of the Great Debate on Immigration* and *From Italian Villages to Greenwich Village: Our Lady of Pompei, 1892–1992,* 1992, Center for Migration Studies.

Robert Carle is a professor of Christian studies and the director of foundation relations, The King's College. He worked in Asia with the United Board for Christian Higher Education and in church-based community development programs for Trinity Church, Wall Street.

Tony Carnes directs the Seminar on Contents and Methods of the Social Sciences, Columbia University, the International Research Institute on Values Changes, and the Research Institute for New Americans. He has published four books and more than seventy articles. His investigative journalism was used in a Pulitzer-nominated series in the *Wall Street Journal,* ABC's *World News Tonight,* CBS's *60 Minutes,* and the *Philadelphia Inquirer.* For his articles in *Christianity Today,* he was given the Best News Reporting Award by the Evangelical Press Association in 1998.

Richard Cimino is the editor and publisher of *Religion Watch.* His recent publications include *Against the Stream: The Adoption of Traditional Christian Faiths by Young Adults* and *Shopping for Faith: American Religion in the New Millennium.*

Mary Cuthrell Curry is an assistant professor of sociology at the University of Houston, Houston, Texas.

Leah Davidson is a supervising psychiatrist at the William Alanson White Institute, a former president of the American Psychoanalytic Institute, a life fellow of the American Academy of Psychoanalysis, and the author of numerous articles on religion and cross-cultural psychology. She also is a life fellow of the American Psychiatric Association and a member of its Committee on Psychiatry and Religion.

Louis A. Decaro Jr. is the pastor of the Broome Street Evangelical Free Church in Jersey City, New Jersey. He also is the author of *On the Side of My People: A Religious Life of Malcolm X* and *Signs of Hope in the City* and the editor of *Malcolm and the Cross: The Nation of Islam, Malcolm X,* both available from New York University Press.

Paul de Vries is the president of the New York Evangelical Seminary and the author of *Taming the Shrewd: Ethics for Modern Business,* among many other books and articles.

Victoria Erickson is an associate professor of sociology of religion and the chaplain of Drew University. She is the author of many papers and books, including *Where Silence Speaks: Feminism, Social Theory, and Religion.*

Susan A. Farrell is an associate professor in behavioral sciences and human services at Kingsborough Community College, City University of New York. She is a coeditor, with Georgie Ann Weatherby, of *The Power of Gender in Religion;* and a coeditor, with Judith Lorber, of *The Social Construction of Gender.* She is a board member of the Women's Ordination Conference, Catholics for a Free Choice (CFFC), and a member of the Women's Alliance for Theology, Ethics, and Ritual (WATER).

Helaine Harris is a researcher at the City University of New York Graduate Center.

Randal L. Hepner is a visiting assistant professor in the anthropology department at Michigan State University, a research associate in the Metropolitan Detroit Congregational Study Project, and the author of "Chanting down Babylon in the Belly of the Beast: The Rastafari Movement in Metropolitan U.S.A.," in Samuel Murrell et al., eds., *Chanting down Babylon: A Rastafari Reader;* and "The House That Rasta Built," in R. Stephen Warner, ed., *Gatherings in Diaspora: Religious Communities and the New Immigrants.*

Tricia Redeker Hepner is an National Science Foundation distinguished doctoral fellow in anthropology and African studies at Michigan State University.

Anna Karpathakis is an assistant professor of sociology at Kingsborough Community College, City University of New York. Her research interests include race/ethnicity and immigrant issues, as well as immigrant religions. She writes on Greek immigrant and Greek American issues and recently coedited a volume on the Greek American family.

Vivian Klaff is an associate professor in the Department of Sociology and Criminal Justice, University of Delaware. She is the cochair of a research group for a survey of the American Jewish population in year 2000. Klaff is the author of *DEM-LAB: Using Computers to Teach Demography*; and "The Changing Jewish Family: Issues of Continuity," in Cardell Jacobson, ed., *Racial and Ethnic Families in the United States*. She is currently working on a monograph based on the 1990 National Jewish Population Survey and the 1990 U.S. Census.

Samuel Kliger is the chairman of the Research Institute for New Americans, Acculturation Program Coordinator, New York Association for New Americans, Inc. He is also the author of three books and sixty articles including, with Tony Carnes, "Religion and Moral Values in Russia" in Anson Shupe and Bronislav Misztal, eds., *Religion, Mobilization and Social Action*.

Ronald Lawson has been on the City University of New York faculty since 1973, first at Hunter College and, for the past twenty years, at Queens College, where he is a professor in the urban studies department. His publications include *Brisbane in the 1890; The Tenant Movement in New York, 1904–1984*; and articles in *Sociology of Religion, Journal for the Scientific Study of Religion, Religious Research Review*, and *Journal of the American Academy of Religion*. He is currently completing the most comprehensive study ever of Seventh-Day Adventism, based on three thousand in-depth interviews in fifty-four countries using both social movement theory as applied to religious movements, and church-sect theory.

James W. Lucas is a lawyer and a long-time observer of Mormons in New York City. He is also the author of *Working Toward Zion: Economic Teachings of Mormonism*.

Mary B. McRae is an associate professor of applied psychology at New York University and teaches courses in group dynamics, cross-cultural counseling, and program development and evaluation. She is a licensed psychologist and an organizational consultant. Her research is in the area of group processes and systems theory as they relate to community based organizations and issues of diversity.

Richard John Neuhaus is a priest in the Archdiocese of New York, president of the Institute on Religion and Public Life, and editor in chief of the monthly journal *FIRST THINGS*.

Ashakant Nimbark is a professor of sociology at Dowling College. His work focuses on early education in India, and he is currently studying the effects of mass media around the world.

Segundo S. Pantoja is an assistant professor of black and Puerto Rican studies at Hunter College, City University of New York. He is a coeditor of *Discovering Latino Religion*. He contributed to the 1995 four-volume PARAL series on Latino religion published by the Bildner Center at the CUNY Graduate School. Currently he is working on the National Survey of Leadership in Latino Parishes and Congregations based at Brooklyn College's Office of Research for Religion in Society and Culture.

María Elizabeth Pérez y González is an assistant professor in the Department of Puerto Rican and Latino Studies, Brooklyn College, City University of New York. She is also a co-investigator of the Latino Congregations in U.S. Study and the author of *Puerto Ricans in the United States*. She is a member of the Evangelical Lutheran Church in America and has a Pentecostal heritage from Puerto Rico that spans four generations.

Mareleyn Schneider is a professor at Yeshiva University teaching sociology, statistics, and anthropology. She is currently editing a book on the World War II letters of an Orthodox Jewish soldier, preparing an illustrated volume on Jewish tombstones, conducting a long-term research project on Jewish education, analyzing mating and dating responses of Jewish youth, and collecting articles on nontraditional Jewish life in America. With Otto Maduro and Janet Jacobs, she is planning to edit a book on Latino Jews. With colleagues from other disciplines, she has begun two works, one examining health-related issues of Jewish women and the other exploring the life of an anonymous biblical woman.

Hannibal Silver is a psychologist and the director of the Redeemer Presbyterian Counseling Center.

Clarence Taylor is a professor of history and African studies at Florida International University. He is the author of *The Black Churches of Brooklyn* and *Knocking at Our Own Door.*

H. Dean Trulear is the vice-president of Public/Private Ventures, a think tank that deals with youth, religion, and crime. He is also a professor of church and society at the New York Theological Seminary and the author of many books and articles on the sociology of religion, African American churches, and theological education.

Index